Stand Up, Speak Out: The Practice and Ethics of Public Speaking Version 1.0

By

Jason S. Wrench, Anne Goding, Danette Ifert Johnson and Bernardo A. Attias

flat**world**
KNOWLEDGE

Stand Up, Speak Out: The Practice and Ethics of Public Speaking Version 1.0

Jason S. Wrench, Anne Goding, Danette Ifert Johnson and Bernardo A. Attias

Published by:

Flat World Knowledge, Inc.
1133 15th Street. NW, 12th Floor
Washington, DC 20005-2710

Brief Contents

Contents

About the Authors

JASON S. WRENCH

Jason S. Wrench (EdD, West Virginia University) is an associate professor in the Communication and Media department at the State University of New York at New Paltz. Dr. Wrench specializes in workplace learning and performance, or the intersection of instructional communication and organizational communication. His varied research interests include communibiology, computer-mediated communication, empirical research methods, humor, risk/crisis communication, and supervisor-subordinate interactions. Dr. Wrench regularly consults with individuals and organizations on workplace communication and as a professional speech coach for senior executives.

Dr. Wrench has published five previous books: *Intercultural Communication: Power in Context, Communication, Affect, and Learning in the Classroom* (2000, Tapestry Press), *Principles of Public Speaking* (2003, The College Network), *Human Communication in Everyday Life: Explanations and Applications* (2008, Allyn & Bacon), *Quantitative Research Methods for Communication: A Hands-On Approach* (2008, Oxford University Press), and *The Directory of Communication Related Mental Measures* (Summer 2010, National Communication Association). He is currently working on five other book projects for Flat World Knowledge, Kendall-Hunt, Allyn & Bacon, and Praeger. Dr. Wrench was the editor of the *Ohio Communication Journal* from 2005 to 2007 and has served as an associate editor for *Communication Research Reports* from 2007 to 2010. Furthermore, Dr. Wrench has published over twenty research articles that have appeared in various journals: *Communication Quarterly, Communication Research Reports, Education, Human Communication, Journal of Homosexuality, Journal of Intercultural Communication, Southern Communication Journal, The Source: A Journal of Education*, and *The NACADA Journal* (National Association of Campus Advising). Many of his writings are available on his website at http://www.JasonSWrench.com.

ANNE GODING

Anne Goding (MS, Eastern Washington University) is a lecturer in the Communication and Media department at the State University of New York at New Paltz. Ms. Goding specializes in the intersections of intercultural communication, storytelling, and public communication. From 1981 to 1992 Ms. Goding worked as a teacher for the Medicine Chief of the Bear Tribe Medicine Society in Spokane, Washington. Ms. Goding taught outdoor summer programs for adults, which included Native American philosophy; ceremonial etiquette in native societies; earth rituals; traditional women's studies emphasizing Native Americans; the Sacred Pipe emphasizing Ojibwe and Paiute-Arapaho traditions; the sweat lodge ceremony and its symbolism emphasizing Ojibwe tradition; and the Vision Quest, a traditional rite of passage for contemporary people. From 1986 to 1989, Ms. Goding also worked as codirector of Bear Tribe Publishing Company.

In 1994 Ms. Goding received a mini-grant from Eastern Washington University Foundation for the development of a teaching package in visual presentation for public speaking. She has presented workshops on public speaking for a range of audiences. Ms. Goding has previously published the article "How Institutional Meanings Displace the Real Environment (Revisiting Rio)" in the *International Journal of Communication*.

DANETTE IFERT JOHNSON

Danette Ifert Johnson is Professor of Communication Studies at Ithaca College. She previously taught at West Virginia Wesleyan College and Texas Tech University. Danette completed her undergraduate studies in history and speech communication at West Virginia Wesleyan College and earned an MA in educational psychology from West Virginia University and an MA and PhD in communication studies from Northwestern University.

Over her almost twenty-year teaching career, she has taught courses ranging from introductory Business & Professional Communication and Public Speaking to graduate courses in Quantitative Research Methods and Interpersonal Influence. She has written over thirty published articles and book chapters, including articles in *Communication Education, Communication Research, Western Journal of Communication,* and *Communication Teacher.* Dr. Johnson has been recognized for her teaching with West Virginia Wesleyan's (WVWC) Community Council Outstanding Faculty Award and WVWC's Honors Faculty Member of the Year. In 2009, she was recognized as a Distinguished Teaching Fellow of the Eastern Communication Association (ECA). She is also a recipient of ECA's Past President's Award for early to mid-career scholarly achievement and service to the organization. Dr. Johnson is a past executive director of ECA and is presently first vice president-elect of the organization.

BERNARDO A. ATTIAS

Bernardo Alexander Attias (PhD, University of Iowa, 1997) is department chair and professor of communication studies at California State University, Northridge, where he has taught since 1994. Dr. Attias teaches a variety of courses, including Rhetorical Theory; Classical Rhetoric; Postmodern Rhetoric; Freedom of Speech; Rhetoric of Peace and Conflict; Rhetoric of Crime and Punishment; Communication and Technology; Intercultural Communication; and Performance, Language, and Cultural Studies. His research is primarily in the areas of rhetorical studies, cultural studies, performance studies, and critical theory; he has written on media coverage of warfare, the politics of psychoanalysis, the history of sexuality, and electronic dance music culture. Dr. Attias is also a DJ and performance artist, and he brings his creative energy and interests into his scholarship and pedagogy.

Acknowledgments

We want to acknowledge our various college/university campuses that have provided us much needed support and goodwill during this entire project. Without our academic homes, projects like these would never take flight.

We would like to acknowledge Janice Walker Anderson for her help in writing the initial draft of the chapter on communication apprehension. Your help with this draft was immensely helpful and your spirit definitely touched the entire project.

We would like to acknowledge the multitude of people who have helped us along the way. To Elsa Peterson, our developmental editor, thank you for your wisdom and edits as we made our way through this project. To Jenn Yee and KB Mello, our editorial supervisors, thank you for your patience. You helped shepherd this project even when we couldn't see the light at the end of the tunnel. Lastly, thank you to Michael Boezi for taking a chance on our writing team and staying with us throughout the entire project. Your leadership is apparent in each page of this book. PS: Thanks again for a great meal and conversation at the Guilded Otter!

Thank you to all of the reviewers who helped us along the way. Your guidance and insight helped reign us in when necessary and helped us create the amazing textbook you now see in front of you.

- Jodie Mandel, College of Southern Nevada
- Emily Brandenberger, Kutztown University
- Harlene Adams, California State University, Sacramento
- Bridgette Colaco, Troy University
- Jason Warren, George Mason University
- Helen Prien, Ferrum College
- Kevin Backstrom, University of Wisconsin Oshkosh
- Zachary Justus, California State University, Chico
- J. M. Grenier, Middlesex Community College
- Brent Adrian, Central Community College–Grand Isle
- Braze Brickwedel, Tallahassee Community College
- Clark Friesen, Lone Star College
- Bryan Crow, Southern Illinois University, Carbondale
- David Bashore, College of the Desert
- Diana Cooley, Lone Star College–North Harris
- Chad D. Malone, Ivy Tech Community College–Columbus, Indiana Campus
- Burton St. John III, Old Dominion University
- Steven D. Cohen, University of Maryland
- Deborah Bridges, University of Houston, Central Campus
- Cameron Basquiat, California State University, Chico

Lastly, thank you to all of the students who have taken our public speaking classes in the past. Teaching is an exercise of experimentation and our past students have definitely been our guinea pigs at times. The cumulated information in this book comes from our own personal experiences with public speaking, the academic literature, and our previous students. Without our previous students, we wouldn't have the knowledge to write a textbook like this one.

Preface

Public speaking in the twenty-first century is an art and a science that has developed over millennia. In a world that is bombarded by information, the skill set of public speaking is more important today than ever. According to an address given by Tony Karrer at the TechKnowledge 2009 Conference, the *New York Times* contains more information in one week than individuals in the 1800s would encounter in a lifetime. Currently, the amount of information available to people doubles every eighteen months and is expected to double weekly by 2015. In a world filled with so much information, knowing how to effectively organize and present one's ideas through oral communication is paramount.

From audience analysis to giving a presentation, *Stand Up, Speak Out: The Practice and Ethics of Public Speaking* will guide students through the speech-making process. We believe that it is important to focus on the practical process of speech making because we want this book to be a user-friendly guide to creating, researching, and presenting public speeches. While both classic and current academic research in public speaking will guide the book, we do not want to lose the focus of helping students become more seasoned and polished public speakers. We believe that a new textbook in public speaking should first, and foremost, be a practical book that helps students prepare and deliver a variety of different types of speeches.

In addition to practicality, we believe that it is important to focus on the ethics of public speaking from both a source's and a receiver's point of view. In 2006 Pearson, Child, Mattern, and Kahl examined the state of ethics in public speaking textbooks. Specifically, the researchers used the National Communication Association (NCA) Credo for Ethical Communication to guide their study of ethics in public speaking textbooks. Ultimately, the researchers focused on eight specific categories of public speaking ethics content areas: freedom of speech, honesty, plagiarism, ethical listening, ethical research, hate words, diversity, and codes of ethics. As a whole, the top ten public speaking books varied in their degrees of exposure to the various ethical issues. We believe that using the NCA Credo for Ethical Communication as the basis for discussing ethics within this book in addition to the latest research in ethics and communication will help students see how ethics can be applied to the public speaking context. The emphasis on ethics in communication is very important across the field, so a public speaking textbook that completely integrates ethical issues instead of sidelining them will be a welcome addition. All four of the coauthors on this text have conducted research on the topic of communication ethics and written about how ethics is important in every facet of our communicative lives.

Overall, we believe that the combination of practicality and ethics will present a new perspective on public speaking that will be welcomed by the field. We believe this book will be both intellectually stimulating and realistically applicable.

REFERENCES

Karrer, T. (2009, January 29). New work literacies and e-learning 2.0. Presentation given at TechKnowledge-09, Las Vegas, Nevada.

Pearson, J. C., Child, J. T., Mattern, J. L., & Kahl, D. H., Jr. (2006). What are students being taught about ethics in public speaking textbooks? *Communication Quarterly, 54,* 507–521. doi: 10.1080/01463370601036689

CHAPTER 1
Why Public Speaking Matters Today

PUBLIC SPEAKING IN THE TWENTY-FIRST CENTURY

Public speaking is the process of designing and delivering a **message** to an audience. Effective public speaking involves understanding your audience and speaking goals, choosing elements for the speech that will engage your audience with your topic, and delivering your message skillfully. Good public speakers understand that they must plan, organize, and revise their material in order to develop an effective speech. This book will help you understand the basics of effective public speaking and guide you through the process of creating your own presentations. We'll begin by discussing the ways in which public speaking is relevant to you and can benefit you in your career, education, and personal life.

© *Thinkstock*

message

Any verbal or nonverbal stimulus that is meaningful to a receiver.

In a world where people are bombarded with messages through television, social media, and the Internet, one of the first questions you may ask is, "Do people still give speeches?" Well, type the words "public speaking" into Amazon.com or Barnesandnoble.com, and you will find more than two thousand books with the words "public speaking" in the title. Most of these and other books related to public speaking are not college textbooks. In fact, many books written about public speaking are intended for very specific audiences: *A Handbook of Public Speaking for Scientists and Engineers* (by Peter Kenny), *Excuse Me! Let Me Speak!: A Young Person's Guide to Public Speaking* (by Michelle J. Dyett-Welcome), *Professionally Speaking: Public Speaking for Health Professionals* (by Frank De Piano and Arnold Melnick), and *Speaking Effectively: A Guide for Air Force Speakers* (by John A. Kline). Although these different books address specific issues related to nurses, engineers, or air force officers, the content is basically the same. If you search for "public speaking" in an online academic database, you'll find numerous articles on public speaking in business magazines (e.g., *BusinessWeek*, *Nonprofit World*) and academic journals (e.g., *Harvard Business Review*, *Journal of Business Communication*). There is so much information available about public speaking because it continues to be relevant even with the growth of technological means of communication. As author and speaker Scott Berkun writes in his blog, "For all our tech, we're still very fond of the most low tech thing there is: a monologue."[1] People continue to spend millions of dollars every year to listen to professional speakers. For example, attendees of the 2010 TED (Technology, Entertainment, Design) conference, which invites speakers from around the world to share their ideas in short, eighteen-minute presentations, paid six thousand dollars per person to listen to fifty speeches over a four-day period.

Technology can also help public speakers reach audiences that were not possible to reach in the past. Millions of people heard about and then watched Randy Pausch's "Last Lecture" online. In this captivating speech, Randy Pausch, a Carnegie Mellon University professor who retired at age forty-six after developing inoperable tumors, delivered his last lecture to the students, faculty, and staff. This inspiring speech was turned into a DVD and a best-selling book that was eventually published in more than thirty-five languages.[2]

We realize that you may not be invited to TED to give the speech of your life or create a speech so inspirational that it touches the lives of millions via YouTube; however, all of us will find ourselves in situations where we will be asked to give a speech, make a presentation, or just deliver a few words. In this chapter, we will first address why public speaking is important, and then we will discuss models that illustrate the process of public speaking itself.

1. WHY IS PUBLIC SPEAKING IMPORTANT?

LEARNING OBJECTIVES

1. Explore three types of public speaking in everyday life: informative, persuasive, and entertaining.
2. Understand the benefits of taking a course in public speaking.
3. Explain the benefits people get from engaging in public speaking.

© Thinkstock

In today's world, we are constantly bombarded with messages both good and bad. No matter where you live, where you work or go to school, or what kinds of media you use, you are probably exposed to hundreds. if not thousands, of advertising messages every day. Researcher Norman W. Edmund estimates that by 2020 the amount of knowledge in the world will double every seventy-three days.[3] Because we live in a world where we are overwhelmed with content, communicating information in a way that is accessible to others is more important today than ever before. To help us further understand why public speaking is important, we will first examine public speaking in everyday life. We will then discuss how public speaking can benefit you personally.

1.1 Everyday Public Speaking

Every single day people across the United States and around the world stand up in front of some kind of audience and speak. In fact, there's even a monthly publication that reproduces some of the top speeches from around the United States called *Vital Speeches of the Day* (http://www.vsotd.com). Although public speeches are of various types, they can generally be grouped into three categories based on their intended purpose: informative, persuasive, and entertaining.

Informative Speaking

informative speaking

Speaking with the purpose of sharing knowledge or information with an audience.

One of the most common types of public speaking is **informative speaking**. The primary purpose of informative presentations is to share one's knowledge of a subject with an audience. Reasons for making an informative speech vary widely. For example, you might be asked to instruct a group of coworkers on how to use new computer software or to report to a group of managers how your latest project is coming along. A local community group might wish to hear about your volunteer activities in New Orleans during spring break, or your classmates may want you to share your expertise on Mediterranean cooking. What all these examples have in common is the goal of imparting information to an audience.

Informative speaking is integrated into many different occupations. Physicians often lecture about their areas of expertise to medical students, other physicians, and patients. Teachers find themselves presenting to parents as well as to their students. Firefighters give demonstrations about how to effectively control a fire in the house. Informative speaking is a common part of numerous jobs and other everyday activities. As a result, learning how to speak effectively has become an essential skill in today's world.

Persuasive Speaking

A second common reason for speaking to an audience is to **persuade** others. In our everyday lives, we are often called on to convince, motivate, or otherwise persuade others to change their beliefs, take an action, or reconsider a decision. Advocating for music education in your local school district, convincing clients to purchase your company's products, or inspiring high school students to attend college all involve influencing other people through public speaking.

For some people, such as elected officials, giving persuasive speeches is a crucial part of attaining and continuing career success. Other people make careers out of speaking to groups of people who pay to listen to them. Motivational authors and speakers, such as Les Brown (http://www.lesbrown.com), make millions of dollars each year from people who want to be motivated to do better in their lives. Brian Tracy, another professional speaker and author, specializes in helping business leaders become more productive and effective in the workplace (http://www.briantracy.com).

Whether public speaking is something you do every day or just a few times a year, persuading others is a challenging task. If you develop the skill to persuade effectively, it can be personally and professionally rewarding.

> **persuade**
>
> The intentional attempt to get another person or persons to change or reinforce specific beliefs, values, and/or behaviors.

Entertaining Speaking

Entertaining speaking involves an array of speaking occasions ranging from introductions to wedding toasts, to presenting and accepting awards, to delivering eulogies at funerals and memorial services in addition to after-dinner speeches and motivational speeches. Entertaining speaking has been important since the time of the ancient Greeks, when Aristotle identified epideictic speaking (speaking in a ceremonial context) as an important type of address. As with persuasive and informative speaking, there are professionals, from religious leaders to comedians, who make a living simply from delivering entertaining speeches. As anyone who has watched an awards show on television or has seen an incoherent best man deliver a wedding toast can attest, speaking to entertain is a task that requires preparation and practice to be effective.

> **entertaining speaking**
>
> Speech designed to captivate an audience's attention and regale or amuse them while delivering a clear message.

1.2   Personal Benefits of Public Speaking

Oral communication skills were the number one skill that college graduates found useful in the business world, according to a study by sociologist Andrew Zekeri.[4] That fact alone makes learning about public speaking worthwhile. However, there are many other benefits of communicating effectively for the hundreds of thousands of college students every year who take public speaking courses. Let's take a look at some of the personal benefits you'll get both from a course in public speaking and from giving public speeches.

Benefits of Public Speaking Courses

In addition to learning the process of creating and delivering an effective speech, students of public speaking leave the class with a number of other benefits as well. Some of these benefits include

- developing critical thinking skills,
- fine-tuning verbal and nonverbal skills,
- overcoming fear of public speaking.

Developing Critical Thinking Skills

One of the very first benefits you will gain from your public speaking course is an increased ability to think critically. Problem solving is one of many critical thinking skills you will engage in during this course. For example, when preparing a persuasive speech, you'll have to think through real problems affecting your campus, community, or the world and provide possible solutions to those problems. You'll also have to think about the positive and negative consequences of your solutions and then communicate your ideas to others. At first, it may seem easy to come up with solutions for a campus problem such as a shortage of parking spaces: just build more spaces. But after thinking and researching further you may find out that building costs, environmental impact from loss of green space, maintenance needs, or limited locations for additional spaces make this solution impractical. Being able to think through problems and analyze the potential costs and benefits of solutions is an essential part of critical thinking and of public speaking aimed at persuading others. These skills will help you not only in public speaking contexts but throughout your life as well. As we stated earlier, college graduates in Zekeri's study rated oral communication skills as the most useful for success in the business world. The second most valuable skill they reported was problem-solving ability, so your public speaking course is doubly valuable!

Another benefit to public speaking is that it will enhance your ability to conduct and analyze research. Public speakers must provide credible evidence within their speeches if they are going to persuade various audiences. So your public speaking course will further refine your ability to find and utilize a range of sources.

Fine-Tuning Verbal and Nonverbal Skills

A second benefit of taking a public speaking course is that it will help you fine-tune your verbal and nonverbal communication skills. Whether you competed in public speaking in high school or this is your first time speaking in front of an audience, having the opportunity to actively practice communication skills and receive professional feedback will help you become a better overall communicator. Often, people don't even realize that they twirl their hair or repeatedly mispronounce words while speaking in public settings until they receive feedback from a teacher during a public speaking course. People around the United States will often pay speech coaches over one hundred dollars per hour to help them enhance their speaking skills. You have a built-in speech coach right in your classroom, so it is to your advantage to use the opportunity to improve your verbal and nonverbal communication skills.

Overcoming Fear of Public Speaking

An additional benefit of taking a public speaking class is that it will help reduce your fear of public speaking. Whether they've spoken in public a lot or are just getting started, most people experience some anxiety when engaging in public speaking. Heidi Rose and Andrew Rancer evaluated students' levels of public speaking anxiety during both the first and last weeks of their public speaking class and found that those levels decreased over the course of the semester.[5] One explanation is that people often have little exposure to public speaking. By taking a course in public speaking, students become better acquainted with the public speaking process, making them more confident and less apprehensive. In addition, you will learn specific strategies for overcoming the challenges of speech anxiety. We will discuss this topic in greater detail in Chapter 3.

Benefits of Engaging in Public Speaking

Once you've learned the basic skills associated with public speaking, you'll find that being able to effectively speak in public has profound benefits, including

- influencing the world around you,
- developing leadership skills,
- becoming a thought leader.

Influencing the World around You

If you don't like something about your local government, then speak out about your issue! One of the best ways to get our society to change is through the power of speech. Common citizens in the United States and around the world, like you, are influencing the world in real ways through the power of speech. Just type the words "citizens speak out" in a search engine and you'll find numerous examples of how common citizens use the power of speech to make real changes in the world—for example, by speaking out against "fracking" for natural gas (a process in which chemicals are injected into rocks in an attempt to open them up for fast flow of natural gas or oil) or in favor of retaining a popular local sheriff. One of the amazing parts of being a citizen in a democracy is the right to stand up and speak out, which is a luxury many people in the world do not have. So if you don't like something, be the force of change you're looking for through the power of speech.

Developing Leadership Skills

Have you ever thought about climbing the corporate ladder and eventually finding yourself in a management or other leadership position? If so, then public speaking skills are very important. Hackman and Johnson assert that effective public speaking skills are a necessity for all leaders.[6] If you want people to follow you, you have to communicate effectively and clearly what followers should do. According to Bender, "Powerful leadership comes from knowing what matters to you. Powerful presentations come from expressing this effectively. It's important to develop both."[7] One of the most important skills for leaders to develop is their public speaking skills, which is why executives spend millions of dollars every year going to public speaking workshops; hiring public speaking coaches; and buying public speaking books, CDs, and DVDs.

Becoming a Thought Leader

Even if you are not in an official leadership position, effective public speaking can help you become a **"thought leader."** Joel Kurtzman, editor of *Strategy & Business*, coined this term to call attention to individuals who contribute new ideas to the world of business. According to business consultant Ken Lizotte, "when your colleagues, prospects, and customers view you as one very smart guy or gal to know, then you're a thought leader."[8] Typically, thought leaders engage in a range of behaviors, including enacting and conducting research on business practices. To achieve thought leader status, individuals must communicate their ideas to others through both writing and public speaking. Lizotte demonstrates how becoming a thought leader can be personally and financially rewarding at the same time: when others look to you as a thought leader, you will be more desired and make more money as a result. Business gurus often refer to "intellectual capital," or the combination of your knowledge and ability to communicate that knowledge to others.[9] Whether standing before a group of executives discussing the next great trend in business or delivering a webinar (a seminar over the web), thought leaders use public speaking every day to create the future that the rest of us live in.

thought leader

An individual who contributes new ideas that help various aspects of society.

KEY TAKEAWAYS

- People have many reasons for engaging in public speaking, but the skills necessary for public speaking are applicable whether someone is speaking for informative, persuasive, or entertainment reasons.
- Taking a public speaking class will improve your speaking skills, help you be a more critical thinker, fine-tune your verbal and nonverbal communication skills, and help you overcome public speaking anxiety.
- Effective public speaking skills have many direct benefits for the individual speaker, including influencing the world around you, developing leadership skills, and becoming a go-to person for ideas and solutions.

EXERCISES

1. Talk to people who are currently working in the career you hope to pursue. Of the three types of public speaking discussed in the text, which do they use most commonly use in their work?
2. Read one of the free speeches available at http://www.vsotd.com. What do you think the speaker was trying to accomplish? What was her or his reason for speaking?
3. Which personal benefit are you most interested in receiving from a public speaking class? Why?

2.   THE PROCESS OF PUBLIC SPEAKING

© *Thinkstock*

As noted earlier, all of us encounter thousands of messages in our everyday environments, so getting your idea heard above all the other ones is a constant battle. Some speakers will try gimmicks, but we strongly believe that getting your message heard depends on three fundamental components: message, skill, and passion. The first part of getting your message across is the message itself. When what you are saying is clear and coherent, people are more likely to pay attention to it. On the other hand, when a message is ambiguous, people will often stop paying attention. Our discussions in the first part of this book involve how to have clear and coherent content.

The second part of getting your message heard is having effective communication skills. You may have the best ideas in the world, but if you do not possess basic public speaking skills, you're going to have a problem getting anyone to listen. In this book, we will address the skills you must possess to effectively communicate your ideas to others.

Lastly, if you want your message to be heard, you must communicate passion for your message. One mistake that novice public speakers make is picking topics in which they have no emotional investment. If an audience can tell that you don't really care about your topic, they will just tune you out. Passion is the extra spark that draws people's attention and makes them want to listen to your message.

In this section, we're going to examine the process of public speaking by first introducing you to a basic model of public speaking and then discussing how public speaking functions as dialogue. These models will give you a basic understanding of the communication process and some challenges that you may face as a speaker.

2.1   Models of Public Speaking

A basic model of human communication is one of the first topics that most communication teachers start with in any class. For our focus on public speaking, we will introduce two widely discussed models in communication: interactional and transactional.

Interactional Model of Public Speaking

Linear Model

The interactional model of public speaking comes from the work of Claude Shannon and Warren Weaver.[10] The original model mirrored how radio and telephone technologies functioned and consisted of three primary parts: source, channel, and receiver. The **source** was the part of a telephone a person spoke into, the **channel** was the telephone itself, and the **receiver** was the part of the phone where one could hear the other person. Shannon and Weaver also recognized that often there is static that interferes with listening to a telephone conversation, which they called noise.

Although there are a number of problems with applying this model to human communication, it does have some useful parallels to public speaking. In public speaking, the source is the person who is giving the speech, the channel is the speaker's use of **verbal** and **nonverbal communication**, and the receivers are the audience members listening to the speech. As with a telephone call, a wide range of distractions (**noise**) can inhibit an audience member from accurately attending to a speaker's speech. Avoiding or adapting to these types of noise is an important challenge for public speakers.

Interactional Model

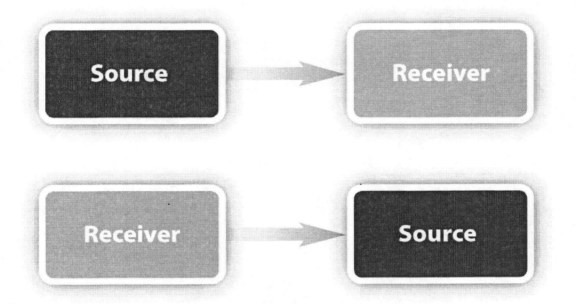

The interactional model of communication developed by Wilbur Schramm builds upon the linear model.[11] Schramm added three major components to the Shannon and Weaver model. First, Schramm identified two basic processes of communication: encoding and decoding. **Encoding** is what a source does when "creating a message, adapting it to the receiver, and transmitting it across some source-selected channel."[12] When you are at home preparing your speech or standing in front of your classroom talking to your peers, you are participating in the encoding process.

The second major process is the **decoding** process, or "sensing (for example, hearing or seeing) a source's message, interpreting the source's message, evaluating the source's message, and responding to the source's message."[13] Decoding is relevant in the public speaking context when, as an audience member, you listen to the words of the speech, pay attention to nonverbal behaviors of the speaker, and attend to any presentation aids that the speaker uses. You must then interpret what the speaker is saying.

Although interpreting a speaker's message may sound easy in theory, in practice many problems can arise. A speaker's verbal message, nonverbal communication, and **mediated** presentation aids can all make a **message** either clearer or harder to understand. For example, unfamiliar vocabulary, speaking too fast or too softly, or small print on presentation aids may make it difficult for you to figure out what the speaker means. Conversely, by providing definitions of complex terms, using well-timed gestures, or displaying graphs of quantitative information, the speaker can help you interpret his or her meaning.

Once you have interpreted what the speaker is communicating, you then evaluate the message. Was it good? Do you agree or disagree with the speaker? Is a speaker's argument logical? These are all questions that you may ask yourself when evaluating a speech.

source

The person(s) who originates a message.

channel

The means by which a message is carried from one person to another (e.g., verbal, nonverbal, or mediated).

receiver

The person(s) who takes delivery of a message.

verbal communication

The use of words to elicit meaning in the mind of a receiver.

nonverbal communication

Any stimuli other than words that can potentially elicit meaning in the mind of a receiver.

noise

Any internal or environmental factor that interferes with the ability to listen effectively. Some of these factors are physical, psychological, physiological, and semantic.

encoding

The process a source goes through when creating a message, adapting it to the receiver, and transmitting it across some source-selected channel.

decoding

Sensing a source's message (through the five senses), interpreting the source's message, and evaluating the source's message.

mediated

The use of some form of technology that intervenes between a source and a receiver of a message.

message

Any verbal or nonverbal stimulus that is meaningful to a receiver.

feedback

A receiver's observable verbal and nonverbal responses to a source's message.

The last part of decoding is "responding to a source's message," when the receiver encodes a message to send to the source. When a receiver sends a message back to a source, we call this process **feedback**. Schramm talks about three types of feedback: direct, moderately direct, and indirect.[14] The first type, direct feedback, occurs when the receiver directly talks to the source. For example, if a speech ends with a question-and-answer period, listeners will openly agree or disagree with the speaker. The second type of feedback, moderately direct, focuses on nonverbal messages sent while a source is speaking, such as audience members smiling and nodding their heads in agreement or looking at their watches or surreptitiously sending text messages during the speech. The final type of feedback, indirect, often involves a greater time gap between the actual message and the receiver's feedback. For example, suppose you run for student body president and give speeches to a variety of groups all over campus, only to lose on student election day. Your audiences (the different groups you spoke to) have offered you indirect feedback on your message through their votes. One of the challenges you'll face as a public speaker is how to respond effectively to audience feedback, particularly the direct and moderately direct forms of feedback you receive during your presentation.

Transactional Model of Public Speaking

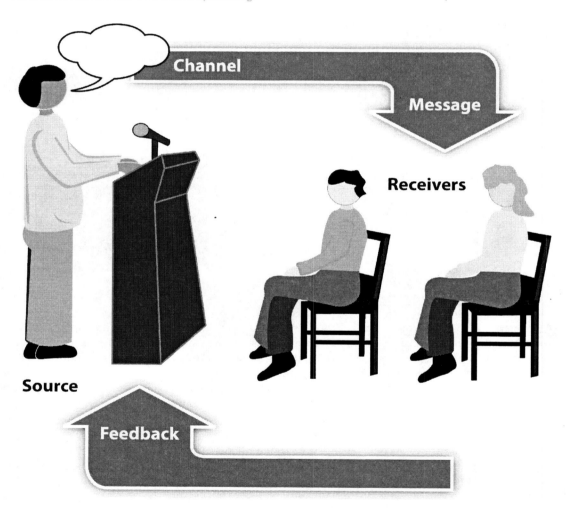

One of the biggest concerns that some people have with the interactional model of communication is that it tends to place people into the category of either source or receiver with no overlap. Even with Schramm's model, encoding and decoding are perceived as distinct for sources and receivers. Furthermore, the interactional model cannot handle situations where multiple sources are interacting at the same time.[15] To address these weaknesses, Dean Barnlund proposed a transactional model of communication.[16] The basic premise of the transactional model is that individuals are sending and receiving messages at the same time. Whereas the interactional model has individuals engaging in the role of either source or receiver and the meaning of a message is sent from the source to the receiver, the transactional model assumes that meaning is cocreated by both people interacting together.

The idea that meanings are cocreated between people is based on a concept called the "field of experience." According to West and Turner, a field of experience involves "how a person's culture, experiences, and heredity influence his or her ability to communicate with another."[17] Our education, race, gender, ethnicity, religion, personality, beliefs, actions, attitudes, languages, social status, past experiences, and customs are all aspects of our field of experience, which we bring to every interaction. For meaning to occur, we must have some shared experiences with our audience; this makes it challenging to speak effectively to audiences with very different experiences from our own. Our goal as public speakers is to build upon shared fields of experience so that we can help audience members interpret our message.

2.2   Dialogic Theory of Public Speaking

Most people think of public speaking as engaging in a monologue where the speaker stands and delivers information and the audience passively listens. Based on the work of numerous philosophers, however, Ronald Arnett and Pat Arneson proposed that all communication, even public speaking, could be viewed as a dialogue.[18] The **dialogic theory** is based on three overarching principles:

1. Dialogue is more natural than monologue.
2. Meanings are in people not words.
3. Contexts and social situations impact perceived meanings.[19]

Let's look at each of these in turn.

Dialogue vs. Monologue

The first tenet of the dialogic perspective is that communication should be a dialogue and not a monologue. Lev Yakubinsky argued that even public speaking situations often turn into dialogues when audience members actively engage speakers by asking questions. He even claimed that nonverbal behavior (e.g., nodding one's head in agreement or scowling) functions as feedback for speakers and contributes to a dialogue.[20] Overall, if you approach your public speaking experience as a dialogue, you'll be more actively engaged as a speaker and more attentive to how your audience is responding, which will, in turn, lead to more actively engaged audience members.

Meanings Are in People, Not Words

Part of the dialogic process in public speaking is realizing that you and your audience may differ in how you see your speech. Hellmut Geissner and Edith Slembeck (1986) discussed Geissner's idea of responsibility, or the notion that the meanings of words must be mutually agreed upon by people interacting with each other.[21] If you say the word "dog" and think of a soft, furry pet and your audience member thinks of the animal that attacked him as a child, the two of you perceive the word from very different vantage points. As speakers, we must do our best to craft messages that take our audience into account and use audience feedback to determine whether the meaning we intend is the one that is received. To be successful at conveying our desired meaning, we must know quite a bit about our audience so we can make language choices that will be the most appropriate for the context. Although we cannot predict how all our audience members will interpret specific words, we do know that—for example—using teenage slang when speaking to the audience at a senior center would most likely hurt our ability to convey our meaning clearly.

Contexts and Social Situations

Russian scholar Mikhail Bahktin notes that human interactions take place according to cultural norms and rules.[22] How we approach people, the words we choose, and how we deliver speeches are all dependent on different speaking contexts and social situations. On September 8, 2009, President Barack Obama addressed school children with a televised speech (http://www.whitehouse.gov/mediaresources/PreparedSchoolRemarks). If you look at the speech he delivered to kids around the country and then at his speeches targeted toward adults, you'll see lots of differences. These dissimilar speeches are necessary because the audiences (speaking to kids vs. speaking to adults) have different experiences and levels of knowledge. Ultimately, good public speaking is a matter of taking into account the cultural background of your audience and attempting to engage your audience in a dialogue from their own vantage point.

Considering the context of a public speech involves thinking about four dimensions: physical, temporal, social-psychological, and cultural.[23]

Physical Dimension

The physical dimension of communication involves the real or touchable environment where communication occurs. For example, you may find yourself speaking in a classroom, a corporate board room,

> **dialogical theory**
>
> Theory of public speaking that views public speaking as a dialogue between the speaker and her or his audience.

or a large amphitheater. Each of these real environments will influence your ability to interact with your audience. Larger physical spaces may require you to use a microphone and speaker system to make yourself heard or to use projected presentation aids to convey visual material.

How the room is physically decorated or designed can also impact your interaction with your audience. If the room is dimly lit or is decorated with interesting posters, audience members' minds may start wandering. If the room is too hot, you'll find people becoming sleepy. As speakers, we often have little or no control over our physical environment, but we always need to take it into account when planning and delivering our messages.

Temporal Dimension

According to Joseph DeVito, the temporal dimension "has to do not only with the time of day and moment in history but also with where a particular message fits into the sequence of communication events."[24] The time of day can have a dramatic effect on how alert one's audience is. Don't believe us? Try giving a speech in front of a class around 12:30 p.m. when no one's had lunch. It's amazing how impatient audience members get once hunger sets in.

In addition to the time of day, we often face temporal dimensions related to how our speech will be viewed in light of societal events. Imagine how a speech on the importance of campus security would be interpreted on the day after a shooting occurred. Compare this with the interpretation of the same speech given at a time when the campus had not had any shootings for years, if ever.

Another element of the temporal dimension is how a message fits with what happens immediately before it. For example, if another speaker has just given an intense speech on death and dying and you stand up to speak about something more trivial, people may downplay your message because it doesn't fit with the serious tone established by the earlier speech. You never want to be the funny speaker who has to follow an emotional speech where people cried. Most of the time in a speech class, you will have no advance notice as to what the speaker before you will be talking about. Therefore, it is wise to plan on being sensitive to previous topics and be prepared to ease your way subtly into your message if the situation so dictates.

Social-Psychological Dimension

The social-psychological dimension of context refers to "status relationships among participants, roles and games that people play, norms of the society or group, and the friendliness, formality, or gravity of the situation."[25] You have to know the types of people in your audience and how they react to a wide range of messages.

Cultural Dimension

The final context dimension Joseph DeVito mentions is the cultural dimension.[26] When we interact with others from different cultures, misunderstandings can result from differing cultural beliefs, norms, and practices. As public speakers engaging in a dialogue with our audience members, we must attempt to understand the cultural makeup of our audience so that we can avoid these misunderstandings as much as possible.

Each of these elements of context is a challenge for you as a speaker. Throughout the rest of the book, we'll discuss how you can meet the challenges presented by the audience and context and become a more effective public speaker in the process.

KEY TAKEAWAYS

- Getting your message across to others effectively requires attention to message content, skill in communicating content, and your passion for the information presented.
- The interactional models of communication provide a useful foundation for understanding communication and outline basic concepts such as sender, receiver, noise, message, channel, encoding, decoding, and feedback. The transactional model builds on the interactional models by recognizing that people can enact the roles of sender and receiver simultaneously and that interactants cocreate meaning through shared fields of experience.
- The dialogic theory of public speaking understands public speaking as a dialogue between speaker and audience. This dialogue requires the speaker to understand that meaning depends on the speaker's and hearer's vantage points and that context affects how we must design and deliver our messages.

EXERCISES

1. Draw the major models of communication on a piece of paper and then explain how each component is important to public speaking.
2. When thinking about your first speech in class, explain the context of your speech using DeVito's four dimensions: physical, temporal, social-psychological, and cultural. How might you address challenges posed by each of these four dimensions?

3.   CHAPTER EXERCISES

END-OF-CHAPTER ASSESSMENT

1. José is a widely sought-after speaker on the topic of environmental pollution. He's written numerous books on the topic and is always seen as the "go-to" guy by news channels when the topic surfaces. What is José?

    a. thought leader

    b. innovator

    c. business strategist

    d. rhetorical expert

    e. intellectual capitalist

2. Fatima is getting ready for a speech she is delivering to the United Nations. She realizes that there are a range of relationships among her various audience members. Furthermore, the United Nations has a variety of norms that are specific to that context. Which of DeVito's (2009) four aspects of communication context is Fatima concerned with?

    a. physical

    b. temporal

    c. social-psychological

    d. cultural

    e. rhetorical

ANSWER KEY

1. a
2. c

ENDNOTES

1. Berkun, S. (2009, March 4). *Does public speaking matter in 2009?* [Web log message]. Retrieved from http://www.scottberkun.com/blog

2. Carnegie Mellon University. (n.d.). Randy Pausch's last lecture. Retrieved June 6, 2011, from http://www.cmu.edu/randyslecture

3. Edmund, N. W. (2005). *End the biggest educational and intellectual blunder in history: A $100,000 challenge to our top educational leaders.* Ft. Lauderdale, FL: Scientific Method Publishing Co.

4. Zekeri, A. A. (2004). College curriculum competencies and skills former students found essential to their careers. *College Student Journal, 38,* 412–422.

5. Rose, H. M., & Rancer, A. S. (1993). The impact of basic courses in oral interpretation and public speaking on communication apprehension. *Communication Reports, 6,* 54–60.

6. Hackman, M. Z., & Johnson, C. E. (2004). *Leadership: A communication perspective* (4th ed.). Long Grove, IL: Waveland.

7. Bender, P. U. (1998). Stand, deliver and lead. *Ivey Business Journal, 62*(3), 46–47.

8. Lizotte, K. (2008). *The expert's edge: Become the go-to authority people turn to every time* [Kindle 2 version]. New York, NY: McGraw-Hill. Retrieved from Amazon.com (locations 72–78)

9. Lizotte, K. (2008). *The expert's edge: Become the go-to authority people turn to every time* [Kindle 2 version]. New York, NY: McGraw-Hill. Retrieved from Amazon.com

10. Shannon, C. E., & Weaver, W. (1949). *The mathematical theory of communication.* Urbana, IL: University of Illinois Press.

11. Schramm, W. (1954). How communication works. In W. Schramm (Ed.), *The process and effects of communication* (pp. 3–26). Urbana, IL: University of Illinois Press.

12. Wrench, J. S., McCroskey, J. C., & Richmond, V. P. (2008). *Human communication in everyday life: Explanations and applications.* Boston, MA: Allyn & Bacon, p. 17.

13. Wrench, J. S., McCroskey, J. C., & Richmond, V. P. (2008). *Human communication in everyday life: Explanations and applications.* Boston, MA: Allyn & Bacon, p. 17.

14. Schramm, W. (1954). How communication works. In W. Schramm (Ed.), *The process and effects of communication* (pp. 3–26). Urbana, IL: University of Illinois Press.

15. Mortenson, C. D. (1972). *Communication: The study of human communication.* New York, NY: McGraw-Hill.

16. Barnlund, D. C. (2008). A transactional model of communication. In C. D. Mortensen (Ed.), *Communication theory* (2nd ed., pp. 47–57). New Brunswick, NJ: Transaction.

17. West, R., & Turner, L. H. (2010). *Introducing communication theory: Analysis and application* (4th ed.). New York, NY: McGraw-Hill, p. 13.

18. Arnett, R. C., & Arneson, P. (1999). *Dialogic civility in a cynical age: Community, hope, and interpersonal relationships.* Albany, NY: SUNY Press.

19. Bakhtin, M. (2001a). The problem of speech genres. (V. W. McGee, Trans., 1986). In P. Bizzell & B. Herzberg (Eds.), *The rhetorical tradition* (pp. 1227–1245). Boston, MA: Bedford/St. Martin's. (Original work published in 1953.); Bakhtin, M. (2001b). Marxism and the philosophy of language. (L. Matejka & I. R. Titunik, Trans., 1973). In P. Bizzell & B. Herzberg (Eds.), *The rhetorical tradition* (pp. 1210–1226). Boston, MA: Medford/St. Martin's. (Original work published in 1953).

20. Yakubinsky, L. P. (1997). On dialogic speech. (M. Eskin, Trans.). *PMLA, 112*(2), 249–256. (Original work published in 1923).

21. Geissner, H., & Slembek, E. (1986). *Miteinander sprechen und handeln* [Speak and act: Living and working together]. Frankfurt, Germany: Scriptor.

22. Bakhtin, M. (2001a). The problem of speech genres. (V. W. McGee, Trans., 1986). In P. Bizzell & B. Herzberg (Eds.), *The rhetorical tradition* (pp. 1227–1245). Boston, MA: Bedford/St. Martin's. (Original work published in 1953.); Bakhtin, M. (2001b). Marxism and the philosophy of language. (L. Matejka & I. R. Titunik, Trans., 1973). In P. Bizzell & B. Herzberg (Eds.), *The rhetorical tradition* (pp. 1210–1226). Boston, MA: Medford/St. Martin's. (Original work published in 1953).

23. DeVito, J. A. (2009). *The interpersonal communication book* (12th ed.). Boston, MA: Allyn & Bacon.

24. DeVito, J. A. (2009). *The interpersonal communication book* (12th ed.). Boston, MA: Allyn & Bacon, p. 13.

25. DeVito, J. A. (2009). *The interpersonal communication book* (12th ed.). Boston, MA: Allyn & Bacon, p. 14.

26. DeVito, J. A. (2009). *The interpersonal communication book* (12th ed.). Boston, MA: Allyn & Bacon.

CHAPTER 2
Ethics Matters: Understanding the Ethics of Public Speaking

ETHICS TODAY

Every day, people around the world make ethical decisions regarding public speech. Is it ever appropriate to lie to a group of people if it's in the group's best interest? As a speaker, should you use evidence within a speech that you are not sure is correct if it supports the speech's core argument? As a listener, should you refuse to listen to a speaker with whom you fundamentally disagree? These three examples represent ethical choices speakers and listeners face in the public speaking context. In this chapter, we will explore what it means to be both an ethical speaker and an ethical listener. To help you understand the issues involved with thinking about ethics, this chapter begins by presenting a model for ethical communication known as the ethics pyramid. We will then show how the National Communication Association (NCA) Credo for Ethical Communication can be applied to public speaking. The chapter will conclude with a general discussion of free speech.

© *Thinkstock*

---

1.   THE ETHICS PYRAMID

LEARNING OBJECTIVE

1. Explain how the three levels of the ethics pyramid might be used in evaluating the ethical choices of a public speaker or listener.

The word "ethics" can mean different things to different people. Whether it is an ethical lapse in business or politics or a disagreement about medical treatments and end-of-life choices, people come into contact with ethical dilemmas regularly. Speakers and listeners of public speech face numerous ethical dilemmas as well. What kinds of support material and sources are ethical to use? How much should a speaker adapt to an audience without sacrificing his or her own views? What makes a speech ethical?

© *Thinkstock*

FIGURE 2.1 Ethical Pyramid

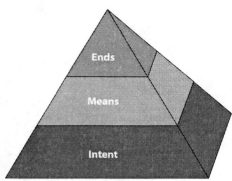

Elspeth Tilley, a public communication ethics expert from Massey University, proposes a structured approach to thinking about ethics.[1] Her ethics pyramid involves three basic concepts: intent, means, and ends. Figure 2.1 illustrates the Tilley pyramid.

1.1 Intent

According to Tilley, the first major consideration to be aware of when examining the ethicality of something is the issue of **intent**. To be an ethical speaker or listener, it is important to begin with ethical intentions. For example, if we agree that honesty is ethical, it follows that ethical speakers will prepare their remarks with the intention of telling the truth to their audiences. Similarly, if we agree that it is ethical to listen with an open mind, it follows that ethical listeners will be intentional about letting a speaker make his or her case before forming judgments.

intent

The degree to which an individual is cognitively aware of her or his behavior, the means one uses, and the ends one achieves.

One option for assessing intent is to talk with others about how ethical they think a behavior is; if you get a variety of answers, it might be a sign that the behavior is not ethical and should be avoided. A second option is to check out existing codes of ethics. Many professional organizations, including the Independent Computer Consultants Association, American Counseling Association, and American Society of Home Inspectors, have codes of conduct or ethical guidelines for their members. Individual corporations such as Monsanto, Coca-Cola, Intel, and ConocoPhillips also have ethical guidelines for how their employees should interact with suppliers or clients. Even when specific ethical codes are not present, you can apply general ethical principles, such as whether a behavior is beneficial for the majority or whether you would approve of the same behavior if you were listening to a speech instead of giving it.

In addition, it is important to be aware that people can engage in unethical behavior unintentionally. For example, suppose we agree that it is unethical to take someone else's words and pass them off as your own—a behavior known as plagiarism. What happens if a speaker makes a statement that he believes he thought of on his own, but the statement is actually quoted from a radio commentator whom he heard without clearly remembering doing so? The plagiarism was unintentional, but does that make it ethical?

1.2 Means

means

The tools or behaviors that one employs to achieve a desired outcome.

Tilley describes the **means** you use to communicate with others as the second level of the ethics pyramid. According to McCroskey, Wrench, and Richmond,[2] "means" are the tools or behaviors we employ to achieve a desired outcome. We must realize that there are a range of possible behavioral choices for any situation and that some choices are good, some are bad, and some fall in between.

For example, suppose you want your friend Marty to spend an hour reviewing a draft of your speech according to criteria, such as audience appropriateness, adequate research, strong support of assertions, and dynamic introduction and conclusion. What means might you use to persuade Marty to do you this favor? You might explain that you value Marty's opinion and will gladly return the favor the next time Marty is preparing a speech (good means), or you might threaten to tell a professor that Marty cheated on a test (bad means). While both of these means may lead to the same end—having Marty agree to review your speech—one is clearly more ethical than the other.

1.3 Ends

ends

The outcomes that one desires to achieve.

The final part of the ethics pyramid is the ends. According to McCroskey, Wrench, and Richmond,[3] **ends** are those outcomes that you desire to achieve. Examples of ends might include persuading your audience to make a financial contribution for your participation in Relay for Life, persuading a group of homeowners that your real estate agency would best meet their needs, or informing your fellow students about newly required university fees. Whereas the means are the behavioral choices we make, the ends are the results of those choices.

Like intentions and means, ends can be good or bad, or they can fall into a gray area where it is unclear just how ethical or unethical they are. For example, suppose a city council wants to balance the city's annual budget. Balancing the budget may be a good end, assuming that the city has adequate tax revenues and areas of discretionary spending for nonessential services for the year in question. However, voters might argue that balancing the budget is a bad end if the city lacks these things for the year in question, because in that case balancing the budget would require raising taxes, curtailing essential city services, or both.

When examining ends, we need to think about both the source and the receiver of the message or behavior. Some end results could be good for the source but bad for the receiver, or vice versa.

Suppose, for example, that Anita belongs to a club that is raffling off a course of dancing lessons. Anita sells Ben a ten-dollar raffle ticket. However, Ben later thinks it over and realizes that he has no desire to take dancing lessons and that if he should win the raffle, he will never take the lessons. Anita's club has gained ten dollars—a good end—but Ben has lost ten dollars—a bad end. Again, the ethical standards you and your audience expect to be met will help in deciding whether a particular combination of speaker and audience ends is ethical.

1.4   Thinking through the Pyramid

Ultimately, understanding ethics is a matter of balancing all three parts of the ethical pyramid: intent, means, and ends. When thinking about the ethics of a given behavior, Tilley recommends asking yourself three basic questions:

1. "Have I discussed the ethicality of the behavior with others and come to a general consensus that the behavior is ethical?"
2. "Does the behavior adhere to known codes of ethics?"
3. "Would I be happy if the outcomes of the behavior were reversed and applied to me?"[4]

While you do not need to ask yourself these three questions before enacting every behavior as you go through a day, they do provide a useful framework for thinking through a behavior when you are not sure whether a given action, or statement, may be unethical. Ultimately, understanding ethics is a matter of balancing all three parts of the ethical pyramid: intent, means, and ends.

KEY TAKEAWAY

- The ethics pyramid is a pictorial way of understanding the three fundamental parts of ethics: intent, means, and ends. Intent exists at the base of the ethical pyramid and serves as a foundation for determining the ethics of specific behavior. Means are the tools one uses to accomplish a goal and constitute the second layer of the ethical pyramid. Finally, ends are the results that occur after a specific behavior has occurred and exist at the top of the pyramid.

EXERCISES

1. Can you think of a time when you intended to have a "good" end and employed "good" means, but you ended up accomplishing a "bad" end? Why do you think our ends are not always in line with our intentions?
2. Ursula is developing a speech on the importance of organ donation. She has found lots of impressive statistics in her research but feels she needs an interesting story to really make an impression on her audience and persuade them to become organ donors. Ursula can't find a true story she really likes, so she takes elements of several stories and pieces them together into a single story. Her speech is a huge success and six of her classmates sign up to be organ donors immediately after her presentation. How do we decide whether Ursula's behavior is ethical?
3. Pablo has been scheduled to work late several nights this week and is very tired by the time his public speaking class rolls around in the late afternoon. One of his classmates gives a speech about environmental sustainability and Pablo does not really pay attention to what the classmate is saying. After the speech, Pablo's teacher asks him to critique the speech. Because he doesn't really know what happened in the speech, Pablo makes a general statement that the speech was pretty good, that the delivery was OK, and that the organization was fine. Using the ethics pyramid as a guide, in what ways might Pablo's response be ethical? In what ways might it be unethical? What are Pablo's responsibilities as an ethical listener?

2. ETHICS IN PUBLIC SPEAKING

LEARNING OBJECTIVES

1. Understand how to apply the National Communication Association (NCA) Credo for Ethical Communication within the context of public speaking.
2. Understand how you can apply ethics to your public speaking preparation process.

The study of ethics in human communication is hardly a recent endeavor. One of the earliest discussions of ethics in communication (and particularly in public speaking) was conducted by the ancient Greek philosopher Plato in his dialogue *Phaedrus*. In the centuries since Plato's time, an entire subfield within the discipline of human communication has developed to explain and understand communication ethics.

2.1 Communication Code of Ethics

In 1999, the National Communication Association officially adopted the Credo for Ethical Communication (see the following sidebar). Ultimately, the NCA Credo for Ethical Communication is a set of beliefs communication scholars have about the ethics of human communication.

National Communication Association Credo for Ethical Communication

Questions of right and wrong arise whenever people communicate. Ethical communication is fundamental to responsible thinking, decision making, and the development of relationships and communities within and across contexts, cultures, channels, and media. Moreover, ethical communication enhances human worth and dignity by fostering truthfulness, fairness, responsibility, personal integrity, and respect for self and others. We believe that unethical communication threatens the quality of all communication and consequently the well-being of individuals and the society in which we live. Therefore we, the members of the National Communication Association, endorse and are committed to practicing the following principles of ethical communication:

- We advocate truthfulness, accuracy, honesty, and reason as essential to the integrity of communication.
- We endorse freedom of expression, diversity of perspective, and tolerance of dissent to achieve the informed and responsible decision making fundamental to a civil society.
- We strive to understand and respect other communicators before evaluating and responding to their messages.
- We promote access to communication resources and opportunities as necessary to fulfill human potential and contribute to the well-being of families, communities, and society.
- We promote communication climates of caring and mutual understanding that respect the unique needs and characteristics of individual communicators.
- We condemn communication that degrades individuals and humanity through distortion, intimidation, coercion, and violence, and through the expression of intolerance and hatred.
- We are committed to the courageous expression of personal convictions in pursuit of fairness and justice.
- We advocate sharing information, opinions, and feelings when facing significant choices while also respecting privacy and confidentiality.
- We accept responsibility for the short- and long-term consequences of our own communication and expect the same of others.

Source: http://www.natcom.org/Default.aspx?id=134&terms=Credo

2.2 Applying the NCA Credo to Public Speaking

The NCA Credo for Ethical Communication is designed to inspire discussions of ethics related to all aspects of human communication. For our purposes, we want to think about each of these principles in terms of how they affect public speaking.

We Advocate Truthfulness, Accuracy, Honesty, and Reason as Essential to the Integrity of Communication

As public speakers, one of the first ethical areas we should be concerned with is information honesty. While there are cases where speakers have blatantly lied to an audience, it is more common for speakers to prove a point by exaggerating, omitting facts that weigh against their message, or distorting information. We believe that speakers build a relationship with their audiences, and that lying, exaggerating, or distorting information violates this relationship. Ultimately, a speaker will be more persuasive by using reason and logical arguments supported by facts rather than relying on emotional appeals designed to manipulate the audience.

© Thinkstock

It is also important to be honest about where all your information comes from in a speech. As speakers, examine your information sources and determine whether they are biased or have hidden agendas. For example, you are not likely to get accurate information about nonwhite individuals from a neo-Nazi website. While you may not know all your sources of information firsthand, you should attempt to find objective sources that do not have an overt or covert agenda that skews the argument you are making. We will discuss more about ethical sources of information in Chapter 7 later in this book.

The second part of information honesty is to fully disclose where we obtain the information in our speeches. As ethical speakers, it is important to always cite your sources of information within the body of a speech. Whether you conducted an interview or read a newspaper article, you must tell your listeners where the information came from. We mentioned earlier in this chapter that using someone else's words or ideas without giving credit is called **plagiarism**. The word "plagiarism" stems from the Latin word *plagiaries*, or kidnapper. The American Psychological Association states in its publication manual that ethical speakers do not claim "words and ideas of another as their own; they give credit where credit is due."[5]

In the previous sentence, we placed quotation marks around the sentence to indicate that the words came from the American Psychological Association and not from us. When speaking informally, people sometimes use "air quotes" to signal direct quotations—but this is not a recommended technique in public speaking. Instead, speakers need to verbally tell an audience when they are using someone else's information. The consequences for failing to cite sources during public speeches can be substantial. When Senator Joseph Biden was running for president of the United States in 1988, reporters found that he had plagiarized portions of his stump speech from British politician Neil Kinnock. Biden was forced to drop out of the race as a result. More recently, the student newspaper at Malone University in Ohio alleged that the university president, Gary W. Streit, had plagiarized material in a public speech. Streit retired abruptly as a result.

Even if you are not running for president of the United States or serving as a college president, citing sources is important to you as a student. Many universities have policies that include dismissal from the institution for student plagiarism of academic work, including public speeches. Failing to cite your sources might result, at best, in lower credibility with your audience and, at worst, in a failing grade on your assignment or expulsion from your school. While we will talk in more detail about plagiarism later in this book, we cannot emphasize enough the importance of giving credit to the speakers and authors whose ideas we pass on within our own speeches and writing.

Speakers tend to fall into one of three major traps with plagiarism. The first trap is failing to tell the audience the source of a direct quotation. In the previous paragraph, we used a direct quotation from the American Psychological Association; if we had not used the quotation marks and clearly listed where the cited material came from, you, as a reader, wouldn't have known the source of that information. To avoid plagiarism, you always need to tell your audience when you are directly quoting information within a speech.

The second plagiarism trap public speakers fall into is paraphrasing what someone else said or wrote without giving credit to the speaker or author. For example, you may have read a book and learned that there are three types of schoolyard bullying. In the middle of your speech you talk about those three types of schoolyard bullying. If you do not tell your audience where you found that information, you are plagiarizing. Typically, the only information you do not need to cite is information that is general knowledge. General knowledge is information that is publicly available and widely known by a large segment of society. For example, you would not need to provide a citation within a speech for the name of Delaware's capital. Although many people do not know the capital of Delaware without looking it up, this information is publicly available and easily accessible, so assigning credit to one specific source is not useful or necessary.

The third plagiarism trap that speakers fall into is re-citing someone else's sources within a speech. To explain this problem, let's look at a brief segment from a research paper written by Wrench, DiMartino, Ramirez, Oviedo, and Tesfamariam:

plagiarism

Using someone else's words or ideas without giving credit.

The main character on the hit Fox television show House, Dr. Gregory House, has one basic mantra, "It's a basic truth of the human condition that everybody lies. The only variable is about what" (Shore & Barclay, 2005). This notion that "everybody lies" is so persistent in the series that t-shirts have been printed with the slogan. Surprisingly, research has shown that most people do lie during interpersonal interactions to some degree. In a study conducted by Turner, Edgley, and Olmstead (1975), the researchers had 130 participants record their own conversations with others. After recording these conversations, the participants then examined the truthfulness of the statements within the interactions. Only 38.5% of the statements made during these interactions were labeled as "completely honest."

In this example, we see that the authors of this paragraph (Wrench, DiMartino, Ramirez, Oviedio, & Tesfamariam) cited information from two external sources: Shore and Barclay and Tummer, Edgley, and Olmstead. These two groups of authors are given credit for their ideas. The authors make it clear that they (Wrench, DiMartino, Ramirez, Oviedio, and Tesfamariam) did not produce the television show *House* or conduct the study that found that only 38.5 percent of statements were completely honest. Instead, these authors cited information found in two other locations. This type of citation is appropriate.

However, if a speaker read the paragraph and said the following during a speech, it would be plagiarism: "According to Wrench DiMartino, Ramirez, Oviedio, and Tesfamariam, in a study of 130 participants, only 38.5 percent of the responses were completely honest." In this case, the speaker is attributing the information cited to the authors of the paragraph, which is not accurate. If you want to cite the information within your speech, you need to read the original article by Turner, Edgley, and Olmstead and cite that information yourself.

There are two main reasons we do this. First, Wrench, DiMartino, Ramirez, Oviedio, and Tesfamariam may have mistyped the information. Suppose the study by Turner, Edgley, and Olstead really actually found that 58.5 percent of the responses were completely honest. If you cited the revised number (38.5 percent) from the paragraph, you would be further spreading incorrect information.

The second reason we do not re-cite someone else's sources within our speeches is because it's intellectually dishonest. You owe your listeners an honest description of where the facts you are relating came from, not just the name of an author who cited those facts. It is more work to trace the original source of a fact or statistic, but by doing that extra work you can avoid this plagiarism trap.

We Endorse Freedom of Expression, Diversity of Perspective, and Tolerance of Dissent to Achieve the Informed and Responsible Decision Making Fundamental to a Civil Society

This ethical principle affirms that a civil society depends on freedom of expression, diversity of perspective, and tolerance of dissent and that informed and responsible decisions can only be made if all members of society are free to express their thoughts and opinions. Further, it holds that diverse viewpoints, including those that disagree with accepted authority, are important for the functioning of a democratic society.

If everyone only listened to one source of information, then we would be easily manipulated and controlled. For this reason, we believe that individuals should be willing to listen to a range of speakers on a given subject. As listeners or consumers of communication, we should realize that this diversity of perspectives enables us to be more fully informed on a subject. Imagine voting in an election after listening only to the campaign speeches of one candidate. The perspective of that candidate would be so narrow that you would have no way to accurately understand and assess the issues at hand or the strengths and weaknesses of the opposing candidates. Unfortunately, some voters do limit themselves to listening only to their candidate of choice and, as a result, base their voting decisions on incomplete—and, not infrequently, inaccurate—information.

Listening to diverse perspectives includes being willing to hear dissenting voices. Dissent is by nature uncomfortable, as it entails expressing opposition to authority, often in very unflattering terms. Legal scholar Steven H. Shiffrin has argued in favor of some symbolic speech (e.g., flag burning) because we as a society value the ability of anyone to express their dissent against the will and ideas of the majority.[6] Ethical communicators will be receptive to dissent, no matter how strongly they may disagree with the speaker's message because they realize that a society that forbids dissent cannot function democratically.

Ultimately, honoring free speech and seeking out a variety of perspectives is very important for all listeners. We will discuss this idea further in the chapter on listening.

We Strive to Understand and Respect Other Communicators before Evaluating and Responding to Their Messages

This is another ethical characteristic that is specifically directed at receivers of a message. As listeners, we often let our perceptions of a speaker's nonverbal behavior—his or her appearance, posture, mannerisms, eye contact, and so on—determine our opinions about a message before the speaker has said a word. We may also find ourselves judging a speaker based on information we have heard about him or her from other people. Perhaps you have heard from other students that a particular teacher is a really boring lecturer or is really entertaining in class. Even though you do not have personal knowledge, you may prejudge the teacher and his or her message based on information you have been given from others. The NCA **credo** reminds us that to be ethical listeners, we need to avoid such judgments and instead make an effort to listen respectfully; only when we have understood a speaker's viewpoint are we ready to begin forming our opinions of the message.

Listeners should try to objectively analyze the content and arguments within a speech before deciding how to respond. Especially when we disagree with a speaker, we might find it difficult to listen to the content of the speech and, instead, work on creating a rebuttal the entire time the speaker is talking. When this happens, we do not strive to understand the speaker and do not respect the speaker.

Of course, this does not just affect the listener in the public speaking situation. As speakers, we are often called upon to evaluate and refute potential arguments against our positions. While we always want our speeches to be as persuasive as possible, we do ourselves and our audiences a disservice when we downplay, distort, or refuse to mention important arguments from the opposing side. Fairly researching and evaluating counterarguments is an important ethical obligation for the public speaker.

credo

A formal statement of core beliefs and principles.

We Promote Access to Communication Resources and Opportunities as Necessary to Fulfill Human Potential and Contribute to the Well-Being of Families, Communities, and Society

Human communication is a skill that can and should be taught. We strongly believe that you can become a better, more ethical speaker. One of the reasons the authors of this book teach courses in public speaking and wrote this college textbook on public speaking is that we, as communication professionals, have an ethical obligation to provide others, including students like you, with resources and opportunities to become better speakers.

We Promote Communication Climates of Caring and Mutual Understanding That Respect the Unique Needs and Characteristics of Individual Communicators

Speakers need to take a two-pronged approach when addressing any audience: caring about the audience and understanding the audience. When you as a speaker truly care about your audience's needs and desires, you avoid setting up a manipulative climate. This is not to say that your audience will always perceive their own needs and desires in the same way you do, but if you make an honest effort to speak to your audience in a way that has their best interests at heart, you are more likely to create persuasive arguments that are not just manipulative appeals.

Second, it is important for a speaker to create an atmosphere of mutual understanding. To do this, you should first learn as much as possible about your audience, a process called audience analysis. We will discuss this topic in more detail in the audience analysis chapter.

To create a climate of caring and mutual respect, it is important for us as speakers to be open with our audiences so that our intentions and perceptions are clear. Nothing alienates an audience faster than a speaker with a hidden agenda unrelated to the stated purpose of the speech. One of our coauthors once listened to a speaker give a two-hour talk, allegedly about workplace wellness, which actually turned out to be an infomercial for the speaker's weight-loss program. In this case, the speaker clearly had a hidden (or not-so-hidden) agenda, which made the audience feel disrespected.

We Condemn Communication That Degrades Individuals and Humanity through Distortion, Intimidation, Coercion, and Violence and through the Expression of Intolerance and Hatred

This ethical principle is very important for all speakers. Hopefully, intimidation, coercion, and violence will not be part of your public speaking experiences, but some public speakers have been known to call for violence and incite mobs of people to commit attrocities. Thus distortion and expressions of intolerance and hatred are of special concern when it comes to public speaking.

distortion

Purposefully twisting information in a way that detracts from its original meaning.

ageist

Language that demeans an individual because of her or his age.

heterosexist

Language that assumes that all members within an audience are heterosexual or is intended to demean nonheterosexual audience members.

racist

Language that demeans an entire race of people, people within a specific ethnic group, or an individual because he or she belongs to a specific race or ethnic group.

sexist

Language that demeans or excludes one of the biological sexes.

Distortion occurs when someone purposefully twists information in a way that detracts from its original meaning. Unfortunately, some speakers take information and use it in a manner that is not in the spirit of the original information. One place we see distortion frequently is in the political context, where politicians cite a statistic or the results of a study and either completely alter the information or use it in a deceptive manner. FactCheck.org, a project of the Annenberg Public Policy Center (http://www.factcheck.org), and the St. Petersburg Times's Politifact (http://www.politifact.com) are nonpartisan organizations devoted to analyzing political messages and demonstrating how information has been distorted.

Expressions of intolerance and hatred that are to be avoided include using **ageist**, **heterosexist**, **racist**, **sexist**, and any other form of speech that demeans or belittles a group of people. Hate speech from all sides of the political spectrum in our society is detrimental to ethical communication. As such, we as speakers should be acutely aware of how an audience may perceive words that could be considered bigoted. For example, suppose a school board official involved in budget negotiations used the word "shekels" to refer to money, which he believes the teachers' union should be willing to give up.[7] The remark would be likely to prompt accusations of anti-Semitism and to distract listeners from any constructive suggestions the official might have for resolving budget issues. Although the official might insist that he meant no offense, he damaged the ethical climate of the budget debate by using a word associated with bigotry.

At the same time, it is important for listeners to pay attention to expressions of intolerance or hatred. Extremist speakers sometimes attempt to disguise their true agendas by avoiding bigoted "buzzwords" and using mild-sounding terms instead. For example, a speaker advocating the overthrow of a government might use the term "regime change" instead of "revolution"; similarly, proponents of genocide in various parts of the world have used the term "ethnic cleansing" instead of "extermination." By listening critically to the gist of a speaker's message as well as the specific language he or she uses, we can see how that speaker views the world.

We Are Committed to the Courageous Expression of Personal Convictions in Pursuit of Fairness and Justice

We believe that finding and bringing to light situations of inequality and injustice within our society is important. Public speaking has been used throughout history to point out inequality and injustice, from Patrick Henry arguing against the way the English government treated the American colonists and Sojourner Truth describing the evils of slavery to Martin Luther King Jr.'s "I Have a Dream" speech and Army Lt. Dan Choi's speeches arguing that the military's "don't ask, don't tell policy" is unjust. Many social justice movements have started because young public speakers have decided to stand up for what they believe is fair and just.

We Advocate Sharing Information, Opinions, and Feelings When Facing Significant Choices While Also Respecting Privacy and Confidentiality

This ethical principle involves balancing personal disclosure with discretion. It is perfectly normal for speakers to want to share their own personal opinions and feelings about a topic; however, it is also important to highlight information within a speech that represents your own thoughts and feelings. Your listeners have a right to know the difference between facts and personal opinions.

Similarly, we have an obligation to respect others' privacy and confidentiality when speaking. If information is obtained from printed or publicly distributed material, it's perfectly appropriate to use that information without getting permission, as long as you cite it. However, when you have a great anecdote one of your friends told you in confidence, or access to information that is not available to the general public, it is best to seek permission before using the information in a speech.

This ethical obligation even has legal implications in many government and corporate contexts. For example, individuals who work for the Central Intelligence Agency are legally precluded from discussing their work in public without prior review by the agency. And companies such as Google also have policies requiring employees to seek permission before engaging in public speaking in which sensitive information might be leaked.

We Accept Responsibility for the Short- and Long-Term Consequences of Our Own Communication and Expect the Same of Others

The last statement of NCA's ethical credo may be the most important one. We live in a society where a speaker's message can literally be heard around the world in a matter of minutes, thanks to our global communication networks. Extreme remarks made by politicians, media commentators, and celebrities, as well as ordinary people, can unexpectedly "go viral" with regrettable consequences. It is not unusual to see situations where a speaker talks hatefully about a specific group, but when one of the speaker's listeners violently attacks a member of the group, the speaker insists that he or she had no way of knowing that this could possibly have happened. Washing one's hands of responsibility is unacceptable: all speakers should accept responsibility for the short-term and long-term consequences of their speeches. Although it is certainly not always the speaker's fault if someone commits an act of violence, the speaker should take responsibility for her or his role in the situation. This process involves being truly reflective and willing to examine how one's speech could have tragic consequences.

Furthermore, attempting to persuade a group of people to take any action means you should make sure that you understand the consequences of that action. Whether you are persuading people to vote for a political candidate or just encouraging them to lose weight, you should know what the short-term and long-term consequences of that decision could be. While our predictions of short-term and long-term consequences may not always be right, we have an ethical duty to at least think through the possible consequences of our speeches and the actions we encourage.

2.3 Practicing Ethical Public Speaking

Thus far in this section we've introduced you to the basics of thinking through the ethics of public speaking. Knowing about ethics is essential, but even more important to being an ethical public speaker is putting that knowledge into practice by thinking through possible ethical pitfalls prior to standing up and speaking out. Table 2.1 is a checklist based on our discussion in this chapter to help you think through some of these issues.

TABLE 2.1 Public Speaking Ethics Checklist

Instructions: For each of the following ethical issues, check either "true" or "false."		True	False
1.	I have knowingly added information within my speech that is false.		
2.	I have attempted to persuade people by unnecessarily tapping into emotion rather than logic.		
3.	I have not clearly cited all the information within my speech.		
4.	I do not know who my sources of information are or what makes my sources credible.		
5.	I wrote my speech based on my own interests and really haven't thought much about my audience.		
6.	I haven't really thought much about my audience's needs and desires.		
7.	I have altered some of the facts in my speech to help me be more persuasive.		
8.	Some of the language in my speech may be considered bigoted.		
9.	My goal is to manipulate my audience to my point of view.		
10.	I sometimes blend in my personal opinions when discussing actual facts during the speech.		
11.	My personal opinions are just as good as facts, so I don't bother to distinguish between the two during my speech.		
12.	I've used information in my speech from a friend or colleague that probably shouldn't be repeated.		
13.	I'm using information in my speech that a source gave me even though it was technically "off the record."		
14.	It's just a speech. I really don't care what someone does with the information when I'm done speaking.		
15.	I haven't really thought about the short- or long-term consequences of my speech.		
Scoring: For ethical purposes, all your answers should have been "false."			

KEY TAKEAWAYS

- All eight of the principles espoused in the NCA Credo for Ethical Communication can be applied to public speaking. Some of the principles relate more to the speaker's role in communication, while others relate to both the speaker's and the audience's role in public speech.
- When preparing a speech, it is important to think about the ethics of public speaking from the beginning. When a speaker sets out to be ethical in his or her speech from the beginning, arriving at ethical speech is much easier.

3. FREE SPEECH

LEARNING OBJECTIVES

1. Define the concept of free speech and discuss its origins.
2. Discuss the First Amendment to the US Constitution in terms of free speech.
3. Describe how free speech relates to other freedoms guaranteed by the First Amendment to the US Constitution.

© Thinkstock

free speech

The right to express information, ideas, and opinions free of government restrictions based on content and subject only to reasonable limitations.

3.1 What Is Free Speech?

Free speech has been a constitutional right since the founding of our nation, and according to *Merriam Webster's Dictionary of Law*, **free speech** entails "the right to express information, ideas, and opinions free of government restrictions based on content and subject only to reasonable limitations (as the power of the government to avoid a clear and present danger) esp. as guaranteed by the First and Fourteenth Amendments to the U.S. Constitution."[8] Free speech is especially important to us as public speakers because expressing information and ideas is the purpose of public speaking. It is also important to audiences of public speeches because free speech allows us to hear and consider multiple points of view so that we can make more informed decisions.

3.2 The First Amendment to the Constitution

Free speech was so important to the founders of the United States that it is included in the first of the ten amendments to the US Constitution that are known as the Bill of Rights. This is not surprising, considering that many American colonists had crossed the Atlantic to escape religious persecution and that England had imposed many restrictions on personal freedoms during the colonial era. The text of the First Amendment reads, "Congress shall make no law respecting an establishment of religion, or prohibiting the free exercise thereof; or abridging the freedom of speech, or of the press; or the right of the people peaceably to assemble, and to petition the Government for a redress of grievances."[9]

The freedoms protected by the First Amendment may seem perfectly natural today, but they were controversial in 1791 when the Bill of Rights was enacted. Proponents argued that individuals needed protection from overreaching powers of government, while opponents believed these protections were unnecessary and that amending them to the Constitution could weaken the union.

Freedom of speech, of the press, of religion, of association, of assembly and petition are all guaranteed in amendments to the US Constitution. Free speech allows us to exercise our other First Amendment rights. Freedom of assembly means that people can gather to discuss and protest issues of importance to them. If free speech were not protected, citizens would not be able to exercise their right to protest about activities such as war or policies such as health care reform.

Free speech does not mean, however, that every US citizen has the legal right to say anything at any time. If your speech is likely to lead to violence or other illegal acts, it is not protected. One recent example is a 2007 Supreme Court decision in the *Morse et al. v. Frederick* case. In this case, a high school student held up a sign reading "Bong Hits 4 Jesus" across from the school during the 2002 Olympic Torch Relay. The principal suspended the teenager, and the teen sued the principal for violating his First Amendment rights. Ultimately, the court decided that the principal had the right to suspend the student because he was advocating illegal behavior.[10]

The meaning of "free speech" is constantly being debated by politicians, judges, and the public, even within the United States, where this right has been discussed for over two hundred years. As US citizens, it is important to be aware of both the protections afforded by free speech and its limits so that we can be both articulate speakers and critical listeners when issues such as antiwar protests at military funerals or speech advocating violence against members of specific groups come up within our communities.

Source: Photo courtesy of Noclip, http://commons.wikimedia.org/wiki/File:Supreme_Court_Front_Dusk.jpg.

KEY TAKEAWAYS

- Freedom of speech is the right to express information, ideas, and opinions free of government restrictions based on content and subject only to reasonable limitations.
- Free speech helps us to enact other freedoms protected by the First Amendment, including freedom of assembly and freedom of religion. Without free speech, we would not be able to assemble in groups to publically debate and challenge government policies or laws. Without free speech, we would not be able to exercise our rights to express our religious views even when they are at odds with popular opinion.

EXERCISES

1. What are your campus's internal codes on speech and free speech? Do you have free speech areas on campus? If so, how are they used and regulated?
2. Some college campuses have experienced controversy in recent years when they invited speakers such as Ward Churchill or those who deny that the Holocaust occurred to campus. Discuss in a small group how these controversies reflect the importance of free speech in our society.

4.   CHAPTER EXERCISES

SPEAKING ETHICALLY

Jerold Follinsworth is an elected official on the verge of giving the most important speech of his entire life, but he doesn't know which speech to give. He looks down at his hands and sees two very different speeches. The speech in his left hand clearly admits to the public that he has been having an affair with a senior staffer. The allegations have been around for a few months, but his office has been denying the allegations as slanderous attacks from his opponents. In his right hand, he has a speech that sidesteps the affair allegations and focuses on an important policy issue. If Jerold gives the speech in his left hand, an important initiative for his state will be defeated by his political enemies. If Jerold gives the speech in his right hand, he will be deceiving the public, but it will lead to increased growth in jobs for his state. Jerold asked his top speech writer to prepare both speeches. As Jerold waits in the wings for his press conference, he's just not sure which speech he should give.

1. What ethical communication choices do you see Jerold as having in this case?
2. How would you analyze Jerold's decision using the ethical pyramid?
3. How would you apply the National Communication Association (NCA) Credo for Ethical Communication to this case?

END-OF-CHAPTER ASSESSMENT

1. Darlene is in the process of preparing a speech on global warming. She knowingly includes a source from a fringe group that has been previously discredited, but she thinks the source will really help her drive her argument home. What combination of the ethics pyramid does this case represent?

    a. intentional use of bad means
    b. intentional use of good means
    c. unintentional use of bad means
    d. unintentional use of good means
    e. intentional use of neutral means

2. Which of the following is *not* an ethical aspect described by the NCA Credo for Ethical Communication?

    a. freedom of expression
    b. access to communication resources and opportunities
    c. accepting responsibility for one's own communication
    d. respecting a source before evaluating her or his message
    e. promoting ethical standards in business

ANSWER KEY

1. a
2. e

ENDNOTES

1. Tilley, E. (2005). The ethics pyramid: Making ethics unavoidable in the public relations process. *Journal of Mass Media Ethics, 20*, 305–320.

2. McCroskey, J. C., Wrench, J. S., & Richmond, V. P. (2003). *Principles of public speaking.* Indianapolis, IN: The College Network.

3. McCroskey, J. C., Wrench, J. S., & Richmond, V. P. (2003). *Principles of public speaking.* Indianapolis, IN: The College Network.

4. Tilley, E. (2005). The ethics pyramid: Making ethics unavoidable in the public relations process. *Journal of Mass Media Ethics, 20*, 305–320.

5. American Psychological Association. (2001). *Publication manual of the American Psychological Association* (5th ed.). Washington, DC: Author, p. 349.

6. Shiffrin, S. H. (1999). *Dissent, injustice and the meanings of America.* Princeton, NJ: Princeton University Press.

7. Associated Press. (2011, May 5). Conn. shekel shellacking. *New York Post.*

8. Freedom of speech. (n.d.). In *Merriam-Webster's dictionary of law.* Retrieved from Dictionary.com website: http://dictionary.reference.com/browse/freedom%20of%20speech

9. National Archives and Records Administration. (2011). Bill of rights transcription. Retrieved from http://www.archives.gov/exhibits/charters/bill_of_rights_transcript.html

10. Supreme Court of the United States. (2007). Syllabus: Morse et al. v. Frederick. No. 06–278. Argued March 19, 2007–Decided June 25, 2007. Retrieved from http://www.supremecourt.gov/opinions/06pdf/06-278.pdf

CHAPTER 3
Speaking Confidently

BATTLING NERVES AND THE UNEXPECTED

One of your biggest concerns about public speaking might be how to deal with nervousness or unexpected events. If that's the case, you're not alone—fear of speaking in public consistently ranks at the top of lists of people's common fears. Some people are not joking when they say they would rather die than stand up and speak in front of a live audience. The fear of public speaking ranks right up there with the fear of flying, death, and spiders.[1] Even if you are one of the fortunate few who don't typically get nervous when speaking in public, it's important to recognize things that can go wrong and be mentally prepared for them. On occasion, everyone misplaces speaking notes, has technical difficulties with a presentation aid, or gets distracted by an audience member. Speaking confidently involves knowing how to deal with these and other unexpected events while speaking.

© Thinkstock

In this chapter, we will help you gain knowledge about speaking confidently by exploring what communication apprehension is, examining the different types and causes of communication apprehension, suggesting strategies you can use to manage your fears of public speaking, and providing tactics you can use to deal with a variety of unexpected events you might encounter while speaking.

1. WHAT IS COMMUNICATION APPREHENSION?

LEARNING OBJECTIVES

1. Explain the nature of communication apprehension.
2. List the physiological symptoms of communication apprehension.
3. Identify different misconceptions about communication anxiety.

"Speech is a mirror of the soul," commented Publilius Syrus, a popular writer in 42 BCE.[2] Other people come to know who we are through our words. Many different social situations, ranging from job interviews to dating to public speaking, can make us feel uncomfortable as we anticipate that we will be evaluated and judged by others. How well we communicate is intimately connected to our self-image, and the process of revealing ourselves to the evaluation of others can be threatening whether we are meeting new acquaintances, participating in group discussions, or speaking in front of an audience.

1.1 Definition of Communication Apprehension

According to James McCroskey, **communication apprehension** is the broad term that refers to an individual's "fear or anxiety associated with either real or anticipated communication with another person or persons."[3] At its heart, communication apprehension is a psychological response to evaluation. This psychological response, however, quickly becomes physical as our body responds to the threat the mind perceives. Our bodies cannot distinguish between psychological and physical threats, so we react as though we were facing a Mack truck barreling in our direction. The body's circulatory and adrenal systems shift into overdrive, preparing us to function at maximum physical efficiency—the "flight or

communication apprehension

The fear or anxiety associated with either real or perceived communication with another person or persons.

fight" response.[4] Yet instead of running away or fighting, all we need to do is stand and talk. When it comes to communication apprehension, our physical responses are often not well adapted to the nature of the threat we face, as the excess energy created by our body can make it harder for us to be effective public speakers. But because communication apprehension is rooted in our minds, if we understand more about the nature of the body's responses to stress, we can better develop mechanisms for managing the body's misguided attempts to help us cope with our fear of social judgment.

1.2   Physiological Symptoms of Communication Apprehension

© Thinkstock

There are a number of physical sensations associated with communication apprehension. We might notice our heart pounding or our hands feeling clammy. We may break out in a sweat. We may have "stomach butterflies" or even feel nauseated. Our hands and legs might start to shake, or we may begin to pace nervously. Our voices may quiver, and we may have a "dry mouth" sensation that makes it difficult to articulate even simple words. Breathing becomes more rapid and, in extreme cases, we might feel dizzy or light-headed. Anxiety about communicating is profoundly disconcerting because we feel powerless to control our bodies. Furthermore, we may become so anxious that we fear we will forget our name, much less remember the main points of the speech we are about to deliver.

The physiological changes produced in the body at critical moments are designed to contribute to the efficient use of muscles and expand available energy. Circulation and breathing become more rapid so that additional oxygen can reach the muscles. Increased circulation causes us to sweat. Adrenaline rushes through our body, instructing the body to speed up its movements. If we stay immobile behind a lectern, this hormonal urge to speed up may produce shaking and trembling. Additionally, digestive processes are inhibited so we will not lapse into the relaxed, sleepy state that is typical after eating. Instead of feeling sleepy, we feel butterflies in the pit of our stomach. By understanding what is happening to our bodies in response to the stress of public speaking, we can better cope with these reactions and channel them in constructive directions.

Any conscious emotional state such as anxiety or excitement consists of two components: a primary reaction of the central nervous system and an intellectual interpretation of these physiological responses. The physiological state we label as communication anxiety does not differ from ones we label rage or excitement. Even experienced, effective speakers and performers experience some communication apprehension. What differs is the mental label that we put on the experience. Effective speakers have learned to channel their body's reactions, using the energy released by these physiological reactions to create animation and stage presence.

1.3   Myths about Communication Apprehension

© Thinkstock

A wealth of conventional wisdom surrounds the discomfort of speaking anxiety, as it surrounds almost any phenomenon that makes us uncomfortable. Most of this "folk" knowledge misleads us, directing our attention away from effective strategies for thinking about and coping with anxiety reactions. Before we look in more detail at the types of communication apprehension, let's dispel some of the myths about it.

1. **People who suffer from speaking anxiety are neurotic.** As we have explained, speaking anxiety is a normal reaction. Good speakers can get nervous just as poor speakers do. Winston Churchill, for example, would get physically ill before major speeches in Parliament. Yet he rallied the British people in a time of crisis. Many people, even the most professional performers, experience anxiety about communicating. Such a widespread problem, Dr. Joyce Brothers contends, "cannot be attributed to deep-seated neuroses."[5]

2. **Telling a joke or two is always a good way to begin a speech.** Humor is some of the toughest material to deliver effectively because it requires an exquisite sense of timing. Nothing is worse than waiting for a laugh that does not come. Moreover, one person's joke is another person's slander. It is extremely easy to offend when using humor. The same material can play very differently with different audiences. For these reasons, it is not a good idea to start with a joke, particularly if it is not well related to your topic. Humor is just too unpredictable and difficult for many novice speakers. If you insist on using humor, make sure the "joke" is on you, not on someone else. Another tip is never to pause and wait for a laugh that may not come. If the audience catches the joke, fine. If not, you're not left standing in awkward silence waiting for a reaction.

3. **Imagine the audience is naked.** This tip just plain doesn't work because imagining the audience naked will do nothing to calm your nerves. As Malcolm Kushner noted, "There are some folks in the audience I wouldn't want to see naked—especially if I'm trying *not* to be frightened."[6] The audience is not some abstract image in your mind. It consists of real individuals who you can connect with through your material. To "imagine" the audience is to misdirect your focus from the real people in front of you to an "imagined" group. What we imagine is usually more threatening than the reality that we face.

4. **Any mistake means that you have "blown it."** We all make mistakes. What matters is not whether we make a mistake but how well we recover. One of the authors of this book was giving a speech and wanted to thank a former student in the audience. Instead of saying "former student," she said, "former friend." After the audience stopped laughing, the speaker remarked, "Well, I guess she'll be a *former* friend now!"—which got more laughter from the audience. A speech does not have to be perfect. You just have to make an effort to relate to the audience naturally and be willing to accept your mistakes.

5. **Avoid speaking anxiety by writing your speech out word for word and memorizing it.** Memorizing your speech word for word will likely make your apprehension worse rather than better. Instead of remembering three to five main points and subpoints, you will try to commit to memory more than a thousand bits of data. If you forget a point, the only way to get back on track is to start from the beginning. You are inviting your mind to go blank by overloading it with details. In addition, audiences do not like to listen to "canned," or memorized, material. Your delivery is likely to suffer if you memorize. Audiences appreciate speakers who talk naturally to them rather than recite a written script.

6. **Audiences are out to get you.** With only a few exceptions, which we will talk about in Section 2, the natural state of audiences is empathy, not antipathy. Most face-to-face audiences are interested in your material, not in your image. Watching someone who is anxious tends to make audience members anxious themselves. Particularly in public speaking classes, audiences want to see you succeed. They know that they will soon be in your shoes and they identify with you, most likely hoping you'll succeed and give them ideas for how to make their own speeches better. If you establish direct eye contact with real individuals in your audience, you will see them respond to what you are saying, and this response lets you know that you are succeeding.

7. **You will look to the audience as nervous as you feel.** Empirical research has shown that audiences do not perceive the level of nervousness that speakers report feeling.[7] Most listeners judge speakers as less anxious than the speakers rate themselves. In other words, the audience is not likely to perceive accurately the level of anxiety you might be experiencing. Some of the most effective speakers will return to their seats after their speech and exclaim they were **so** nervous. Listeners will respond, "You didn't look nervous." Audiences do not necessarily perceive our fears. Consequently, don't apologize for your nerves. There is a good chance the audience will not notice if you do not point it out to them.

8. **A little nervousness helps you give a better speech.** This "myth" is true! Professional speakers, actors, and other performers consistently rely on the heightened arousal of nervousness to channel extra energy into their performance. People would much rather listen to a speaker who is alert and enthusiastic than one who is relaxed to the point of boredom. Many professional speakers say that the day they stop feeling nervous is the day they should stop speaking in public. The goal is to control those nerves and channel them into your presentation.

KEY TAKEAWAYS

- Communication apprehension refers to the fear or anxiety people experience at the thought of being evaluated by others. Some anxiety is a normal part of the communication process.
- The psychological threat individuals perceive in the communication situation prompts physiological changes designed to help the body respond. These physical reactions to stress create the uncomfortable feelings of unease called speech anxiety and may include sweaty palms, shaking, butterflies in the stomach, and dry mouth.
- A great deal of conventional advice for managing stage fright is misleading, including suggestions that speech anxiety is neurotic, that telling a joke is a good opening, that imagining the audience naked is helpful, that any mistake is fatal to an effective speech, that memorizing a script is useful, that audiences are out to get you, and that your audience sees how nervous you really are.

2. ALL ANXIETY IS NOT THE SAME: SOURCES OF COMMUNICATION APPREHENSION

LEARNING OBJECTIVES

1. Distinguish among the four different types of communication apprehension.
2. Identify various factors that cause communication apprehension.

We have said that experiencing some form of anxiety is a normal part of the communication process. Most people are anxious about being evaluated by an audience. Interestingly, many people assume that their nervousness is an experience unique to them. They assume that other people do not feel anxious when confronting the threat of public speaking.[8] Although anxiety is a widely shared response to the stress of public speaking, not all anxiety is the same. Many researchers have investigated the differences between apprehension grounded in personality characteristics and anxiety prompted by a particular situation at a particular time.[9] McCroskey argues there are four types of communication apprehension: anxiety related to trait, context, audience, and situation.[10] If you understand these different types of apprehension, you can gain insight into the varied communication factors that contribute to speaking anxiety.

2.1 Trait Anxiety

trait anxiety

Anxiety prompted by a personality trait that describes how people *generally* feel about communication across situations and time periods.

Some people are just more disposed to communication apprehension than others. As Witt, Brown, Roberts, Weisel, Sawyer, and Behnke explain, "**Trait anxiety** measures how people *generally* feel across situations and time periods."[11] This means that some people feel more uncomfortable than the average person regardless of the context, audience, or situation. It doesn't matter whether you are raising your hand in a group discussion, talking with people you meet at a party, or giving speeches in a class, you're likely to be uncomfortable in all these settings if you experience trait anxiety. While trait anxiety is not the same as shyness, those with high trait anxiety are more likely to avoid exposure to public speaking situations, so their nervousness might be compounded by lack of experience or skill.[12] People who experience trait anxiety may never like public speaking, but through preparation and practice, they can learn to give effective public speeches when they need to do so.

2.2   Context Anxiety

Context anxiety refers to anxiety prompted by specific communication contexts. Some of the major context factors that can heighten this form of anxiety are formality, uncertainty, and novelty.

Formality

Some individuals can be perfectly composed when talking at a meeting or in a small group; yet when faced with a more formal public speaking setting, they become intimidated and nervous. As the formality of the communication context increases, the stakes are raised, sometimes prompting more apprehension. Certain communication contexts, such as a press conference or a courtroom, can make even the most confident individuals nervous. One reason is that these communication contexts presuppose an adversarial relationship between the speaker and some audience members.

Uncertainty

In addition, it is hard to predict and control the flow of information in such contexts, so the level of uncertainty is high. The feelings of context anxiety might be similar to those you experience on the first day of class with a new instructor: you don't know what to expect, so you are more nervous than you might be later in the semester when you know the instructor and the class routine better.

Novelty

Additionally, most of us are not experienced in high-tension communication settings. The novelty of the communication context we encounter is another factor contributing to apprehension. Anxiety becomes more of an issue in communication environments that are new to us, even for those who are normally comfortable with speaking in public.

Most people can learn through practice to cope with their anxiety prompted by formal, uncertain, and novel communication contexts. Fortunately, most public speaking classroom contexts are not adversarial. The opportunities you have to practice giving speeches reduces the novelty and uncertainty of the public speaking context, enabling most students to learn how to cope with anxiety prompted by the communication context.

© Thinkstock

context anxiety

The anxiety prompted by specific communication contexts such as group discussions, interpersonal interactions, or public speaking.

2.3   Audience Anxiety

For some individuals, it is not the communication context that prompts anxiety; it is the people in the audience they face. **Audience anxiety** describes communication apprehension prompted by specific audience characteristics. These characteristics include similarity, subordinate status, audience size, and familiarity.

You might have no difficulty talking to an audience of your peers in student government meetings, but an audience composed of parents and students on a campus visit might make you nervous because of the presence of parents in the audience. The degree of perceived similarity between you and your audience can influence your level of speech anxiety. We all prefer to talk to an audience that we believe shares our values more than to one that does not. The more dissimilar we are compared to our audience members, the more likely we are to be nervous. Studies have shown that subordinate status can also contribute to speaking anxiety.[13] Talking in front of your boss or teacher may be intimidating, especially if you are being evaluated. The size of the audience can also play a role: the larger the audience, the more threatening it may seem. Finally, familiarity can be a factor. Some of us prefer talking to strangers rather than to people we know well. Others feel more nervous in front of an audience of friends and family because there is more pressure to perform well.

audience anxiety

The communication apprehension prompted by specific types of audiences.

2.4   Situational Anxiety

Situational anxiety, McCroskey explains, is the communication apprehension created by "the unique combination of influences generated by audience, time and context."[14] Each communication event involves several dimensions: physical, temporal, social-psychological, and cultural. These dimensions combine to create a unique communication situation that is different from any previous

situational anxiety

Communication apprehension created by the specific combination of audience, time, and setting.

communication event. The situation created by a given audience, in a given time, and in a given context can coalesce into situational anxiety.

For example, I once had to give a presentation at a general faculty meeting on general education assessment. To my surprise, I found myself particularly nervous about this speech. The audience was familiar to me but was relatively large compared to most classroom settings. I knew the audience well enough to know that my topic was controversial for some faculty members who resented the mandate for assessment coming from top administration. The meeting occurred late on a Friday afternoon, and my presentation was scheduled more than an hour into the two-hour meeting. All these factors combined to produce situational anxiety for me. While I successfully applied the principles that we will discuss in Section 3 for managing stage fright, this speaking situation stands out in my mind as one of the most nerve-wracking speaking challenges I have ever faced.

KEY TAKEAWAYS

- Communication apprehension stems from many sources, including the speaker's personality characteristics, communication context, nature of the audience, or situation.
- Many factors exaggerate communication apprehension. Formality, familiarity, novelty, perceived similarity, and subordinate status are a few of the factors that influence our tendency to feel anxious while speaking.

EXERCISE

1. Make a list of sources of your communication apprehension. What factors contribute most to your anxiety about public speaking?

---

3. REDUCING COMMUNICATION APPREHENSION

LEARNING OBJECTIVES

1. Explain steps for managing anxiety in the speech preparation process.
2. Identify effective techniques for coping with anxiety during delivery.
3. Recognize the general options available for stress reduction and anxiety management.

Experiencing some nervousness about public speaking is normal. The energy created by this physiological response can be functional if you harness it as a resource for more effective public speaking. In this section, we suggest a number of steps that you can take to channel your stage fright into excitement and animation. We will begin with specific speech-related considerations and then briefly examine some of the more general anxiety management options available.

3.1 Speech-Related Considerations

© Thinkstock

Communication apprehension does not necessarily remain constant throughout all the stages of speech preparation and delivery. One group of researchers studied the ebb and flow of anxiety levels at four stages in the delivery of a speech. They compared indicators of physiological stress at different milestones in the process:

- anticipation (the minute prior to starting the speech),
- confrontation (the first minute of the speech),
- adaptation (the last minute of the speech), and
- release (the minute immediately following the end of the speech).[15]

These researchers found that anxiety typically peaked at the anticipatory stage. In other words, we are likely to be most anxious right before we get up to speak. As we progress through our speech, our level of anxiety is likely to decline. Planning your speech to incorporate techniques for managing your nervousness at different times will help you decrease the overall level of stress you experience. We also offer a number of suggestions for managing your reactions while you are delivering your speech.

Think Positively

As we mentioned earlier, communication apprehension begins in the mind as a psychological response. This underscores the importance of a speaker's psychological attitude toward speaking. To prepare yourself mentally for a successful speaking experience, we recommend using a technique called **cognitive restructuring**. Cognitive restructuring is simply changing how you label the physiological responses you will experience. Rather than thinking of public speaking as a dreaded obligation, make a conscious decision to consider it an exciting opportunity. The first audience member that you have to convince is yourself, by deliberately replacing negative thoughts with positive ones. If you say something to yourself often enough, you will gradually come to believe it.

We also suggest practicing what communication scholars Metcalfe, Beebe, and Beebe call **positive self-talk** rather than **negative self-talk**.[16] If you find yourself thinking, "I'm going to forget everything when I get to the front of the room," turn that negative message around to a positive one. Tell yourself, "I have notes to remind me what comes next, and the audience won't know if I don't cover everything in the order I planned." The idea is to dispute your negative thoughts and replace them with positive ones, even if you think you are "conning" yourself. By monitoring how you talk about yourself, you can unlearn old patterns and change the ways you think about things that produce anxiety.

cognitive restructuring
A technique of deliberately replacing negative cognitions with positive ones.

positive self-talk
A habit of thinking in positive terms about your capabilities.

negative self-talk
A habit of thinking in negative terms about your skills and abilities.

Reducing Anxiety through Preparation

As we have said earlier in this chapter, uncertainty makes for greater anxiety. Nothing is more frightening than facing the unknown. Although no one can see into the future and predict everything that will happen during a speech, every speaker can and should prepare so that the "unknowns" of the speech event are kept to a minimum. You can do this by gaining as much knowledge as possible about whom you will be addressing, what you will say, how you will say it, and where the speech will take place.

Analyze Your Audience

The audience that we imagine in our minds is almost always more threatening than the reality of the people sitting in front of us. The more information you have about the characteristics of your audience, the more you will be able to craft an effective message. Since your stage fright is likely to be at its highest in the beginning of your speech, it is helpful to open the speech with a technique to prompt an audience response. You might try posing a question, asking for a show of hands, or sharing a story that you know is relevant to your listeners' experience. When you see the audience responding to you by nodding, smiling, or answering questions, you will have directed the focus of attention from yourself to the audience. Such responses indicate success; they are positively reinforcing, and thus reduce your nervousness.

Clearly Organize Your Ideas

Being prepared as a speaker means knowing the main points of your message so well that you can remember them even when you are feeling highly anxious, and the best way to learn those points is to create an outline for your speech. With a clear outline to follow, you will find it much easier to move from one point to the next without stumbling or getting lost.

A note of caution is in order: you do not want to react to the stress of speaking by writing and memorizing a manuscript. Your audience will usually be able to tell that you wrote your speech out verbatim, and they will tune out very quickly. You are setting yourself up for disaster if you try to memorize a written text because the pressure of having to remember all those particulars will be tremendous. Moreover, if you have a momentary memory lapse during a memorized speech, you may have a lot of trouble continuing without starting over at the beginning.

What you do want to prepare is a simple outline that reminds you of the progression of ideas in your speech. What is important is the order of your points, not the specifics of each sentence. It is perfectly fine if your speech varies in terms of specific language or examples each time you practice it.

It may be a good idea to reinforce this organization through visual aids. When it comes to managing anxiety, visual aids have the added benefit of taking attention off the speaker.

Adapt Your Language to the Oral Mode

Another reason not to write out your speech as a manuscript is that to speak effectively you want your language to be adapted to the oral, not the written, mode. You will find your speaking anxiety more manageable if you speak in the oral mode because it will help you to feel like you are having a conversation with friends rather than delivering a formal proclamation.

Appropriate oral style is more concrete and vivid than written style. Effective speaking relies on verbs rather than nouns, and the language is less complex. Long sentences may work well for novelists such as William Faulkner or James Joyce, where readers can go back and reread passages two, three, or even seven or eight times. Your listeners, though, cannot "rewind" you in order to catch ideas they miss the first time through.

Don't be afraid to use personal pronouns freely, frequently saying "I" and "me"—or better yet, "us" and "we." Personal pronouns are much more effective in speaking than language constructions, such as the following "this author," because they help you to build a connection with your audience. Another oral technique is to build audience questions into your speech. Rhetorical questions, questions that do not require a verbal answer, invite the audience to participate with your material by thinking about the implications of the question and how it might be answered. If you are graphic and concrete in your language selection, your audience is more likely to listen attentively. You will be able to see the audience listening, and this feedback will help to reduce your anxiety.

Practice in Conditions Similar to Those You Will Face When Speaking

It is not enough to practice your speech silently in your head. To reduce anxiety and increase the likelihood of a successful performance, you need to practice out loud in a situation similar to the one you will face when actually performing your speech. Practice delivering your speech out loud while standing on your feet. If you make a mistake, do not stop to correct it but continue all the way through your speech; that is what you will have to do when you are in front of the audience.

If possible, practice in the actual room where you will be giving your speech. Not only will you have a better sense of what it will feel like to actually speak, but you may also have the chance to practice using presentation aids and potentially avoid distractions and glitches like incompatible computers, blown projector bulbs, or sunlight glaring in your eyes.

Two very useful tools for anxiety-reducing practice are a clock and a mirror. Use the clock to time your speech, being aware that most novice speakers speak too fast, not too slowly. By ensuring that you are within the time guidelines, you will eliminate the embarrassment of having to cut your remarks short because you've run out of time or of not having enough to say to fulfill the assignment. Use the mirror to gauge how well you are maintaining eye contact with your audience; it will allow you to check that you are looking up from your notes. It will also help you build the habit of using appropriate facial expressions to convey the emotions in your speech. While you might feel a little absurd practicing your speech out loud in front of a mirror, the practice that you do before your speech can make you much less anxious when it comes time to face the audience.

Watch What You Eat

A final tip about preparation is to watch what you eat immediately before speaking. The butterflies in your stomach are likely to be more noticeable if you skip normal meals. While you should eat normally, you should avoid caffeinated drinks because they can make your shaking hands worse. Carbohydrates operate as natural sedatives, so you may want to eat carbohydrates to help slow down your metabolism and to avoid fried or very spicy foods that may upset your stomach. Especially if you are speaking in the morning, be sure to have breakfast. If you haven't had anything to eat or drink since dinner the night before, dizziness and light-headedness are very real possibilities.

Reducing Nervousness during Delivery

Anticipate the Reactions of Your Body

deep breathing

A relaxation technique that involves expanding the diaphragm to increase air flow.

There are a number of steps you can take to counteract the negative physiological effects of stress on the body. **Deep breathing** will help to counteract the effects of excess adrenaline. You can place symbols in your notes, like "slow down" or ☺, that remind you to pause and breathe during points in your speech. It is also a good idea to pause a moment before you get started to set an appropriate pace from the onset. Look at your audience and smile. It is a reflex for some of your audience members to smile back. Those smiles will reassure you that your audience members are friendly.

Physical movement helps to channel some of the excess energy that your body produces in response to anxiety. If at all possible, move around the front of the room rather than remaining imprisoned behind the lectern or gripping it for dear life (avoid pacing nervously from side to side, however). Move closer to the audience and then stop for a moment. If you are afraid that moving away from the lectern will reveal your shaking hands, use note cards rather than a sheet of paper for your outline. Note cards do not quiver like paper, and they provide you with something to do with your hands.

Vocal warm-ups are also important before speaking. Just as athletes warm up before practice or competition and musicians warm up before playing, speakers need to get their voices ready to speak. Talking with others before your speech or quietly humming to yourself can get your voice ready for your presentation. You can even sing or practice a bit of your speech out loud while you're in the shower (just don't wake the neighbors), where the warm, moist air is beneficial for your vocal mechanism. Gently yawning a few times is also an excellent way to stretch the key muscle groups involved in speaking.

Immediately before you speak, you can relax the muscles of your neck and shoulders, rolling your head gently from side to side. Allow your arms to hang down your sides and stretch out your shoulders. **Isometric exercises** that involve momentarily tensing and then relaxing specific muscle groups are an effective way to keep your muscles from becoming stiff.

isometric exercises

A form of exercise in which you systematically tense and then relax certain muscle groups.

Focus on the Audience, Not on Yourself

During your speech, make a point of establishing direct eye contact with your audience members. By looking at individuals, you establish a series of one-to-one contacts similar to interpersonal communication. An audience becomes much less threatening when you think of them not as an anonymous mass but as a collection of individuals.

A colleague once shared his worst speaking experience when he reached the front of the room and forgot everything he was supposed to say. When I asked what he saw when he was in the front of the room, he looked at me like I was crazy. He responded, "I didn't see anything. All I remember is a mental image of me up there in the front of the room blowing it." Speaking anxiety becomes more intense if you focus on yourself rather than concentrating on your audience and your material.

Maintain Your Sense of Humor

No matter how well we plan, unexpected things happen. That fact is what makes the public speaking situation so interesting. When the unexpected happens to you, do not let it rattle you. At the end of a class period late in the afternoon of a long day, a student raised her hand and asked me if I knew that I was wearing two different colored shoes, one black and one blue. I looked down and saw that she was right; my shoes did not match. I laughed at myself, complimented the student on her observational abilities and moved on with the important thing, the material I had to deliver.

3.2   Stress Management Techniques

Even when we employ positive thinking and are well prepared, some of us still feel a great deal of anxiety about public speaking. When that is the case, it can be more helpful to use stress management than to try to make the anxiety go away.

One general technique for managing stress is **positive visualization**. Visualization is the process of seeing something in your mind's eye; essentially it is a form of self-hypnosis. Frequently used in sports training, positive visualization involves using the imagination to create images of relaxation or ultimate success. Essentially, you imagine in great detail the goal for which you are striving, say, a rousing round of applause after you give your speech. You mentally picture yourself standing at the front of the room, delivering your introduction, moving through the body of your speech, highlighting your presentation aids, and sharing a memorable conclusion. If you imagine a positive outcome, your body will respond to it as through it were real. Such mind-body techniques create the psychological grounds for us to achieve the goals we have imagined. As we discussed earlier, communication apprehension has a psychological basis, so mind-body techniques such as visualization can be important to reducing anxiety. It's important to keep in mind, though, that visualization does not mean you can skip practicing your speech out loud. Just as an athlete still needs to work out and practice the sport, you need to practice your speech in order to achieve the positive results you visualize.

positive visualization

Using the imagination to control stress and create images of success.

Systematic desensitization is a behavioral modification technique that helps individuals overcome anxiety disorders. People with phobias, or irrational fears, tend to avoid the object of their fear. For example, people with a phobia of elevators avoid riding in elevators—and this only adds to their fear because they never "learn" that riding in elevators is usually perfectly safe. Systematic desensitization changes this avoidance pattern by gradually exposing the individual to the object of fear until it can be tolerated.

systematic desensitization

A behavioral modification technique that reduces anxiety by gradually exposing the individual to the object or situation they fear while teaching them basic relaxation techniques.

First, the individual is trained in specific muscle relaxation techniques. Next, the individual learns to respond with conscious relaxation even when confronted with the situation that previously caused them fear. James McCroskey used this technique to treat students who suffered from severe, trait-based communication apprehension.[17] He found that "the technique was eighty to ninety percent effective" for the people who received the training.[18] If you're highly anxious about public speaking, you might begin a program of systematic desensitization by watching someone else give a speech. Once you are able to do this without discomfort, you would then move to talking about giving a speech yourself, practicing, and, eventually, delivering your speech.

The success of techniques such as these clearly indicates that increased exposure to public speaking reduces overall anxiety. Consequently, you should seek out opportunities to speak in public rather than avoid them. As the famous political orator William Jennings Bryan once noted, "The ability to speak effectively is an acquirement rather than a gift."[19]

EXERCISES

1. Go to http://www.hypknowsis.com and practice a few of the simple beginning visualization exercises presented there.
2. Make a plan for managing your anxiety before and during your speech that includes specific techniques you want to try before your next public speaking assignment.

4. COPING WITH THE UNEXPECTED

LEARNING OBJECTIVES

1. Identify common difficulties that may fluster even experienced speakers.
2. Describe some basic strategies for dealing with unexpected events during a public speech.

Even the most prepared, confident public speaker may encounter unexpected challenges during the speech. This section discusses some common unexpected events and addresses some general strategies for combating the unexpected when you encounter it in your own speaking.

© Thinkstock

4.1 Speech Content Issues

Nearly every experienced speaker has gotten to the middle of a presentation and realized that a key notecard is missing or that he or she skipped important information from the beginning of the speech. When encountering these difficulties, a good strategy is to pause for a moment to think through what you want to do next. Is it important to include the missing information, or can it be omitted without hurting the audience's ability to understand the rest of your speech? If it needs to be included, do you want to add the information now, or will it fit better later in the speech? It is often difficult to remain silent when you encounter this situation, but pausing for a few seconds will help you to figure out what to do and may be less distracting to the audience than sputtering through a few "ums" and "uhs."

4.2 Technical Difficulties

Technology has become a very useful aid in public speaking, allowing us to use audio or video clips, presentation software, or direct links to websites. However, one of the best known truisms about technology is that it does break down. Web servers go offline, files will not download in a timely manner, and media are incompatible with the computer in the presentation room. It is important to always have a backup plan, developed in advance, in case of technical difficulties with your presentation materials. As you develop your speech and visual aids, think through what you will do if you cannot show a particular graph or if your presentation slides are hopelessly garbled. Although your beautifully prepared chart may be superior to the oral description you can provide, your ability to provide a succinct oral description when technology fails can give your audience the information they need.

4.3 External Distractions

Although many public speaking instructors directly address audience etiquette during speeches, you're still likely to encounter an audience member who walks in late, a ringing cell phone, or even a car alarm going off outside your classroom. If you are distracted by external events like these, it is often useful, and sometimes necessary (as in the case of the loud car alarm), to pause and wait so that you can regain the audience's attention and be heard.

Whatever the unexpected event, your most important job as a speaker is to maintain your composure. It is important not to get upset or angry because of these types of glitches—and, once again, the key to this is being fully prepared. If you keep your cool and quickly implement a "plan B" for moving forward with your speech, your audience is likely to be impressed and may listen even more attentively to the rest of your presentation.

KEY TAKEAWAY

1. Plan ahead for how to cope with unexpected difficulties such as forgetting part of your speech content, having technical trouble with visual aids, or being interrupted by external distractions.

EXERCISES

1. Talk to people who engage in public speaking regularly (e.g., teachers and professionals) and find out what unexpected events have happened when they were giving speeches. What did they do to deal with these unexpected happenings?
2. Fill out the Personal Report of Communication Apprehension (PRCA24). The measure can be found at http://www.jamescmccroskey.com/measures/prca24.htm.

5. CHAPTER EXERCISES

TEST YOUR KNOWLEDGE OF COMMUNICATION APPREHENSION

Myths or Facts about Communication Apprehension

Instructions: For each of the following questions, check either "myth" or "fact."	Myth	Fact
1. Audiences will be able to tell how nervous you feel.		
2. Some stage fright might be a good thing, as you can channel it to make your delivery more energetic.		
3. Most audiences are basically hostile, looking to see you make a fool of yourself.		
4. Experienced speakers don't feel any stage fright.		
5. Most speakers tend to relax as they progress through their speeches.		
6. Moving around the front of the room during your speech will make you less nervous.		
7. Most audiences would rather see a speaker do well.		
8. Focusing on yourself rather than the audience is an effective way to reduce your stage fright.		
9. The positive or negative label you ascribe to the public speaking situation will influence how nervous you feel.		
10. Telling a joke in your introduction is guaranteed to get the audience on your side.		
Scoring: Myths: 1, 3, 4, 8, and 10; Facts: 2, 5, 6, 7, and 9		

ENDNOTES

1. Wallechinsky, D., Wallace, I., & Wallace, A. (1977). *The people's almanac presents the book of lists*. New York, NY: Morrow. See also Boyd, J. H., Rae, D. S., Thompson, J. W., Burns, B. J., Bourdon, K., Locke, B. Z., & Regier, D. A. (1990). Phobia: Prevalence and risk factors. *Social Psychiatry and Psychiatric Epidemiology, 25*(6), 314–323.

2. Bartlett, J. (comp.). (1919). *Familiar quotations* (10th ed.). Rev. and enl. by Nathan Haskell Dole. Boston, MA: Little, Brown, and Company. Retrieved from Bartleby.com website: http://www.bartleby.com/100

3. McCroskey, J. C. (2001). *An introduction to rhetorical communication*. Boston, MA: Allyn & Bacon, p. 40.

4. Sapolsky, R. M. (2004). *Why zebras don't get ulcers* (3rd ed.). New York, NY: Henry Holt.

5. Brothers, J. (2008, July 1). Public speaking among people's top fears. *Seattle Pi.* Retrieved from http://www.seattlepi.com

6. Kushner, M. (1999). *Public speaking for dummies*. New York, NY: IDG Books Worldwide, p. 242.

7. Clevenger, T. J. (1959). A synthesis of experimental research in stage fright. *Quarterly Journal of Speech, 45,* 135–159. See also Savitsky, K., & Gilovich, T. (2003). The illusion of transparency and the alleviation of speech anxiety. *Journal of Experimental Social Psychology, 39,* 601–625.

8. McCroskey, J. C. (2001). *An introduction to rhetorical communication*. Boston, MA: Allyn & Bacon.

9. Witt, P. L., Brown, K. C., Roberts, J. B., Weisel, J., Sawyer, C., & Behnke, R. (2006, March). Somatic anxiety patterns before, during and after giving a public speech. *Southern Communication Journal, 71,* 87–100.

10. McCroskey, J. C. (2001). *An introduction to rhetorical communication*. Boston, MA: Allyn & Bacon.

11. Witt, P. L., Brown, K. C., Roberts, J. B., Weisel, J., Sawyer, C., & Behnke, R. (2006, March). Somatic anxiety patterns before, during and after giving a public speech. *Southern Communication Journal, 71,* 88.

12. Witt, P. L., Brown, K. C., Roberts, J. B., Weisel, J., Sawyer, C., & Behnke, R. (2006, March). Somatic anxiety patterns before, during and after giving a public speech. *Southern Communication Journal, 71,* 87–100.

13. Witt, P. L., Brown, K. C., Roberts, J. B., Weisel, J., Sawyer, C., & Behnke, R. (2006, March). Somatic anxiety patterns before, during and after giving a public speech. *Southern Communication Journal, 71,* 87–100.

14. McCroskey, J. C. (2001). *An introduction to rhetorical communication*. Boston, MA: Allyn & Bacon, p. 43.

15. Witt, P. L., Brown, K. C., Roberts, J. B., Weisel, J., Sawyer, C., & Behnke, R. (2006, March). Somatic anxiety patterns before, during and after giving a public speech. *Southern Communication Journal, 71,* 89.

16. Metcalfe, S. (1994). *Building a speech*. New York, NY: The Harcourt Press; Beebe, S.A., & Beebe, S. J. (2000). *Public speaking: An audience centered approach*. Boston, MA: Allyn & Bacon.

17. McCroskey, J. C. (1972). The implementation of a large-scale program of systematic desensitization for communication apprehension. *The Speech Teacher, 21,* 255–264.

18. McCroskey, J. C. (2001). *An introduction to rhetorical communication*. Boston, MA: Allyn & Bacon, p. 57.

19. Carnegie, D. (1955). *Public speaking and influencing men in business*. New York, NY: American Book Stratford Press, Inc.

CHAPTER 4
The Importance of Listening

"Are you listening to me?" This question is often asked because the speaker thinks the listener is nodding off or daydreaming. We sometimes think that listening means we only have to sit back, stay barely awake, and let a speaker's words wash over us. While many Americans look upon being active as something to admire, to engage in, and to excel at, listening is often understood as a "passive" activity. More recently, *O, the Oprah Magazine* featured a cover article with the title, "How to Talk So People *Really* Listen: Four Ways to Make Yourself Heard." This title leads us to expect a list of ways to leave the listening to others and insist that they do so, but the article contains a surprise ending. The final piece of advice is this: "You can't go wrong by showing interest in what other people say and making them feel important. In other words, the better *you* listen, the more you'll be listened to."[1]

© *Thinkstock*

You may have heard the adage, "We have two ears but only one mouth"—an easy way to remember that listening can be twice as important as talking. As a student, you most likely spend many hours in a classroom doing a large amount of focused listening, yet sometimes it is difficult to apply those efforts to communication in other areas of your life. As a result, your listening skills may not be all they could be. In this chapter, we will examine listening versus hearing, listening styles, listening difficulties, listening stages, and listening critically.

1. LISTENING VS. HEARING

LEARNING OBJECTIVES

1. Understand the differences between listening and hearing.
2. Explain the benefits of listening.

1.1 Listening or Hearing

Hearing is an accidental and automatic brain response to sound that requires no effort. We are surrounded by sounds most of the time. For example, we are accustomed to the sounds of airplanes, lawn mowers, furnace blowers, the rattling of pots and pans, and so on. We hear those incidental sounds and, unless we have a reason to do otherwise, we train ourselves to ignore them. We learn to filter out sounds that mean little to us, just as we choose to hear our ringing cell phones and other sounds that are more important to us.

© *Thinkstock*

hearing

An accidental and automatic brain response to sound.

FIGURE 4.1 Hearing vs. Listening

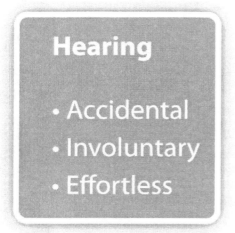

Listening, on the other hand, is purposeful and focused rather than accidental. As a result, it requires motivation and effort. **Listening**, at its best, is active, focused, concentrated attention for the purpose of understanding the meanings expressed by a speaker. We do not always listen at our best, however, and later in this chapter we will examine some of the reasons why and some strategies for becoming more active critical listeners.

1.2 Benefits of Listening

Listening should not be taken for granted. Before the invention of writing, people conveyed virtually all knowledge through some combination of showing and telling. Elders recited tribal histories to attentive audiences. Listeners received religious teachings enthusiastically. Myths, legends, folktales, and stories for entertainment survived only because audiences were eager to listen. Nowadays, however, you can gain information and entertainment through reading and electronic recordings rather than through real-time listening. If you become distracted and let your attention wander, you can go back and replay a recording. Despite that fact, you can still gain at least four compelling benefits by becoming more active and competent at real-time listening.

You Become a Better Student

When you focus on the material presented in a classroom, you will be able to identify not only the words used in a lecture but their emphasis and their more complex meanings. You will take better notes, and you will more accurately remember the instructor's claims, information, and conclusions. Many times, instructors give verbal cues about what information is important, specific expectations about assignments, and even what material is likely to be on an exam, so careful listening can be beneficial.

You Become a Better Friend

When you give your best attention to people expressing thoughts and experiences that are important to them, those individuals are likely to see you as someone who cares about their well-being. This fact is especially true when you give your attention only and refrain from interjecting opinions, judgments, and advice.

People Will Perceive You as Intelligent and Perceptive

When you listen well to others, you reveal yourself as being curious and interested in people and events. In addition, your ability to understand the meanings of what you hear will make you a more knowledgeable and thoughtful person.

Good Listening Can Help Your Public Speaking

When you listen well to others, you start to pick up more on the stylistic components related to how people form arguments and present information. As a result, you have the ability to analyze what you think works and doesn't work in others' speeches, which can help you transform your speeches in the process. For example, really paying attention to how others cite sources orally during their speeches may give you ideas about how to more effectively cite sources in your presentation.

KEY TAKEAWAYS

- Hearing is the physiological process of attending to sound within one's environment; listening, however, is a focused, concentrated approach to understanding the message a source is sending.
- Learning how to be an effective listener has numerous advantages. First, effective listening can help you become a better student. Second, effective listening can help you become more effective in your interpersonal relationships. Third, effective listening can lead others to perceive you as more intelligent. Lastly, effective listening can help you become a stronger public speaker.

EXERCISE

1. With a partner, discuss how you find out when you haven't been listening carefully. What are some of the consequences of poor listening?

2.   LISTENING STYLES

LEARNING OBJECTIVES

1. Understand the nature of listening styles.
2. Explain the people listening style.
3. Explain the action listening style.
4. Explain the content listening style.
5. Explain the time listening style.

If listening were easy, and if all people went about it in the same way, the task for a public speaker would be much easier. Even Aristotle, as long ago as 325 BC, recognized that listeners in his audience were varied in **listening style**. He differentiated them as follows:

© *Thinkstock*

listening style

The preferred focus of a listener's attention in a given situation. An effective listener is able to adapt his or her listening style to the context.

Rhetoric falls into three divisions, determined by the three classes of listeners to speeches. For of the three elements in speech-making—speaker, subject, and person addressed—it is the last one, the hearer, that determines the speech's end and object. The hearer must be either a judge, with a decision to make about things past or future, or an observer. A member of the assembly decides about future events, a juryman about past events: while those who merely decide on the orator's skill are observers.[2]

Thus Aristotle classified listeners into those who would be using the speech to make decisions about past events, those who would make decisions affecting the future, and those who would evaluate the speaker's skills. This is all the more remarkable when we consider that Aristotle's audiences were composed exclusively of male citizens of one city-state, all prosperous property owners.

Our audiences today are likely to be much more heterogeneous. Think about the classroom audience that will listen to your speeches in this course. Your classmates come from many religious and ethnic backgrounds. Some of them may speak English as a second language. Some might be survivors of war-torn parts of the world such as Bosnia, Darfur, or northwest China. Being mindful of such differences will help you prepare a speech in which you minimize the potential for misunderstanding.

Part of the potential for misunderstanding is the difference in listening styles. In an article in the *International Journal of Listening*, Watson, Barker, and Weaver[3] identified four listening styles: people, action, content, and time.

2.1 People

people-oriented listening

Listening that is focused on the speaker. The listener is most interested in the personality or experience of the speaker and the parts of the message related to those interests.

The **people-oriented listener** is interested in the speaker. People-oriented listeners listen to the message in order to learn how the speaker thinks and how they feel about their message. For instance, when people-oriented listeners listen to an interview with a famous rap artist, they are likely to be more curious about the artist as an individual than about music, even though the people-oriented listener might also appreciate the artist's work. If you are a people-oriented listener, you might have certain questions you hope will be answered, such as: Does the artist feel successful? What's it like to be famous? What kind of educational background does he or she have? In the same way, if we're listening to a doctor who responded to the earthquake crisis in Haiti, we might be more interested in the doctor as a person than in the state of affairs for Haitians. Why did he or she go to Haiti? How did he or she get away from his or her normal practice and patients? How many lives did he or she save? We might be less interested in the equally important and urgent needs for food, shelter, and sanitation following the earthquake.

The people-oriented listener is likely to be more attentive to the speaker than to the message. If you tend to be such a listener, understand that the message is about what is important to the speaker.

2.2 Action

action-oriented listening

Listening focused on what is expected of the listener. The action-oriented listener is less interested in the underlying rationale than in learning what action to take.

Action-oriented listeners are primarily interested in finding out what the speaker wants. Does the speaker want votes, donations, volunteers, or something else? It's sometimes difficult for an action-oriented speaker to listen through the descriptions, evidence, and explanations with which a speaker builds his or her case.

Action-oriented listening is sometimes called task-oriented listening. In it, the listener seeks a clear message about what needs to be done, and might have less patience for listening to the reasons behind the task. This can be especially true if the reasons are complicated. For example, when you're a passenger on an airplane waiting to push back from the gate, a flight attendant delivers a brief speech called the preflight safety briefing. The flight attendant does not read the findings of a safety study or the regulations about seat belts. The flight attendant doesn't explain that the content of his or her speech is actually mandated by the Federal Aviation Administration. Instead, the attendant says only to buckle up so we can leave. An action-oriented listener finds "buckling up" a more compelling message than a message about the underlying reasons.

2.3 Content

Content-oriented listeners are interested in the message itself, whether it makes sense, what it means, and whether it's accurate. When you give a speech, many members of your classroom audience will be content-oriented listeners who will be interested in learning from you. You therefore have an obligation to represent the truth in the fullest way you can. You can emphasize an idea, but if you exaggerate, you could lose credibility in the minds of your content-oriented audience. You can advocate ideas that are important to you, but if you omit important limitations, you are withholding part of the truth and could leave your audience with an inaccurate view.

Imagine you're delivering a speech on the plight of orphans in Africa. If you just talk about the fact that there are over forty-five million orphans in Africa but don't explain why, you'll sound like an infomercial. In such an instance, your audience's response is likely to be less enthusiastic than you might want. Instead, content-oriented listeners want to listen to well-developed information with solid explanations.

content-oriented listening

Listening focused on the information and meanings in the message. This listener gives less attention to the speaker than to the message, its meanings, and its credibility.

2.4 Time

People using a **time-oriented listening** style prefer a message that gets to the point quickly. Time-oriented listeners can become impatient with slow delivery or lengthy explanations. This kind of listener may be receptive for only a brief amount of time and may become rude or even hostile if the speaker expects a longer focus of attention. Time-oriented listeners convey their impatience through eye rolling, shifting about in their seats, checking their cell phones, and other inappropriate behaviors. If you've been asked to speak to a group of middle-school students, you need to realize that their attention spans are simply not as long as those of college students. This is an important reason speeches to young audiences must be shorter, or broken up by more variety than speeches to adults.

In your professional future, some of your audience members will have real time constraints, not merely perceived ones. Imagine that you've been asked to deliver a speech on a new project to the board of directors of a local corporation. Chances are the people on the board of directors are all pressed for time. If your speech is long and filled with overly detailed information, time-oriented listeners will simply start to tune you out as you're speaking. Obviously, if time-oriented listeners start tuning you out, they will not be listening to your message. This is not the same thing as being a time-oriented listener who might be less interested in the message content than in its length.

time-oriented listening

Listening focused on reaching the end of the message.

KEY TAKEAWAYS

- A listening style is a general manner in which an individual attends to the messages of another person.
- People-oriented listeners pay attention to the personal details of a speaker and not to the speaker's actual message.
- Action-oriented listeners pay attention to the physical actions a speaker wants the listener to engage in.
- Content-oriented listeners pay attention to the meaning and credibility of a speaker's message.
- Time-oriented listeners pay attention to messages that are short and concise as a result of limited attention spans or limited time commitments.

EXERCISES

1. In a small group, discuss what each person's usual listening style is. Under what circumstances might you practice a different listening style?
2. Make a list of benefits and drawbacks to each of the listening styles discussed in this section.
3. As you prepare for your next speech, identify ways that you can adapt your message to each of the listening styles noted in this section.

3.   WHY LISTENING IS DIFFICULT

LEARNING OBJECTIVES

1. Understand the types of noise that can affect a listener's ability to attend to a message.
2. Explain how a listener's attention span can limit the listener's ability to attend to a speaker's message.
3. Analyze how a listener's personal biases can influence her or his ability to attend to a message.
4. Define receiver apprehension and the impact it can have on a listener's ability to attend to a message.

© Thinkstock

noise

Any internal or environmental factor that interferes with the ability to listen effectively. Some of these factors are physical, psychological, physiological, and semantic.

physical noise

Various sounds in an environment that interfere with a source's ability to hear.

psychological noise

Distractions to a speaker's message caused by a receiver's internal thoughts.

physiological noise

Distractions to a speaker's message caused by a listener's own body.

semantic noise

When a receiver experiences confusion over the meaning of a source's word choice.

At times, everyone has difficulty staying completely focused during a lengthy presentation. We can sometimes have difficulty listening to even relatively brief messages. Some of the factors that interfere with good listening might exist beyond our control, but others are manageable. It's helpful to be aware of these factors so that they interfere as little as possible with understanding the message.

3.1   Noise

Noise is one of the biggest factors to interfere with listening; it can be defined as anything that interferes with your ability to attend to and understand a message. There are many kinds of noise, but we will focus on only the four you are most likely to encounter in public speaking situations: physical noise, psychological noise, physiological noise, and semantic noise.

Physical Noise

Physical noise consists of various sounds in an environment that interfere with a source's ability to hear. Construction noises right outside a window, planes flying directly overhead, or loud music in the next room can make it difficult to hear the message being presented by a speaker even if a microphone is being used. It is sometimes possible to manage the context to reduce the noise. Closing a window might be helpful. Asking the people in the next room to turn their music down might be possible. Changing to a new location is more difficult, as it involves finding a new location and having everyone get there.

Psychological Noise

Psychological noise consists of distractions to a speaker's message caused by a receiver's internal thoughts. For example, if you are preoccupied with personal problems, it is difficult to give your full attention to understanding the meanings of a message. The presence of another person to whom you feel attracted, or perhaps a person you dislike intensely, can also be psychosocial noise that draws your attention away from the message.

Physiological Noise

Physiological noise consists of distractions to a speaker's message caused by a listener's own body. Maybe you're listening to a speech in class around noon and you haven't eaten anything. Your stomach may be growling and your desk is starting to look tasty. Maybe the room is cold and you're thinking more about how to keep warm than about what the speaker is saying. In either case, your body can distract you from attending to the information being presented.

Semantic Noise

Semantic noise occurs when a receiver experiences confusion over the meaning of a source's word choice. While you are attempting to understand a particular word or phrase, the speaker continues to present the message. While you are struggling with a word interpretation, you are distracted from listening to the rest of the message. One of the authors was listening to a speaker who mentioned using a sweeper to clean carpeting. The author was confused, as she did not see how a broom would be effective in cleaning carpeting. Later, the author found out that the speaker was using the word "sweeper" to refer to a vacuum cleaner; however, in the meantime, her listening was hurt by her inability to understand what the speaker meant. Another example of semantic noise is euphemism. Euphemism is diplomatic language used for delivering unpleasant information. For instance, if someone is said to be "flexible with the truth," it might take us a moment to understand that the speaker means this person sometimes lies.

FIGURE 4.2 Types of Noise

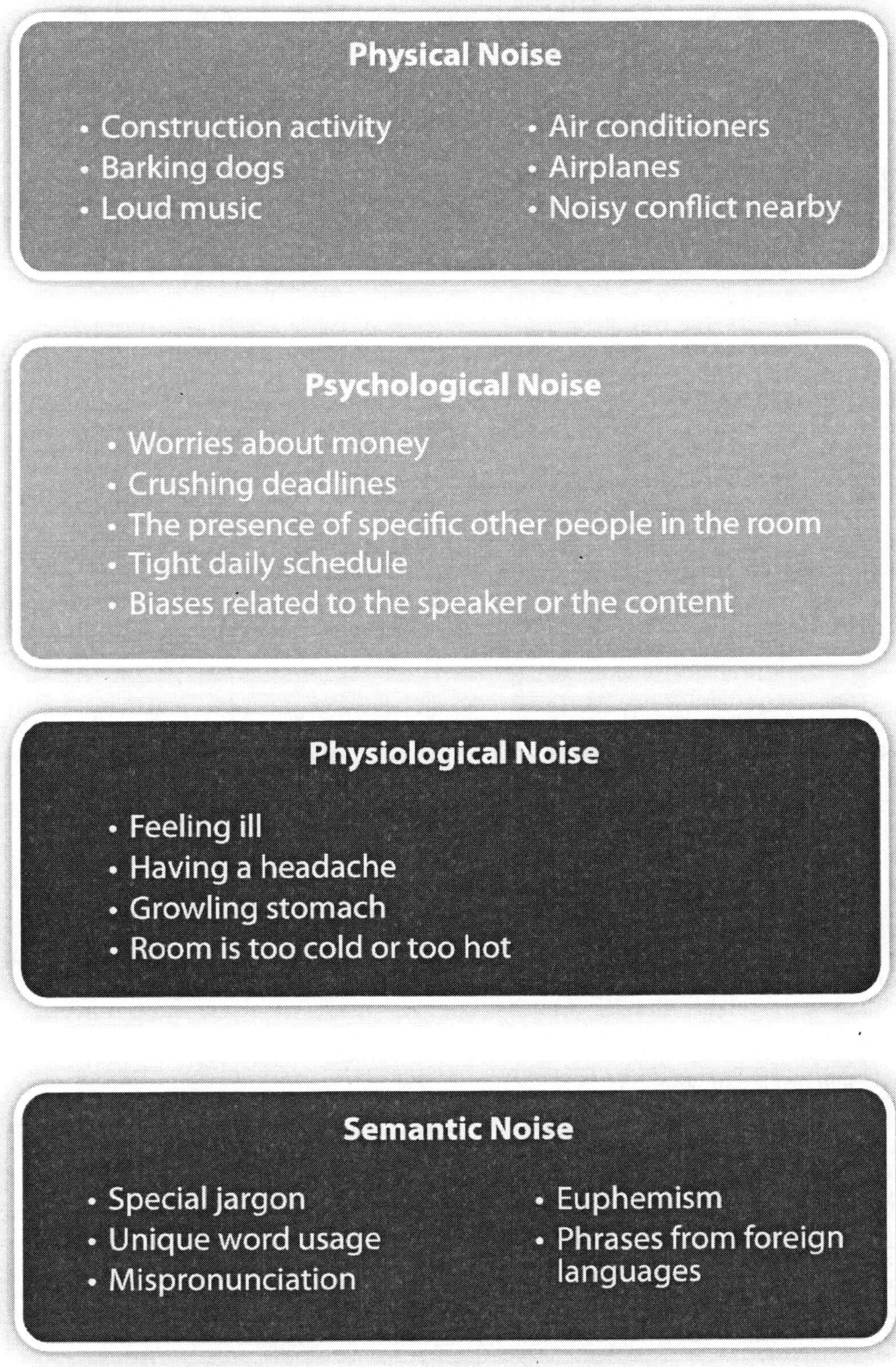

Physical Noise

- Construction activity
- Barking dogs
- Loud music
- Air conditioners
- Airplanes
- Noisy conflict nearby

Psychological Noise

- Worries about money
- Crushing deadlines
- The presence of specific other people in the room
- Tight daily schedule
- Biases related to the speaker or the content

Physiological Noise

- Feeling ill
- Having a headache
- Growling stomach
- Room is too cold or too hot

Semantic Noise

- Special jargon
- Unique word usage
- Mispronunciation
- Euphemism
- Phrases from foreign languages

distractions

Internal or external factors that interfere with a listener's ability to give full attention to a message.

Many **distractions** are the fault of neither the listener nor the speaker. However, when you are the speaker, being aware of these sources of noise can help you reduce some of the noise that interferes with your audience's ability to understand you.

3.2   Attention Span

attention span

The length of time a listener can maintain focused attention to a message.

A person can only maintain focused attention for a finite length of time. In his 1985 book *Amusing Ourselves to Death: Public Discourse in the Age of Show Business*, New York University's Steinhardt School of Education professor Neil Postman argued that modern audiences have lost the ability to sustain attention to a message.[4] More recently, researchers have engaged in an ongoing debate over whether Internet use is detrimental to **attention span**.[5] Whether or not these concerns are well founded, you have probably noticed that even when your attention is "glued" to something in which you are deeply interested, every now and then you pause to do something else, such as getting a drink of water, stretching, or looking out the window.

The limits of the human attention span can interfere with listening, but listeners and speakers can use strategies to prevent this interference. As many classroom instructors know, listeners will readily renew their attention when the presentation includes frequent breaks in pacing.[6] For example, a fifty- to seventy-five-minute class session might include some lecture material alternated with questions for class discussion, video clips, handouts, and demonstrations. Instructors who are adept at holding listeners' attention also move about the front of the room, writing on the board, drawing diagrams, and intermittently using slide transparencies or PowerPoint slides.

If you have instructors who do a good job of keeping your attention, they are positive role models showing strategies you can use to accommodate the limitations of your audience's attention span.

3.3   Receiver Biases

receiver biases

Preconceived ideas that interfere with accurately understanding and remembering a message. These biases can refer either to the speaker or to the topic.

opinions

Opinions are beliefs we have about the worth of things we know or believe we know.

Good listening involves keeping an open mind and withholding judgment until the speaker has completed the message. Conversely, biased listening is characterized by jumping to conclusions; the biased listener believes, "I don't need to listen because I already know what I think." **Receiver biases** can refer to two things: biases with reference to the speaker and preconceived ideas and **opinions** about the topic or message. Both can be considered noise. Everyone has biases, but good listeners have learned to hold them in check while listening.

The first type of bias listeners can have is related to the speaker. Often a speaker stands up and an audience member simply doesn't like the speaker, so the audience member may not listen to the speaker's message. Maybe you have a classmate who just gets under your skin for some reason, or maybe you question a classmate's competence on a given topic. When we have preconceived notions about a speaker, those biases can interfere with our ability to listen accurately and competently to the speaker's message.

The second type of bias listeners can have is related to the topic or content of the speech. Maybe the speech topic is one you've heard a thousand times, so you just tune out the speech. Or maybe the speaker is presenting a topic or position you fundamentally disagree with. When listeners have strong preexisting opinions about a topic, such as the death penalty, religious issues, affirmative action, abortion, or global warming, their biases may make it difficult for them to even consider new information about the topic, especially if the new information is inconsistent with what they already believe to be true. As listeners, we have difficulty identifying our biases, especially when they seem to make sense. However, it is worth recognizing that our lives would be very difficult if no one ever considered new points of view or new information. We live in a world where everyone can benefit from clear thinking and open-minded listening.

3.4   Listening or Receiver Apprehension

listening or receiver apprehension

The listener's anxiety about his or her ability to understand the information, concepts, or vocabulary in a message.

Listening or receiver apprehension is the fear that you might be unable to understand the message or process the information correctly or be able to adapt your thinking to include the new information coherently.[7] In some situations, you might worry that the information presented will be "over your head"—too complex, technical, or advanced for you to understand adequately.

Many students will actually avoid registering for courses in which they feel certain they will do poorly. In other cases, students will choose to take a challenging course only if it's a requirement. This avoidance might be understandable but is not a good strategy for success. To become educated people, students should take a few courses that can shed light on areas where their knowledge is limited.

As a speaker, you can reduce listener apprehension by defining terms clearly and using simple visual aids to hold the audience's attention. You don't want to underestimate or overestimate your audience's knowledge on a subject, so good audience analysis is always important. If you know your audience doesn't have special knowledge on a given topic, you should start by defining important terms. Research has shown us that when listeners do not feel they understand a speaker's message, their apprehension about receiving the message escalates. Imagine that you are listening to a speech about chemistry and the speaker begins talking about "colligative properties." You may start questioning whether you're even in the right place. When this happens, apprehension clearly interferes with a listener's ability to accurately and competently understand a speaker's message. As a speaker, you can lessen the listener's apprehension by explaining that colligative properties focus on *how much* is dissolved in a solution, not on *what* is dissolved in a solution. You could also give an example that they might readily understand, such as saying that it doesn't matter what kind of salt you use in the winter to melt ice on your driveway, what is important is how much salt you use.

KEY TAKEAWAYS

- Listeners are often unable to accurately attend to messages because of four types of noise. Physical noise is caused by the physical setting a listener is in. Psychological noise exists within a listener's own mind and prevents him or her from attending to a speaker's message. Physiological noise exists because a listener's body is feeling some sensation that prevents him or her from attending to a speaker's message. Semantic noise is caused by a listener's confusion over the meanings of words used by a speaker.

- All audiences have a limited attention span. As a speaker, you must realize how long you can reasonably expect an audience to listen to your message.

- Listeners must be aware of the biases they have for speakers and the topics speakers choose. Biases can often prevent a listener from accurately and competently listening to a speaker's actual message.

- Receiver apprehension is the fear that a listener might be unable to understand the message, process the information correctly, or adapt thinking to include new information coherently. Speakers need to make sure their messages are appropriate to the audience's knowledge level and clearly define and explain all terms that could lead to increased anxiety.

EXERCISES

1. In a group, discuss what distracts you most from listening attentively to a speaker. Have you found ways to filter out or manage the distraction?

2. This chapter refers to psychological noise as one of the distractions you might experience. Identify strategies you have successfully used to minimize the impact of the specific psychological noises you have experienced.

3. Make a list of biases you might have as a listener. You can think about how you'd answer such questions as, With whom would I refuse to be seen socially or in public? Who would I reject as a trustworthy person to help if I were in danger? What topics do I refuse to discuss? The answers to these questions might provide useful insights into your biases as a listener.

4. STAGES OF LISTENING

LEARNING OBJECTIVES

1. Explain the receiving stage of listening.
2. Explain the understanding stage of listening.
3. Explain the remembering stage of listening.
4. Explain the evaluating stage of listening.
5. Explain the responding stage of listening.
6. Understand the two types of feedback listeners give to speakers.

FIGURE 4.3 Stages of Feedback

 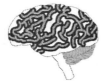  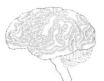 

| Stage 1 Receiving | Stage 2 Understanding | Stage 2 Remembering | Stage 2 Evaluating | Stage 5 Feedback |

As you read earlier, there are many factors that can interfere with listening, so you need to be able to manage a number of mental tasks at the same time in order to be a successful listener. Author Joseph DeVito has divided the listening process into five stages: receiving, understanding, remembering, evaluating, and responding.[8]

4.1 Receiving

receiving

The process of hearing and giving focused attention to a speaker's message.

Receiving is the intentional focus on hearing a speaker's message, which happens when we filter out other sources so that we can isolate the message and avoid the confusing mixture of incoming stimuli. At this stage, we are still only hearing the message. Notice in Figure 4.3 that this stage is represented by the ear because it is the primary tool involved with this stage of the listening process.

One of the authors of this book recalls attending a political rally for a presidential candidate at which about five thousand people were crowded into an outdoor amphitheater. When the candidate finally started speaking, the cheering and yelling was so loud that the candidate couldn't be heard easily despite using a speaker system. In this example, our coauthor had difficulty receiving the message because of the external noise. This is only one example of the ways that hearing alone can require sincere effort, but you must hear the message before you can continue the process of listening.

4.2 Understanding

understanding

The effort to learn the speaker's meanings.

In the **understanding** stage, we attempt to learn the meaning of the message, which is not always easy. For one thing, if a speaker does not enunciate clearly, it may be difficult to tell what the message was—did your friend say, "I think she'll be late for class," or "my teacher delayed the class"? Notice in Figure 4.3 that stages two, three, and four are represented by the brain because it is the primary tool involved with these stages of the listening process.

Even when we have understood the words in a message, because of the differences in our backgrounds and experience, we sometimes make the mistake of attaching our own meanings to the words of others. For example, say you have made plans with your friends to meet at a certain movie theater, but you arrive and nobody else shows up. Eventually you find out that your friends are at a different theater all the way across town where the same movie is playing. Everyone else understood that the meeting place was the "west side" location, but you wrongly understood it as the "east side" location and therefore missed out on part of the fun.

The consequences of ineffective listening in a classroom can be much worse. When your professor advises students to get an "early start" on your speech, he or she probably hopes that you will begin your research right away and move on to developing a thesis statement and outlining the speech as soon as possible. However, students in your class might misunderstand the instructor's meaning in several ways. One student might interpret the advice to mean that as long as she gets started, the rest of the assignment will have time to develop itself. Another student might instead think that to start early is to start on the Friday before the Monday due date instead of Sunday night.

So much of the way we understand others is influenced by our own perceptions and experiences. Therefore, at the understanding stage of listening we should be on the lookout for places where our perceptions might differ from those of the speaker.

4.3   Remembering

Remembering begins with listening; if you can't remember something that was said, you might not have been listening effectively. Wolvin and Coakley note that the most common reason for not remembering a message after the fact is because it wasn't really learned in the first place.[9] However, even when you are listening attentively, some messages are more difficult than others to understand and remember. Highly complex messages that are filled with detail call for highly developed listening skills. Moreover, if something distracts your attention even for a moment, you could miss out on information that explains other new concepts you hear when you begin to listen fully again.

It's also important to know that you can improve your memory of a message by processing it meaningfully—that is, by applying it in ways that are meaningful to you. [10] Instead of simply repeating a new acquaintance's name over and over, for example, you might remember it by associating it with something in your own life. "Emily," you might say, "reminds me of the Emily I knew in middle school," or "Mr. Impiari's name reminds me of the Impala my father drives."

Finally, if understanding has been inaccurate, recollection of the message will be inaccurate too.

remembering
The ability to recall accurately the content of a message.

4.4   Evaluating

The fourth stage in the listening process is **evaluating**, or judging the value of the message. We might be thinking, "This makes sense" or, conversely, "This is very odd." Because everyone embodies biases and perspectives learned from widely diverse sets of life experiences, evaluations of the same message can vary widely from one listener to another. Even the most open-minded listeners will have opinions of a speaker, and those opinions will influence how the message is evaluated. People are more likely to evaluate a message positively if the speaker speaks clearly, presents ideas logically, and gives reasons to support the points made.

Unfortunately, personal opinions sometimes result in prejudiced evaluations. Imagine you're listening to a speech given by someone from another country and this person has an accent that is hard to understand. You may have a hard time simply making out the speaker's message. Some people find a foreign accent to be interesting or even exotic, while others find it annoying or even take it as a sign of ignorance. If a listener has a strong bias against foreign accents, the listener may not even attempt to attend to the message. If you mistrust a speaker because of an accent, you could be rejecting important or personally enriching information. Good listeners have learned to refrain from making these judgments and instead to focus on the speaker's meanings.

evaluating
The listener's process of judging the value of a message or a speaker.

4.5   Responding

Responding—sometimes referred to as feedback—is the fifth and final stage of the listening process. It's the stage at which you indicate your involvement. Almost anything you do at this stage can be interpreted as feedback. For example, you are giving positive feedback to your instructor if at the end of class you stay behind to finish a sentence in your notes or approach the instructor to ask for clarification. The opposite kind of feedback is given by students who gather their belongings and rush out the door as soon as class is over. Notice in Figure 4.3 that this stage is represented by the lips because we often give feedback in the form of verbal feedback; however, you can just as easily respond nonverbally.

responding
The verbal and nonverbal feedback given by listeners during and after the presentation of a message.

Formative Feedback

Not all response occurs at the end of the message. Formative feedback is a natural part of the ongoing transaction between a speaker and a listener. As the speaker delivers the message, a listener signals his or her involvement with focused attention, note-taking, nodding, and other behaviors that indicate understanding or failure to understand the message. These signals are important to the speaker, who is interested in whether the message is clear and accepted or whether the content of the message is meeting the resistance of preconceived ideas. Speakers can use this feedback to decide whether additional examples, support materials, or explanation is needed.

Summative Feedback

Summative feedback is given at the end of the communication. When you attend a political rally, a presentation given by a speaker you admire, or even a class, there are verbal and nonverbal ways of indicating your appreciation for or your disagreement with the messages or the speakers at the end of the message. Maybe you'll stand up and applaud a speaker you agreed with or just sit staring in silence after listening to a speaker you didn't like. In other cases, a speaker may be attempting to persuade you to donate to a charity, so if the speaker passes a bucket and you make a donation, you are providing feedback on the speaker's effectiveness. At the same time, we do not always listen most carefully to the messages of speakers we admire. Sometimes we simply enjoy being in their presence, and our summative feedback is not about the message but about our attitudes about the speaker. If your feedback is limited to something like, "I just love your voice," you might be indicating that you did not listen carefully to the content of the message.

There is little doubt that by now, you are beginning to understand the complexity of listening and the great potential for errors. By becoming aware of what is involved with active listening and where difficulties might lie, you can prepare yourself both as a listener and as a speaker to minimize listening errors with your own public speeches.

KEY TAKEAWAYS

- The receiving stage of listening is the basic stage where an individual hears a message being sent by a speaker.
- The understanding stage of listening occurs when a receiver of a message attempts to figure out the meaning of the message.
- The remembering stage of listening is when a listener either places information into long-term memory or forgets the information presented.
- The evaluating stage of listening occurs when a listener judges the content of the message or the character of the speaker.
- The responding stage of listening occurs when a listener provides verbal or nonverbal feedback about the speaker or message.
- During the responding stage of listening, listeners can provide speakers with two types of feedback designed to help a speaker know whether a listener is understanding and what the listener thinks of a message. Formative feedback is given while the speaker is engaged in the act of speech making. Summative feedback is given at the conclusion of a speech.

EXERCISES

1. Make a list of some of the abstract words you have misunderstood. What were the consequences of the misunderstanding?
2. Reflect on your listening in class or in other settings where remembering information is important. What keeps you from remembering important information accurately?
3. Give an example of a time when you felt that your message was misunderstood or treated with shallow attention. How did you know your message had been misunderstood or rejected? What does this mean you must do as a student of public speaking?

5. LISTENING CRITICALLY

LEARNING OBJECTIVES

1. Define and explain critical listening and its importance in the public speaking context.
2. Understand six distinct ways to improve your ability to critically listen to speeches.
3. Evaluate what it means to be an ethical listener.

As a student, you are exposed to many kinds of messages. You receive messages conveying academic information, institutional rules, instructions, and warnings; you also receive messages through political discourse, advertisements, gossip, jokes, song lyrics, text messages, invitations, web links, and all other manner of communication. You know it's not all the same, but it isn't always clear how to separate the truth from the messages that are misleading or even blatantly false. Nor is it always clear which messages are intended to help the listener and which ones are merely self-serving for the speaker. Part of being a good listener is to learn when to use caution in evaluating the messages we hear.

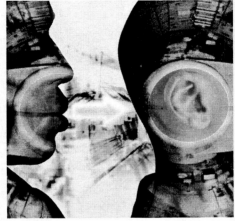
© *Thinkstock*

Critical listening in this context means using careful, systematic thinking and reasoning to see whether a message makes sense in light of factual evidence. Critical listening can be learned with practice but is not necessarily easy to do. Some people never learn this skill; instead, they take every message at face value even when those messages are in conflict with their knowledge. Problems occur when messages are repeated to others who have not yet developed the skills to discern the difference between a valid message and a mistaken one. Critical listening can be particularly difficult when the message is complex. Unfortunately, some speakers may make their messages intentionally complex to avoid critical scrutiny. For example, a city treasurer giving a budget presentation might use very large words and technical jargon, which make it difficult for listeners to understand the proposed budget and ask probing questions.

critical listening

The process of examining claims made in a speech in order to assess their relevance and credibility.

5.1 Six Ways to Improve Your Critical Listening

Critical listening is first and foremost a skill that can be learned and improved. In this section, we are going to explore six different techniques you can use to become a more critical listener.

Recognizing the Difference between Facts and Opinions

Senator Daniel Patrick Moynihan is credited with saying, "Everyone is entitled to their own opinions, but they are not entitled to their own facts."[11] Part of critical listening is learning to separate opinions from facts, and this works two ways: critical listeners are aware of whether a speaker is delivering a factual message or a message based on opinion, and they are also aware of the interplay between their own opinions and facts as they listen to messages.

In American politics, the issue of health care reform is heavily laden with both opinions and facts, and it is extremely difficult to sort some of them out. A clash of fact versus opinion happened on September 9, 2010, during President Obama's nationally televised speech to a joint session of Congress outlining his health care reform plan. In this speech, President Obama responded to several rumors about the plan, including the claim "that our reform effort will insure illegal immigrants. This, too, is false—the reforms I'm proposing would not apply to those who are here illegally." At this point, one congressman yelled out, "You lie!" Clearly, this congressman did not have a very high opinion of either the health care reform plan or the president. However, when the nonpartisan watch group Factcheck.org examined the language of the proposed bill, they found that it had a section titled "No Federal Payment for Undocumented Aliens."[12]

Often when people have a negative opinion about a topic, they are unwilling to accept facts. Instead, they question all aspects of the speech and have a negative predisposition toward both the speech and the speaker.

This is not to say that speakers should not express their opinions. Many of the greatest speeches in history include personal opinions. Consider, for example, Martin Luther King Jr.'s famous "I Have a Dream" speech, in which he expressed his personal wish for the future of American society. Critical listeners may agree or disagree with a speaker's opinions, but the point is that they know when a message they are hearing is based on opinion and when it is factual.

Uncovering Assumptions

assumptions

Assumptions are inferences we form in the absence of factual information. Some assumptions turn out to be accurate, but many are incomplete or just plain wrong.

If something is factual, supporting evidence exists. However, we still need to be careful about what evidence does and does not mean. **Assumptions** are gaps in a logical sequence that listeners passively fill with their own ideas and opinions and may or may not be accurate. When listening to a public speech, you may find yourself being asked to assume something is a fact when in reality many people question that fact. For example, suppose you're listening to a speech on weight loss. The speaker talks about how people who are overweight are simply not motivated or lack the self-discipline to lose weight. The speaker has built the speech on the assumption that motivation and self-discipline are the only reasons why people can't lose weight. You may think to yourself, what about genetics? By listening critically, you will be more likely to notice unwarranted assumptions in a speech, which may prompt you to question the speaker if questions are taken or to do further research to examine the validity of the speaker's assumptions. If, however, you sit passively by and let the speaker's assumptions go unchallenged, you may find yourself persuaded by information that is not factual.

When you listen critically to a speech, you might hear information that appears unsupported by evidence. You shouldn't accept that information unconditionally. You would accept it under the condition that the speaker offers credible evidence that directly supports it.

TABLE 4.1 Facts vs. Assumptions

Facts	Assumptions
Facts are verified by clear, unambiguous evidence.	Assumptions are not supported by evidence.
Most facts can be tested.	Assumptions about the future cannot be tested in the present.

Be Open to New Ideas

Sometimes people are so fully invested in their perceptions of the world that they are unable to listen receptively to messages that make sense and would be of great benefit to them. Human progress has been possible, sometimes against great odds, because of the mental curiosity and discernment of a few people. In the late 1700s when the technique of vaccination to prevent smallpox was introduced, it was opposed by both medical professionals and everyday citizens who staged public protests.[13] More than two centuries later, vaccinations against smallpox, diphtheria, polio, and other infectious diseases have saved countless lives, yet popular opposition continues.

In the world of public speaking, we must be open to new ideas. Let's face it, people have a tendency to filter out information they disagree with and to filter in information that supports what they already believe. Nicolaus Copernicus was a sixteenth-century astronomer who dared to publish a treatise explaining that the earth revolves around the sun, which was a violation of Catholic doctrine. Copernicus's astronomical findings were labeled heretical and his treatise banned because a group of people at the time were not open to new ideas. In May of 2010, almost five hundred years after his death, the Roman Catholic Church admitted its error and reburied his remains with the full rites of Catholic burial.[14]

While the Copernicus case is a fairly dramatic reversal, listeners should always be open to new ideas. We are not suggesting that you have to agree with every idea that you are faced with in life; rather, we are suggesting that you at least listen to the message and then evaluate the message.

Rely on Reason and Common Sense

common sense

Common sense in listening is an approach to considering the ideas in a speech. If the ideas seem to be consistent with each other and with daily reality, they might have merit. However, common sense in public speaking is not a substitute for factual evidence.

If you are listening to a speech and your **common sense** tells you that the message is illogical, you very well might be right. You should be thinking about whether the speech seems credible and coherent. In this way, your use of common sense can act as a warning system for you.

One of our coauthors once heard a speech on the environmental hazards of fireworks. The speaker argued that fireworks (the public kind, not the personal kind people buy and set off in their backyards) were environmentally hazardous because of litter. Although there is certainly some paper that makes it to the ground before burning up, the amount of litter created by fireworks displays is relatively small compared to other sources of litter, including trash left behind by all the spectators watching fireworks at public parks and other venues. It just does not make sense to identify a few bits of charred paper as a major environmental hazard.

If the message is inconsistent with things you already know, if the argument is illogical, or if the language is exaggerated, you should investigate the issues before accepting or rejecting the message. Often, you will not be able to take this step during the presentation of the message; it may take longer to collect enough knowledge to make that decision for yourself.

However, when you are the speaker, you should not substitute common sense for evidence. That's why during a speech it's necessary to cite the authority of scholars whose research is irrefutable, or at least highly credible. It is all too easy to make a mistake in reasoning, sometimes called fallacy, in stating your case. We will discuss these fallacies in more detail in Chapter 8. One of the most common fallacies is *post hoc, ergo propter hoc*, a "common sense" form of logic that translates roughly as "after the fact, therefore because of the fact." The argument says that if A happened first, followed by B, then A caused B. We know the outcome cannot occur earlier than the cause, but we also know that the two events might be related indirectly or that causality works in a different direction. For instance, imagine a speaker arguing that because the sun rises after a rooster's crow, the rooster caused the sun to rise. This argument is clearly illogical because roosters crow many times each day, and the sun's rising and setting do not change according to crowing or lack thereof. But the two events are related in a different way. Roosters tend to wake up and begin crowing at first light, about forty-five minutes before sunrise. Thus it is the impending sunrise that causes the predawn crowing.

In Chapter 2, we pointed out that what is "common sense" for people of one generation or culture may be quite the opposite for people of a different generation or culture. Thus it is important not to assume that your audience shares the beliefs that are, for you, common sense. Likewise, if the message of your speech is complex or controversial, you should consider the needs of your audience and do your best to explain its complexities factually and logically, not intuitively.

Relate New Ideas to Old Ones

As both a speaker and a listener, one of the most important things you can do to understand a message is to relate new ideas to previously held ideas. Imagine you're giving a speech about biological systems and you need to use the term "homeostasis," which refers to the ability of an organism to maintain stability by making constant adjustments. To help your audience understand homeostasis, you could show how homeostasis is similar to adjustments made by the thermostats that keep our homes at a more or less even temperature. If you set your thermostat for seventy degrees and it gets hotter, the central cooling will kick in and cool your house down. If your house gets below seventy degrees, your heater will kick in and heat your house up. Notice that in both cases your thermostat is making constant adjustments to stay at seventy degrees. Explaining that the body's homeostasis works in a similar way will make it more relevant to your listeners and will likely help them both understand and remember the idea because it links to something they have already experienced.

If you can make effective comparisons while you are listening, it can deepen your understanding of the message. If you can provide those comparisons for your listeners, you make it easier for them to give consideration to your ideas.

Take Notes

Note-taking is a skill that improves with practice. You already know that it's nearly impossible to write down everything a speaker says. In fact, in your attempt to record everything, you might fall behind and wish you had divided your attention differently between writing and listening.

Careful, selective note-taking is important because we want an accurate record that reflects the meanings of the message. However much you might concentrate on the notes, you could inadvertently leave out an important word, such as *not*, and undermine the reliability of your otherwise carefully written notes. Instead, if you give the same care and attention to listening, you are less likely to make that kind of a mistake.

It's important to find a balance between listening well and taking good notes. Many people struggle with this balance for a long time. For example, if you try to write down only key phrases instead of full sentences, you might find that you can't remember how two ideas were related. In that case, too few notes were taken. At the opposite end, extensive note-taking can result in a loss of emphasis on the most important ideas.

To increase your critical listening skills, continue developing your ability to identify the central issues in messages so that you can take accurate notes that represent the meanings intended by the speaker.

5.2   Listening Ethically

© *Thinkstock*

ethical listening

Courteous attention to a speaker and thoughtful consideration of the message.

Ethical listening rests heavily on honest intentions. We should extend to speakers the same respect we want to receive when it's our turn to speak. We should be facing the speaker with our eyes open. We should not be checking our cell phones. We should avoid any behavior that belittles the speaker or the message.

Scholars Stephanie Coopman and James Lull emphasize the creation of a climate of caring and mutual understanding, observing that "respecting others' perspectives is one hallmark of the effective listener."[15] Respect, or unconditional positive regard for others, means that you treat others with consideration and decency whether you agree with them or not. Professors Sprague, Stuart, and Bodary[16] also urge us to treat the speaker with respect even when we disagree, don't understand the message, or find the speech boring.

Doug Lipman (1998),[17] a storytelling coach, wrote powerfully and sensitively about listening in his book:

> *Like so many of us, I used to take listening for granted, glossing over this step as I rushed into the more active, visible ways of being helpful. Now, I am convinced that listening is the single most important element of any helping relationship.*
>
> *Listening has great power. It draws thoughts and feelings out of people as nothing else can. When someone listens to you well, you become aware of feelings you may not have realized that you felt. You have ideas you may have never thought before. You become more eloquent, more insightful.…*
>
> *As a helpful listener, I do not interrupt you. I do not give advice. I do not do something else while listening to you. I do not convey distraction through nervous mannerisms. I do not finish your sentences for you. In spite of all my attempts to understand you, I do not assume I know what you mean.*
>
> *I do not convey disapproval, impatience, or condescension. If I am confused, I show a desire for clarification, not dislike for your obtuseness. I do not act vindicated when you misspeak or correct yourself.*
>
> *I do not sit impassively, withholding participation.*
>
> *Instead, I project affection, approval, interest, and enthusiasm. I am your partner in communication. I am eager for your imminent success, fascinated by your struggles, forgiving of your mistakes, always expecting the best. I am your delighted listener.[18]*

This excerpt expresses the decency with which people should treat each other. It doesn't mean we must accept everything we hear, but ethically, we should refrain from trivializing each other's concerns. We have all had the painful experience of being ignored or misunderstood. This is how we know that one of the greatest gifts one human can give to another is listening.

KEY TAKEAWAYS

- Critical listening is the process a listener goes through using careful, systematic thinking and reasoning to see whether a speaker's message makes sense in light of factual evidence. When listeners are not critical of the messages they are attending to, they are more likely to be persuaded by illogical arguments based on opinions and not facts.

- Critical listening can be improved by employing one or more strategies to help the listener analyze the message: recognize the difference between facts and opinions, uncover assumptions given by the speaker, be open to new ideas, use both reason and common sense when analyzing messages, relate new ideas to old ones, and take useful notes.

- Being an ethical listener means giving respectful attention to the ideas of a speaker, even though you may not agree with or accept those ideas.

EXERCISES

1. Think of a time when you were too tired or distracted to give your full attention to the ideas in a speech. What did you do? What should you have done?

2. Give an example of a mistake in reasoning that involved the speaker mistaking an assumption for fact.

6. CHAPTER EXERCISES

SPEAKING ETHICALLY

Imagine that you're in the audience when the main speaker proposes an action that is so offensive to you that you earnestly want to stand up and walk right out of the room. You are sitting near the end of a row, so it would be possible to do so. You notice that other people are listening intently. You hope others will not assume that by your presence, you show that you agree. What is the most ethical choice?

1. Continue listening to be sure your understanding is accurate and to see whether the speaker explains the point of view in a way that makes it more acceptable.

2. Interrupt the speaker so other listeners won't be "taken in" by the message.

3. Walk out as a symbolic gesture of disagreement.

END-OF-CHAPTER ASSESSMENT

1. The difference between hearing and listening is

    a. very small; the two processes amount to about the same thing
    b. hearing is mindful and intentional, but listening is effortless
    c. hearing is effortless, but listening is mindful and intentional
    d. hearing requires strong motivation and attention, but listening is an automatic human response to speech
    e. hearing depends on listening, but listening does not depend on hearing

2. Although you are a strong advocate of First Amendment rights, especially the protection of religious freedom, you find an exception to your beliefs when a speaker defends the rights of separatist religious sects to practice polygamy. Which of these responses is most ethical?

    a. Wait until the end of the presentation, then stand up and insist that the speaker listen to your rebuttal, just as you have listened to him or her.
    b. Seek a way to infiltrate the sect in order to investigate the truth of what's really going on.
    c. Go home to look up passages in the Bible that either support or refute the speakers claims, then write an anonymous letter to a newspaper opinion page.
    d. Sit quietly and listen to the speech to decide whether the message contains elements of value or whether to leave your original opinion unmodified.
    e. Have a sense of humor; lighten the mood with a little laughter.

3. Which of the following statements is best?

    a. A fact is carefully reasoned.
    b. A fact is verifiable by authoritative evidence.
    c. A carefully considered opinion is as good as factual evidence.
    d. Assumptions are always wrong.
    e. Opinions, even expert opinions, never belong in human discourse.

4. What is critical listening?

    a. negative judgments listeners develop during a speech
    b. the practice of detecting flaws in a speech
    c. a listener's use of his or her opinions in order to mentally refute factual details in the speech
    d. the rejection of a message
    e. careful scrutiny of the ideas and logical elements of a speech

5. Listening to a speech with an open mind means

    a. accepting the claims and conclusions of the speech
    b. listening in order to learn
    c. listening in order to quote the speaker later
    d. replacing your outdated knowledge with the newer information in the speech
    e. you must allow the speaker his or her First Amendment rights

ANSWER KEY

1. c
2. d
3. b
4. e
5. b

ENDNOTES

1. Jarvis, T. (2009, November). How to talk so people *really* listen: Four ways to make yourself heard. *O, the Oprah Magazine*. Retrieved from http://www.oprah.com/relationships/Communication-Skills-How-to-Make-Yourself-Heard

2. Aristotle. (c. 350 BCE). *Rhetoric* (W. Rhys Roberts, Trans.). Book I, Part 3, para. 1. Retrieved from http://classics.mit.edu/Aristotle/rhetoric.1.i.html

3. Watson, K. W., Barker, L. L., & Weaver, J. B., III. (1995). The listening styles profile (LSP-16): Development and validation of an instrument to assess four listening styles. *International Journal of Listening, 9*, 1–13.

4. Postman, N. (1985). *Amusing ourselves to death: Public discourse in the age of show business*. New York: Viking Press.

5. Carr, N. (2010, May 24). The Web shatters focus, rewires brains. *Wired Magazine*. Retrieved from http://www.wired.com/magazine/2010/05/ff_nicholas_carr/all/1

6. Middendorf, J., & Kalish, A. (1996). The "change-up" in lectures. *The National Teaching and Learning Forum, 5*(2).

7. Wheeless, L. R. (1975). An investigation of receiver apprehension and social context dimensions of communication apprehension. *Speech Teacher, 24*, 261–268.

8. DeVito, J. A. (2000). *The elements of public speaking* (7th ed.). New York, NY: Longman.

9. Wolvin, A., & Coakley, C. G. (1996). *Listening* (5th ed.). Boston, MA: McGraw-Hill.

10. Gluck, M. A., Mercado, E., & Myers, C. E. (2008). *Learning and memory: From brain to behavior*. New York: Worth Publishers, pp. 172–173.

11. Wikiquote. (n.d.). Daniel Patrick Moynihan. Retrieved from http://en.wikiquote.org/wiki/Daniel_Patrick_Moynihan

12. Factcheck.org, a Project of the Annenberg Public Policy Center of the University of Pennsylvania. (2009, September 10). Obama's health care speech. Retrieved from http://www.factcheck.org/2009/09/obamas-health-care-speech

13. Edward Jenner Museum. (n.d.). Vaccination. Retrieved from http://www.jennermuseum.com/Jenner/vaccination.html

14. Owen, R. (2010, May 23). Catholic church reburies "heretic" Nicolaus Copernicus with honour. *Times Online*. Retrieved from http://www.timesonline.co.uk/tol/news/world/europe/article7134341.ece

15. Coopman, S. J., & Lull, J. (2008). *Public speaking: The evolving art*. Cengage Learning, p. 60.

16. Sprague, J., Stuart, D., & Bodary, D. (2010). *The speaker's handbook* (9th ed.). Boston, MA: Wadsworth Cengage.

17. Lippman, D. (1998). *The storytelling coach: How to listen, praise, and bring out people's best*. Little Rock, AR: August House.

18. Lippman, D. (1998). *The storytelling coach: How to listen, praise, and bring out people's best*. Little Rock, AR: August House, pp. 110–111.

CHAPTER 5
Audience Analysis

WHAT IS AN AUDIENCE ANALYSIS?

One of the consequences of the First Amendment to the Constitution, which protects our right to speak freely, is that we focus so much on what we want to say that we often overlook the question of who our audience is. Does your audience care what you as a speaker think? Can they see how your speech applies to their lives and interests? The act of public speaking is a shared activity that involves interaction between speaker and audience. In order for your speech to get a fair hearing, you need to create a relationship with your listeners. Scholars Sprague, Stuart, and Bodary explain, "Speakers do not give speeches *to* audiences; they jointly create meaning *with* audiences."[1] The success of your speech rests in large part on how your audience receives and understands it.

© *Thinkstock*

Think of a time when you heard a speech that sounded "canned" or that fell flat because the audience didn't "get it." Chances are that this happened because the speaker neglected to consider that public speaking is an **audience-centered** activity. Worse, lack of consideration for one's audience can result in the embarrassment of alienating listeners by telling a joke they don't appreciate, or using language they find offensive. The best way to reduce the risk of such situations is to conduct an audience analysis as you prepare your speech.

Audience analysis is the process of gathering information about the people in your audience so that you can understand their needs, expectations, beliefs, values, attitudes, and likely opinions. In this chapter, we will first examine some reasons why audience analysis is important. We will then describe three different types of audience analysis and some techniques to use in conducting audience analysis. Finally, we will explain how you can use your audience analysis not only during the creation of your speech but also while you are delivering it.

audience-centered

The emphasis of a speaker on the importance of the audience's characteristics and needs.

audience analysis

The process of gathering certain kinds of information about the people in your audience and using that information to understand the beliefs, values, needs, attitudes, and opinions they hold.

1. WHY CONDUCT AN AUDIENCE ANALYSIS?

1.1   Acknowledge the Audience

© Thinkstock

Picture yourself in front of the audience, about to deliver your speech. This is the moment when your relationship with your audience begins, and the quality of this relationship will influence how receptive they will be to your ideas, or at least how willing they'll be to listen to what you have to say. One of the best ways to initiate this relationship is by finding a way to acknowledge your audience. This can be as simple as establishing eye contact and thanking them for coming to hear your presentation. If they've braved bad weather, are missing a world-class sports event, or are putting up with an inconvenience such as a stuffy conference room, tell them how much you appreciate their presence in spite of the circumstances. This can go a long way toward getting them "on board" with your message.

For a political candidate who is traveling from town to town giving what may be perceived as the same campaign speech time and time again, a statement like "It's great to be here in Springfield, and I want to thank the West Valley League of Women Voters and our hosts, the Downtown Senior Center, for the opportunity to be with you today" lets the audience know that the candidate has at least taken the trouble to tailor the speech to the present audience. Stephanie Coopman and James Lull tell us that Microsoft chairman Bill Gates often adapts to his audiences by thanking them for their participation in the computer industry or for their preparation to participate in an electronic world. The authors say, "Even those brief acknowledgments let audience members know that Gates had prepared his speech with them in mind."[2] We will cover audience acknowledgment further in Chapter 10.

1.2   Choose a Worthwhile Topic

Your selection of a topic should reflect your regard for the audience. There is no universal list of good or bad topics, but you have an ethical responsibility to select a topic that will be worth listening to. As a student, you are probably sensitive to how unpleasant it would be to listen to a speech on a highly complex or technical topic that you found impossible to understand. However, have you considered that audiences do not want to waste their time or attention listening to a speech that is too simple? Many students find themselves tempted to choose an easy topic, or a topic they already know a great deal about. This is an understandable temptation; if you are like most students, you have many commitments and the demands on your time are considerable. Many experts encourage students to begin with something they already know. However, our experience tells us that students often do this simply to reduce their workload. For example, if the purpose of your speech is to inform or persuade students in your public speaking class, a topic such as fitness, drunk driving, the Greek system (campus fraternities and sororities), or credit card responsibility may be easy for you to address, but it is unlikely to go very far toward informing your audience, and in all likelihood, it will not be persuading them either. Instead, your audience members and your professor will quickly recognize that you were thinking of your own needs rather than those of your audience.

To avoid this trap, it behooves you to seek a topic that will be novel and interesting both for you and for your audience. It will also be important to do some credible research in order to ensure that even the most informed audience members will learn something from you. There are many topics that could provide a refreshing departure from your usual academic studies. Topics such as the Bermuda Triangle, biopiracy, the environmental niche of sharks, the green lifestyle, and the historic Oneida Community all provide interesting views of human and natural phenomena not usually provided in public education. Such topics might be more likely to hold the interest of your classroom audience than topics they've heard about time and time again.

You should be aware that your audience will not have the same set of knowledge that you do. For instance, if you are speaking about biopiracy, you should probably define it and give a clear example. If your speech is on the green lifestyle, it would be important to frame it as a realistic choice, not a goal so remote as to be hopeless. In each case, you should use audience analysis to consider how your audience will respond to you, your topic, and your message.

Clarity

Nothing is more lamentable than a rhetorical actor who endeavors to make grandiose the impressions of others through the utilization of an elephantine albeit nonsensical **argot**—or nothing is worse than a speaker who tries to impress the audience with a giant vocabulary that no one understands. In the first portion of the preceding sentence, we pulled out as many polysyllabic words as we could find. Unfortunately, most people will just find the sentence wordy and the meaning will pass right over their heads. As such, we as public speakers must ensure that we are clear in what we say.

Make sure that you state your topic clearly at the outset, using words that your audience will understand. Letting them know what to expect from your speech shows consideration for them as listeners and lets them know that you value their time and attention.

Throughout your speech, define your terms clearly and carefully in order to avoid misleading or alarming people by mistake. Be careful not to use jargon or "insider" language that will exclude listeners who aren't "in the know." If you approach audience analysis in haste, you might find yourself presenting a speech with no clear message. You might avoid making any statements outright from fear of offending. It is much better to know to whom you're speaking and to present a clear, decisive message that lets listeners know what you think.

Controversial Topics Are Important and Risky

Some of the most interesting topics are controversial. They are **controversial topics** because people have deeply felt values and beliefs on different sides of those topics. For instance, before you choose nuclear energy as your topic, investigate the many voices speaking out both in favor and against increasing its use. Many people perceive nuclear energy as a clean, reliable, and much-needed source of energy. Others say that even the mining of uranium is harmful to the environment, that we lack satisfactory solutions for storing nuclear waste, and that nuclear power plants are vulnerable to errors and attacks. Another group might view the issue economically, believing that industry needs nuclear energy. Engineers might believe that if the national grid could be modernized, we would have enough energy, and that we should strive to use and waste less energy until modernization is feasible. Some might feel deep concern about our reliance on foreign oil. Others might view nuclear energy as more tried-and-true than other alternatives. The topic is extremely controversial, and yet it is interesting and very important.

You shouldn't avoid controversy altogether, but you should choose your topic carefully. Moreover, how you treat your audience is just as important as how you treat your topic. If your audience has widely diverse views, take the time to acknowledge the concerns they have. Treat them as intelligent people, even if you don't trust the completeness or the accuracy of their beliefs about your topic.

1.3   Adapt Your Speech to Audience Needs

When preparing a speech for a classroom audience consisting of other students and your professor, you may feel that you know their interests and expectations fairly well. However, we learn public speaking in order to be able to address other audiences where we can do some good. In some cases, your audience might consist of young children who are not ready to accept the fact that a whale is not a fish or that the moon is always round even though it sometimes appears to be a crescent or a half circle. In other cases, your audience might include retirees living on fixed incomes and who therefore might not agree that raising local taxes is a vital "investment in the future."

Even in an audience that appears to be *homogeneous*—composed of people who are very similar to one another—different listeners will understand the same ideas in different ways. Every member of every audience has his or her own **frame of reference**—the unique set of perspectives, experience, knowledge, and values belonging to every individual. An audience member who has been in a car accident caused by a drunk driver might not appreciate a lighthearted joke about barhopping. Similarly, stressing the importance of graduate school might be discouraging to audience members who don't know whether they can even afford to stay in college to complete an undergraduate degree.

argot

Specialized vocabulary or jargon of a particular profession or social group.

controversial topics

Topics surrounded by diverse and deeply felt feelings and opinions.

frame of reference

An individual's unique set of perspectives, experience, knowledge, and values.

demographic information

Information about the audience's gender, age range, marital status, ethnicity, socioeconomic status, and other variables that can influence their frame of reference.

psychographic information

The audience's set of beliefs, values, religions, and life experiences.

racism

The assumption that one race is superior to another.

ethnocentrism

The belief that one's own culture is the standard to which other cultures should aspire.

sexism

The assumption that one sex is weaker, less intelligent, less competent, or less deserving than the other.

ageism

The attitude of valuing youth and devaluing age.

elitism

The practice of thinking the best of those with the highest status and prestige and treating them preferentially.

These examples illustrate why audience analysis—the process of learning all you reasonably can about your audience—is so centrally important. Audience analysis includes consideration of **demographic information**, such as the gender, age range, marital status, race, and ethnicity of the people in your audience. Another, perhaps less obvious, demographic factor is *socioeconomic status*, which refers to a combination of characteristics including income, wealth, level of education, and occupational prestige. Each of these dimensions gives you some information about which kinds of topics, and which aspects of various topics, will be well received.

Suppose you are preparing to give an informative speech about early childhood health care. If your audience is a group of couples who have each recently had a new baby and who live in an affluent suburb, you can expect that they will be young adults with high socioeconomic status; they will likely be eager to know about the very best available health care for their children, whether they are healthy or have various medical problems. In contrast, if your audience is a group of nurses, they may differ in age, but will be similar in education and occupational prestige. They will already know quite a lot about the topic, so you will want to find an aspect that may be new for them, such as community health care resources for families with limited financial resources or for referring children with special needs. As another example, if you are addressing a city council committee that is considering whether to fund a children's health care initiative, your audience is likely to have very mixed demographics.

Audience analysis also takes into account what market researchers call **psychographic information**, which is more personal and more difficult to predict than demographics. Psychographic information involves the beliefs, attitudes, and values that your audience members embrace. Respecting your audience means that you avoid offending, excluding, or trivializing the beliefs and values they hold. Returning to the topic of early childhood health care, you can expect new parents to be passionate about wanting the best for their child. The psychographics of a group of nurses would revolve around their professional competence and the need to provide "standard of care" for their patients. In a city council committee meeting, the topic of early childhood health care may be a highly personal and emotional issue for some of your listeners, while for others it may be strictly a matter of dollars and cents.

Consider Audience Diversity

Diversity is a key dimension of audience membership and, therefore, of audience analysis. While the term "diversity" is often used to refer to racial and ethnic minorities, it is important to realize that audiences can be diverse in many other ways as well. Being mindful of diversity means being respectful of all people and striving to avoid **racism**, **ethnocentrism**, **sexism**, **ageism**, **elitism**, and other assumptions. An interesting "ism" that is not often mentioned is *chronocentrism*, or the assumption that people today are superior to people who lived in earlier eras.[3]

Sociologists John R. Logan and Wenquan Zhang analyzed racial and ethnic diversity in US cities and observed a pattern that rewrites the traditional "rules" of neighborhood change.[4] Whereas in our grandparents' day a racially mixed neighborhood was one with African American and white residents, in recent decades, many more people from a variety of Asian and Latin American countries have immigrated to the United States. As a result, many cities have neighborhoods that are richly diverse with Asian, Hispanic, and African American cultural influences as well as those of white European Americans. Each cultural group consists of people from many communities and occupations. Each cultural group came to the United States for different reasons and came from different communities and occupations within their original cultures. Even though it can be easy to assume that people from a culture are exactly like each other, we undermine our credibility when we create our message as though members of these cultures are carbon copies of each other.

One of the author's classes included two students from China. During a discussion of cultural similarity and difference, one remarked, "I thought we would have the same tastes in food because we are both from China, but she likes different spices and cooking techniques than I do."

While race, ethnicity, and culture may be relatively visible aspects of diversity, there are many other aspects that are less obvious, so your audience is often more diverse than you might initially think. Suppose you are going to give a talk on pool safety to residents of a very affluent suburban community—will all your audience members be wealthy? No. There might be some who are unemployed, some who are behind on their mortgage payments, some who live in rented rooms, not to mention some who work as babysitters or housekeepers. Furthermore, if your listeners have some characteristic in common, it doesn't mean that they all think alike. For instance, if your audience consists of people who are members of military families, don't assume that they all have identical beliefs about national security. If there are many business students in your audience, don't assume they all agree about the relative importance of ethics and profits. Instead, recognize that a range of opinion exists.

This is where the *frame of reference* we mentioned earlier becomes an important concept. People have a wide variety of reasons for making the choices they make and for doing the things they do. For instance, a business student, while knowing that profitability is important, might have a strong interest in green lifestyles, low energy use, and alternative energy sources, areas of economic development that might require a great deal of investment before profits are realized. In fact, some business students may want to be involved in a paradigm shift away from "business as usual."

These examples illustrate how important it is to use audience analysis to avoid *stereotyping*—taking for granted that people with a certain characteristic in common have the same likes, dislikes, values, and beliefs. All members of our audiences deserve to have the same sensitivity and the same respect extended to them as unique individuals. Respecting diversity is not merely a responsibility within public speaking; it should be a responsibility we strive to embrace in all our human interactions.

Avoid Offending Your Audience

It might seem obvious that speakers should use audience analysis to avoid making offensive remarks, but even very experienced speakers sometimes forget this basic rule. If you were an Anglo-American elected official addressing a Latino audience, would you make a joke about a Mexican American person's name sounding similar to the name of a popular brand of tequila? In fact, a state governor did just that in June 2011. Not suprisingly, news organizations covering the event reported that the joke fell flat.[5] People are members of groups they didn't choose and can't change. We didn't choose our race, ethnicity, sex, age, sexual orientation, intellectual potential, or appearance. We already know that jokes aimed at people because of their membership in these groups are not just politically incorrect but also ethically wrong.

It is not only insensitive humor that can offend an audience. Speakers also need to be aware of language and nonverbal behaviors that state or imply a negative message about people based on their various membership groups. Examples include language that suggests that all scientists are men, that all relationships are heterosexual, or that all ethnic minorities are unpatriotic. By the same token, we should avoid embedding assumptions about people in our messages. Even the most subtle suggestion may not go unnoticed. For example, if, in your speech, you assume that elderly people are frail and expensively medicated, you may offend people whose elder loved ones do not conform in any way to your assumptions.

Scholars Samovar and McDaniel tell us that ethical language choices require four guidelines:

1. Be accurate; present the facts accurately.

2. Be aware of the emotional impact; make sure that you don't manipulate feelings.

3. Avoid hateful words; refrain from language that disparages or belittles people.

4. Be sensitive to the audience; know how audience members prefer to be identified (e.g., Native American instead of Indian, women instead of girls, African American instead of black, disabled instead of crippled).[6]

If you alienate your audience, they will stop listening. They will refuse to accept your message, no matter how true or important it is. They might even become hostile. If you fail to recognize the complexity of your audience members and if you treat them as stereotypes, they will resent your assumptions and doubt your credibility.

1.4   Ethical Speaking Is Sincere Speaking

Ethos is the term Aristotle used to refer to what we now call **credibility**: the perception that the speaker is honest, knowledgeable, and rightly motivated. Your ethos, or credibility, must be established as you build rapport with your listeners. Have you put forth the effort to learn who they are and what you can offer to them in your speech? Do you respect them as individual human beings? Do you respect them enough to serve their needs and interests? Is your topic relevant and appropriate for them? Is your approach honest and sensitive to their preexisting beliefs? Your ability to answer these questions in a constructive way must be based on the best demographic and psychographic information you can use to learn about your listeners.

The audience needs to know they can trust the speaker's motivations, intentions, and knowledge. They must believe that the speaker has no hidden motives, will not manipulate or trick them, and has their best interests at heart.

In order to convey regard and respect for the audience, you must be sincere. You must examine the motives behind your topic choice, the true purpose of your speech, and your willingness to do the work of making sure the content of the speech is true and represents reality. This can be difficult for students who face time constraints and multiple demands on their efforts. However, the attitude you assume for this task represents, in part, the kind of professional, citizen, parent, and human being you want to be. Even if you've given this issue little thought up to now, you can examine your motives and the integrity of your research and message construction. Ethically, you should.

ethos

Aristotle's term for credibility; the perception that the speaker is honest, knowledgeable, and rightly motivated.

credibility

The perception that the speaker is honest, knowledgeable, and rightly motivated.

EXERCISES

1. Brainstorm a list of topics for an informative or persuasive speech. By yourself or with a partner, identify the kinds of information you need about your audience in order to make ethical decisions about how you approach the speech.
2. Make a list of values or opinions you have that might not conform to popular views. Why might these be important for a speaker to know before attempting to inform or persuade you?
3. Pretend you have been asked to give a speech about environmental conservation in the United States. What audience beliefs, attitudes, values, concerns, and other variables should you consider?

2. THREE TYPES OF AUDIENCE ANALYSIS

LEARNING OBJECTIVES

1. Understand how to gather and use demographic information.
2. Understand how to gather and use psychographic information.
3. Understand how to gather and use situational information.

© Thinkstock

While audience analysis does not guarantee against errors in judgment, it will help you make good choices in topic, language, style of presentation, and other aspects of your speech. The more you know about your audience, the better you can serve their interests and needs. There are certainly limits to what we can learn through information collection, and we need to acknowledge that before making assumptions, but knowing how to gather and use information through audience analysis is an essential skill for successful speakers.

2.1 Demographic Analysis

As indicated earlier, demographic information includes factors such as gender, age range, marital status, race and ethnicity, and socioeconomic status. In your public speaking class, you probably already know how many students are male and female, their approximate ages, and so forth. But how can you assess the demographics of an audience ahead of time if you have had no previous contact with them? In many cases, you can ask the person or organization that has invited you to speak; it's likely that they can tell you a lot about the demographics of the people who are expected to come to hear you.

Whatever method you use to gather demographics, exercise respect from the outset. For instance, if you are collecting information about whether audience members have ever been divorced, be aware that not everyone will want to answer your questions. You can't require them to do so, and you may not make assumptions about their reluctance to discuss the topic. You must allow them their privacy.

Age

There are certain things you can learn about an audience based on age. For instance, if your audience members are first-year college students, you can assume that they have grown up in the post-9/11 era and have limited memory of what life was like before the "war on terror." If your audience includes people in their forties and fifties, it is likely they remember a time when people feared they would contract the AIDS virus from shaking hands or using a public restroom. People who are in their sixties today came of age during the 1960s, the era of the Vietnam War and a time of social confrontation and experimentation. They also have frames of reference that contribute to the way they think, but it may not be easy to predict which side of the issues they support.

Gender

Gender can define human experience. Clearly, most women have had a different cultural experience from that of men within the same culture. Some women have found themselves excluded from certain careers. Some men have found themselves blamed for the limitations imposed on women. In books such as *You Just Don't Understand* and *Talking from 9 to 5*, linguist Deborah Tannen has written extensively on differences between men's and women's communication styles. Tannen explains, "This is not to say that all women and all men, or all boys and girls, behave any one way. Many factors influence our styles, including regional and ethnic backgrounds, family experience and individual personality. But gender is a key factor, and understanding its influence can help clarify what happens when we talk."[7]

Marriage tends to impose additional roles on both men and women and divorce even more so, especially if there are children. Even if your audience consists of young adults who have not yet made occupational or marital commitments, they are still aware that gender and the choices they make about issues such as careers and relationships will influence their experience as adults.

Culture

In past generations, Americans often used the metaphor of a "melting pot" to symbolize the assimilation of immigrants from various countries and cultures into a unified, harmonious "American people." Today, we are aware of the limitations in that metaphor, and have largely replaced it with a multiculturalist view that describes the American fabric as a "patchwork" or a "mosaic." We know that people who immigrate do not abandon their cultures of origin in order to conform to a standard American identity. In fact, cultural continuity is now viewed as a healthy source of identity.

We also know that subcultures and cocultures exist within and alongside larger cultural groups. For example, while we are aware that Native American people do not all embrace the same values, beliefs, and customs as mainstream white Americans, we also know that members of the Navajo nation have different values, beliefs, and customs from those of members of the Sioux or the Seneca. We know that African American people in urban centers like Detroit and Boston do not share the same cultural experiences as those living in rural Mississippi. Similarly, white Americans in San Francisco may be culturally rooted in the narrative of distant ancestors from Scotland, Italy, or Sweden or in the experience of having emigrated much more recently from Australia, Croatia, or Poland.

Not all cultural membership is visibly obvious. For example, people in German American and Italian American families have widely different sets of values and practices, yet others may not be able to differentiate members of these groups. Differences are what make each group interesting and are important sources of knowledge, perspectives, and creativity.

Religion

There is wide variability in religion as well. The Pew Forum on Religion and Public Life found in a nationwide survey that 84 percent of Americans identify with at least one of a dozen major religions, including Christianity, Judaism, Buddhism, Islam, Hinduism, and others. Within Christianity alone, there are half a dozen categories including Roman Catholic, Mormon, Jehovah's Witness, Orthodox (Greek and Russian), and a variety of Protestant denominations. Another 6 percent said they were unaffiliated but religious, meaning that only one American in ten is atheist, agnostic, or "nothing in particular."[8]

Even within a given denomination, a great deal of diversity can be found. For instance, among Roman Catholics alone, there are people who are devoutly religious, people who self-identify as Catholic but do not attend mass or engage in other religious practices, and others who faithfully make confession and attend mass but who openly question Papal doctrine on various issues. Catholicism among immigrants from the Caribbean and Brazil is often blended with indigenous religion or with religion imported from the west coast of Africa. It is very different from Catholicism in the Vatican.

The dimensions of diversity in the religion demographic are almost endless, and they are not limited by denomination. Imagine conducting an audience analysis of people belonging to an individual congregation rather than a denomination: even there, you will most likely find a multitude of variations that involve how one was brought up, adoption of a faith system as an adult, how strictly one observes religious practices, and so on.

Yet, even with these multiple facets, religion is still a meaningful demographic lens. It can be an indicator of probable patterns in family relationships, family size, and moral attitudes.

Group Membership

In your classroom audience alone, there will be students from a variety of academic majors. Every major has its own set of values, goals, principles, and codes of ethics. A political science student preparing for law school might seem to have little in common with a student of music therapy, for instance. In addition, there are other group memberships that influence how audience members understand the world. Fraternities and sororities, sports teams, campus organizations, political parties, volunteerism, and cultural communities all provide people with ways of understanding the world as it is and as we think it should be.

Because public speaking audiences are very often members of one group or another, group membership is a useful and often easy to access facet of audience analysis. The more you know about the associations of your audience members, the better prepared you will be to tailor your speech to their interests, expectations, and needs.

Education

Education is expensive, and people pursue education for many reasons. Some people seek to become educated, while others seek to earn professional credentials. Both are important motivations. If you know the education levels attained by members of your audience, you might not know their motivations, but you will know to what extent they could somehow afford the money for an education, afford the time to get an education, and survive educational demands successfully.

The kind of education is also important. For instance, an airplane mechanic undergoes a very different kind of education and training from that of an accountant or a software engineer. This means that not only the attained level of education but also the particular field is important in your understanding of your audience.

Occupation

People choose occupations for reasons of motivation and interest, but their occupations also influence their perceptions and their interests. There are many misconceptions about most occupations. For instance, many people believe that teachers work an eight-hour day and have summers off. When you ask teachers, however, you might be surprised to find out that they take work home with them for evenings and weekends, and during the summer, they may teach summer school as well as taking courses in order to keep up with new developments in their fields. But even if you don't know those things, you would still know that teachers have had rigorous generalized and specialized qualifying education, that they have a complex set of responsibilities in the classroom and the institution, and that, to some extent, they have chosen a relatively low-paying occupation over such fields as law, advertising, media, fine and performing arts, or medicine. If your audience includes doctors and nurses, you know that you are speaking to people with differing but important philosophies of health and illness. Learning about those occupational realities is important in avoiding wrong assumptions and stereotypes. We insist that you not assume that nurses are merely doctors "lite." Their skills, concerns, and responsibilities are almost entirely different, and both are crucially necessary to effective health care.

2.2 Psychographic Analysis

Earlier, we mentioned psychographic information, which includes such things as values, opinions, attitudes, and beliefs. Authors Grice and Skinner present a model in which values are the basis for beliefs, attitudes, and behaviors.[9] Values are the foundation of their pyramid model. They say, "A value expresses a judgment of what is desirable and undesirable, right and wrong, or good and evil. Values are usually stated in the form of a word or phrase. For example, most of us probably share the values of equality, freedom, honesty, fairness, justice, good health, and family. These values compose the principles or standards we use to judge and develop our beliefs, attitudes, and behaviors."

It is important to recognize that, while demographic information as discussed in Section 2 is fairly straightforward and verifiable, psychographic information is much less clear-cut. Two different people who both say they believe in equal educational opportunity may have very different interpretations of what "equal opportunity" means. People who say they don't buy junk food may have very different standards for what specific kinds of foods are considered "junk food."

We also acknowledge that people inherit some values from their family upbringing, cultural influences, and life experiences. The extent to which someone values family loyalty and obedience to parents, thrift, humility, and work may be determined by these influences more than by individual choice.

Psychographic analysis can reveal preexisting notions that limit your audience's frame of reference. By knowing about such notions ahead of time, you can address them in your speech. Audiences are likely to have two basic kinds of preexisting notions: those about the topic and those about the speaker.

Preexisting Notions about Your Topic

Many things are a great deal more complex than we realize. Media stereotypes often contribute to our oversimplifications. For instance, one of your authors, teaching public speaking in the past decade, was surprised to hear a student claim that "the hippies meant well, but they did it wrong." Aside from the question of the "it" that was done wrong, there was a question about how little the student actually knew about the diverse hippy cultures and their aspirations. The student seemed unaware that some of "the hippies" were the forebears of such things as organic bakeries, natural food co-ops, urban gardens, recycling, alternative energy, wellness, and other arguably positive developments.

It's important to know your audience in order to make a rational judgment about how their views of your topic might be shaped. In speaking to an audience that might have differing definitions, you should take care to define your terms in a clear, honest way.

At the opposite end from oversimplification is the level of sophistication your audience might embody. Your audience analysis should include factors that reveal it. Suppose you are speaking about trends in civil rights in the United States. You cannot pretend that advancement of civil rights is virtually complete nor can you claim that no progress has been made. It is likely that in a college classroom, the audience will know that although much progress has been made, there are still pockets of prejudice, discrimination, and violence. When you speak to an audience that is cognitively complex, your strategy must be different from one you would use for an audience that is less educated in the topic. With a cognitively complex audience, you must acknowledge the overall complexity while stating that your focus will be on only one dimension. With an audience that's uninformed about your topic, that strategy in a persuasive speech could confuse them; they might well prefer a black-and-white message with no gray areas. You must decide whether it is ethical to represent your topic this way.

When you prepare to do your audience analysis, include questions that reveal how much your audience already knows about your topic. Try to ascertain the existence of stereotyped, oversimplified, or prejudiced attitudes about it. This could make a difference in your choice of topic or in your approach to the audience and topic.

Preexisting Notions about You

People form opinions readily. For instance, we know that students form impressions of teachers the moment they walk into our classrooms on the first day. You get an immediate impression of our age, competence, and attitude simply from our appearance and nonverbal behavior. In addition, many have heard other students say what they think of us.

The same is almost certainly true of you. But it's not always easy to get others to be honest about their impressions of you. They're likely to tell you what they think you want to hear. Sometimes, however, you do know what others think. They might think of you as a jock, a suit-wearing conservative, a nature lover, and so on. Based on these impressions, your audience might expect a boring speech, a shallow speech, a sermon, and so on. However, your concern should still be serving your audience's needs and interests, not debunking their opinions of you or managing your image. In order to help them be receptive, you address their interests directly, and make sure they get an interesting, ethical speech.

2.3   Situational Analysis

The next type of analysis is called the **situational audience analysis** because it focuses on characteristics related to the specific speaking situation. The situational audience analysis can be divided into two main questions:

1. How many people came to hear my speech and why are they here? What events, concerns, and needs motivated them to come? What is their interest level, and what else might be competing for their attention?
2. What is the physical environment of the speaking situation? What is the size of the audience, layout of the room, existence of a podium or a microphone, and availability of digital media for visual aids? Are there any distractions, such as traffic noise?

situational audience analysis

Audience analysis that focuses on situational factors such as the size of the audience, the physical setting, and the disposition of the audience toward the topic, the speaker, and the occasion.

Audience Size

In a typical class, your audience is likely to consist of twenty to thirty listeners. This audience size gives you the latitude to be relatively informal within the bounds of good judgment. It isn't too difficult to let each audience member feel as though you're speaking to him or her. However, you would not become so informal that you allow your carefully prepared speech to lapse into shallow entertainment. With larger audiences, it's more difficult to reach out to each listener, and your speech will tend to be more formal, staying more strictly within its careful outline. You will have to work harder to prepare visual and audio material that reaches the people sitting at the back of the room, including possibly using amplification.

Occasion

There are many occasions for speeches. Awards ceremonies, conventions and conferences, holidays, and other celebrations are some examples. However, there are also less joyful reasons for a speech, such as funerals, disasters, and the delivery of bad news. As always, there are likely to be mixed reactions. For instance, award ceremonies are good for community and institutional morale, but we wouldn't be surprised to find at least a little resentment from listeners who feel deserving but were overlooked. Likewise, for a speech announcing bad news, it is likely that at least a few listeners will be glad the bad news wasn't even worse. If your speech is to deliver bad news, it's important to be honest but also to avoid traumatizing your audience. For instance, if you are a condominium board member speaking to a residents' meeting after the building was damaged by a hurricane, you will need to provide accurate data about the extent of the damage and the anticipated cost and time required for repairs. At the same time, it would be needlessly upsetting to launch into a graphic description of injuries suffered by people, animals, and property in neighboring areas not connected to your condomium complex.

Some of the most successful speeches benefit from situational analysis to identify audience concerns related to the occasion. For example, when the president of the United States gives the annual State of the Union address, the occasion calls for commenting on the condition of the nation and outlining the legislative agenda for the coming year. The speech could be a formality that would interest only "policy wonks," or with the use of good situational audience analysis, it could be a popular event reinforcing the connection between the president and the American people. In January 2011, knowing that the United States' economy was slowly recovering and that jobless rates were still very high, President Barack Obama and his staff knew that the focus of the speech had to be on jobs. Similarly, in January 2003, President George W. Bush's State of the Union speech focused on the "war on terror" and his reasons for justifying the invasion of Iraq. If you look at the history of State of the Union Addresses, you'll often find that the speeches are tailored to the political, social, and economic situations facing the United States at those times.

Voluntariness of Audience

A **voluntary audience** gathers because they want to hear the speech, attend the event, or participate in an event. A classroom audience, in contrast, is likely to be a captive audience. **Captive audiences** are required to be present or feel obligated to do so. Given the limited choices perceived, a captive audience might give only grudging attention. Even when there's an element of choice, the likely consequences of nonattendance will keep audience members from leaving. The audience's relative perception of choice increases the importance of holding their interest.

Whether or not the audience members chose to be present, you want them to be interested in what you have to say. Almost any audience will be interested in a topic that pertains directly to them. However, your audience might also be receptive to topics that are indirectly or potentially pertinent to their lives. This means that if you choose a topic such as advances in the treatment of spinal cord injury or advances in green technology, you should do your best to show how these topics are potentially relevant to their lives or careers.

However, there are some topics that appeal to audience curiosity even when it seems there's little chance of direct pertinence. For instance, topics such as Blackbeard the pirate or ceremonial tattoos among the Maori might pique the interests of various audiences. Depending on the instructions you get from your instructor, you can consider building an interesting message about something outside the daily foci of our attention.

Physical Setting

The physical setting can make or break even the best speeches, so it is important to exercise as much control as you can over it. In your classroom, conditions might not be ideal, but at least the setting is familiar. Still, you know your classroom from the perspective of an audience member, not a speaker standing in the front—which is why you should seek out any opportunity to rehearse your speech during a minute when the room is empty. If you will be giving your presentation somewhere else, it is a good idea to visit the venue ahead of time if at all possible and make note of any factors that will affect how you present your speech. In any case, be sure to arrive well in advance of your speaking time so that you will have time to check that the microphone works, to test out any visual aids, and to request any needed adjustments in lighting, room ventilation, or other factors to eliminate distractions and make your audience more comfortable.

---

voluntary audience

An audience attending a speech of their own free will.

captive audience

An audience that perceives little or no choice about attendance.

KEY TAKEAWAYS

- Demographic audience analysis focuses on group memberships of audience members.
- Another element of audience is psychographic information, which focuses on audience attitudes, beliefs, and values.
- Situational analysis of the occasion, physical setting, and other factors are also critical to effective audience analysis.

EXERCISES

1. List the voluntary (political party, campus organization, etc.) and involuntary (age, race, sex, etc.) groups to which you belong. After each group, write a sentence or phrase about how that group influences your experience as a student.
2. Visit http://www.claritas.com/MyBestSegments/Default.jsp and http://homes.point2.com and report on the demographic information found for several different towns or zip codes. How would this information be useful in preparing an audience analysis?
3. In a short paragraph, define the term "fairness." Compare your definition with someone else's definition. What factors do you think contributed to differences in definition?
4. With a partner, identify an instance when you observed a speaker give a poor speech due to failing to analyze the situation. What steps could the speaker have taken to more effectively analyze the situation?

3. CONDUCTING AUDIENCE ANALYSIS

LEARNING OBJECTIVES

1. Learn several tools for gathering audience information.
2. Create effective tools for gathering audience information.

Now that we have described what audience analysis is and why it is important, let's examine some details of how to conduct it. Exactly how can you learn about the people who will make up your audience?

3.1 Direct Observation

One way to learn about people is to observe them. By observing nonverbal patterns of behavior, you can learn a great deal as long as you are careful how you interpret the behaviors. For instance, do people greet each other with a handshake, a hug, a smile, or a nod? Do members of opposite sexes make physical contact? Does the setting suggest more conservative behavior? By listening in on conversations, you can find out the issues that concern people. Are people in the campus center talking about political unrest in the Middle East? About concerns over future Pell Grant funding? We suggest that you consider the ethical dimensions of eavesdropping, however. Are you simply overhearing an open conversation, or are you prying into a highly personal or private discussion?

© *Thinkstock*

3.2 Interviews and Surveys

interview

A one-on-one exchange in which you ask questions of a respondent.

respondent

Someone who responds to a survey, questionnaire, interview, or focus group.

survey

A set of written questions with multiple-choice questions and/or open-ended questions.

Because your demographic analysis will be limited to your most likely audience, your most accurate way to learn about them is to seek personal information through interviews and surveys. An **interview** is a one-on-one exchange in which you ask questions of a **respondent**, whereas a **survey** is a set of questions administered to several—or, preferably, many—respondents. Interviews may be conducted face-to-face, by phone, or by written means, such as texting. They allow more in-depth discussion than surveys, and they are also more time consuming to conduct. Surveys are also sometimes conducted face-to-face or by phone, but online surveys are increasingly common. You may collect and tabulate survey results manually, or set up an automated online survey through the free or subscription portals of sites like Survey Monkey and Zoomerang. Using an online survey provides the advantage of keeping responses anonymous, which may increase your audience members' willingness to participate and to answer personal questions. Surveys are an efficient way to collect information quickly; however, in contrast to interviews, they don't allow for follow-up questions to help you understand why your respondent gave a certain answer.

When you use interviews and surveys, there are several important things to keep in mind:

- Make sure your interview and survey questions are directly related to your speech topic. Do not use interviews to delve into private areas of people's lives. For instance, if your speech is about the debate between creationism and evolution, limit your questions to their opinions about that topic; do not meander into their beliefs about sexual behavior or their personal religious practices.

- Create and use a standard set of questions. If you "ad lib" your questions so that they are phrased differently for different interviewees, you will be comparing "apples and oranges" when you compare the responses you've obtained.

- Keep interviews and surveys short, or you could alienate your audience long before your speech is even outlined. Tell them the purpose of the interview or survey and make sure they understand that their participation is voluntary.

- Don't rely on just a few respondents to inform you about your entire audience. In all likelihood, you have a cognitively diverse audience. In order to accurately identify trends, you will likely need to interview or survey at least ten to twenty people.

In addition, when you conduct interviews and surveys, keep in mind that people are sometimes less than honest in describing their beliefs, attitudes, and behavior. This widely recognized weakness of interviews and survey research is known as *socially desirable responding*: the tendency to give responses that are considered socially acceptable. Marketing professor Ashok Lalwani divides socially desirable responding into two types: (1) impression management, or intentionally portraying oneself in a favorable light and (2) self-deceptive enhancement, or exaggerating one's good qualities, often unconsciously.[10]

You can reduce the effects of socially desirable responding by choosing your questions carefully. As marketing consultant Terry Vavra advises, "one should never ask what one can't logically expect respondents to honestly reveal."[11] For example, if you want to know audience members' attitudes about body piercing, you are likely to get more honest answers by asking "Do you think body piercing is attractive?" rather than "How many piercings do you have and where on your body are they located?"

3.3 Focus Groups

focus group

A group of three to eight people who meet together to respond to questions asked by the researcher. A focus group is usually an anonymous group and their responses can be freewheeling. With permission, their discussion can be recorded.

A **focus group** is a small group of people who give you feedback about their perceptions. As with interviews and surveys, in a focus group you should use a limited list of carefully prepared questions designed to get at the information you need to understand their beliefs, attitudes, and values specifically related to your topic.

If you conduct a focus group, part of your task will be striking a balance between allowing the discussion to flow freely according to what group members have to say and keeping the group focused on the questions. It's also your job to guide the group in maintaining responsible and respectful behavior toward each other.

In evaluating focus group feedback, do your best to be receptive to what people had to say, whether or not it conforms to what you expected. Your purpose in conducting the group was to understand group members' beliefs, attitudes, and values about your topic, not to confirm your assumptions.

3.4 Using Existing Data about Your Audience

Occasionally, existing information will be available about your audience. For instance, if you have a student audience, it might not be difficult to find out what their academic majors are. You might also be able to find out their degree of investment in their educations; for instance, you could reasonably assume that the seniors in the audience have been successful students who have invested at least three years pursuing a higher education. Sophomores have at least survived their first year but may not have matched the seniors in demonstrating strong values toward education and the work ethic necessary to earn a degree.

In another kind of an audience, you might be able to learn other significant facts. For instance, are they veterans? Are they retired teachers? Are they members of a voluntary civic organization such as the Lions Club or Mothers Against Drunk Driving (MADD)? This kind of information should help you respond to their concerns and interests.

In other cases, you may be able to use demographics collected by public and private organizations. Demographic analysis is done by the US Census Bureau through the American Community Survey, which is conducted every year, and through other specialized demographic surveys.[12] The Census Bureau analysis generally captures information about people in all the regions of the United States, but you can drill down in census data to see results by state, by age group, by gender, by race, and by other factors.

Demographic information about narrower segments of the United States, down to the level of individual zip codes, is available through private organizations such as The Nielsen Company (http://www.claritas.com/MyBestSegments/Default.jsp?ID=20&SubID=&pageName=ZIP%2BCode%2BLook-up), Sperling's Best Places (http://www.bestplaces.net), and Point2Homes (http://homes.point2.com). Sales and marketing professionals use this data, and you may find it useful for your audience analysis as well.

KEY TAKEAWAYS

- Several options exist for learning about your audience, including direct observation, interviews, surveys, focus groups, and using existing research about your audience.
- In order to create effective tools for audience analysis, interview and survey questions must be clear and to the point, focus groups must be facilitated carefully, and you must be aware of multiple interpretations of direct observations or existing research about your audience.

EXERCISES

1. Write a coherent set of four clear questions about a given issue, such as campus library services, campus computer centers, or the process of course registration. Make your questions concrete and specific in order to address the information you seek. Do not allow opportunities for your respondent to change the subject. Test out your questions on a classmate.

2. Write a set of six questions about public speaking anxiety to be answered on a Likert-type scale (strongly agree, agree, neither agree nor disagree, disagree, and strongly disagree).

3. Create a seven-question set designed to discover your audience's attitudes about your speech topic. Have a partner evaluate your questions for clarity, respect for audience privacy, and relevance to your topic.

4. USING YOUR AUDIENCE ANALYSIS

© Thinkstock

A good audience analysis takes time, thought, preparation, implementation, and processing. If done well, it will yield information that will help you interact effectively with your audience. Professional speakers, corporate executives, sales associates, and entertainers all rely on audience analysis to connect with their listeners. So do political candidates, whose chances of gaining votes depend on crafting the message and mood to appeal to each specific audience. One audience might be preoccupied with jobs, another with property taxes, and another with crime. Similarly, your audience analysis should help you identify the interests of your audience. Ultimately, a successful audience analysis can guide you in preparing the basic content of your speech and help you adjust your speech "on the fly."

4.1 Prepare Content with Your Audience in Mind

The first thing a good audience analysis can do is help you focus your content for your specific audience. If you are planning on a delivering a persuasive speech on why people should become vegans and you find out through analysis that half of your audience are daughters and sons of cattle ranchers, you need to carefully think through your approach to the content. Maybe you'll need to tweak your topic to focus on just the benefits of veganism without trying to persuade the audience explicitly. The last thing you want to do as a speaker is stand before an audience who is highly negative toward your topic before you ever open your mouth. While there will always be some naysayers in any audience, if you think through your topic with your audience in mind, you may be able to find a topic that will be both interesting to you as a speaker and beneficial to your audience as well.

In addition to adjusting the topic of your speech prior to the speaking event, you can also use your audience analysis to help ensure that the content of your speech will be as clear and understandable as humanly possible. We can use our audience analysis to help sure that we are clear.

idiom

A word or phrase where the meaning cannot be predicted from normal, dictionary definitions.

One area of clarity to be careful of is the use of idioms your audience may not know. An **idiom** is a word or phrase where the meaning cannot be predicted from normal, dictionary definitions. Many idioms are culturally or temporally based. For example, the phrase "according to Hoyle" indicates that something is done "by the book" or "by the rules," as in "These measurements aren't according to Hoyle, but they're close enough to give a general idea." Most of us have no clue who Hoyle was or what this idiom means. It refers to Edmond Hoyle, who wrote some of the most popular card-playing rule books back in the 1700s in England. Today, card game enthusiasts may understand the intent of "according to Hoyle," but for most people it no longer carries specific meaning. When thinking about your speech, be careful not to accidentally use idioms that you find commonplace but your audience may not.

4.2 Adjusting Your Speech Based on Your Analysis

In addition to using audience analysis to help formulate speech content, we can also use our audience analysis to make adjustments during the actual speech. These adjustments can pertain to the audience and to the physical setting.

The feedback you receive from your audience during your speech is a valuable indication of ways to adjust your presentation. If you're speaking after lunch and notice audience members looking drowsy, you can make adjustments to liven up the tone of your speech. You could use humor. You could raise your voice slightly. You could pose some questions and ask for a show of hands to get your listeners actively involved. As another example, you may notice from frowns and headshaking that some listeners aren't convinced by the arguments you are presenting. In this case, you could spend more time on a specific area of your speech and provide more evidence than you originally intended. Good speakers can learn a lot by watching their audience while speaking and then make specific adjustments to both the content and delivery of the speech to enhance the speech's ultimate impact.

The second kind of adjustment has to do with the physical setting for your speech. For example, your situational analysis may reveal that you'll be speaking in a large auditorium when you had expected a nice, cozy conference room. If you've created visual aids for a small, intimate environment, you may have to omit it, or tell your listeners that they can view it after the presentation. You may also need to account for a microphone. If you're lucky enough to have a cordless microphone, then you won't have to make too many adjustments to your speaking style. If, on the other hand, the microphone is corded or is attached to an unmovable podium, you'll have to make adjustments to how you deliver the presentation.

In preparing a speech about wealth distribution in the United States, one of our students had the opposite problem. Anticipating a large room, she had planned to use a one-hundred-foot tape measure to illustrate the percentage of the nation's wealth owned by the top one-fifth of the population. However, when she arrived she found that the room was only twelve by twenty feet, so that she had to walk back and forth zigzagging the tape from end to end to stretch out one hundred feet. Had she thought more creatively about how to adapt to the physical setting, she could have changed her plans to use just ten feet of the tape measure to symbolize 100 percent of the wealth. We will discuss the physical setting further in Chapter 14.

KEY TAKEAWAYS

- You can use your audience analysis to provide you further information about what types of content would be appropriate and meaningful for your specific audience.
- You can use your audience analysis to help you make adjustments to your speech in terms of both how you present the speech within a given environment and also how you adapt your content and delivery based on audience feedback during the speech.

EXERCISES

1. Choose a topic. Then write a different concrete thesis statement for each of six different audiences: students, military veterans, taxpayers, registered nurses, crime victims, and professional athletes, for instance.
2. Think of a controversial topic and list all the various perspectives about it that you can think of or discover. If people of various perspectives were in your audience, how might you acknowledge them during your introduction?

5. CHAPTER EXERCISES

SPEAKING ETHICALLY

You've got to be kidding me, Fatima thought to herself as she received the e-mail from her boss. She reread the e-mail hoping that something would change on the screen: "Fatima, I need you to prepare a presentation on what our company has done in the past year for Mrs. Jorgensen. She's old, keep it simple. Leave out any of the complex material because it will probably just bore her anyways.—John."

Fatima joined R & R Consulting right after Anthony Jorgensen, the founder and CEO, had passed away. While Penelope Jorgensen inherited the major stake in the firm and was still listed as the firm's CEO, the day-to-day running of operations was given to John Preston, the chief operating officer.

Fatima stared at her screen and wondered to what extent she should follow John's advice and "keep it simple." She'd only met Mrs. Jorgensen twice, but she'd always seemed to be pretty knowledgeable about the inner workings of the firm. Sure Mrs. Jorgensen wasn't an expert in the field, but should she be treated like a helpless little old lady? *Not only is that sexist, it's completely ageist! On the other hand, John's words may have been chosen poorly, but maybe all Mrs. Jorgensen really wanted was a quick snapshot of what's going on here?*

Fatima sat in silence for a few minutes, opened up PowerPoint, and just stared at her monitor trying to figure out the best way to proceed.

1. Do you think John's e-mail to Fatima expressed unethical audience analysis? Why or why not?
2. How do you think Fatima should proceed?

END-OF-CHAPTER ASSESSMENT

1. George wants to persuade his audience to purchase more locally produced foods. He decides he needs to know how his audience members already feel about this topic and whether they know about locally produced options. George's audience analysis focuses on gathering

    a. demographic information
    b. psychographic information
    c. situational information
    d. statistical information
    e. religious information

2. Freya wants to give her classroom an informative speech on the dangers of drunk driving. You suggest that this might not be a good topic because the audience of college students probably

    a. will not understand the topic
    b. will not be interested in drinking
    c. are not culturally diverse
    d. do not believe in drinking because of their religious background
    e. already know a lot about the topic

3. Yukhi will be giving a speech at the local Elks Lodge in a few weeks and wants to know more about her audience. She decides to attend one of the group's meetings so she gets a sense of what the group does and who its members are. Yukhi is engaging in which method of audience analysis?

    a. interviews
    b. focus group
    c. survey
    d. experiment
    e. direct observation

ANSWER KEY

1. b
2. e
3. e

ENDNOTES

1. Sprague, J., Stuart, D., & Bodary, D. (2010). *The speaker's handbook* (9th ed.). Boston, MA: Wadsworth Cengage.

2. Coopman, S. J., & Lull, J. (2009). *Public speaking: The evolving art.* Boston, MA: Wadsworth Cengage.

3. Russell, J. (1991). Inventing the flat earth. *History Today, 41*(8), 13–19.

4. Logan, J. R., and Zhang, C. (2010). Global neighborhoods: New pathways to diversity and separation. *American Journal of Sociology, 115*, 1069–1109.

5. Shahid, A. (2011, June 24). Rick Perry's Jose Cuervo joke at Latino convention bombs in Texas, as governor mulls 2012 GOP bid. *New York Daily News.* Retrieved from http://www.nydailynews.com/news/politics/2011/06/24/
2011-06-24_rick_perrys_jose_cuervo_joke_at_latino_convention_
bombs_in_texas_as_governor_mul.html

6. Samovar, L. A., & McDaniel, E. R. (2007). *Public speaking in a multicultural society.* Los Angeles, CA: Roxbury.

7. Tannen, D. (1994, December 11). The talk of the sandbox: How Johnny and Suzy's playground chatter prepares them for life at the office. *The Washington Post.* Retrieved from http://www9.georgetown.edu/faculty/tannend/sandbox.htm

8. Pew Forum on Religion & Public Life. (2008, February). Summary of key findings. In *U.S. religious landscape survey.* Retrieved from http://religions.pewforum.org/reports#

9. Grice, G. L., & Skinner, J. F. (2009). *Mastering public speaking: The handbook* (7th ed.). Boston, MA: Pearson.

10. Lalwani, A. K. (2009, August). The distinct influence of cognitive busyness and need for closure on cultural differences in socially desirable responding. *Journal of Consumer Research, 36*, 305–316. Retrieved from http://business.utsa.edu/marketing/
files/phdpapers/lalwani2_2009-jcr.pdf

11. Vavra, T. G. (2009, June 14). The truth about truth in survey research. Retrieved from http://www.terryvavra.com/customer-research/
the-truth-about-truth-in-survey-research

12. Bureau of the Census. (2011). About the American community survey. Retrieved from http://www.census.gov/acs/www/about_the_survey/
american_community_survey/; Bureau of the Census. (2011). Demographic surveys. Retrieved from http://www.census.gov/aboutus/sur_demo.html

CHAPTER 6
Finding a Purpose and Selecting a Topic

FINDING YOUR PURPOSE

In the 2004 Tony Award–winning musical *Avenue Q*, the lead character sings a song about finding his purpose in life: "I don't know how I know / But I'm gonna find my purpose / I don't know where I'm gonna look / But I'm gonna find my purpose." Although the song is about life in general, the lyrics are also appropriate when thinking about the purpose of your speech. You may know that you have been assigned to deliver a speech, but finding a purpose and topic seems like a formidable task. You may be asking yourself questions like, "What if the topic I pick is too common?"; "What if no one is interested in my topic?"; "What if my topic is too huge to cover in a three- to five-minute speech?"; or many others.

Finding a speech's purpose and topic isn't as complex or difficult as you might believe. This may be hard to accept right now, but trust us. After you read this chapter, you'll understand how to go about finding interesting topics for a variety of different types of speeches. In this chapter, we are going to explain how to identify the general purpose of a speech. We will also discuss how to select a topic, what to do if you're just drawing a blank, and four basic questions you should ask yourself about the speech topic you ultimately select. Finally, we will explain how to use your general purpose and your chosen topic to develop the specific purpose of your speech.

© Thinkstock

1. GENERAL PURPOSES OF SPEAKING

LEARNING OBJECTIVES

1. Differentiate among the three types of general speech purposes.
2. Examine the basics of informative speech topics and some common forms of informative speeches.
3. Examine the basics of persuasive speech topics and some common forms of persuasive speeches.
4. Examine the basics of entertaining speech topics and some common forms of entertaining speeches.

© Thinkstock

general purpose

The broad goal that someone has for creating and delivering a speech.

inform

A general purpose designed to help audience members acquire information that they currently do not possess.

What do you think of when you hear the word "purpose"? Technically speaking, a purpose can be defined as why something exists, how we use an object, or why we make something. For the purposes of public speaking, all three can be applicable. For example, when we talk about a speech's purpose, we can question why a specific speech was given; we can question how we are supposed to use the information within a speech; and we can question why we are personally creating a speech. For this specific chapter, we are more interested in that last aspect of the definition of the word "purpose": why we give speeches.

Ever since scholars started writing about public speaking as a distinct phenomenon, there have been a range of different systems created to classify the types of speeches people may give. Aristotle talked about three speech purposes: deliberative (political speech), forensic (courtroom speech), and epideictic (speech of praise or blame). Cicero also talked about three purposes: judicial (courtroom speech), deliberative (political speech), and demonstrative (ceremonial speech—similar to Aristotle's epideictic). A little more recently, St. Augustine of Hippo also wrote about three specific speech purposes: to teach (provide people with information), to delight (entertain people or show people false ideas), and to sway (persuade people to a religious ideology). All these systems of identifying public speeches have been attempts at helping people determine the general purpose of their speech. A **general purpose** refers to the broad goal in creating and delivering a speech.

These typologies or classification systems of public speeches serve to demonstrate that general speech purposes have remained pretty consistent throughout the history of public speaking. Modern public speaking scholars typically use a classification system of three general purposes: to inform, to persuade, and to entertain.

1.1 To Inform

The first general purpose that some people have for giving speeches is to **inform**. Simply put, this is about helping audience members acquire information that they do not already possess. Audience members can then use this information to understand something (e.g., speech on a new technology, speech on a new virus) or to perform a new task or improve their skills (e.g., how to swing a golf club, how to assemble a layer cake). The most important characteristic of informative topics is that the goal is to gain knowledge. Notice that the goal is not to encourage people to use that knowledge in any specific way. When a speaker starts encouraging people to use knowledge in a specific way, he or she is no longer informing but is persuading.

Let's look at a real example of how an individual can accidentally go from informing to persuading. Let's say you are assigned to inform an audience about a new vaccination program. In an informative speech, the purpose of the speech is to explain to your audience what the program is and how it works. If, however, you start encouraging your audience to participate in the vaccination program, you are no longer informing them about the program but rather persuading them to become involved in the program. One of the most common mistakes new public speaking students make is to blur the line between informing and persuading.

Why We Share Knowledge

Knowledge sharing is the process of delivering information, skills, or expertise in some form to people who could benefit from it. In fact, understanding and exchanging knowledge is so important that an entire field of study, called *knowledge management*, has been created to help people (especially businesses) become more effective at harnessing and exchanging knowledge. In the professional world, sharing knowledge is becoming increasingly important. Every year, millions of people attend some kind of knowledge sharing conference or convention in hopes of learning new information or skills that will help them in their personal or professional lives.[1]

People are motivated to share their knowledge with other people for a variety of reasons.[2] For some, the personal sense of achievement or of responsibility drives them to share their knowledge (internal motivational factors). Others are driven to share knowledge because of the desire for recognition or the possibility of job enhancement (external motivational factors). Knowledge sharing is an important part of every society, so learning how to deliver informative speeches is a valuable skill.

knowledge sharing

The process an individual goes through when information, skills, or expertise is delivered in some form to other person's who could benefit from having that information, those skills, or the expertise.

Common Types of Informative Topics

O'Hair, Stewart, and Rubenstein identified six general types of informative speech topics: objects, people, events, concepts, processes, and issues. [3] The first type of informative speech relates to objects, which can include how objects are designed, how they function, and what they mean. For example, a student of one of our coauthors gave a speech on the design of corsets, using a mannequin to demonstrate how corsets were placed on women and the amount of force necessary to lace one up.

The second type of informative speech focuses on people. People-based speeches tend to be biography-oriented. Such topics could include recounting an individual's achievements and explaining why he or she is important in history. Some speakers, who are famous themselves, will focus on their own lives and how various events shaped who they ultimately became. Dottie Walters is most noted as being the first female in the United States to run an advertising agency. In addition to her work in advertising, Dottie also spent a great deal of time as a professional speaker. She often would tell the story about her early years in advertising when she would push around a stroller with her daughter inside as she went from business to business trying to generate interest in her copywriting abilities. You don't have to be famous, however, to give a people-based speech. Instead, you could inform your audience about a historical or contemporary hero whose achievements are not widely known.

The third type of informative speech involves explaining the significance of specific events, either historical or contemporary. For example, you could deliver a speech on a specific battle of World War II or a specific presidential administration. If you're a history buff, event-oriented speeches may be right up your alley. There are countless historical events that many people aren't familiar with and would find interesting. You could also inform your audience about a more recent or contemporary event. Some examples include concerts, plays, and arts festivals; athletic competitions; and natural phenomena, such as storms, eclipses, and earthquakes. The point is to make sure that an informative speech is talking about the event (who, what, when, where, and why) and not attempting to persuade people to pass judgment upon the event or its effects.

The fourth type of informative speech involves concepts, or "abstract and difficult ideas or theories."[4] For example, if you want to explain a specific communication theory, E. M. Griffin provides an excellent list of communication theories on his website, http://www.afirstlook.com/main.cfm/theory_list. Whether you want to discuss theories related to business, sociology, psychology, religion, politics, art, or any other major area of study, this type of speech can be very useful in helping people to understand complex ideas.

The fifth type of informative speech involves processes. The process speech can be divided into two unique types: how-it-functions and how-to-do. The first type of process speech helps audience members understand how a specific object or system works. For example, you could explain how a bill becomes a law in the United States. There is a very specific set of steps that a bill must go through before it becomes a law, so there is a very clear process that could be explained to an audience. The how-to-do speech, on the other hand, is designed to help people come to an end result of some kind. For example, you could give a speech on how to quilt, how to change a tire, how to write a résumé, and millions of other how-to oriented topics. In our experience, the how-to speech is probably the most commonly delivered informative speech in public speaking classes.

The final type of informative speech involves issues, or "problems or matters of dispute."[5] This informative speech topic is probably the most difficult for novice public speakers because it requires walking a fine line between informing and persuading. If you attempt to deliver this type of speech, remember the goal is to be balanced when discussing both sides of the issue. To see an example of how you can take a very divisive topic and make it informative, check out the series *Point/Counterpoint* published by Chelsea House (http://chelseahouse.infobasepublishing.com). This series of books covers everything from the pros and cons of blogging to whether the United States should have mandatory military service.

Sample: Jessy Ohl's Informative Speech

The following text represents an informative speech prepared and delivered by an undergraduate student named Jessy Ohl. While this speech is written out as a text for purposes of analysis, in your public speaking course, you will most likely be assigned to speak from an outline or notes, not a fully written script. As you read through this sample speech, notice how Ms. Ohl uses informative strategies to present the information without trying to persuade her audience.

In 1977, a young missionary named Daniel Everett traveled deep into the jungles of Brazil to spread the word of God. However, he soon found himself working to translate the language of a remote tribe that would ultimately change his faith, lead to a new profession, and pit him in an intellectual fistfight with the world-famous linguist Noam Chomsky. As New Scientist Magazine of January 2008 explains, Everett's research on a small group of 350 people called the Pirahã tribe has revealed a language that has experts and intellectuals deeply disturbed.

While all languages are unique, experts like Noam Chomsky have argued that they all have universal similarities, such as counting, that are hard-wired into the human brain. So as National Public Radio reported on April 8, 2007, without the ability to count, conceptualize time or abstraction, or create syntax, the Pirahã have a language that by all accounts shouldn't exist.

Daniel Everett is now a professor of linguistics at Illinois State University, and he has created controversy by calling for a complete reevaluation of all linguistic theory in light of the Pirahã. Exploration of the Pirahã could bring further insight into the understanding of how people communicate and even, perhaps, what it means to be human. Which is why we must: first, examine the unique culture of the Pirahã; second, explore what makes their language so surprising; and finally, discover the implications the Pirahã have for the way we look at language and humanity.

Taking a closer look at the tribe's culture, we can identify two key components of Pirahã culture that help mold language: first, isolation; and second, emphasis on reality.

First, while globalization has reached nearly every corner of the earth, it has not been able to penetrate the Pirahã natives in the slightest. As Dr. Everett told the New Yorker of April 16, 2007, no group in history has resisted change like the Pirahã. "They reject everything from outside their world" as unnecessary and silly. Distaste for all things foreign is the reason why the people have rejected technology, farming, religion, and even artwork.

The lack of artwork illustrates the second vital part of Pirahã culture: an emphasis on reality. According to the India Statesman of May 22, 2006, all Pirahã understanding is based around the concept of personal experience. If something cannot be felt, touched, or experienced directly then to them, it doesn't exist, essentially eliminating the existence of abstract thought. Since art is often a representation of reality, it has no value among the people. During his work as a missionary, Everett was amazed to find that the natives had no interest in the story of Jesus once they found out that he was dead. The Pirahã psyche is so focused on the present that the people have no collective memory, history, written documents, or creation myths. They are unable to even remember the names of dead grandparents because once something or someone cannot be experienced, they are no longer important.

Since his days as a missionary, Everett remains the only Western professor able to translate Pirahã. His research has discovered many things missing with the language: words for time, direction, and color. But more importantly, Pirahã also lacks three characteristics previously thought to be essential to all languages: complexity, counting, and recursion.

First, the Pirahã language seems incredibly simple. Now, this isn't meant to imply that the people are uncivilized or stupid, but instead, they are minimalist. As I mentioned earlier, they only talk in terms of direct experience. The London Times of January 13, 2007, notes that with only eight consonants and three vowels, speakers rely on the use of tone, pitch, and humming to communicate. In fact, Pirahã almost sounds more like song than speech.

Second, Noam Chomsky's famous universal grammar theory includes the observation that every language has a means of counting. However, as reported in the June 2007 issue of Prospect Magazine, the Pirahã only have words for "one, two, and MANY." This demonstrates the Pirahã's inability to conceptualize a difference between three and five or three and a thousand. Dr. Everett spent six months attempting to teach even a single Pirahã person to count to ten, but his efforts were in vain, as tribal members considered the new numbers and attempts at math "childish."

Third, and the biggest surprise for researchers, is the Pirahã's apparent lack of recursion. Recursion is the ability to link several thoughts together. It is characterized in Christine Kenneally's 2007 book, The Search for the Origins of Language, as the fundamental principle of all language and the source of limitless expression. Pirahã is unique since the language does not have any conjunctions or linking words. Recursion is so vital for expression that the Chicago Tribune of June 11, 2007, reports that a language without recursion is like disproving gravity.

Although the Pirahã don't care what the outside world thinks of them, their language and world view has certainly ruffled feathers. And while civilization hasn't been able to infiltrate the Pirahã, it may ultimately be the Pirahã that teaches civilization a thing or two, which brings us to implications on the communicative, philosophical, and cultural levels. By examining the culture, language, and implications of the Pirahã tribe we are able to see how this small Brazilian village could shift the way that we think and talk about the world. Daniel Everett's research hasn't made him more popular with his colleagues. But his findings do show that more critical research is needed to make sure that our understanding of language is not lost in translation.

1.2   To Persuade

The second general purpose people can have for speaking is to **persuade**. When we speak to persuade, we attempt to get listeners to embrace a point of view or to adopt a behavior that they would not have done otherwise. A persuasive speech can be distinguished from an informative speech by the fact that it includes a call for action for the audience to make some change in their behavior or thinking.

Why We Persuade

The reasons behind persuasive speech fall into two main categories, which we will call "pure persuasion" and "manipulative persuasion." **Pure persuasion** occurs when a speaker urges listeners to engage in a specific behavior or change a point of view because the speaker truly believes that the change is in the best interest of the audience members. For example, you may decide to give a speech on the importance of practicing good oral hygiene because you truly believe that oral hygiene is important and that bad oral hygiene can lead to a range of physical, social, and psychological problems. In this case, the speaker has no ulterior or hidden motive (e.g., you are not a toothpaste salesperson).

Manipulative persuasion, on the other hand, occurs when a speaker urges listeners to engage in a specific behavior or change a point of view by misleading them, often to fulfill an ulterior motive beyond the face value of the persuasive attempt. We call this form of persuasion manipulative because the speaker is not being honest about the real purpose for attempting to persuade the audience. Ultimately, this form of persuasion is perceived as highly dishonest when audience members discover the ulterior motive. For example, suppose a physician who also owns a large amount of stock in a pharmaceutical company is asked to speak before a group of other physicians about a specific disease. Instead of informing the group about the disease, the doctor spends the bulk of his time attempting to persuade the audience that the drug his company manufactures is the best treatment for that specific disease.

Obviously, the key question for persuasion is the speaker's intent. Is the speaker attempting to persuade the audience because of a sincere belief in the benefits of a certain behavior or point of view? Or is the speaker using all possible means—including distorting the truth—to persuade the audience because he or she will derive personal benefits from their adopting a certain behavior or point of view? Unless your speech assignment specifically calls for a speech of manipulative persuasion, the usual (and ethical) understanding of a "persuasive speech" assignment is that you should use the pure form of persuasion.

persuade

The process an individual goes through attempting to get another person to behave in a manner or embrace a point of view related to values, attitudes, or beliefs that he or she would not have done otherwise.

pure persuasion

Occurs when a speaker urges listeners to engage in a specific behavior or change a point of view because the speaker truly believes that the change is in the best interest of the audience members.

manipulative persuasion

Occurs when a speaker urges listeners to engage in a specific behavior or change a point of view by misleading them, often to fulfill an ulterior motive beyond the face value of the persuasive attempt.

Persuasion: Behavior versus Attitudes, Values, and Beliefs

As we've mentioned in the preceding sections, persuasion can address behaviors—observable actions on the part of listeners—and it can also address intangible thought processes in the form of attitudes, values, and beliefs.

When the speaker attempts to persuade an audience to change behavior, we can often observe and even measure how successful the persuasion was. For example, after a speech attempting to persuade the audience to donate money to a charity, the charity can measure how many donations were received. The following is a short list of various behavior-oriented persuasive speeches we've seen in our own classes: washing one's hands frequently and using hand sanitizer, adapting one's driving habits to improve gas mileage, using open-source software, or drinking one soft drink or soda over another. In all these cases, the goal is to make a change in the basic behavior of audience members.

The second type of persuasive topic involves a change in attitudes, values, or beliefs. An **attitude** is defined as an individual's general predisposition toward something as being good or bad, right or wrong, negative or positive. If you believe that dress codes on college campuses are a good idea, you want to give a speech persuading others to adopt a positive attitude toward campus dress codes.

A speaker can also attempt to persuade listeners to change some value they hold. **Value** refers to an individual's perception of the usefulness, importance, or worth of something. We can value a college education, we can value technology, and we can value freedom. Values, as a general concept, are fairly ambiguous and tend to be very lofty ideas. Ultimately, what we value in life actually motivates us to engage in a range of behaviors. For example, if you value protecting the environment, you may recycle more of your trash than someone who does not hold this value. If you value family history and heritage, you may be more motivated to spend time with your older relatives and ask them about their early lives than someone who does not hold this value.

Lastly, a speaker can attempt to persuade people to change their personal beliefs. **Beliefs** are propositions or positions that an individual holds as true or false without positive knowledge or proof. Typically, beliefs are divided into two basic categories: core and dispositional. **Core beliefs** are beliefs that people have actively engaged in and created over the course of their lives (e.g., belief in a higher power, belief in extraterrestrial life forms). **Dispositional beliefs**, on the other hand, are beliefs that people have not actively engaged in; they are judgments based on related subjects, which people make when they encounter a proposition. Imagine, for example, that you were asked the question, "Can gorillas speak English?" While you may never have met a gorilla or even seen one in person, you can make instant judgments about your understanding of gorillas and fairly certainly say whether you believe that gorillas can speak English.

When it comes to persuading people to alter beliefs, persuading audiences to change core beliefs is more difficult than persuading audiences to change dispositional beliefs. If you find a topic related to dispositional beliefs, using your speech to help listeners alter their processing of the belief is a realistic possibility. But as a novice public speaker, you are probably best advised to avoid core beliefs. Although core beliefs often appear to be more exciting and interesting than dispositional ones, you are very unlikely to alter anyone's core beliefs in a five- to ten-minute classroom speech.

Sample: Jessy Ohl's Persuasive Speech

The following speech was written and delivered by an undergraduate student named Jessy Ohl. As with our earlier example, while this speech is written out as a text for purposes of analysis, in your public speaking course, you will most likely be assigned to speak from an outline or notes, not a fully written script.

Take a few minutes and compare this persuasive speech to the informative speech Ms. Ohl presented earlier in this chapter. What similarities do you see? What differences do you see? Does this speech seek to change the audience's behavior? Attitudes? Values? Dispositional or core beliefs? Where in the speech do you see one or more calls for action?

---

attitude

An individual's general predisposition toward something as being good or bad, right or wrong, negative or positive, and so on.

value

An individual's perception of the usefulness, importance, or worth of something.

beliefs

Propositions or positions that an individual holds as true or false without positive knowledge or proof.

core beliefs

Beliefs that people have actively engaged in and created over the course of their lives.

dispositional beliefs

Beliefs that people have not actively engaged in; judgments based on related subjects, which people make when they encounter a proposition.

With a declining population of around 6,000, my home town of Denison, Iowa, was on the brink of extinction when a new industry rolled in bringing jobs and revenue. However, as the Canadian Globe and Mail of July 23, 2007, reports, the industry that saved Denison may ultimately lead to its demise.

Denison is one of 110 communities across the country to be revolutionized by the production of corn ethanol. Ethanol is a high-powered alcohol, derived from plant matter, that can be used like gasoline. According to the Omaha World Herald of January 8, 2008, our reliance on foreign oil combined with global warming concerns have many holding corn ethanol as our best energy solution. But despite the good intentions of helping farmers and lowering oil consumption, corn ethanol is filled with empty promises. In fact, The Des Moines Register of March 1, 2008, concludes that when ethanol is made from corn, all of its environmental and economic benefits disappear. With oil prices at 100 dollars per barrel, our nation is in an energy crisis, and luckily, the production of ethanol can be a major help for both farmers and consumers, if done correctly. Unfortunately, the way we make ethanol—over 95% from corn—is anything but correct. Although hailed as a magic bullet, corn ethanol could be the worst agricultural catastrophe since the Dust Bowl.

The serious political, environmental, and even moral implications demand that we critically rethink this so-called yellow miracle by: first, examining the problems created by corn ethanol; second, exploring why corn ethanol has gained such power; and finally, discovering solutions to prevent a corn ethanol disaster.

Now, if you have heard anything about the problems of corn ethanol, it probably dealt with efficiency. As the Christian Science Monitor of November 15, 2007, notes, it takes a gallon of gasoline or more to make a gallon of ethanol. And while this is an important concern, efficiency is the least of our worries. Turning this crop into fuel creates two major problems for our society: first, environmental degradation; and second, acceleration of global famine.

First, corn ethanol damages the environment as much as, if not more than, fossil fuels. The journal Ethanol and Bio-diesel News of September 2007 asserts that the production of corn ethanol is pushing natural resources to the breaking point. Since the Dust Bowl, traditional farming practices have required farmers to "rotate" crops. But with corn ethanol being so profitable, understandably, farmers have stopped rotating crops, leading to soil erosion, deforestation, and fertilizer runoff—making our soil less fertile and more toxic. And the story only gets worse once the ethanol is manufactured. According to National Public Radio's Talk of the Nation of February 10, 2008, corn ethanol emits more carbon monoxide and twice the amount of carcinogens into the air as traditional gasoline.

The second problem created from corn ethanol is the acceleration of global famine. According to the US Grains Council, last year, 27 million tons of corn, traditionally used as food, was turned into ethanol, drastically increasing food prices. The March 7, 2007, issue of The Wall Street Journal explains that lower supplies of corn needed for necessities such as farm feed, corn oil, and corn syrup have increased our food costs in everything from milk to bread, eggs, and even beer as much as 25 percent. The St. Louis Post Dispatch of April 12, 2007, reports that the amount of corn used to fill one tank of gas could feed one person for an entire year. In October, Global protests over corn ethanol lead the United Nations to call its production "a crime against humanity."

If you weren't aware of the environmental or moral impacts of corn ethanol, you're not alone. The Financial Times of May 27, 2007, reports that the narrative surrounding corn ethanol as a homegrown fuel is so desirable that critical thinking is understandably almost nonexistent. To start thinking critically about corn ethanol, we need to examine solutions on both the federal and personal levels.

First, at the federal level, our government must end the ridiculously high subsidies surrounding corn ethanol. On June 24, 2007, The Washington Post predicted that subsidies on corn ethanol would cost the federal government an extra 131 billion dollars by 2010.

This isn't to say that the federal government should abandon small farmers. Instead, let's take the excitement around alternative fuels and direct it toward the right kinds of ethanol. The

Economist of June 2, 2007, reports that other materials such as switch grass and wood chips can be used instead of corn. And on July 6, 2011, The New York Times reported on ethanol made from corn cobs, leaves, and husks, which leaves the corn kernels to be used as food. The government could use the money paid in subsidies to support this kind of responsible production of ethanol. The point is that ethanol done right can honestly help with energy independence.

On the personal level, we have all participated in the most important step, which is being knowledgeable about the true face of corn ethanol. However, with big business and Washington proclaiming corn ethanol's greatness, we need to spread the word. So please, talk to friends and family about corn ethanol while there is still time. To make this easier, visit my website, at http://www.responsibleethanol.com. Here you will find informational materials, links to your congressional representatives, and ways to invest in switch grass and wood ethanol.

Today, we examined the problems of corn ethanol in America and discovered solutions to make sure that our need for energy reform doesn't sacrifice our morality. Iowa is turning so much corn into ethanol that soon the state will have to import corn to eat. And while my hometown of Denison has gained much from corn ethanol, we all have much more to lose from it.

1.3 To Entertain

The final general purpose people can have for public speaking is to entertain. Whereas informative and persuasive speech making is focused on the end result of the speech process, entertainment speaking is focused on the theme and occasion of the speech. An entertaining speech can be either informative or persuasive at its root, but the context or theme of the speech requires speakers to think about the speech primarily in terms of audience enjoyment.

Why We Entertain

Entertaining speeches are very common in everyday life. The fundamental goal of an entertaining speech is audience enjoyment, which can come in a variety of forms. Entertaining speeches can be funny or serious. Overall, entertaining speeches are not designed to give an audience a deep understanding of life but instead to function as a way to divert an audience from their day-to-day lives for a short period of time. This is not to say that an entertaining speech cannot have real content that is highly informative or persuasive, but its goal is primarily about the entertaining aspects of the speech and not focused on the informative or persuasive quality of the speech.

Common Forms of Entertainment Topics

There are three basic types of entertaining speeches: the after-dinner speech, the ceremonial speech, and the inspirational speech. The after-dinner speech is a form of speaking where a speaker takes a serious speech topic (either informative or persuasive) and injects a level of humor into the speech to make it entertaining. Some novice speakers will attempt to turn an after-dinner speech into a stand-up comedy routine, which doesn't have the same focus.[6] After-dinner speeches are first and foremost speeches.

A ceremonial speech is a type of entertaining speech where the specific context of the speech is the driving force of the speech. Common types of ceremonial speeches include introductions, toasts, and eulogies. In each of these cases, there are specific events that drive the speech. Maybe you're introducing an individual who is about to receive an award, giving a toast at your best friend's wedding, or delivering the eulogy at a relative's funeral. In each of these cases, the speech and the purpose of the speech is determined by the context of the event and not by the desire to inform or persuade.

The final type of entertaining speech is one where the speaker's primary goal is to inspire her or his audience. Inspirational speeches are based in emotion with the goal to motivate listeners to alter their lives in some significant way. Florence Littauer, a famous professional speaker, delivers an emotionally charged speech titled "Silver Boxes." In the speech, Mrs. Littauer demonstrates how people can use positive comments to encourage others in their daily lives. The title comes from a story she tells at the beginning of the speech where she was teaching a group of children about using positive speech, and one of the children defined positive speech as giving people little silver boxes with bows on top (http://server.firefighters.org/catalog/2009/45699.mp3).

Sample: Adam Fink's Entertainment Speech

The following speech, by an undergraduate student named Adam Fink, is an entertainment speech. Specifically, this speech is a ceremonial speech given at Mr. Fink's graduation. As with our earlier examples, while this speech is written out as a text for purposes of analysis, in your public speaking course you will most likely be assigned to speak from an outline or notes, not a fully written script. Notice that the tenor of this speech is persuasive but that it persuades in a more inspiring way than just building and proving an argument.

Good evening! I've spent the last few months looking over commencement speeches on YouTube. The most notable ones had eight things in common. They reflected on the past, pondered about the future. They encouraged the honorees. They all included some sort of personal story and application. They made people laugh at least fifteen times. They referred to the university as the finest university in the nation or world, and last but not least they all greeted the people in attendance. I'll begin by doing so now.

President Holst, thank you for coming. Faculty members and staff, salutations to you all. Distinguished guests, we are happy to have you. Family members and friends, we could not be here without you. Finally, ladies and gentlemen of the class of 2009, welcome to your commencement day here at Concordia University, Saint Paul, this, the finest university in the galaxy, nay, universe. Really, it's right up there with South Harlem Institute of Technology, the School of Hard Knocks, and Harvard. Check and check!

Graduates, we are not here to watch as our siblings, our parents, friends, or other family walk across this stage. We are here because today is our graduation day. I am going to go off on a tangent for a little bit. Over the past umpteen years, I have seen my fair share of graduations and ceremonies. In fact, I remember getting dragged along to my older brothers' and sisters' graduations, all 8,000 of them—at least it seems like there were that many now. Seriously, I have more family members than friends. I remember sitting here in these very seats, intently listening to the president and other distinguished guests speak, again saying welcome and thank you for coming. Each year, I got a little bit better at staying awake throughout the entire ceremony. Every time I would come up with something new to keep myself awake, daydreams, pinching my arms, or pulling leg hair; I was a very creative individual. I am proud to say that I have been awake for the entirety of this ceremony. I would like to personally thank my classmates and colleagues sitting around me for slapping me every time I even thought about dozing off. Personal story, check—and now, application!

Graduates, don't sleep through life. If you need a close friend or colleague to keep you awake, ask. Don't get bored with life. In the words of one of my mentors, the Australian film director, screen writer, and producer Baz Luhrman, "Do one thing every day that scares you." Keep yourself on your toes. Stay occupied but leave room for relaxation; embrace your hobbies. Don't get stuck in a job you hate. I am sure many of you have seen the "Did You Know?" film on YouTube. The film montages hundreds of statistics together, laying down the ground work to tell viewers that we are approaching a crossroad. The way we live is about to change dramatically. We are living in exponential times. It's a good thing that we are exponential people.

We are at a crossing point here, now. Each of us is graduating; we are preparing to leave this place we have called home for the past few years. It's time to move on and flourish. But let's not leave this place for good. Let us walk away with happy memories. We have been fortunate enough to see more change in our time here than most alumni see at their alma mater in a lifetime. We have seen the destruction of Centennial, Minnesota, and Walther. Ladies, it might not mean a lot to you, but gentlemen, we had some good times there. We have seen the building and completion of the new Residence Life Center. We now see the beginnings of our very own stadium. We have seen enough offices and departments move to last any business a lifetime. Let us remember these things, the flooding of the knoll, Ultimate Frisbee beginning at ten o'clock at night, and two back-to-back Volleyball National Championship teams, with one of those championship games held where you are sitting now. I encourage all of you to walk out of this place with flashes of the old times flickering through your brains. Reflection, check!

Honorees, in the words of Michael Scott, only slightly altered, "They have no idea how high [we] can fly." Right now you are surrounded by future politicians, film critics, producers, directors, actors, actresses, church workers, artists, the teachers of tomorrow, musicians, people who will change the world. We are all held together right here and now, by a common bond of unity. We are one graduating class.

In one of his speeches this year, President Barack Obama said, "Generations of Americans have connected their stories to the larger American story through service and helped move our country forward. We need that service now." He is right. America needs selfless acts of service.

Hebrews 10:23–25 reads, "Let us hold unswervingly to the hope we profess, for he who promised is faithful. And let us consider how we may spur one another on toward love and good deeds. Let us not give up meeting together, as some are in the habit of doing, but let us encourage one another—and all the more as you see the Day approaching." Let us not leave this place as enemies but rather as friends and companions. Let us come back next fall for our first reunion, the Zero Class Reunion hosted by the wonderful and amazing workers in the alumni department. Let us go and make disciples of all nations, guided by His Word. Let us spread God's peace, joy, and love through service to others. Congratulations, graduates! I hope to see you next homecoming. Encouragement, check!

KEY TAKEAWAYS

- There are three general purposes that all speeches fall into: to inform, to persuade, and to entertain. Depending on what your ultimate goal is, you will start by picking one of these general purposes and then selecting an appropriate speech pattern that goes along with that general purpose.
- Informative speeches can focus on objects, people, events, concepts, processes, or issues. It is important to remember that your purpose in an informative speech is to share information with an audience, not to persuade them to do or believe something.
- There are two basic types of persuasion: pure and manipulative. Speakers who attempt to persuade others for pure reasons do so because they actually believe in what they are persuading an audience to do or think. Speakers who persuade others for manipulative reasons do so often by distorting the support for their arguments because they have an ulterior motive in persuading an audience to do or think something. If an audience finds out that you've been attempting to manipulate them, they will lose trust in you.
- Entertainment speeches can be after-dinner, ceremonial, or inspirational. Although there may be informative or persuasive elements to your speech, your primary reason for giving the speech is to entertain the audience.

2. SELECTING A TOPIC

LEARNING OBJECTIVES

1. Understand the four primary constraints of topic selection.
2. Demonstrate an understanding of how a topic is narrowed from a broad subject area to a manageable specific purpose.

One of the most common stumbling blocks for novice public speakers is selecting their first speech topic. Generally, your public speaking instructor will provide you with some fairly specific parameters to make this a little easier. You may be assigned to tell about an event that has shaped your life or to demonstrate how to do something. Whatever your basic parameters, at some point you as the speaker will need to settle on a specific topic. In this section, we're going to look at some common constraints of public speaking, picking a broad topic area, and narrowing your topic.

2.1   Common Constraints of Public Speaking

© Thinkstock

When we use the word "constraint" with regard to public speaking, we are referring to any limitation or restriction you may have as a speaker. Whether in a classroom situation or in the boardroom, speakers are typically given specific instructions that they must follow. These instructions constrain the speaker and limit what the speaker can say. For example, in the professional world of public speaking, speakers are often hired to speak about a specific topic (e.g., time management, customer satisfaction, entrepreneurship). In the workplace, a supervisor may assign a subordinate to present certain information in a meeting. In these kinds of situations, when a speaker is hired or assigned to talk about a specific topic, he or she cannot decide to talk about something else.

Furthermore, the speaker may have been asked to speak for an hour, only to show up and find out that the event is running behind schedule, so the speech must now be made in only thirty minutes. Having prepared sixty minutes of material, the speaker now has to determine what stays in the speech and what must go. In both of these instances, the speaker is constrained as to what he or she can say during a speech. Typically, we refer to four primary constraints: purpose, audience, context, and time frame.

Purpose

The first major constraint someone can have involves the general purpose of the speech. As mentioned earlier, there are three general purposes: to inform, to persuade, and to entertain. If you've been told that you will be delivering an informative speech, you are automatically constrained from delivering a speech with the purpose of persuading or entertaining. In most public speaking classes, this is the first constraint students will come in contact with because generally teachers will tell you the exact purpose for each speech in the class.

Audience

The second major constraint that you need to consider as a speaker is the type of audience you will have. As discussed in the chapter on audience analysis, different audiences have different political, religious, and ideological leanings. As such, choosing a speech topic for an audience that has a specific mindset can be very tricky. Unfortunately, choosing what topics may or may not be appropriate for a given audience is based on generalizations about specific audiences. For example, maybe you're going to give a speech at a local meeting of Democratic leaders. You may think that all Democrats are liberal or progressive, but there are many conservative Democrats as well. If you assume that all Democrats are liberal or progressive, you may end up offending your audience by making such a generalization without knowing better. Obviously, the best way to prevent yourself from picking a topic that is inappropriate for a specific audience is to really know your audience, which is why we recommend conducting an audience analysis, as described in Chapter 5.

Context

The third major constraint relates to the context. For speaking purposes, the context of a speech is the set of circumstances surrounding a particular speech. There are countless different contexts in which we can find ourselves speaking: a classroom in college, a religious congregation, a corporate boardroom, a retirement village, or a political convention. In each of these different contexts, the expectations for a speaker are going to be unique and different. The topics that may be appropriate in front of a religious group may not be appropriate in the corporate boardroom. Topics appropriate for the corporate boardroom may not be appropriate at a political convention.

Time Frame

The last—but by no means least important—major constraint that you will face is the time frame of your speech. In speeches that are under ten minutes in length, you must narrowly focus a topic to one major idea. For example, in a ten-minute speech, you could not realistically hope to discuss the entire topic of the US Social Security program. There are countless books, research articles, websites, and other forms of media on the topic of Social Security, so trying to crystallize all that information into ten minutes is just not realistic.

Instead, narrow your topic to something that is more realistically manageable within your allotted time. You might choose to inform your audience about Social Security disability benefits, using one individual disabled person as an example. Or perhaps you could speak about the career of Robert J. Myers, one of the original architects of Social Security.[7] By focusing on information that can be covered within your time frame, you are more likely to accomplish your goal at the end of the speech.

2.2 Selecting a Broad Subject Area

subject area

A broad area of knowledge (e.g., art, business, history, physical sciences, social sciences, humanities, education).

Once you know what the basic constraints are for your speech, you can then start thinking about picking a topic. The first aspect to consider is what subject area you are interested in examining. A **subject area** is a broad area of knowledge. Art, business, history, physical sciences, social sciences, humanities, and education are all examples of subject areas. When selecting a topic, start by casting a broad net because it will help you limit and weed out topics quickly.

Furthermore, each of these broad subject areas has a range of subject areas beneath it. For example, if we take the subject area "art," we can break it down further into broad categories like art history, art galleries, and how to create art. We can further break down these broad areas into even narrower subject areas (e.g., art history includes prehistoric art, Egyptian art, Grecian art, Roman art, Middle Eastern art, medieval art, Asian art, Renaissance art, modern art). As you can see, topic selection is a narrowing process.

2.3 Narrowing Your Topic

Narrowing your topic to something manageable for the constraints of your speech is something that takes time, patience, and experience. One of the biggest mistakes that new public speakers make is not narrowing their topics sufficiently given the constraints. In the previous section, we started demonstrating how the narrowing process works, but even in those examples, we narrowed subject areas down to fairly broad areas of knowledge.

Think of narrowing as a funnel. At the top of the funnel are the broad subject areas, and your goal is to narrow your topic further and further down until just one topic can come out the other end of the funnel. The more focused your topic is, the easier your speech is to research, write, and deliver. So let's take one of the broad areas from the art subject area and keep narrowing it down to a manageable speech topic. For this example, let's say that your general purpose is to inform, you are delivering the speech in class to your peers, and you have five to seven minutes. Now that we have the basic constraints, let's start narrowing our topic. The broad area we are going to narrow in this example is Middle Eastern art. When examining the category of Middle Eastern art, the first thing you'll find is that Middle Eastern art is generally grouped into four distinct categories: Anatolian, Arabian, Mesopotamian, and Syro-Palestinian. Again, if you're like us, until we started doing some research on the topic, we had no idea that the historic art of the Middle East was grouped into these specific categories. We'll select Anatolian art, or the art of what is now modern Turkey.

You may think that your topic is now sufficiently narrow, but even within the topic of Anatolian art, there are smaller categories: pre-Hittite, Hittite, Uratu, and Phrygian periods of art. So let's narrow our topic again to the Phrygian period of art (1200–700 BCE). Although we have now selected a specific period of art history in Anatolia, we are still looking at a five-hundred-year period in which a great deal of art was created. One famous Phrygian king was King Midas, who according to myth was given the ears of a donkey and the power of a golden touch by the Greek gods. As such, there is an interesting array of art from the period of Midas and its Greek counterparts representing Midas. At this point, we could create a topic about how Phrygian and Grecian art differed in their portrayals of King Midas. We now have a topic that is unique, interesting, and definitely manageable in five to seven minutes. You may be wondering how we narrowed the topic down; we just started doing a little research using the Metropolitan Museum of Art's website (http://www.metmuseum.org).

Overall, when narrowing your topic, you should start by asking yourself four basic questions based on the constraints discussed earlier in this section:

1. Does the topic match my intended general purpose?
2. Is the topic appropriate for my audience?
3. Is the topic appropriate for the given speaking context?
4. Can I reasonably hope to inform or persuade my audience in the time frame I have for the speech?

KEY TAKEAWAYS

- Selecting a topic is a process. We often start by selecting a broad area of knowledge and then narrowing the topic to one that is manageable for a given rhetorical situation.
- When finalizing a specific purpose for your speech, always ask yourself four basic questions: (1) Does the topic match my intended general purpose?; (2) Is the topic appropriate for my audience?; (3) Is the topic appropriate for the given speaking context?; and (4) Can I reasonably hope to inform or persuade my audience in the time frame I have for the speech?

EXERCISES

1. Imagine you've been asked to present on a new technology to a local business. You've been given ten minutes to speak on the topic. Given these parameters, take yourself through the narrowing process from subject area (business) to a manageable specific purpose.
2. Think about the next speech you'll be giving in class. Show how you've gone from a large subject area to a manageable specific purpose based on the constraints given to you by your professor.

3. WHAT IF YOU DRAW A BLANK?

Uh-oh, what if you have no clue what to speak about at all? Thankfully, there are many places where you can get help finding a good topic for you. In this section, we're going to talk about a range of ways to find the best topic.

3.1 Conduct a Personal Inventory

The first way to find a good topic is to conduct what we call a personal inventory. A **personal inventory** is a detailed and descriptive list about an individual. In this case, we want you to think about you. Here are some basic questions to get you started:

- What's your major?
- What are your hobbies?
- What jobs have you had?
- What extracurricular activities have you engaged in?
- What clubs or groups do you belong to?
- What political issues interest you?
- Where have you traveled in life?
- What type of volunteer work have you done?
- What goals do you have in life?
- What social problems interest you?
- What books do you read?
- What movies do you watch?
- What games do you play?
- What unique skills do you possess?

© Thinkstock

personal inventory

A detailed and descriptive list about an individual.

After responding to these questions, you now have a range of areas that are unique to you that you could realistically develop into a speech. Here are some unique inventory items that could be turned into speeches for some of the authors of this textbook:

Jason S. Wrench

1. Grew up as an air force dependent and lived on the island of Crete
2. Is a puppeteer
3. Has two puggles (half pug/half beagle) named Daikin and Teddy

Anne Goding

1. Worked as a teacher for the Medicine Chief of the Bear Tribe Medicine Society in Spokane, Washington
2. Was codirector of Bear Tribe Publishing Company
3. Specializes in storytelling

Danette Ifert-Johnson

1. Is an avid fan of the Baltimore Orioles
2. Spent a month in South Korea as part of a study/travel group
3. Is a history buff who likes visiting historic sites and national parks

Bernardo Attias

1. Briefly lived in the Dominican Republic with his family as a young boy
2. Is a DJ
3. Occasionally practices yoga

We wanted to note these interesting facts about our personal lives to illustrate the fact that each and every one of us has done unique and interesting things in our lives that could make really interesting and informative, persuasive, or entertaining speeches.

3.2   Use Finding Aids

If you're still just stumped after conducting a personal inventory, the next recommendation we have for helping you find a good topic is to use a finding aid. A **finding aid** is a tool that will help you find lists of possible topics. Let's look at four of them: best-seller lists, organizations that tally information, media outlets, and the Internet.

finding aid

A tool that will help you find lists of possible topics.

Best-Seller Lists

A best-seller list is a list of books that people are currently buying. These lists often contain various subdivisions including fiction, nonfiction, business, advice, or graphic novels. Table 6.1 contains a range of best-seller lists to examine:

TABLE 6.1 Best-Seller Lists

Name	Website
New York Times	http://www.nytimes.com/pages/books/bestseller
Amazon.com	http://www.amazon.com/gp/bestsellers/books
USA Today	http://www.usatoday.com/life/books/leb1.htm
American Booksellers	http://www.bookweb.org/indiebound/bestsellers.html
Publisher's Weekly	http://www.publishersweekly.com
The Washington Post	http://www.washingtonpost.com/wp-srv/artsandliving/books/bestsellers-list
Business Week	http://www.businessweek.com/lifestyle/books.htm
CNN	http://www.cnn.com/books/bestsellers

It is important to realize that your goal in looking at best-seller lists is not to choose a book to serve as the topic of your speech—unless you've been assigned to give a book review! The point is that while all these lists indicate what people are reading, you can use them to find out what topics people are generally interested in right now.

Polling Organizations

In addition to numerous sources for best sellers, there are also a number of polling organizations that regularly conduct research on the American public. Not only are these organizations good for finding interesting research, but generally the most recent polls are an indication of what people are interested in understanding today. For example, The Gallup Organization regularly conducts polls to find out Americans' perceptions of current political issues, business issues, social issues, and a whole range of other interesting information. Often just looking at the Gallup Organization's website can help you find very interesting speech topics.

TABLE 6.2 Tallied Information

Name	Website
The Gallup Organization	http://www.gallup.com
US Census Bureau	http://www.census.gov
Polling Report	http://www.pollingreport.com
Rasmussen Reports	http://www.rasmussenreports.com
Zogby International	http://www.zogby.com
Pew Research Center	http://pewresearch.org

Media Outlets

The next great ways to find interesting topics for your speeches are watching television and listening to the radio. The evening news, the History Channel, and the National Geographic channel can all provide ideas for many different speech topics. There are even a host of television shows that broadcast the latest and most interesting topics weekly (e.g., *Dateline, 20/20, 60 Minutes*). Here are some recent segments from *20/20* that could make interesting speeches: former *Tarzan* actor, Steve Sipek, has lived with tigers for forty years; the science behind the *Bachelor* phenomenon; the world of childhood schizophrenia; and a girl born with a rare "mermaid" condition.

As for listening to the radio, talk radio is often full of interesting possibilities for speech topics. Many of the most prominent talk radio shows have two or three hours to fill five days a week, so the shows' producers are always looking for interesting topics. Why not let those producers do the investigative work for you? If you're listening to talk radio and hear an interesting topic, write it down and think about using it for your next speech.

As with the best-seller list, it is important to realize that your goal is not to use a given television or radio program as the basis for your speech, much less to repeat the exact arguments that a talk radio host or caller has made. We are not advocating stealing someone's ideas—you need to do your own thinking to settle on your speech topic. You can certainly use ideas from the media as contributions to your speech; however, if you do this, it is only ethical to make sure that you correctly cite the show where you heard about the topic by telling your audience the title, station, and date when you heard it.

The Internet

You can, of course, also look for interesting speech topics online. While the Internet may not always provide the most reliable information, it is a rich source of interesting topics. For example, to browse many interesting blogs, check out http://www.blogcatalog.com/ or http://www.findblogs.com/. Both websites link to hundreds of blogs you could peruse, searching for a topic that inspires you.

If you find yourself really stumped, there are even a handful of websites that specialize in helping people, just like you, find speech topics. Yes, that's right! Some insightful individuals have posted long lists of possible topics for your next speech right on the Internet. Here are some we recommend:

- http://www.hawaii.edu/mauispeech/html/infotopichelp.html
- http://web.sau.edu/WastynRonaldO/topics.html
- http://daphne.palomar.edu/kerbe/documents/inform_speech_topics.pdf
- http://cas.bethel.edu/dept/comm/nfa/journal/vol9no2-6.pdf

Using the Internet is a great way to find a topic, but you'll still need to put in the appropriate amount of your own thinking and time to really investigate your topic once you've found one that inspires you.

3.3   Poll Your Audience for Interests and Needs

The last way you can find a great topic is to conduct a simple poll of your audience to see what their interests and needs are. Let's handle these two methods separately. When you ask potential audience members about their interests, it's not hard to quickly find that patterns of interests exist in every group. You can find out about interests by either formally handing people a questionnaire or just asking people casually. Suppose it's your turn to speak at your business club's next meeting. If you start asking your fellow club members and other local business owners if there are any specific problems their businesses are currently facing, you will probably start to see a pattern develop. While you may not be an expert on the topic initially, you can always do some research to see what experts have said on the topic and pull together a speech using that research.

The second type of poll you may conduct of your potential audience is what we call a needs analysis. A **needs analysis** involves a set of activities designed to determine your audience's needs, wants, wishes, or desires. The purpose of a needs analysis is to find a gap in information that you can fill as a speaker. Again, you can use either informal or formal methods to determine where a need is. Informally, you may ask people if they have problems with something specific like writing a business plan or cooking in a wok. The only problem that can occur with the informal method is that you often find out that people overestimate their own knowledge about a topic. Someone may think they know how to use a wok even though they've never owned one and never cooked in one. For that reason, we often use more formal methods of assessing needs.

The formal process for conducting a needs analysis is threefold: (1) find a gap in knowledge, (2) figure out the cause, and (3) identify solutions. First, you need to find that a gap in knowledge actually exists. Overall, this isn't very hard to do. You can have people try to accomplish a task or just orally have them explain a task to you, and if you find that they are lacking you'll know that there is a possible need. Second, you need to figure out what is causing the gap. One of the mistakes that people make is

needs analysis

A set of activities designed to determine your audience's needs, wants, wishes, and desires.

assuming that all gaps exist because of a lack of information. This is not necessarily true—it can also be because of lack of experience. For example, people may have learned how to drive a car in a driver education class, but if they've never been behind the wheel of a car, they're not really going to know how to drive. Would giving a speech on how to drive a car at this point be useful? No. Instead, these people need practice, not another speech. Lastly, when you determine that the major cause of the need is informational, it's time to determine the best way to deliver that information.

KEY TAKEAWAYS

- Conducting a personal inventory is a good way to start the topic selection process. When we analyze our own experiences, interests, knowledge, and passions, we often find topics that others will also find interesting and useful.
- A speaker can investigate finding aids when searching for a good topic. Various finding aids have their positives and negatives, so we recommend investigating several different finding aids to see what topic ideas inspire you.
- One way to ensure a successful speech is to identify your audience's interests or needs. When the speaker's topic is immediately useful for the audience, the audience will listen to the speech and appreciate it.

EXERCISES

1. Look at the questions posed in this chapter related to conducting a personal inventory. Do you see any potential speech ideas developing from your personal inventory? If yes, which one do you think would impact your audience the most?
2. Take a broad subject area and then use two of the different finding aids to see what types of topics appear. Are you finding similarities or differences? The goal of this activity is to demonstrate how taking a very broad topic can be narrowed down to a more manageable topic using finding aids.
3. For an upcoming speech in your public speaking class, create a simple survey to determine your audience's needs. Find out what your audience may find interesting. Remember, the goal is to find out what your audience needs, not necessarily what you think your audience needs.

4. SPECIFIC PURPOSES

LEARNING OBJECTIVES

1. Understand the process of extending a general purpose into a specific purpose.
2. Integrate the seven tips for creating specific purposes.

© Thinkstock

Once you have chosen your general purpose and your topic, it's time to take your speech to the next phase and develop your specific purpose. A **specific purpose** starts with one of the three general purposes and then specifies the actual topic you have chosen and the basic objective you hope to accomplish with your speech. Basically, the specific purpose answers the *who, what, when, where,* and *why* questions for your speech.

4.1 Getting Specific

When attempting to get at the core of your speech (the specific purpose), you need to know a few basic things about your speech. First, you need to have a general purpose. Once you know whether your goal is to inform, persuade, or entertain, picking an appropriate topic is easier. Obviously, depending on the general purpose, you will have a range of different types of topics. For example, let's say you want to give a speech about hygiene. You could still give a speech about hygiene no matter what your general purpose is, but the specific purpose would vary depending on whether the general purpose is to inform (discussing hygiene practices around the globe), to persuade (discussing why people need to adopt a specific hygiene practice), or to entertain (discussing some of the strange and unique hygiene practices that people have used historically). Notice that in each of these cases, the general purpose alters the topic, but all three are still fundamentally about hygiene.

Now, when discussing specific purposes, we are concerned with who, what, when, where, why, and how questions for your speech. Let's examine each of these separately. First, you want to know who is going to be in your audience. Different audiences, as discussed in the chapter on audience analysis, have differing desires, backgrounds, and needs. Keeping your audience first and foremost in your thoughts when choosing a specific purpose will increase the likelihood that your audience will find your speech meaningful.

Second is the "what" question, or the basic description of your topic. When picking an effective topic, you need to make sure that the topic is appropriate for a variety of constraints or limitations within a speaking context.

Third, you need to consider when your speech will be given. Different speeches may be better for different times of the day. For example, explaining the importance of eating breakfast and providing people with cereal bars may be a great topic at 9:00 a.m. but may not have the same impact if you're giving it at 4:00 p.m.

Fourth, you need to consider where your speech will be given. Are you giving a speech in front of a classroom? A church? An executive meeting? Depending on the location of your speech, different topics may or may not be appropriate.

The last question you need to answer within your speech is why. Why does your audience need to hear your speech? If your audience doesn't care about your specific purpose, they are less likely to attend to your speech. If it's a topic that's a little more off-the-wall, you'll really need to think about why they should care.

Once you've determined the *who, what, when, where,* and *why* aspects of your topic, it's time to start creating your actual specific purpose. First, a specific purpose, in its written form, should be a short, declarative sentence that emphasizes the main topic of your speech. Let's look at an example:

Topic	The military
Narrower Topic	The military's use of embedded journalists
Narrowed Topic	The death of British reporter Rupert Hamer in 2010 in a roadside bombing in Nawa, Afghanistan, along with five US Marines

In this example, we've quickly narrowed a topic from a more general topic to a more specific topic. Let's now look at that topic in terms of a general purpose and specific purpose:

General Purpose	To inform
Specific Purpose	To inform my audience about the danger of embedded journalism by focusing on the death of British reporter Rupert Hamer
General Purpose	To persuade
Specific Purpose	To persuade a group of journalism students to avoid jobs as embedded journalists by using the death of British reporter Rupert Hamer as an example of what can happen

For the purpose of this example, we used the same general topic area, but demonstrated how you could easily turn the topic into either an informative speech or a persuasive speech. In the first example, the speaker is going to talk about the danger embedded journalists face. In this case, the speaker isn't attempting to alter people's ideas about embedded journalists, just make them more aware of the dangers. In the second case, the specific purpose is to persuade a group of journalism students (the audience) to avoid jobs as embedded journalists.

4.2   Your Specific Statement of Purpose

To form a clear and succinct statement of the specific purpose of your speech, start by naming your general purpose (to inform, to persuade, or to entertain). Follow this by a capsule description of your audience (my peers in class, a group of kindergarten teachers, etc.). Then complete your statement of purpose with a prepositional phrase (a phrase using "to," "about," "by," or another preposition) that summarizes your topic. As an example, "My specific purpose is to persuade the students in my residence hall to protest the proposed housing cost increase" is a specific statement of purpose, while "My speech will be about why we should protest the proposed housing cost increase" is not.

Specific purposes should be statements, not questions. If you find yourself starting to phrase your specific purpose as a question, ask yourself how you can reword it as a statement. Table 6.3 provides several more examples of good specific purpose statements.

TABLE 6.3 My Specific Purpose Is...

General Purpose	Audience	Topic
To inform	my audience	**about** the usefulness of scrapbooking to save a family's memories.
To persuade	a group of kindergarten teachers	**to** adopt a new disciplinary method for their classrooms.
To entertain	a group of executives	**by** describing the lighter side of life in "cubicle-ville."
To inform	community members	**about** the newly proposed swimming pool plans that have been adopted.
To persuade	my peers in class	**to** vote for me for class president.
To entertain	the guests attending my mother's birthday party	**by** telling a humorous story followed by a toast.

4.3   Basic Tips for Creating Specific Purposes

Now that we've examined what specific purposes are, we are going to focus on a series of tips to help you write specific purposes that are appropriate for a range of speeches.

Audience, Audience, Audience

First and foremost, you always need to think about your intended audience when choosing your specific purpose. In the previous section, we talked about a speech where a speaker is attempting to persuade a group of journalism students to not take jobs as embedded journalists. Would the same speech be successful, or even appropriate, if given in your public speaking class? Probably not. As a speaker, you may think your topic is great, but you always need to make sure you think about your audience when selecting your specific purpose. For this reason, when writing your specific purpose, start off your sentence by including the words "my audience" or actually listing the name of your audience: a group of journalism students, the people in my congregation, my peers in class, and so on. When you place your audience first, you're a lot more likely to have a successful speech.

Matching the Rhetorical Situation

After your audience, the second most important consideration about your specific purpose pertains to the rhetorical situation of your speech. The **rhetorical situation** is the set of circumstances surrounding your speech (e.g., speaker, audience, text, and context). When thinking about your specific purpose, you want to ensure that all these components go together. You want to make sure that you are the appropriate speaker for a topic, the topic is appropriate for your audience, the text of your speech is appropriate, and the speech is appropriate for the context. For example, speeches that you give in a classroom may not be appropriate in a religious context and vice versa.

rhetorical situation

The set of circumstances surrounding your speech (e.g., speaker, audience, text, and context).

Make It Clear

The specific purpose statement for any speech should be direct and not too broad, general, or vague. Consider the lack of clarity in the following specific purpose: "To persuade the students in my class to drink more." Obviously, we have no idea what the speaker wants the audience to drink: water, milk, orange juice? Alcoholic beverages? Furthermore, we have no way to quantify or make sense of the word "more." "More" assumes that the students are already drinking a certain amount, and the speaker wants them to increase their intake. If you want to persuade your listeners to drink eight 8-ounce glasses of water per day, you need to say so clearly in your specific purpose.

Another way in which purpose statements are sometimes unclear comes from the use of colloquial language. While we often use colloquialisms in everyday life, they are often understood only by a limited number of people. It may sound like fun to have a specific purpose like, "To persuade my audience to get jiggy," but if you state this as your purpose, many people probably won't know what you're talking about at all.

Don't Double Up

You cannot hope to solve the entire world's problems in one speech, so don't even try. At the same time, you also want to make sure that you stick to one specific purpose. Chances are it will be challenging enough to inform your audience about one topic or persuade them to change one behavior or opinion. Don't put extra stress on yourself by adding topics. If you find yourself using the word "and" in your specific topic statement, you're probably doubling up on topics.

Can I Really Do This in Five to Seven Minutes?

When choosing your specific purpose, it's important to determine whether it can be realistically covered in the amount of time you have. Time limits are among the most common constraints for students in a public speaking course. Usually speeches early in the term have shorter time limits (three to five minutes), and speeches later in the term have longer time limits (five to eight minutes). While eight minutes may sound like an eternity to be standing up in front of the class, it's actually a very short period of time in which to cover a topic. To determine whether you think you can accomplish your speech's purpose in the time slot, ask yourself how long it would take to make you an informed person on your chosen topic or to persuade you to change your behavior or attitudes.

If you cannot reasonably see yourself becoming informed or persuaded during the allotted amount of time, chances are you aren't going to inform or persuade your audience either. The solution, of course, is to make your topic narrower so that you can fully cover a limited aspect of it.

KEY TAKEAWAYS

- Moving from a general to specific purpose requires you to identify the *who, what, when, where,* and *why* of your speech.
- State your specific purpose in a sentence that includes the general purpose, a description of the intended audience, and a prepositional phrase summarizing the topic.
- When creating a specific purpose for your speech, first, consider your audience. Second, consider the rhetorical situation. Make sure your specific purpose statement uses clear language, and that it does not try to cover more than one topic.
- Make sure you can realistically accomplish your specific purpose within the allotted time.

EXERCISES

1. You've been asked to give a series of speeches on the importance of health care in poverty-stricken countries. One audience will consist of business men and women, one audience will consist of religious leaders, and another audience will consist of high school students. How would you need to adjust your speech's purpose for each of these different audiences? How do these different audiences alter the rhetorical situation?
2. For the following list of topics, think about how you could take the same topic and adjust it for each of the different general purposes (inform, persuade, and entertain). Write out the specific purpose for each of your new speech topics. Here are the three general topic areas to work with: the First Amendment to the US Constitution, iPods, and literacy in the twenty-first century.

5. CONCLUSION

After reading this chapter, we hope that you now have a better understanding not only of the purpose of your speech but also of how to find a really interesting topic for yourself and your audience. We started this chapter citing lyrics from the *Avenue Q* song "Purpose." While the character is trying to find his purpose in life, we hope this chapter has helped you identify your general purpose, choose a topic that will interest you and your audience, and use these to develop a specific purpose statement for your speech.

6. CHAPTER EXERCISES

SPEAKING ETHICALLY

Rona is a huge supporter of Gerry Mitchell in the mayoral campaign. Rona decides to volunteer for Mitchell's campaign and is soon asked to speak at various rallies when Mitchell can't attend.

One Saturday evening, Rona is asked to speak before a group of retirees at a local retirement center. As a campaign insider, Rona knows that Mitchell has privately acknowledged that he's probably going to have to drastically cut city support for a number of programs that help the elderly. Of course, this information hasn't been made public. Rona also realizes that the group she is speaking before would not vote for Mitchell if they knew what his future plans are.

1. If Rona attempts to persuade the retirees without divulging the information about the future cuts, is she a pure persuader or a manipulative persuader?

2. Does a political operative have an ethical·obligation to be honest when the information being disseminated to a group of people isn't complete?

3. If you were Rona, what would you do?

END-OF-CHAPTER ASSESSMENT

1. Modern scholars generally describe the three general purposes of speaking as
   a. entertain, persuade, and debate
   b. persuade, inform, and perpetuate
   c. celebrate, perpetuate, and inform
   d. inform, persuade, and entertain
   e. deliberative, epideictic, and forensic

2. "To persuade a group of local residents to buy a car from Mitken's Car Dealership" is an example of which type of purpose?
   a. celebratory
   b. specific
   c. systematic
   d. supplemental
   e. general

3. Benji wanted to speak on the elements of jazz music, but his instructor told the class that they could only choose from a specific list of topics. This is an example of
   a. poor topic selection
   b. constraints
   c. a bad speech
   d. poor narrowing
   e. topic shortage aversion

4. Which of the following would be a good scope for a speech that is five to seven minutes in length?
   a. the history of the United States
   b. military maneuvers in the nineteenth century
   c. women in the Battle of Lewisburg
   d. religion in Asia
   e. changes in state-sponsored militias

5. Tika is speaking on the benefits of sleep, but does not include a call for action to get more sleep. Which type of general purpose does Tika have?
   a. to inform
   b. to persuade
   c. to entertain
   d. to console
   e. to educate

ANSWER KEY

1. d
2. b
3. b
4. c
5. a

ENDNOTES

1. Atwood, C. G. (2009). *Knowledge management basics*. Alexandria, VA: ASTD Press.

2. Hendriks, P. (1999). Why share knowledge? The influence of ICT on the motivation for knowledge sharing. *Knowledge and Process Management, 6*, 91–100.

3. O'Hair, D., Stewart, R., & Rubenstein, H. (2007). *A speaker's guidebook: Text and reference* (3rd ed.). Boston, MA: Bedford/St. Martins.

4. O'Hair, D., Stewart, R., & Rubenstein, H. (2007). *A speaker's guidebook: Text and reference* (3rd ed.). Boston, MA: Bedford/St. Martins, p. 95.

5. O'Hair, D., Stewart, R., & Rubenstein, H. (2007). *A speaker's guidebook: Text and reference* (3rd ed.). Boston, MA: Bedford/St. Martins, p. 25.

6. Roye, S. (2010). Austan Goolsbee a funny stand-up comedian? Not even close... [Web log post]. Retrieved from http://www.realfirststeps.com/1184/austan-goolsbee-funny-standup-comedian-close

7. See, for example, Social Security Administration (1996). Robert J. Myers oral history interview. Retrieved from http://www.ssa.gov/history/myersorl.html

CHAPTER 7
Researching Your Speech

LIBRARIES AND LIBRARIANS ARE OUR FRIENDS

If you hear the word "research" and get a little queasy inside, you're hardly alone. Many people dread the idea of having to research something, whether for a speech or a paper. However, there are amazing people who are like wizards of information called librarians, and they live in a mystical place of knowledge called the library. OK, so maybe they're not wizards and libraries aren't mystical, but librarians and libraries are definitely a good speaker's best friend. Whether you are dealing with a librarian at a public library or an academic library, librarians have many tricks and shortcuts up their sleeves to make hunting for information easier and faster.[1] You may find it odd that we decided to start a chapter on research discussing librarians, but we strongly believe that interacting with librarians and using libraries effectively is the first step to good research.

© *Thinkstock*

To help make your interactions with research librarians more fulfilling, we sent out an e-mail to research librarians who belong to the American Library Association asking them for tips on working with a research librarian. Thankfully, the research librarians were very willing to help us help you. Listed below are some of the top tips we received from research librarians (in no particular order)[2] :

1. Your librarian is just as knowledgeable about information resources and the research process as your professor is about his or her discipline. Collaborate with your librarian so that you can benefit from his or her knowledge.

2. Try to learn from the librarian so that you can increase your research skills. You'll need these skills as you advance in your academic coursework, and you'll rely on these skills when you're in the workplace.

3. When we are in our offices, we aren't on reference desk duty. Whether an office door is open or closed, please knock first and wait to be invited in. With that said, if we are at the reference desk, we are there to help you. Please ask! You aren't interrupting. Helping students does *not* bother us. It is our job and profession, and we like doing it.

4. I'm here to teach you, not go to bat for you. Please don't expect me to write a note to your instructor because the materials (reference, reserve, or whatever) weren't available.

5. Please, please, please don't interrupt me when I am working with another student. This happens regularly and we work on a first-come, first-serve basis. Wait your turn.

6. If we help you find sources, please take a look at them, so we will be more likely to want to help you in the future.

7. Research is a process, not an event. If you haven't allocated enough time for your project, the librarian can't bail you out at the very last minute

8. Don't expect the librarian to do the work that you should be doing. It is your project and your grade. The librarian can lead you to the resources, but you have to select the best sources for your particular project. This takes time and effort on your part.

9. Reference librarians are professional searchers who went to graduate school to learn how to do research. Reference librarians are here to help no matter how stupid a student thinks her or his question is.

10. Good research takes time and, while there are shortcuts, students should still expect to spend some time with a librarian and to trawl through the sources they find.

11. Students should also know that we ask questions like, "Where have you looked so far?" and "Have you had a library workshop before?" for a reason. It may sound like we're deferring the question, but what we're trying to do is gauge how much experience the student has with research and to avoid going over the same ground twice.

12. Students should approach a librarian sooner rather than later. If a student isn't finding what they need within fifteen minutes or so, they need to come find a librarian. Getting help early will save the student a lot of time and energy.

13. If you don't have a well-defined topic to research, or if you don't know what information resources you're hoping to find, come to the reference desk with a copy of your class assignment. The librarian will be glad to help you to select a topic that's suitable for your assignment and to help you access the resources you need. Having at least a general topic in mind and knowing what the assignment entails (peer-reviewed only, three different types of sources, etc.) helps immensely.

14. Most academic librarians are willing to schedule in-depth research consultations with students. If you feel you'll need more time and attention than you might normally receive at the reference desk or if you're shy about discussing your research interest in a public area, ask the librarian for an appointment.

15. Students, if they know their topic, should be as specific as possible in what they ask for. Students who are struggling with identifying a narrow topic should seek help from either their professors or librarians. We can't help you find sources if your topic isn't really very clear.

16. Students need to learn that many questions do not have ready-made or one-stop answers. Students need to understand that an interface with a reference librarian is a dialog and part of a recursive, repetitive process. They need to make time for this process and assume an active role in the exchange.

17. Students should understand that information can come in a variety of formats. If a student asks for a "book about" something without providing any other details about the information needed, that student could come away empty handed. Instead, students should get in the habit of asking for "information about" something first.

18. "Gee thanks!" every now and then will win every librarian's heart!

1. WHAT IS RESEARCH?

LEARNING OBJECTIVES

1. Explain why research is fun and useful.
2. Differentiate between primary and secondary research.

Say it with me: "Research is fun!" OK, now we know that some of you just looked at that sentence and totally disagree, but we're here to tell you that research is fun. Now, this doesn't mean that research is easy. In fact, research can be quite difficult and time consuming, but it's most definitely fun. Let us explain why. First, when conducting research you get to ask questions and actually find answers. If you have ever wondered what the best strategies are when being interviewed for a job, research will tell you. If you've ever wondered what it takes to be a NASCAR driver, an astronaut, a marine biologist, or a university professor, once again, research is one of the easiest ways to find answers to questions you're interested in knowing. Second, research can open a world you never knew existed. We often find ideas we had never considered and learn facts we never knew when we go through the research process. Lastly, research can lead you to new ideas and activities. Maybe you want to learn how to compose music, draw, learn a foreign language, or write a screenplay; research is always the best step toward learning anything.

© Thinkstock

For the purposes of this book, we define **research** as scholarly investigation into a topic in order to discover, revise, or report facts, theories, and applications. Now you'll notice that there are three distinct parts of research: discovering, revising, and reporting. The first type of research is when people conduct some kind of study and find something completely new. For example, in 1928 Alexander Fleming accidentally discovered the first antibiotic, penicillin. Before this discovery, there were no antibiotics and simple infections killed people regularly. In this case, Fleming conducted research and discovered something not known to scientists before that time.

The second type of research occurs when people revise existing facts, theories, and applications. The bulk of the work of modern scientists is not really in discovering new things, but rather trying to improve older discoveries. For example, to improve upon the work of Fleming's first antibiotic, a group of Croatian researchers created azithromycin. Today azithromycin is licensed by Pfizer Inc. under the name Zithromax. In essence, the Croatian scientists built on the work of Fleming and ultimately revised our ability to treat infectious diseases. Today, azithromycin is one of the most prescribed antibiotics in the world.

The last part of research is called the reporting function of research. This is the phase when you accumulate information about a topic and report that information to others. For example, in the previous two paragraphs, we conducted research on the history of antibiotics and provided you with that information. We did not discover anything, nor did we revise anything; we are just reporting the research.

In addition to the three functions of research, there are also three end results that researchers strive toward: facts, theories, and applications. First, a **fact** is a truth that is arrived at through the scientific process. For example, in the world of psychology, it is a fact that the human brain influences human behavior. Centuries ago, people believed that human behavior was a result of various combinations of black and yellow biles running through our bodies. However, research failed to find support for this idea, whereas research increasingly found support for the connection between the brain and behavior. Facts are difficult to attain—it can take generations of research before a theory gains acceptance as a scientific fact.

Second, researchers conduct research to understand, contradict, or support theories. A **theory** is a proposed explanation for a phenomenon that can be tested scientifically. Scientists work with theories for a very long time, testing them under a variety of conditions attempting to replicate earlier findings or to identify conditions under which earlier findings do not hold true. For example, one theory that often surprises people is the universal theory of gravity. Many people believe that our understanding of gravity is set in stone, and much of physics relies on the assumption that gravity exists, but gravity is not a fact. The fact that the theory of gravity explains is that if I hold my keys out and let go, they will fall to the floor. Physicists are still debating how gravity actually functions and speculating about other explanations for why my keys will fall to the floor. So from a researcher's perspective, very few things are scientific facts.

research

The scholarly investigation into a topic in order to discover, revise, or report facts, theories, and applications.

fact

A truth that is arrived at through the scientific process.

theory

A proposed explanation for a phenomenon that can be scientifically tested.

Lastly, researchers often look for new applications for something that already exists. For example, botulism was at one point a dreaded bacterium that plagued the US food supply and led to many deaths. In the 1980s, an ophthalmologist named Allan Scott started using a version of botulism to treat muscle spasms in a drug called onabotulinumtoxinA—better known by the brand name Botox.[3] Richard Clark, a plastic surgeon, reported in a 1989 article that the drug also had the side effect of decreasing wrinkles.[4] From deadly bacteria to medical cure to one of the most commonly used cosmetic drugs in the world, the history of Botox has been a constant stream of new applications.

1.1 Primary Research

Research generally falls into one of two categories: primary and secondary. **Primary research** is carried out to discover or revise facts, theories, and applications and is reported by the person conducting the research. Primary research can be considered an active form of research because the researcher is actually conducting the research for the purpose of creating new knowledge. For the purposes of your speech, you may utilize two basic categories of primary research: surveys and interviews.

Surveys You Conduct

The first type of primary research you might conduct is a survey. A survey is a collection of facts, figures, or opinions gathered from participants used to indicate how everyone within a target group may respond. Maybe you're going to be speaking before a board of education about its plans to build a new library, so you create a survey and distribute it to all your neighbors seeking their feedback on the project. During your speech, you could then discuss your survey and the results you found.

Depending on the amount of time you have and the funding available, there are a number of different ways you could survey people. The most expensive method of surveying is sending surveys through the postal system. Unfortunately, most people do not respond to surveys they receive through the mail, so the number of completed surveys you get back tends to be very low (often under 20 percent).

To make surveying cheaper, many people prefer to use the Internet or to approach people face-to-face and ask them to participate. Internet surveying can be very useful and cheap, but you'll still have the same problem mail surveys do—getting people to fill out your survey. Face-to-face surveying, on the other hand, is time consuming but generally results in a higher number of completed surveys.

Ultimately, when determining whether you should conduct a survey, Wrench, Thomas-Maddox, Richmond, and McCroskey suggest that you ask yourself four basic questions.[5] First, "Do you know what you want to ask?" Surveys, by their very nature, are concrete—once you've handed it to one person, you need to hand out the same form to every person to be able to compare results. If you're not sure what questions need to be asked, then a survey is not appropriate. Second, "Do you really need to collect data?" Often you can find information in textbooks, scholarly articles, magazines, and other places. If the information already exists, then why are you duplicating the information? Third, "Do your participants know the information you want to find out, or if they do know, will they tell you?" One of the biggest mistakes novice survey researchers make is to ask questions that their participants can't or won't answer. Asking a young child for her or his parents' gross income doesn't make sense, but then neither does asking an adult how many times they've been to see a physician in the past ten years. The flip side to this question is, "Will your participants tell you?" If the information could be potentially damaging, people are more likely to either lie on a survey or leave the question blank.

The last question is, "Is your goal generalizable?" **Generalizability** occurs when we attempt to survey a small number of people in the hopes of representing a much larger group of people. For example, maybe you want to find out how people in your community feel about a new swimming pool. The whole community may contain one thousand families, but it would be impractical to try to survey all those families, so you decide to survey two hundred families instead. The ultimate question for researchers is whether those two hundred families can be generalized to the one thousand families. The number may be large enough (as opposed to surveying, say, twenty families), but if the two hundred families you survey only represent the rich part of town, then your sample (the two hundred families) is not generalizable to the entire population (one thousand families).

Interviews You Conduct

The second type of primary research you might conduct is an interview. An interview is a conversation in which the interviewer asks a series of questions aimed at learning facts, figures, or opinions from one or more respondents. As with a survey, an interviewer generally has a list of prepared questions to ask; but unlike a survey, an interview allows for follow-up questions that can aid in understanding why a respondent gave a certain answer. Sometimes interviews are conducted on a one-on-one basis, but other times interviews are conducted with a larger group, which is commonly referred to as a focus group.

primary research

Research carried out to discover or revise facts, theories, and applications that is reported by the person(s) conducting the research.

generalizability

Surveying a small sample with the intent of it representing a larger population.

One-on-one interviews enable an interviewer to receive information about a given topic with little or no interference from others. Focus groups are good for eliciting information, but they are also good for seeing how groups of people interact and perceive topics. Often information that is elicited in a one-on-one interview is different from the information gained from a group of people interacting.

If you're preparing for a speech on implementing project management skills for student organizations, you may want to interview a handful of student organization leaders for their input. You may also want to get a group of students who have led successful projects for their student organizations and see what they did right. You could also get a group of students who have had bad project outcomes and try to understand what went wrong. Ultimately, you could use all this information not only to help you understand the needs student organizations have concerning project management but also to provide support for the recommendations you make during your speech.

1.2 Secondary Research

Secondary research is carried out to discover or revise facts, theories, and applications—similar to primary research—but it is reported by someone not involved in conducting the actual research. Most of what we consider "research" falls into the category of secondary research. If you've ever written a paper for one of your classes and had to cite sources, then you've conducted secondary research. Secondary research is when you report the results of someone else's primary research. If you read an academic article about an experiment that a group of researchers conducted and then tell your audience about that study, you are delivering information secondhand to your audience. You as the speaker did not conduct the study, so you are reporting what someone else has written.

One place where secondary research can get people into trouble is when they attempt to use someone else's secondary research. In a book titled *Unleashing the Power of PR: A Contrarian's Guide to Marketing and Communication*, Mark Weiner cites research conducted by the investment firm Veronis Suhler Stevenson Partners.[6] It might be tempting to leave out Weiner's book and just cite the Veronis Suhler Stevenson Partners' research instead. While this may be easier, it's not exactly ethical. Mark Weiner spent time conducting research and locating primary research; when you steal one of his sources, it's like you're stealing part of the work he's done. Your secondary research should still be *your* research. If you haven't laid eyes on the original study (e.g., Veronis Suhler Stevenson Partners' study), you shouldn't give your audience the impression that you have. An exception to this rule is if you are citing a translation of something originally written in a foreign language—and in that case, you still need to mention that you're using a translation and not the original.

Aside from the ethics of telling your audience where you got your information, you need to be aware that published sources sometimes make mistakes when citing information, so you could find yourself incorrectly providing information based on a mistake in Weiner's book. Think of it like the old game of "Telephone," in which you tell one person a phrase, that person turns to the next person and repeats the phrase, and by the time thirty people have completed the process, the final phrase doesn't remotely resemble the original. When people pass information along without verifying it themselves, there is always an increased likelihood of error.

secondary research

Research carried out to discover or revise facts, theories, and applications that is reported by someone not involved in conducting the actual research.

KEY TAKEAWAYS

- Research is a fascinating and fun process because it allows us to find answers to questions, it exposes us to new ideas, and it can lead us to pursue new activities.
- Primary and secondary sources are quite common in research literature. Primary research is where the author has conducted the research him or herself and secondary research is when an author reports on research conducted by others.

EXERCISES

1. Make a list of research projects you have conducted in your academic career. Did your research help revise facts, theories, or applications?
2. With a group of classmates, identify when it is better to use primary research and when it is better to use secondary research.

2.   DEVELOPING A RESEARCH STRATEGY

L E A R N I N G   O B J E C T I V E S

1. Differentiate between research time and speech preparation time.
2. Understand how to establish research needs before beginning research.
3. Explain the difference between academic and nonacademic sources.
4. Identify appropriate nonacademic sources (e.g., books, special-interest periodicals, newspapers and blogs, and websites).
5. Identify appropriate academic sources (e.g., scholarly books, scholarly articles, computerized databases, and scholarly information on the web).
6. Evaluate George's (2008) six questions to analyze sources.

© Thinkstock

project life cycle

The phases that connect the beginning of a project to its end.

In the previous section we discussed what research was and the difference between primary and secondary research. In this section, we are going to explore how to develop a research strategy. Think of a research strategy as your personal map. The end destination is the actual speech, and along the way, there are various steps you need to complete to reach your destination: the speech. From the day you receive your speech assignment, the more clearly you map out the steps you need to take leading up to the date when you will give the speech, the easier your speech development process will be. In the rest of this section, we are going to discuss time management, determining your research needs, finding your sources, and evaluating your sources.

2.1   Alloting Time

First and foremost, when starting a new project, no matter how big or small, it is important to seriously consider how much time that project is going to take. To help us discuss the issue of time with regard to preparing your speech, we're going to examine what the Project Management Institute refers to as the **project life cycle**, or "the phases that connect the beginning of a project to its end."[7] Often in a public speaking class, the time you have is fairly concrete. You may have two or three weeks between speeches in a semester course or one to two weeks in a quarter course. In either case, from the moment your instructor gives you the assigned speech, the proverbial clock is ticking. With each passing day, you are losing precious time in your speech preparation process. Now, we realize that as a college student you probably have many things vying for your time in life: school, family, jobs, friends, or dating partners. For this reason, you need to really think through how much time it's going to take you to complete your preparation in terms of both research and speech preparation.

Research Time

The first step that takes a good chunk of your time is researching your speech. Whether you are conducting primary research or relying on secondary research sources, you're going to be spending a significant amount of time researching.

As Howard and Taggart point out in their book *Research Matters*, research is not just a one-and-done task.[8] As you develop your speech, you may realize that you want to address a question or issue that didn't occur to you during your first round of research, or that you're missing a key piece of information to support one of your points. For these reasons, it's always wise to allow extra time for targeted research later in your schedule.

You also need to take into account the possibility of meeting with a research librarian. Although research librarians have many useful tips and tricks, they have schedules just like anyone else. If you know you are going to need to speak with a librarian, try to set up an appointment ahead of time for the date when you think you'll have your questions organized, and be ready to meet.

A good rule of thumb is to devote no more than one-third of your speech preparation time to research (e.g., if you have three weeks before your speech date, your research should be done by the end of the first week). If you are not careful, you could easily end up spending all your time on research and waiting until the last minute to actually prepare your speech, which is highly inadvisable.

Speech Preparation Time

The second task in speech preparation is to sit down and actually develop your speech. During this time period, you will use the information you collected during your research to fully flesh out your ideas into a complete speech. You may be making arguments using the research or creating visual aids. Whatever you need to complete during this time period, you need to give yourself ample time to actually prepare your speech. One common rule of thumb is one day of speech preparation per one minute of actual speaking time.

By allowing yourself enough time to prepare your speech, you're also buffering yourself against a variety of things that can go wrong both in life and with your speech. Let's face it, life happens. Often events completely outside our control happen, and these events could negatively impact our ability to prepare a good speech. When you give yourself a little time buffer, you're already insulated from the possible negative effects on your speech if something goes wrong.

The last part of speech preparation is practice. Although some try to say that practice makes perfect, we realize that perfection is never realistic because no one is perfect. We prefer this mantra: "Practice makes permanent."

And by "practice," we mean actual rehearsals in which you deliver your speech out loud. Speakers who only script out their speeches or only think through them often forget their thoughts when they stand in front of an audience. Research has shown that when individuals practice, their speech performance in front of an audience is more closely aligned with their practice than people who just think about their speeches. In essence, you need to allow yourself to become comfortable not only with the text of the speech but also with the nonverbal delivery of the speech, so giving yourself plenty of speech preparation time also gives you more practice time. We will discuss speech development and practice further in other chapters.

2.2   Determining Your Needs

When starting your research, you want to start by asking yourself what you think you need. Obviously, you'll need to have a good idea about what your topic is before just randomly looking at information in a library or online. Your instructor may provide some very specific guidance for the type of information he or she wants to see in your speech, so that's a good place to start determining your basic needs.

Once you have a general idea of your basic needs, you can start to ask yourself a series of simple questions:

1. What do I, personally, know about my topic?
2. Do I have any clear gaps in my knowledge of my topic?
3. Do I need to conduct primary research for my speech?
4. What type of secondary research do I need?
    a. Do I need research related to facts?
    b. Do I need research related to theories?
    c. Do I need research related to applications?

The clearer you are about the type of research you need at the onset of the research process, the easier it will be to locate specific information.

2.3   Finding Resources

Once you have a general idea about the basic needs you have for your research, it's time to start tracking down your secondary sources. Thankfully, we live in a world that is swimming with information. Back in the decades when the authors of this textbook first started researching, we all had to go to a library and search through a physical card catalog to find books. If you wanted to research a topic in magazine or journal articles, you had to look up key terms in a giant book, printed annually, known as an index of periodicals. Researchers could literally spend hours in the library and find just one or two sources that were applicable to their topic.

Today, on the other hand, information is quite literally at our fingertips. Not only is information generally more accessible, it is also considerably easier to access. In fact, we have the opposite problem from a couple of decades ago—we have too much information at our fingertips. In addition, we now have to be more skeptical about where that information is coming from. In this section we're going to discuss how to find information in both nonacademic and academic sources.

Nonacademic Information Sources

Nonacademic information sources are sometimes also called popular press information sources; their primary purpose is to be read by the general public. Most nonacademic information sources are written at a sixth- to eighth-grade reading level, so they are very accessible. Although the information often contained in these sources is often quite limited, the advantage of using nonacademic sources is that they appeal to a broad, general audience.

Books

The first source we have for finding secondary information is books. Now, the authors of your text are admitted bibliophiles—we love books. Fiction, nonfiction, it doesn't really matter, we just love books. And, thankfully, we live in a world where books abound and reading has never been easier. Unless your topic is very cutting-edge, chances are someone has written a book about your topic at some point in history.

Historically, the original purpose of libraries was to house manuscripts that were copied by hand and stored in library collections. After Gutenberg created the printing press, we had the ability to mass produce writing, and the handwritten manuscript gave way to the printed manuscript. In today's modern era, we are seeing another change where printed manuscript is now giving way, to some extent, to the electronic manuscript. Amazon.com's Kindle, Barnes & Noble's Nook, Apple's iPad, and Sony's e-Ink-based readers are examples of the new hardware enabling people to take entire libraries of information with them wherever they go. We now can carry the amount of information that used to be housed in the greatest historic libraries in the palms of our hands. When you sit back and really think about it, that's pretty darn cool!

In today's world, there are three basic types of libraries you should be aware of: physical library, physical/electronic library, and e-online library. The physical library is a library that exists only in the physical world. Many small community or county library collections are available only if you physically go into the library and check out a book. We highly recommend doing this at some point. Libraries today generally model the US Library of Congress's card catalog system. As such, most library layouts are similar. This familiar layout makes it much easier to find information if you are using multiple libraries. Furthermore, because the Library of Congress catalogs information by type, if you find one book that is useful for you, it's very likely that surrounding books on the same shelf will also be useful. When people don't take the time to physically browse in a library, they often miss out on some great information.

The second type of library is the library that has both physical and electronic components. Most college and university libraries have both the physical stacks (where the books are located) and electronic databases containing e-books. The two largest e-book databases are ebrary (http://www.ebrary.com) and NetLibrary (http://www.netlibrary.com). Although these library collections are generally cost-prohibitive for an individual, more and more academic institutions are subscribing to them. Some libraries are also making portions of their collections available online for free: Harvard University's Digital Collections (http://digitalcollections.harvard.edu), New York Public Library's E-book Collection (http://ebooks.nypl.org), The British Library's Online Gallery (http://www.bl.uk/onlinegallery/ttp/ttpbooks.html#), and the US Library of Congress (http://www.loc.gov).

One of the greatest advantages to using libraries for finding books is that you can search not only their books, but often a wide network of other academic institutions' books as well. Furthermore, in today's world, we have one of the greatest online card catalogs ever created—and it wasn't created for libraries at all! Retail bookseller sites like Amazon.com can be a great source for finding books that may be applicable to your topic, and the best part is, you don't actually need to purchase the book if you use your library, because your library may actually own a copy of a book you find on a bookseller site. You can pick a topic and then search for that topic on a bookseller site. If you find a book that you think may be appropriate, plug that book's title into your school's electronic library catalog. If your library owns the book, you can go to the library and pick it up today.

If your library doesn't own it, do you still have an option other than buying the book? Yes: interlibrary loans. An **interlibrary loan** is a process where librarians are able to search other libraries to locate the book a researcher is trying to find. If another library has that book, then the library asks to borrow it for a short period of time. Depending on how easy a book is to find, your library could receive it in a couple of days or a couple of weeks. Keep in mind that interlibrary loans take time, so do not expect to get a book at the last minute. The more lead time you provide a librarian to find a book you are looking for, the greater the likelihood that the book will be sent through the mail to your library on time.

The final type of library is a relatively new one, the library that exists only online. With the influx of computer technology, we have started to create vast stores of digitized content from around the world. These online libraries contain full-text documents free of charge to everyone. Some online libraries we recommend are Project Gutenberg (http://www.gutenberg.org), Google Books (http://books.google.com), Read Print (http://www.readprint.com), Open Library (http://openlibrary.org), and Get Free e-Books (http://www.getfreeebooks.com). This is a short list of just a handful of the libraries that are now offering free e-content.

interlibrary loaning

The process where librarians are able to search other libraries in an attempt to see if they possess the book a researcher is trying to find and then have the external library loan the book to the researcher's library.

General-Interest Periodicals

The second category of information you may seek out includes **general-interest periodicals**. These are magazines and newsletters published on a fairly systematic basis. Some popular magazines in this category include *The New Yorker, People, Reader's Digest, Parade, Smithsonian*, and *The Saturday Evening Post*. These magazines are considered "general interest" because most people in the United States could pick up a copy of these magazines and find them interesting and topical.

Special-Interest Periodicals

Special-interest periodicals are magazines and newsletters that are published for a narrower audience. In a 2005 article, *Business Wire* noted that in the United States there are over ten thousand different magazines published annually, but only two thousand of those magazines have significant circulation. [9] Some more widely known special-interest periodicals are *Sports Illustrated, Bloomberg's Business Week, Gentleman's Quarterly, Vogue, Popular Science*, and *House and Garden*. But for every major magazine, there are a great many other lesser-known magazines like *American Coin Op Magazine, Varmint Hunter, Shark Diver Magazine, Pet Product News International, Water Garden News*, to name just a few.

Newspapers and Blogs

Another major source of nonacademic information is newspapers and blogs. Thankfully, we live in a society that has a free press. We've opted to include both newspapers and blogs in this category. A few blogs (e.g., *The Huffington Post, Talkingpoints Memo, News Max, The Daily Beast, Salon*) function similarly to traditional newspapers. Furthermore, in the past few years we've lost many traditional newspapers around the United States; cities that used to have four or five daily papers may now only have one or two.

According to newspapers.com, the top ten newspapers in the United States are *USA Today*, the *Wall Street Journal*, the *New York Times*, the *Los Angeles Times*, the *Washington Post*, the *New York Daily News*, the *Chicago Tribune*, the *New York Post, Long Island Newsday*, and the *Houston Chronicle*. Most colleges and universities subscribe to a number of these newspapers in paper form or have access to them electronically. Furthermore, LexisNexis, a database many colleges and universities subscribe to, has access to full text newspaper articles from these newspapers and many more around the world.

In addition to traditional newspapers, blogs are becoming a mainstay of information in today's society. In fact, since the dawn of the twenty-first century many major news stories have been broken by professional bloggers rather than traditional newspaper reporters.[10] Although anyone can create a blog, there are many reputable blog sites that are run by professional journalists. As such, blogs can be a great source of information. However, as with all information on the Internet, you often have to wade through a lot of junk to find useful, accurate information.

We do not personally endorse any blogs, but according to Technorati.com, the top ten most commonly read blogs in the world are as follows:

1. *The Huffington Post* (http://www.huffingtonpost.com)
2. *Gizmodo* (http://www.gizmodo.com)
3. *TechCrunch* (http://www.techcrunch.com)
4. *The Corner* (http://corner.nationalreview.com)
5. *Mashable!* (http://mashable.com)
6. *Engadget* (http://www.engadget.com)
7. *Boing Boing* (http://www.boingboing.net)
8. *Gawker* (http://www.gawker.com)
9. *The Daily Beast* (http://www.thedailybeast.com)
10. *TMZ* (http://www.tmz.com)

Encyclopedias

Another type of source that you may encounter is the encyclopedia. **Encyclopedias** are information sources that provide short, very general information about a topic. Encyclopedias are available in both print and electronic formats, and their content can range from eclectic and general (e.g., *Encyclopædia Britannica*) to the very specific (e.g., *Encyclopedia of 20th Century Architecture*, or *Encyclopedia of Afterlife Beliefs and Phenomena*). It is important to keep in mind that encyclopedias are designed to give only brief, fairly superficial summaries of a topic area. Thus they may be useful for finding out what something is if it is referenced in another source, but they are generally not a useful source for your actual speech. In fact, many instructors do not allow students to use encyclopedias as sources for their speeches for this very reason.

general-interest periodicals

Magazines and newsletters that are published on a fairly systematic basis that appeal to a broad range of readers (e.g., *The New Yorker, People, Reader's Digest, Parade*, and *The Saturday Evening Post*).

special-interest periodicals

Magazines and newsletters that are published on a fairly systematic basis that appeal to a narrow range of readers (e.g., *Sports Illustrated, Bloomberg's Business Week, Gentleman's Quarterly, Vogue, Popular Science*, and *Home and Garden*).

encyclopedias

Information sources that provide short, very general information about a topic.

One of the most popular online encyclopedic sources is Wikipedia. Like other encyclopedias, it can be useful for finding out basic information (e.g., what baseball teams did Catfish Hunter play for?) but will not give you the depth of information you need for a speech. Also keep in mind that Wikipedia, unlike the general and specialized encyclopedias available through your library, can be edited by anyone and therefore often contains content errors and biased information. If you are a fan of *The Colbert Report*, you probably know that host Stephen Colbert has, on several occasions, asked viewers to change Wikipedia content to reflect his views of the world. This is just one example of why one should always be careful of information on the web, but this advice is even more important when considering group-edited sites such as Wikipedia.

Websites

Websites are the last major source of nonacademic information. In the twenty-first century we live in a world where there is a considerable amount of information readily available at our fingertips. Unfortunately, you can spend hours and hours searching for information and never quite find what you're looking for if you don't devise an Internet search strategy. First, you need to select a good search engine to help you find appropriate information. Table 7.1 contains a list of common search engines and the types of information they are useful for finding.

TABLE 7.1 Search Engines

http://www.google.com	General search engines
http://www.yahoo.com	
http://www.bing.com	
http://www.ask.com	
http://www.about.com	
http://www.usa.gov	Searches US government websites
http://www.hon.ch/MedHunt	Searches only trustworthy medical websites
http://medlineplus.gov	Largest search engine for medical related research
http://www.bizrate.com	Comparison shopping search engine
http://www.ameristat.org	Provides statistics about the US population
http://artcyclopedia.com	Searches for art-related information
http://www.flipdog.com	Searches for job postings across job search websites

Academic Information Sources

After nonacademic sources, the second major source for finding information comes from academics. The main difference between academic or scholarly information and the information you get from the popular press is oversight. In the nonacademic world, the primary gatekeeper of information is the editor, who may or may not be a content expert. In academia, we have established a way to perform a series of checks to ensure that the information is accurate and follows agreed-upon academic standards. For example, this book, or portions of this book, were read by dozens of academics who provided feedback. Having this extra step in the writing process is time consuming, but it provides an extra level of confidence in the relevance and accuracy of the information. In this section, we will discuss scholarly books and articles, computerized databases, and finding scholarly information on the web.

Scholarly Books

College and university libraries are filled with books written by academics. According to the Text and Academic Authors Association (http://www.taaonline.net), there are two types of scholarly books: textbooks and academic books. **Textbooks** are books that are written about a segment of content within a field of academic study and are written for undergraduate or graduate student audiences. These books tend to be very specifically focused. Take this book, for instance. We are not trying to introduce you to the entire world of human communication, just one small aspect of it: public speaking. Textbooks tend to be written at a fairly easy reading level and are designed to transfer information in a manner that mirrors classroom teaching to some extent. Also, textbooks are secondary sources of information. They are designed to survey the research available in a particular field rather than to present new research.

Academic books are books that are primarily written for other academics for informational and research purposes. Generally speaking, when instructors ask for you to find scholarly books, they are referring to academic books. Thankfully, there are hundreds of thousands of academic books published on almost every topic you can imagine. In the field of communication, there are a handful of major publishers who publish academic books: SAGE (http://www.sagepub.com), Routledge

textbooks

Books that are written about a segment of content within a field of academics study and are written for specific academic levels (i.e., K–12, undergraduate, graduate, etc.).

academic books

Books that are primarily written for other academics for informational and research purposes.

(http://www.routledge.com),   Jossey-Bass   (http://www.josseybass.com),   Pfeiffer
(http://www.pfeiffer.com), the American Psychological Association (http://www.apa.org/pubs/books),
and the National Communication Association (http://www.ncastore.com), among others. In addition
to the major publishers who publish academic books, there are also many university presses who publish   academic   books: SUNY   Press   (http://www.sunypress.edu),   Oxford   University   Press
(http://www.oup.com/us), University of South Carolina Press (http://www.sc.edu/uscpress), Baylor
University   Press   (http://www.baylorpress.com),   University   of   Illinois   Press
(http://www.press.uillinois.edu), and the University of Alabama Press (http://www.uapress.ua.edu) are
just a few of them.

Scholarly Articles

Because most academic writing comes in the form of scholarly articles or journal articles, that is the
best place for finding academic research on a given topic. Every academic subfield has its own journals,
so you should never have a problem finding the best and most recent research on a topic. However,
scholarly articles are written for a scholarly audience, so reading scholarly articles takes more time than
if you were to read a magazine article in the popular press. It's also helpful to realize that there may be
parts of the article you simply do not have the background knowledge to understand, and there is nothing wrong with that. Many research studies are conducted by quantitative researchers who rely on statistics to examine phenomena. Unless you have training in understanding the statistics, it is difficult to
interpret the statistical information that appears in these articles. Instead, focus on the beginning part
of the article where the author(s) will discuss previous research (secondary research), and then focus at
the end of the article, where the author(s) explain what was found in their research (primary research).

Computerized Databases

Finding academic research is easier today than it ever has been in the past because of large computer
databases containing research. Here's how these databases work. A database company signs contracts
with publishers to gain the right to store the publishers' content electronically. The database companies
then create thematic databases containing publications related to general areas of knowledge (business,
communication, psychology, medicine, etc.). The database companies then sell subscriptions to these
databases to libraries.

The largest of these database companies is a group called EBSCO Publishing, which runs both
EBSCO   Host   (an   e-journal   provider)   and   NetLibrary   (a   large   e-book   library)
(http://www.ebscohost.com). Some of the more popular databases that EBSCO provides to colleges and
universities are: Academic Search Complete, Business Source Complete, Communication and Mass
Media Complete, Education Research Complete, Humanities International Complete, Philosopher's
Index, Political Science Complete, PsycArticles, and Vocational and Career Collection. Academic
Search Complete is the broadest of all the databases and casts a fairly wide net across numerous fields.
Information that you find using databases can contain both nonacademic and academic information,
so EBSCO Host has built in a number of filtering options to help you limit the types of information
available.

We strongly recommend checking out your library's website to see what databases they have available and if they have any online tutorials for finding sources using the databases to which your library
subscribes.

Scholarly Information on the Web

In addition to the subscription databases that exist on the web, there are also a number of great sources
for scholarly information on the web. As mentioned earlier, however, finding scholarly information on
the web poses a problem because anyone can post information on the web. Fortunately, there are a
number of great websites that attempt to help filter this information for us.

TABLE 7.2 Scholarly Information on the Web

Website	Type of Information
http://www.doaj.org	The Directory of Open Access Journals is an online database of all freely available academic journals online.
http://scholar.google.com	Google Scholar attempts to filter out nonacademic information. Unfortunately, it tends to return a large number of for-pay site results.
http://www.cios.org	Communication Institute for Online Scholarship is a clearinghouse for online communication scholarship. This site contains full-text journals and books.
http://xxx.lanl.gov	This is an open access site devoted to making physical science research accessible.
http://www.biomedcentral.com	BioMed Central provides open-access medical research.
http://www.osti.gov/eprints	The E-print Network provides access to a range of scholarly research that interests people working for the Department of Energy.
http://www.freemedicaljournals.com	This site provides the public with free access to medical journals.
http://highwire.stanford.edu	This is the link to Stanford University's free, full-text science archives.
http://www.plosbiology.org	This is the Public Library of Science's journal for biology.
http://www.scirus.com	Scrius is a search engine designed to allow researchers to search for journal content, scientists' homepages, courseware, and preprint material.
http://www.ipl.org	The Internet Public Library provides subject guides, reference works, and a number of databases.
http://vlib.org	The WWW Virtual Library provides annotated lists of websites compiled by scholars in specific areas.

Tips for Finding Information Sources

Now that we've given you plenty of different places to start looking for research, we need to help you sort through the research. In this section, we're going to provide a series of tips that should make this process easier and help you find appropriate information quickly. And here is our first tip: We cannot recommend Mary George's book *The Elements of Library Research: What Every Student Needs to Know* more highly. Honestly, we wish this book had been around when we were just learning how to research.

Create a Research Log

research log

A step-by-step account of the process of identifying, obtaining, and evaluating sources for a specific project.

Nothing is more disheartening than when you find yourself at 1:00 a.m. asking, "Haven't I already read this?" We've all learned the tough lessons of research, and this is one that keeps coming back to bite us in the backside if we're not careful. According to a very useful book called *The Elements of Library Research* by M. W. George, a **research log** is a "step-by-step account of the process of identifying, obtaining, and evaluating sources for a specific project, similar to a lab note-book in an experimental setting."[11] In essence, George believes that keeping a log of what you've done is very helpful because it can help you keep track of what you've read thus far. You can use a good old-fashioned notebook, or if you carry around your laptop or netbook with you, you can always keep it digitally. While there are expensive programs like Microsoft Office OneNote that can be used for note keeping, there are also a number of free tools that could be adapted as well. The websites in Table 7.3 will help you find templates and tools for electronic note taking.

TABLE 7.3 Note-Taking Help

Website	Type of Information
Templates	
http://www.uleth.ca/lib/guides/research-log.doc	Word Document template created by the University of Lethbridge
http://www.comcol.umass.edu/dbc/rtfs/research_log_template.rtf	RTF file template created by the University of Massachusetts at Amherst
http://www.tarleton.edu/departments/library/library_module/unit3/researchlog.doc	Word Document template created by Tarleton State University
http://www.uvm.edu/~lkutner/researchlogexampletemplate.doc	Word Document template created by the University of Vermont
http://knowledgecenter.unr.edu/instruction/help/liblog.rtf	Word Document template created by the University of Nevada
Software Packages	
http://office.microsoft.com/en-us/onenote	Microsoft Office OneNote comes with MS Office Professional or is free to try for thirty days. It is also available for forty-five dollars for students through an academic discount program. There is a free app version available for the iPhone or iPad.
http://www.evernote.com	Evernote has both a free version and a subscription version and is similar to MS OneNote. You can also get this one for your smart phone, iPad, or home computer (PC or MAC) and easily sync files between all of your electronic devices.
http://notebook.zoho.com/nb/login.do?serviceurl=%2Fnb%2Findex.do	This is an online, web-based note-taking system that has no cost.
http://journler.com	This is good note-taking software, but it currently costs $34.95 for a single-user subscription.
http://www.thebrain.com	If you're more of a visual organizer, The Brain offers a free program for visually organizing information. You can also purchase more expensive packages as necessary.

Start with Background Information

It's not unusual for students to try to jump right into the meat of a topic, only to find out that there is a lot of technical language they just don't understand. For this reason, you may want to start your research with sources written for the general public. Generally, these lower-level sources are great for background information on a topic and are helpful when trying to learn the basic vocabulary of a subject area.

Search Your Library's Computers

Once you've started getting a general grasp of the broad content area you want to investigate, it's time to sit down and see what your school's library has to offer. If you do not have much experience in using your library's website, see if the website contains an online tutorial. Most schools offer online tutorials to show students the resources that students can access. If your school doesn't have an online tutorial, you may want to call your library and schedule an appointment with a research librarian to learn how to use the school's computers. Also, if you tell your librarian that you want to learn how to use the library, he or she may be able to direct you to online resources that you may have missed.

Try to search as many different databases as possible. Look for relevant books, e-books, newspaper articles, magazine articles, journal articles, and media files. Modern college and university libraries have a ton of sources, and one search may not find everything you are looking for on the first pass. Furthermore, don't forget to think about synonyms for topics. The more synonyms you can generate for your topic, the better you'll be at finding information.

Learn to Skim

If you sit down and try to completely read every article or book you find, it will take you a very long time to get through all the information. Start by reading the introductory paragraphs. Generally, the first few paragraphs will give you a good idea about the overall topic. If you're reading a research article, start by reading the abstract. If the first few paragraphs or abstract don't sound like they're applicable, there's a good chance the source won't be useful for you. Second, look for highlighted, italicized, or bulleted information. Generally, authors use highlighting, italics, and bullets to separate information to make it jump out for readers. Third, look for tables, charts, graphs, and figures. All these forms are separated from the text to make the information more easily understandable for a reader, so seeing if the content is relevant is a way to see if it helps you. Fourth, look at headings and subheadings.

Headings and subheadings show you how an author has grouped information into meaningful segments. If you read the headings and subheadings and nothing jumps out as relevant, that's another indication that there may not be anything useful in that source. Lastly, take good notes while you're skimming. One way to take good notes is to attach a sticky note to each source. If you find relevant information, write that information on the sticky note along with the page number. If you don't find useful information in a source, just write "nothing" on the sticky note and move on to the next source. This way when you need to sort through your information, you'll be able to quickly see what information was useful and locate the information. Other people prefer to create a series of note cards to help them organize their information. Whatever works best for you is what you should use.

Read Bibliographies/Reference Pages

backtracking

The process where a researcher uses a printed bibliography or reference page to find other useful research materials and then finds those cited materials and reads them for herself or himself.

After you've finished reading useful sources, see who those sources cited on their bibliographies or reference pages. We call this method **backtracking**. Often the sources cited by others can lead us to even better sources than the ones we found initially.

Ask for Help

Don't be afraid to ask for help. As we said earlier in this chapter, reference librarians are your friends. They won't do your work for you, but they are more than willing to help if you ask.

2.4   Evaluating Resources

The final step in research occurs once you've found resources relevant to your topic: evaluating the quality of those resources. Below is a list of six questions to ask yourself about the sources you've collected; these are drawn from the book *The Elements of Library Research* by M. W. George.[12]

What Is the Date of Publication?

The first question you need to ask yourself is the date of the source's publication. Although there may be classic studies that you want to cite in your speech, generally, the more recent the information, the better your presentation will be. As an example, if you want to talk about the current state of women's education in the United States, relying on information from the 1950s that debated whether "coeds" should attend class along with male students is clearly not appropriate. Instead you'd want to use information published within the past five to ten years.

Who Is the Author?

The next question you want to ask yourself is about the author. Who is the author? What are her or his credentials? Does he or she work for a corporation, college, or university? Is a political or commercial agenda apparent in the writing? The more information we can learn about an author, the better our understanding and treatment of that author's work will be. Furthermore, if we know that an author is clearly biased in a specific manner, ethically we must tell our audience members. If we pretend an author is unbiased when we know better, we are essentially lying to our audience.

Who Is the Publisher?

In addition to knowing who the author is, we also want to know who the publisher is. While there are many mainstream publishers and academic press publishers, there are also many fringe publishers. For example, maybe you're reading a research report published by the Cato Institute. While the Cato Institute may sound like a regular publisher, it is actually a libertarian think tank (http://www.cato.org). As such, you can be sure that the information in its publications will have a specific political bias. While the person writing the research report may be an upstanding author with numerous credits, the Cato Institute only publishes reports that adhere to its political philosophy. Generally, a cursory examination of a publisher's website is a good indication of the specific political bias. Most websites will have an "About" section or an "FAQ" section that will explain who the publisher is.

Is It Academic or Nonacademic?

The next question you want to ask yourself is whether the information comes from an academic or a nonacademic source. Because of the enhanced scrutiny academic sources go through, we argue that you can generally rely more on the information contained in academic sources than nonacademic sources. One very notorious example of the difference between academic versus nonacademic information can be seen in the problem of popular-culture author John Gray, author of *Men are From Mars, Women are From Venus*. Gray, who received a PhD via a correspondence program from Columbia Pacific University in 1982, has written numerous books on the topic of men and women. Unfortunately, the academic research on the subject of sex and gender differences is often very much at odds with Gray's writing. For a great critique of Gray's writings, check out Julia Wood's article in the *Southern Communication Journal*.[13] Ultimately, we strongly believe that using academic publications is always in your best interest because they generally contain the most reliable information.

What Is the Quality of the Bibliography/Reference Page?

Another great indicator of a well-thought-out and researched source is the quality of its bibliography or reference page. If you look at a source's bibliography or reference page and it has only a couple of citations, then you can assume that either the information was not properly cited or it was largely made up by someone. Even popular-press books can contain great bibliographies and reference pages, so checking them out is a great way to see if an author has done her or his homework prior to writing a text. As noted above, it is also an excellent way to find additional resources on a topic.

Do People Cite the Work?

The last question to ask about a source is, "Are other people actively citing the work?" One way to find out whether a given source is widely accepted is to see if numerous people are citing it. If you find an article that has been cited by many other authors, then clearly the work has been viewed as credible and useful. If you're doing research and you keep running across the same source over and over again, that is an indication that it's an important study that you should probably take a look at. Many colleges and universities also subscribe to Science Citation Index (SCI), Social Sciences Citation Index (SSCI), or the Arts and Humanities Citation Index (AHCI), which are run through Institute for Scientific Information's Web of Knowledge database service (http://isiwebofknowledge.com). All these databases help you find out where information has been cited by other researchers.

KEY TAKEAWAYS

- In conducting research for a speech, commit adequate time and plan your schedule. Consider both the research time, or time spent gathering information, and the preparation time needed to organize and practice your speech.
- Get a general idea of your research needs even before going to the library so that you can take the most advantage of the library's resources and librarians' help.
- We live in a world dominated by information, but some information is filtered and some is not. It's important to know the difference between academic and nonacademic sources.
- Nonacademic sources are a good place to gain general knowledge of a topic; these include books, general or special-interest periodicals, newspapers and blogs, and websites.
- Academic sources offer more specialized, higher-level information; they include books, articles, computer databases, and web resources.
- A fundamental responsibility is to evaluate the sources you choose to use in order to ensure that you are presenting accurate and up-to-date information in your speech.

EXERCISES

1. Find an academic and a nonacademic source about the same topic. How is the writing style different? How useful is the content in each source? Which source has more authority? Why?
2. Download one of the freeware software packages for creating a research log for one of your speech preparations. Do you like using the software? Is the software cumbersome or helpful? Would you use the software for organizing other speeches or other research projects? Why?
3. Find a politically oriented website and analyze the material using George's six questions for evaluating sources.[14] What does your analysis say about the material on the website?

3. CITING SOURCES

LEARNING OBJECTIVES

1. Understand what style is.
2. Know which academic disciplines you are more likely to use, American Psychological Association (APA) versus Modern Language Association (MLA) style.
3. Cite sources using the sixth edition of the American Psychological Association's Style Manual.
4. Cite sources using the seventh edition of the Modern Language Association's Style Manual.
5. Explain the steps for citing sources within a speech.
6. Differentiate between direct quotations and paraphrases of information within a speech.
7. Understand how to use sources ethically in a speech.
8. Explain twelve strategies for avoiding plagiarism.

© Thinkstock

By this point you're probably exhausted after looking at countless sources, but there's still a lot of work that needs to be done. Most public speaking teachers will require you to turn in either a bibliography or a reference page with your speeches. In this section, we're going to explore how to properly cite your sources for a Modern Language Association (MLA) list of works cited or an American Psychological Association (APA) reference list. We're also going to discuss plagiarism and how to avoid it.

3.1 Why Citing Is Important

Citing is important because it enables readers to see where you found information cited within a speech, article, or book. Furthermore, not citing information properly is considered plagiarism, so ethically we want to make sure that we give credit to the authors we use in a speech. While there are numerous citation styles to choose from, the two most common style choices for public speaking are APA and MLA.

3.2 APA versus MLA Source Citations

style

Those components or features of a literary composition or oral presentation that have to do with the form of expression rather than the content expressed (e.g., language, punctuation, parenthetical citations, and endnotes).

APA style

Form of style agreed upon by the American Psychological Association and is commonly used by social scientists.

MLA style

Form of style agreed upon by the Modern Language Association and is commonly used by scholars in the humanities.

Style refers to those components or features of a literary composition or oral presentation that have to do with the form of expression rather than the content expressed (e.g., language, punctuation, parenthetical citations, and endnotes). The APA and the MLA have created the two most commonly used style guides in academia today. Generally speaking, scholars in the various social science fields (e.g., psychology, human communication, business) are more likely to use **APA style**, and scholars in the various humanities fields (e.g., English, philosophy, rhetoric) are more likely to use **MLA style**. The two styles are quite different from each other, so learning them does take time.

APA Citations

The first common reference style your teacher may ask for is APA. As of July 2009, the American Psychological Association published the sixth edition of the *Publication Manual of the American Psychological Association* (http://www.apastyle.org).[15] The sixth edition provides considerable guidance on working with and citing Internet sources. Table 7.4 provides a list of common citation examples that you may need for your speech.

TABLE 7.4 APA Sixth Edition Citations

Research Article in a Journal—One Author	Harmon, M. D. (2006). Affluenza: A world values test. *The International Communication Gazette, 68*, 119–130. doi: 10.1177/1748048506062228
Research Article in a Journal—Two to Five Authors	Hoffner, C., & Levine, K. J. (2005). Enjoyment of mediated fright and violence: A meta-analysis. *Media Psychology, 7*, 207–237. doi: 10.1207/S1532785XMEP0702_5
Book	Eysenck, H. J. (1982). *Personality, genetics, and behavior: Selected papers*. New York, NY: Praeger Publishers.
Book with 6 or More Authors	Huston, A. C., Donnerstein, E., Fairchild, H., Feshbach, N. D., Katz, P. A., Murray, J. P.,…Zuckerman, D. (1992). *Big world, small screen: The role of television in American society*. Lincoln, NE: University of Nebraska Press.
Chapter in an Edited Book	Tamobrini, R. (1991). Responding to horror: Determinants of exposure and appeal. In J. Bryant & D. Zillman (Eds.), *Responding to the screen: Reception and reaction processes* (pp. 305–329). Hillsdale, NJ: Lawrence Erlbaum.
Newspaper Article	Thomason, D. (2010, March 31). Dry weather leads to burn ban. *The Sentinel Record*, p. A1.
Magazine Article	Finney, J. (2010, March–April). The new "new deal": How to communicate a changed employee value proposition to a skeptical audience—and realign employees within the organization. *Communication World, 27*(2), 27–30.
Preprint Version of an Article	Laudel, G., & Gläser, J. (in press). Tensions between evaluations and communication practices. *Journal of Higher Education Policy and Management*. Retrieved from http://www.laudel.info/pdf/Journal%20articles/06%20Tensions.pdf
Blog	Wrench, J. S. (2009, June 3). AMA's managerial competency model [Web log post]. Retrieved from http://workplacelearning.info/blog/?p=182
Wikipedia	Organizational Communication. (2009, July 11). [Wiki entry]. Retrieved from http://en.wikipedia.org/wiki/Organizational_communication
Vlog	Wrench, J. S. (2009, May 15). Instructional communication [Video file]. Retrieved from http://www.learningjournal.com/Learning-Journal-Videos/instructional-communication.htm
Discussion Board	Wrench, J. S. (2009, May 21). NCA's i-tunes project [Online forum comment]. Retrieved from http://www.linkedin.com/groupAnswers?viewQuestionAndAnswers
E-mail List	McAllister, M. (2009, June 19). New listserv: Critical approaches to ads/consumer culture & media studies [Electronic mailing list message]. Retrieved from http://lists.psu.edu/cgi-bin/wa?A2=ind0906&L=CRTNET&T=0&F=&S=&P=20514
Podcast	Wrench, J. S. (Producer). (2009, July 9). *Workplace bullying* [Audio podcast]. Retrieved from http://www.communicast.info
Electronic-Only Book	Richmond, V. P., Wrench, J. S., & Gorham, J. (2009). *Communication, affect, and learning in the classroom* (3rd ed.). Retrieved from http://www.jasonswrench.com/affect
Electronic-Only Journal Article	Molyneaux, H., O'Donnell, S., Gibson, K., & Singer, J. (2008). Exploring the gender divide on YouTube: An analysis of the creation and reception of vlogs. *American Communication Journal, 10*(1). Retrieved from http://www.acjournal.org
Electronic Version of a Printed Book	Wood, A. F., & Smith, M. J. (2004). *Online communication: Linking technology, identity & culture* (2nd ed.). Retrieved from http://books.google.com/books
Online Magazine	Levine, T. (2009, June). To catch a liar. *Communication Currents, 4*(3). Retrieved from http://www.communicationcurrents.com
Online Newspaper	Clifford, S. (2009, June 1). Online, "a reason to keep going." *The New York Times*. Retrieved from http://www.nytimes.com
Entry in an Online Reference Work	Viswanth, K. (2008). Health communication. In W. Donsbach (Ed.), *The international encyclopedia of communication*. Retrieved from http://www.communicationencyclopedia.com. doi: 10.1111/b.9781405131995.2008.x
Entry in an Online Reference Work, No Author	Communication. (n.d.). In *Random House dictionary* (9th ed.). Retrieved from http://dictionary.reference.com/browse/communication
E-Reader Device	Lutgen-Sandvik, P., & Davenport Sypher, B. (2009). *Destructive organizational communication: Processes, consequences, & constructive ways of organizing*. [Kindle version]. Retrieved from http://www.amazon.com

MLA Citations

The second common reference style your teacher may ask for is MLA. In March 2009, the Modern Language Association published the seventh edition of the *MLA Handbook for Writers of Research Papers*[16] (http://www.mla.org/style). The seventh edition provides considerable guidance for citing online sources and new media such as graphic narratives. Table 7.5 provides a list of common citations you may need for your speech.

TABLE 7.5 MLA Seventh Edition Citations

Research Article in a Journal—One Author	Harmon, Mark D. "Affluenza: A World Values Test." *The International Communication Gazette* 68 (2006): 119–130. Print.
Research Article in a Journal—Two to Four Authors	Hoffner, Cynthia A., and Kenneth J. Levine, "Enjoyment of Mediated Fright and Violence: A Meta-analysis." *Media Psychology* 7 (2005): 207–237. Print.
Book	Eysenck, Hans J. *Personality, Genetics, and Behavior: Selected Papers.* New York: Praeger Publishers, 1982. Print.
Book with Four or More Authors	Huston, Aletha C., et al., *Big World, Small Screen: The Role of Television in American Society.* Lincoln, NE: U of Nebraska P, 1992. Print.
Chapter in an Edited Book	Tamobrini, Ron. "Responding to Horror: Determinants of Exposure and Appeal." *Responding to the Screen: Reception and Reaction Processes.* Eds. Jennings Bryant and Dolf Zillman. Hillsdale, NJ: Lawrence Erlbaum, 1991. 305–329. Print.
Newspaper Article	Thomason, Dan. "Dry Weather Leads to Burn Ban." *The Sentinel Record* 31 Mar. 2010: A1. Print.
Magazine Article	Finney, John. "The New 'New Deal': How to Communicate a Changed Employee Value Proposition to a Skeptical Audience—And Realign Employees Within the Organization." *Communication World* Mar.–Apr. 2010: 27–30. Print.
Preprint Version of an Article	*Grit Laudel's* Website. 15 July 2009. Pre-print version of Laudel, Grit and Gläser, Joken. "Tensions Between Evaluations and Communication Practices." *Journal of Higher Education Policy and Management.*
Blog	Wrench, Jason S. " AMA's Managerial Competency Model." *Workplace Learning and Performance Network Blog.* workplacelearning.info/blog, 3 Jun. 2009. Web. 31 Mar. 2010.
Wikipedia	"Organizational Communication." *Wikipedia.* Wikimedia Foundation, n.d. Web. 31 Mar. 2010.
Vlog	Wrench, Jason S. "Instructional Communication." *The Learning Journal Videos.* LearningJournal.com, 15 May 2009. Web. 1 Aug. 2009.
Discussion Board	Wrench, Jason S. "NCA's i-Tunes Project." *National Communication Association LinkedIn Group.* Web. 1 August 2009.
E-mail List	McAllister, Matt. "New Listerv: Critical Approaches to Ads/Consumer Culture & Media Studies." Online posting. 19 June 2009. CRTNet. Web. 1 August 2009. ⟨mattmc@psu.edu⟩
Podcast	"Workplace Bullying." Narr. Wrench, Jason S. and P. Lutgen-Sandvik. CommuniCast.info, 9 July 2009. Web. 31 Mar. 2010.
Electronic-Only Book	Richmond, Virginia P., Jason S. Wrench, and Joan Gorham. *Communication, Affect, and Learning in the Classroom.* 3rd ed. http://www.jasonswrench.com/affect/. Web. 31 Mar. 2010.
Electronic-Only Journal Article	Molyneaux, Heather, Susan O'Donnell, Kerri Gibson, and Janice Singer. "Exploring the Gender Divide on YouTube: An Analysis of the Creation and Reception of Vlogs." *American Communication Journal* 10.1 (2008): n.pag. Web. 31 Mar. 2010.
Electronic Version of a Printed Book	Wood, Andrew F., and Matthew. J. Smith. *Online Communication: Linking Technology, Identity & Culture.* 2nd ed. 2005. Web. 31 Mar. 2010.
Online Magazine	Levine, Timothy. "To Catch a Liar." *Communication Currents.* N.p. June 2009. Web. 31 Mar. 2010.
Online Newspaper	Clifford, Stephanie. "Online, 'A Reason to Keep Going.'" *The New York Times.* 1 Jun. 2009. Web. 31 Mar. 2010.
Entry in an Online Reference Work	Viswanth, K. "Health Communication." *The International Encyclopedia of Communication.* 2008. Web. 31 Mar. 2010.
Entry in an Online Reference Work, No Author	"Communication." *Random House Dictionary Online.* 9th ed. 2009. Web. 31 Mar. 2010.
E-Reader Device	Lutgen-Sandvik, Pamela, and Beverly Davenport Sypher. *Destructive Organizational Communication: Processes, Consequences, & Constructive Ways of Organizing.* New York: Routledge, 2009. Kindle.

3.3 Citing Sources in a Speech

Once you have decided what sources best help you explain important terms and ideas in your speech or help you build your arguments, it's time to place them into your speech. In this section, we're going to quickly talk about using your research effectively within your speeches. Citing sources within a speech is a three-step process: set up the citation, give the citation, and explain the citation.

First, you want to set up your audience for the citation. The setup is one or two sentences that are general statements that lead to the specific information you are going to discuss from your source. Here's an example: "Workplace bullying is becoming an increasing problem for US organizations." Notice that this statement doesn't provide a specific citation yet, but the statement introduces the basic topic.

Second, you want to deliver the source; whether it is a direct quotation or a paraphrase of information from a source doesn't matter at this point. A **direct quotation** is when you cite the actual words from a source with no changes. To **paraphrase** is to take a source's basic idea and condense it using your own words. Here's an example of both:

direct quotation

Citing the actual words from a source with no changes.

paraphrase

Taking the central idea or theme from another speaker or author and adapting it in one's own words.

| Direct Quotation | In a 2009 report titled *Bullying: Getting Away With It*, the Workplace Bullying Institute wrote, "Doing nothing to the bully (ensuring impunity) was the most common employer tactic (54%)." |
| Paraphrase | According to a 2009 study by the Workplace Bullying Institute titled *Bullying: Getting Away With It*, when employees reported bullying, 54 percent of employers did nothing at all. |

You'll notice that in both of these cases, we started by citing the author of the study—in this case, the Workplace Bullying Institute. We then provided the title of the study. You could also provide the name of the article, book, podcast, movie, or other source. In the direct quotation example, we took information right from the report. In the second example, we summarized the same information.[17]

Let's look at another example of direct quotations and paraphrases, this time using a person, rather than an institution, as the author.

| Direct Quotation | In her book *The Elements of Library Research: What Every Student Needs to Know*, Mary George, senior reference librarian at Princeton University's library, defines insight as something that "occurs at an unpredictable point in the research process and leads to the formulation of a thesis statement and argument. Also called an 'Aha' moment or focus." |
| Paraphrase | In her book *The Elements of Library Research: What Every Student Needs to Know*, Mary George, senior reference librarian at Princeton University's library, tells us that insight is likely to come unexpectedly during the research process; it will be an "aha!" moment when we suddenly have a clear vision of the point we want to make. |

Notice that the same basic pattern for citing sources was followed in both cases.

The final step in correct source citation within a speech is the explanation. One of the biggest mistakes of novice public speakers (and research writers) is that they include a source citation and then do nothing with the citation at all. Instead, take the time to explain the quotation or paraphrase to put into the context of your speech. Do not let your audience draw their own conclusions about the quotation or paraphrase. Instead, help them make the connections you want them to make. Here are two examples using the examples above:

| Bullying Example | Clearly, organizations need to be held accountable for investigating bullying allegations. If organizations will not voluntarily improve their handling of this problem, the legal system may be required to step in and enforce sanctions for bullying, much as it has done with sexual harassment. |
| Aha! Example | As many of us know, reaching that "aha!" moment does not always come quickly, but there are definitely some strategies one can take to help speed up this process. |

Notice how in both of our explanations we took the source's information and then added to the information to direct it for our specific purpose. In the case of the bullying citation, we then propose that businesses should either adopt workplace bullying guidelines or face legal intervention. In the case of the "aha!" example, we turn the quotation into a section on helping people find their thesis or topic. In both cases, we were able to use the information to further our speech.

Using Sources Ethically

The last section of this chapter is about using sources in an ethical manner. Whether you are using primary or secondary research, there are five basic ethical issues you need to consider.

Avoid Plagiarism

First, and foremost, if the idea isn't yours, you need to cite where the information came from during your speech. Having the citation listed on a bibliography or reference page is only half of the correct citation. You must provide correct citations for all your sources within the speech as well. In a very helpful book called *Avoiding Plagiarism: A Student Guide to Writing Your Own Work*, Menager-Beeley and Paulos provide a list of twelve strategies for avoiding plagiarism:[18]

1. *Do your own work, and use your own words.* One of the goals of a public speaking class is to develop skills that you'll use in the world outside academia. When you are in the workplace and the "real world," you'll be expected to think for yourself, so you might as well start learning this skill now.

2. *Allow yourself enough time to research the assignment.* One of the most commonly cited excuses students give for plagiarism is that they didn't have enough time to do the research. In this chapter, we've stressed the necessity of giving yourself plenty of time. The more complete your research strategy is from the very beginning, the more successful your research endeavors will be in the long run. Remember, not having adequate time to prepare is no excuse for plagiarism.

3. *Keep careful track of your sources.* A common mistake that people can make is that they forget where information came from when they start creating the speech itself. Chances are you're going to look at dozens of sources when preparing your speech, and it is very easy to suddenly find yourself believing that a piece of information is "common knowledge" and not citing that information within a speech. When you keep track of your sources, you're less likely to inadvertently lose sources and not cite them correctly.

4. *Take careful notes.* However you decide to keep track of the information you collect (old-fashioned pen and notebook or a computer software program), the more careful your note-taking is, the less likely you'll find yourself inadvertently not citing information or citing the information incorrectly. It doesn't matter what method you choose for taking research notes, but whatever you do, you need to be systematic to avoid plagiarizing.

5. *Assemble your thoughts, and make it clear who is speaking.* When creating your speech, you need to make sure that you clearly differentiate your voice in the speech from the voice of specific authors of the sources you quote. The easiest way to do this is to set up a direct quotation or a paraphrase, as we've described in the preceding sections. Remember, audience members cannot see where the quotation marks are located within your speech text, so you need to clearly articulate with words and vocal tone when you are using someone else's ideas within your speech.

6. *If you use an idea, a quotation, paraphrase, or summary, then credit the source.* We can't reiterate it enough: if it is not your idea, you need to tell your audience where the information came from. Giving credit is especially important when your speech includes a statistic, an original theory, or a fact that is not common knowledge.

7. *Learn how to cite sources correctly both in the body of your paper and in your List of Works Cited (Reference Page).* Most public speaking teachers will require that you turn in either a bibliography or reference page on the day you deliver a speech. Many students make the mistake of thinking that the bibliography or reference page is all they need to cite information, and then they don't cite any of the material within the speech itself. A bibliography or reference page enables a reader or listener to find those sources after the fact, but you must also correctly cite those sources within the speech itself; otherwise, you are plagiarizing.

8. *Quote accurately and sparingly.* A public speech should be based on factual information and references, but it shouldn't be a string of direct quotations strung together. Experts recommend that no more than 10 percent of a paper or speech be direct quotations.[19] When selecting direct quotations, always ask yourself if the material could be paraphrased in a manner that would make it clearer for your audience. If the author wrote a sentence in a way that is just perfect, and you don't want to tamper with it, then by all means directly quote the sentence. But if you're just quoting because it's easier than putting the ideas into your own words, this is not a legitimate reason for including direct quotations.

9. *Paraphrase carefully.* Modifying an author's words in this way is not simply a matter of replacing some of the words with synonyms. Instead, as Howard and Taggart explain in *Research Matters*, "paraphrasing force[s] you to understand your sources and to capture their meaning accurately in original words and sentences."[20] Incorrect paraphrasing is one of the most common forms of inadvertent plagiarism by students. First and foremost, paraphrasing is putting the author's argument, intent, or ideas into *your* own words.

10. *Do not patchwrite (patchspeak).* Menager-Beeley and Paulos define patchwriting as consisting "of mixing several references together and arranging paraphrases and quotations to constitute much of the paper. In essence, the student has assembled others' work with a bit of embroidery here

and there but with little original thinking or expression."[21] Just as students can patchwrite, they can also engage in patchspeaking. In patchspeaking, students rely completely on taking quotations and paraphrases and weaving them together in a manner that is devoid of the student's original thinking.

11. *Summarize, don't auto-summarize.* Some students have learned that most word processing features have an auto-summary function. The auto-summary function will take a ten-page document and summarize the information into a short paragraph. When someone uses the auto-summary function, the words that remain in the summary are still those of the original author, so this is not an ethical form of paraphrasing.

12. *Do not rework another student's paper (speech) or buy paper mill papers (speech mill speeches).* In today's Internet environment, there are a number of storehouses of student speeches on the Internet. Some of these speeches are freely available, while other websites charge money for getting access to one of their canned speeches. Whether you use a speech that is freely available or pay money for a speech, you are engaging in plagiarism. This is also true if the main substance of your speech was copied from a web page. Any time you try to present someone else's ideas as your own during a speech, you are plagiarizing.

Avoid Academic Fraud

While there are numerous websites where you can download free speeches for your class, this is tantamount to fraud. If you didn't do the research and write your own speech, then you are fraudulently trying to pass off someone else's work as your own. In addition to being unethical, many institutions have student codes that forbid such activity. Penalties for academic fraud can be as severe as suspension or expulsion from your institution.

Don't Mislead Your Audience

If you know a source is clearly biased, and you don't spell this out for your audience, then you are purposefully trying to mislead or manipulate your audience. Instead, if the information may be biased, tell your audience that the information may be biased and allow your audience to decide whether to accept or disregard the information.

Give Author Credentials

You should always provide the author's credentials. In a world where anyone can say anything and have it published on the Internet or even publish it in a book, we have to be skeptical of the information we see and hear. For this reason, it's very important to provide your audience with background about the credentials of the authors you cite.

Use Primary Research Ethically

Lastly, if you are using primary research within your speech, you need to use it ethically as well. For example, if you tell your survey participants that the research is anonymous or confidential, then you need to make sure that you maintain their anonymity or confidentiality when you present those results. Furthermore, you also need to be respectful if someone says something is "off the record" during an interview. We must always maintain the privacy and confidentiality of participants during primary research, unless we have their express permission to reveal their names or other identifying information.

- Style focuses on the components of your speech that make up the form of your expression rather than your content.
- Social science disciplines, such as psychology, human communication, and business, typically use APA style, while humanities disciplines, such as English, philosophy, and rhetoric, typically use MLA style.
- The APA sixth edition and the MLA seventh edition are the most current style guides and the tables presented in this chapter provide specific examples of common citations for each of these styles.
- Citing sources within your speech is a three-step process: set up the citation, provide the cited information, and interpret the information within the context of your speech.
- A direct quotation is any time you utilize another individual's words in a format that resembles the way they were originally said or written. On the other hand, a paraphrase is when you take someone's ideas and restate them using your own words to convey the intended meaning.
- Ethically using sources means avoiding plagiarism, not engaging in academic fraud, making sure not to mislead your audience, providing credentials for your sources so the audience can make judgments about the material, and using primary research in ways that protect the identity of participants.
- Plagiarism is a huge problem and creeps its way into student writing and oral presentations. As ethical communicators, we must always give credit for the information we convey in our writing and our speeches.

EXERCISES

1. List what you think are the benefits of APA style and the benefits of MLA style. Why do you think some people prefer APA style over MLA style or vice versa?
2. Find a direct quotation within a magazine article. Paraphrase that direct quotation. Then attempt to paraphrase the entire article as well. How would you cite each of these orally within the body of your speech?
3. Which of Menager-Beeley and Paulos (2009) twelve strategies for avoiding plagiarism do you think you need the most help with right now? Why? What can you do to overcome and avoid that pitfall?

4. CHAPTER EXERCISES

SPEAKING ETHICALLY

Jonathan sat staring at his computer screen. The previous two days had been the most disastrous weekend of his entire life. First, his girlfriend broke up with him on Friday and informed him that she was dating his best friend behind his back. Then he got a phone call from his mother informing him that his childhood dog had been hit by a car. And if that wasn't enough, his car died on the way to work, and since it was his third unexcused absence from work, he was fired.

In the midst of all these crises, Jonathan was supposed to be preparing his persuasive speech for his public speaking class. Admittedly, Jonathan had had the two weeks prior to work on the speech, but he had not gotten around to it and thought he could pull it together over the weekend. Now at 1:00 a.m. on Monday morning, he finally got a chance to sit down at his computer to prepare the speech he was giving in nine and a half hours.

His topic was prison reform. He searched through a number of websites and finally found one that seemed really relevant. As he read through the first paragraph, he thought to himself, *this is exactly what I want to say.* After two paragraphs the information just stopped, and the website asked him to pay $29.95 for the rest of the speech. Without even realizing it, Jonathan had found a speech mill website. Jonathan found himself reaching for his wallet thinking, *well it says what I want it to say, so why not?*

1. If you were a student in Jonathan's class and he confided in you that he had used a speech mill for his speech, how would you react?
2. If you were Jonathan, what ethical choices could you have made?
3. Is it ever ethical to use a speech written by a speech mill?

END-OF-CHAPTER ASSESSMENT

1. Which of the following is *not* a recommendation for using research librarians provided by the members of the American Library Association?

    a. Be willing to do your own work.

    b. Academic librarians are willing to schedule in-depth research consultations with students.

    c. You don't need to bring a copy of the assignment when meeting with a librarian.

    d. Good research takes time.

    e. Students need to learn that many questions do not have ready-made or one-stop answers.

2. Samantha has handed out a survey to her peers on their perceptions of birth control. During her speech, Samantha explains the results from her survey. What type of research has Samantha utilized in her speech?

    a. primary

    b. secondary

    c. recency

    d. qualitative

    e. critical

3. Michael is giving a speech on dogs and picks up a copy of *Pet Fancy* magazine at his local bookstore. What type of source has Michael selected?

    a. general-interest periodical

    b. special-interest periodical

    c. Academic journal

    d. nonacademic literature supplement

    e. gender-based interest periodical

4. Jose is having problems finding sources related to his topic. He found one academic journal article that was really useful. He decides to read the references listed on the reference page of the article. He finds a couple that sound really promising so he goes to the library and finds those articles. What process has Jose engaged in?

    a. primary literature search

    b. secondary literature search

    c. backtracking

    d. source evaluation

    e. reference extending

5. What are the components or features of a literary composition or oral presentation that have to do with the form of expression rather than the content expressed (e.g., language, punctuation, parenthetical citations, and endnotes)?

    a. citation functions

    b. referencing functions

    c. grammatical parameters

    d. communicative techniques

    e. style

ANSWER KEY

1. c
2. a
3. b
4. c
5. e

ENDNOTES

1. George, M. W. (2008). *The elements of library research: What every student needs to know*. Princeton, NJ: Princeton University Press.

2. Author Note: We wish to thank the numerous reference librarians who went out of their way to help us develop our top eighteen tips to working with reference librarians. We opted to keep their comments anonymous, but we want to thank them here.

   - Debra Rollins, Louisiana State University-Alexandria
   - William Badke, Trinity Western University
   - Ingrid Hendrix, University of New Mexico
   - Ward Price, Ivy Tech Community College, Northeast
   - Tracy L. Stout, Missouri State University
   - Sandra J. Ley, Pima Community College
   - Annie Smith, Utah Valley University Library
   - Sharlee Jeser-Skaggs, Richland College Library
   - Leslie N. Todd, University of the Incarnate Word
   - Susan G Ryberg, Mount Olive College
   - Kathleen A. Hana, Indiana University-Purdue University Indianapolis University Library
   - Red Wassenich, Austin Community College
   - Elizabeth Kettell, University of Rochester Medical Center

3. Williamson, B. (2011, July 12). The wonders and dangers of Botox. *Australian Broadcasting Corporation, Adelaide*. Retrieved July 14, 2011, from http://www.abc.net.au/local/stories/2011/07/11/3266766.htm

4. Clark, R. P., & Berris, C. E. (1989, August). Botulinum toxin: A treatment for facial asymmetry caused by facial nerve paralysis. *Plastic & Reconstructive Surgery, 84*(2), 353–355.

5. Wrench, J. S., Thomas-Maddox, C., Richmond, V. P., & McCroskey, J. C. (2008). *Quantitative methods for communication researchers: A hands on approach*. New York, NY: Oxford University Press.

6. Weiner, M. (2006). *Unleashing the power of PR: A contrarian's guide to marketing and communication*. San Francisco, CA: Jossey-Bass and the International Association of Business Communicators.

7. Project Management Institute. (2004). *A guide to the project management body of knowledge: PMBOK® guide* (3rd ed.). Newton Square, PA: Author, p. 19.

8. Howard, R. M., & Taggart, A. R. (2010). *Research matters*. New York: McGraw-Hill, pp. 102–103.

9. Total number of magazines published in the US is greater than 10,000 but only about 2,000 have significant circulation. (2005, September 21). *Business Wire*. Retrieved from http://findarticles.com.

10. Ochman, B. L. (2007, June 29). The top 10 news stories broken by bloggers. *TechNewsWorld*. [Web log post]. Retrieved July 14, 2011, from http://www.mpdailyfix.com/technewsworld-the-top-10-news-stories-broken-by-bloggers.

11. George, M. W. (2008). *The elements of library research: What every student needs to know*. Princeton, NJ: Princeton University Press, p. 183.

12. George, M. W. (2008). *The elements of library research: What every student needs to know*. Princeton, NJ: Princeton University Press.

13. Wood, J. T. (2002). A critical response to John Gray's Mars and Venus portrayals of men and women. *Southern Communication Journal, 67*, 201–210.

14. George, M. W. (2008). *The elements of library research: What every student needs to know*. Princeton, NJ: Princeton University Press.

15. American Psychological Association. (2010). *Publication manual of the American Psychological Association* (6th ed.). Washington, DC: Author. See also American Psychological Association. (2010). *Concise rules of APA Style: The official pocket style guide from the American Psychological Association* (6th ed.). Washington, DC: Author.

16. Modern Language Association. (2009). *MLA handbook for writers of research papers* (7th ed.). New York, NY: Modern Language Association.

17. Workplace Bullying Institute. (2009). Bullying: Getting away with it WBI Labor Day Study—September, 2009. Retrieved July 14, 2011, from http://www.workplacebullying.org/res/WBI2009-B-Survey.html

18. Menager-Beeley, R., & Paulos, L. (2009). *Understanding plagiarism: A student guide to writing your own work*. Boston, MA: Houghton Mifflin Harcourt, pp. 5–8.

19. Menager-Beeley, R., & Paulos, L. (2009). *Understanding plagiarism: A student guide to writing your own work*. Boston, MA: Houghton Mifflin Harcourt.

20. Howard, R. M., & Taggart, A. R. (2010). *Research matters*. New York, NY: McGraw-Hill, p. 131.

21. Menager-Beeley, R., & Paulos, L. (2009). *Understanding plagiarism: A student guide to writing your own work*. Boston, MA: Houghton Mifflin Harcourt, pp. 7–8.

CHAPTER 8
Supporting Ideas and Building Arguments

Every day, all around the country, people give speeches that contain generalities and vagueness. Students on your campus might claim that local policies are biased against students, but may not explain why. Politicians may make claims in their speeches about "family values" without defining what those values are or throw out statistics without giving credit to where they found those numbers. Indeed, the nonpartisan websites FactCheck.org and Politifact.com are dedicated to investigating and dispelling the claims that politicians make in their speeches.

In this chapter, we explore the nature of supporting ideas in public speaking and why support is essential to effective presentations. We will then discuss how to use support to build stronger arguments within a speech.

© Thinkstock

1. USING RESEARCH AS SUPPORT

LEARNING OBJECTIVES

1. Define the term "support."
2. Understand three reasons we use support in speeches.
3. Explain four criteria used to evaluate support options.

In public speaking, the word **"support"** refers to a range of strategies that are used to develop the central idea and specific purpose by providing corroborating evidence. Whether you are speaking to inform, persuade, or entertain, using support helps you create a more substantive and polished speech. We sometimes use the words "support" or "evidence" synonymously or interchangeably because both are designed to help ground a speech's specific purpose. However, "evidence" tends to be associated specifically with persuasive speeches, so we opt to use the more general term "support" for most of this chapter. In this section, we are going to explore why speakers use support.

1.1 Why We Use Support

Speakers use support to help provide a foundation for their message. You can think of support as the legs on a table. Without the legs, the table becomes a slab of wood or glass lying on the ground; as such, it cannot fully serve the purpose of a table. In the same way, without support, a speech is nothing more than fluff. Audience members may ignore the speech's message, dismissing it as just so much hot air. In addition to being the foundation that a speech stands on, support also helps us clarify content, increase speaker credibility, and make the speech more vivid.

© Thinkstock

support

The range of strategies a public speaker can use to develop the central idea and specific purpose by providing corroborating evidence.

To Clarify Content

The first reason to use support in a speech is to clarify content. Speakers often choose a piece of support because a previous writer or speaker has phrased something in a way that evokes a clear mental picture of the point they want to make. For example, suppose you're preparing a speech about hazing in college fraternities. You may read your school's code of student conduct to find out how your campus defines hazing. You could use this definition to make sure your audience understands what hazing is and what types of behaviors your campus identifies as hazing.

To Add Credibility

Another important reason to use support is because it adds to your credibility as a speaker. The less an audience perceives you as an expert on a given topic, the more important it is to use a range of support. By doing so, you let your audience know that you've done your homework on the topic.

At the same time, you could hurt your credibility if you use inadequate support or support from questionable sources. Your credibility will also suffer if you distort the intent of a source to try to force it to support a point that the previous author did not address. For example, the famous 1798 publication by Thomas Malthus, *An Essay on the Principle of Population*, has been used as support for various arguments far beyond what Malthus could have intended. Malthus's thesis was that as the human population increases at a greater rate than food production, societies will go to war over scarce food resources.[1] Some modern writers have suggested that, according to the Malthusian line of thinking, almost anything that leads to a food shortage could lead to nuclear war. For example, better health care leads to longer life spans, which leads to an increased need for food, leading to food shortages, which lead to nuclear war. Clearly, this argument makes some giant leaps of logic that would be hard for an audience to accept.

For this reason, it is important to evaluate your support to ensure that it will not detract from your credibility as a speaker. Here are four characteristics to evaluate when looking at support options: accuracy, authority, currency, and objectivity.

Accuracy

One of the quickest ways to lose credibility in the eyes of your audience is to use support that is inaccurate or even questionably accurate. Admittedly, determining the accuracy of support can be difficult if you are not an expert in a given area, but here are some questions to ask yourself to help assess a source's accuracy:

- Does the information within one piece of supporting evidence completely contradict other supporting evidence you've seen?
- If the support is using a statistic, does the supporting evidence explain where that statistic came from and how it was determined?
- Does the logic behind the support make sense?

One of this book's authors recently observed a speech in which a student said, "The amount of pollution produced by using paper towels instead of hand dryers is equivalent to driving a car from the east coast to St. Louis." The other students in the class, as well as the instructor, recognized that this information sounded wrong and asked questions about the information source, the amount of time it would take to produce this much pollution, and the number of hand dryers used. The audience demonstrated strong listening skills by questioning the information, but the speaker lost credibility by being unable to answer their questions.

Authority

The second way to use support in building your credibility is to cite authoritative sources—those who are experts on the topic. In today's world, there are all kinds of people who call themselves "experts" on a range of topics. There are even books that tell you how to get people to regard you as an expert in a given industry.[2] Today there are "experts" on every street corner or website spouting off information that some listeners will view as legitimate.

So what truly makes someone an expert? Bruce D. Weinstein, a professor at West Virginia University's Center for Health Ethics and Law, defined **expertise** as having two senses. In his definition, the first sense of expertise is "knowledge *in* or *about* a particular field, and statements about it generally take the form, 'S is an expert *in* or *about* D.'... The second sense of expertise refers to domains of demonstrable skills, and statements about it generally take the form, 'S is an expert *at skill* D.'"[3] Thus, to be an expert, someone needs to have considerable knowledge on a topic or considerable skill in accomplishing something.

As a novice researcher, how can you determine whether an individual is truly an expert? Unfortunately, there is no clear-cut way to wade through the masses of "experts" and determine each one's legitimacy quickly. However, Table 8.1 presents a list of questions based on the research of Marie-Line Germain that you can ask yourself to help determine whether someone is an expert.[4]

expertise

Knowledge in or about a particular field or domains of demonstrable skills.

TABLE 8.1 Who Is an Expert?

Questions to Ask Yourself	Yes	No
1. Is the person widely recognizable as an expert?		
2. Does the person have an appropriate degree/training/certification to make her or him an expert?		
3. Is the person a member of a recognized profession in her or his claimed area of expertise?		
4. Has the person published articles or books (not self-published) on the claimed area of expertise?		
5. Does the person have appropriate experience in her or his claimed area of expertise?		
6. Does the person have clear knowledge about her or his claimed area of expertise?		
7. Is the person clearly knowledgeable about the field related to her or his claimed area of expertise?		
8. When all is said and done, does the person truly have the qualifications to be considered an expert in her or his claimed area of expertise?		

You don't have to answer "yes" to all the preceding questions to conclude that a source is credible, but a string of "no" answers should be a warning signal. In a *Columbia Journalism Review* article, Allisa Quart raised the question of expert credibility regarding the sensitive subject of autism. Specifically, Quart questioned whether the celebrity spokesperson and autism advocate Jennifer McCarthy (http://www.generationrescue.org/) qualifies as an expert. Quart notes that McCarthy "insists that vaccines caused her son's neurological disorder, a claim that has near-zero support in scientific literature."[5] Providing an opposing view is a widely read blog called *Respectful Insolence* (http://scienceblogs.com/insolence/), whose author is allegedly a surgeon/scientist who often speaks out about autism and "antivaccination lunacy." Respectful Insolence received the 2008 Best Weblog Award from *MedGagdet: The Internet Journal of Emerging Medical Technologies*. We used the word "allegedly" when referring to the author of *Respectful Insolence* because as the website explains that the author's name, Orac, is the "*nom de* blog of a (not so) humble pseudonymous surgeon/scientist with an ego just big enough to delude himself that someone, somewhere might actually give a rodent's posterior about his miscellaneous verbal meanderings, but just barely small enough to admit to himself that few will."[6]

When comparing the celebrity Jenny McCarthy to the blogger Orac, who do you think is the better expert? Were you able to answer "yes" to the questions in Table 8.1 for both "experts"? If not, why not? Overall, determining the authority of support is clearly a complicated task, and one that you should spend time thinking about as you prepare the support for your speech.

Currency

The third consideration in using support to build your credibility is how current the information is. Some ideas stay fairly consistent over time, like the date of the Japanese attack on Pearl Harbor or the mathematical formula for finding the area of a circle, but other ideas change wildly in a short period of time, including ideas about technology, health treatments, and laws.

Although we never want to discount classic supporting information that has withstood the test of time, as a general rule for most topics, we recommend that information be less than five years old. Obviously, this is just a general guideline and can change depending on the topic. If you're giving a speech on the history of mining in West Virginia, then you may use support from sources that are much older. However, if you're discussing a medical topic, then your support information should probably be from the past five years or less. Some industries change even faster, so the best support may come from the past month. For example, if are speaking about advances in word processing, using information about Microsoft Word from 2003 would be woefully out-of-date because two upgrades have been released since 2003 (2007 and 2010). As a credible speaker, it is your responsibility to give your audience up-to-date information.

Objectivity

The last question you should ask yourself when examining support is whether the person or organization behind the information is objective or biased. **Bias** refers to a predisposition or preconception of a topic that prevents impartiality. Although there is a certain logic to the view that every one of us is innately biased, as a credible speaker, you want to avoid just passing along someone's unfounded bias in your speech. Ideally you would use support that is unbiased; Table 8.2 provides some questions to ask yourself when evaluating a potential piece of support to detect bias.

bias

A predisposition or preconception of a topic that prevents impartiality.

TABLE 8.2 Is a Potential Source of Support Biased?

Questions to Ask Yourself	Yes	No
1. Does the source represent an individual's, an organization's, or another group's viewpoint?		
2. Does the source sound unfair in its judgment, either for or against a specific topic?		
3. Does the source sound like personal prejudices, opinions, or thoughts?		
4. Does the source exist only on a website (i.e., not in print or any other format)?		
5. Is the information published or posted anonymously or pseudonymously?		
6. Does the source have any political or financial interests related to the information being disseminated?		
7. Does the source demonstrate any specific political orientation, religious affiliation, or other ideology?		
8. Does the source's viewpoint differ from all other information you've read?		

As with the questions in Table 8.1 about expertise, you don't have to have all "no" or "yes" responses to decide on bias. However, being aware of the possibility of bias and where your audience might see bias will help you to select the best possible support to include in your speech.

To Add Vividness

vividness

A speaker's ability to present information in a striking, exciting manner.

In addition to clarifying content and enhancing credibility, support helps make a speech more vivid. **Vividness** refers to a speaker's ability to present information in a striking, exciting manner. The goal of vividness is to make your speech more memorable. One of the authors still remembers a vivid example from a student speech given several years ago. The student was speaking about the importance of wearing seat belts and stated that the impact from hitting a windshield at just twenty miles per hour without a seat belt would be equivalent to falling out of the window of their second-floor classroom and landing face-first on the pavement below. Because they were in that classroom several times each week, students were easily able to visualize the speaker's analogy and it was successful at creating an image that is remembered years later. Support helps make your speech more interesting and memorable to an audience member.

KEY TAKEAWAYS

- The strategies a public speaker can use to provide corroborating evidence for the speech's central idea and specific purpose are called support.
- There are three primary reasons to use support: to clarify content, to increase speaker credibility, and to make the speech more vivid.
- A good piece of support should be accurate, authoritative, current, and unbiased.

EXERCISES

1. Find an article online about a topic on which you are interested in speaking. Examine it for the four aspects of effective sources (e.g., accuracy, authority, currency, and objectivity). Do you think this source is credible? Why?
2. Find a speech on the Vital Speeches of the Day website (http://www.vsotd.com) and try to identify the types of support the speaker utilized. Is the speaker's use of support effective? Why or why not?

2. EXPLORING TYPES OF SUPPORT

LEARNING OBJECTIVES

1. Understand how speakers can use statistics to support their speeches.
2. Differentiate among the five types of definitions.
3. Differentiate among four types of supportive examples.
4. Explain how narratives can be used to support informative, persuasive, and entertaining speeches.
5. Differentiate between the two forms of testimony.
6. Differentiate between two types of analogies that can be used as support.

Now that we've explained why support is important, let's examine the various types of support that speakers often use within a speech: facts and statistics, definitions, examples, narratives, testimony, and analogies.

2.1 Facts and Statistics

As we discussed in Chapter 7, a fact is a truth that is arrived at through the scientific process. Speakers often support a point or specific purpose by citing facts that their audience may not know. A typical way to introduce a fact orally is "Did you know that...?"

© *Thinkstock*

Many of the facts that speakers cite are based on statistics. **Statistics** is the mathematical subfield that gathers, analyzes, and makes inferences about collected data. Data can come in a wide range of forms—the number of people who buy a certain magazine, the average number of telephone calls made in a month, the incidence of a certain disease. Though few people realize it, much of our daily lives are governed by statistics. Everything from seat-belt laws, to the food we eat, to the amount of money public schools receive, to the medications you are prescribed are based on the collection and interpretation of numerical data.

It is important to realize that a public speaking textbook cannot begin to cover statistics in depth. If you plan to do statistical research yourself, or gain an understanding of the intricacies of such research, we strongly recommend taking a basic class in statistics or quantitative research methods. These courses will better prepare you to understand the various statistics you will encounter.

However, even without a background in statistics, finding useful statistical information related to your topic is quite easy. Table 8.3 provides a list of some websites where you can find a range of statistical information that may be useful for your speeches.

statistics

The mathematical subfield that gathers, analyzes, and makes inferences about collected data.

TABLE 8.3 Statistics-Oriented Websites

Website	Type of Information
http://www.bls.gov/bls/other.htm	Bureau of Labor Statistics provides links to a range of websites for labor issues related to a vast range of countries.
http://www.fedstats.gov	Federal Stats provides information on the US federal government.
http://bjs.ojp.usdoj.gov	Bureau of Justice Statistics provides information on crime statistics in the United States.
http://www.census.gov	US Census Bureau provides a wide range of information about people living in the United States.
http://www.cdc.gov/nchs/datawh.htm	National Center for Health Statistics is a program conducted by the US Centers for Disease Control and Prevention. It provides information on a range of health issues in the United States.
http://www.stats.org	STATS is a nonprofit organization that helps people understand quantitative data. It also provides a range of data on its website.
http://www.ropercenter.uconn.edu	Roper Center for Public Opinion provides data related to a range of issues in the United States.
http://www.nielsen.com	Nielsen provides data on consumer use of various media forms.
http://www.gallup.com	Gallup provides public opinion data on a range of social and political issues in the United States and around the world.
http://www.adherents.com	Adherents provides both domestic and international data related to religious affiliation.
http://people-press.org	Pew Research Center provides public opinion data on a range of social and political issues in the United States and around the world.

Statistics are probably the most used—and misused—form of support in any type of speaking. People like numbers. People are impressed by numbers. However, most people do not know how to correctly interpret numbers. Unfortunately, there are many speakers who do not know how to interpret them either or who intentionally manipulate them to mislead their listeners. As the saying popularized by Mark Twain goes, "There are three kinds of lies: lies, damned lies, and statistics."[7]

To avoid misusing statistics when you speak in public, do three things. First, be honest with yourself and your audience. If you are distorting a statistic or leaving out other statistics that contradict your point, you are not living up to the level of honesty your audience is entitled to expect. Second, run a few basic calculations to see if a statistic is believable. Sometimes a source may contain a mistake—for example, a decimal point may be in the wrong place or a verbal expression like "increased by 50 percent" may conflict with data showing an increase of 100 percent. Third, evaluate sources (even those in Table 8.3, which are generally reputable) according to the criteria discussed earlier in the chapter: accuracy, authority, currency, and objectivity.

2.2   Definitions

Imagine that you gave a speech about the use of presidential veto and your audience did not know the meaning of the word "veto." In order for your speech to be effective, you would need to define what a veto is and what it does. Making sure everyone is "on the same page" is a fundamental task of any communication. As speakers, we often need to clearly define what we are talking about to make sure that our audience understands our meaning. The goal of a definition is to help speakers communicate a word or idea in a manner that makes it understandable for their audiences. For the purposes of public speaking, there are four different types of definitions that may be used as support: lexical, persuasive, stipulative, and theoretical.

Lexical Definitions

lexical definition

"Dictionary" definition that specifically states how a word is used within a specific language.

A **lexical definition** is one that specifically states how a word is used within a specific language. For example, if you go to Dictionary.com and type in the word "speech," here is the lexical definition you will receive:

—noun

1. *the faculty or power of speaking; oral communication; ability to express one's thoughts and emotions by speech sounds and gesture: Losing her speech made her feel isolated from humanity.*

2. *the act of speaking: He expresses himself better in speech than in writing.*

3. *something that is spoken; an utterance, remark, or declaration: We waited for some speech that would indicate her true feelings.*

4. *a form of communication in spoken language, made by a speaker before an audience for a given purpose: a fiery speech.*

5. *any single utterance of an actor in the course of a play, motion picture, etc.*

6. *the form of utterance characteristic of a particular people or region; a language or dialect.*

7. *manner of speaking, as of a person: Your slovenly speech is holding back your career.*

8. *a field of study devoted to the theory and practice of oral communication.*

Lexical definitions are useful when a word may be unfamiliar to an audience and you want to ensure that the audience has a basic understanding of the word. However, our ability to understand lexical definitions often hinges on our knowledge of other words that are used in the definition, so it is usually a good idea to follow a lexical definition with a clear explanation of what it means in your own words.

Persuasive Definitions

Persuasive definitions are designed to motivate an audience to think in a specific manner about the word or term. Political figures are often very good at defining terms in a way that are persuasive. Frank Luntz, a linguist and political strategist, is widely regarded as one of the most effective creators of persuasive definitions.[8] Luntz has the ability to take terms that people don't like and repackage them into persuasive definitions that give the original term a much more positive feel. Here are some of Luntz's more famous persuasive definitions:

> **persuasive definition**
>
> Definition designed to persuade an audience into thinking in a specific manner about the word or term.

- Oil drilling → energy exploration
- Estate tax → death tax
- School vouchers → opportunity scholarships
- Eavesdropping → electronic intercepts
- Global warming → climate change

Luntz has essentially defined the terms in a new way that has a clear political bent and that may make the term more acceptable to some audiences, especially those who do not question the lexical meaning of the new term. For example, "oil drilling" may have negative connotations among citizens who are concerned about the environmental impact of drilling, whereas "energy exploration" may have much more positive connotations among the same group.

Stipulative Definitions

A **stipulative definition** is a definition assigned to a word or term by the person who coins that word or term for the first time. In 1969, Laurence Peter and Raymond Hull wrote a book called *The Peter Principle: Why Things Always Go Wrong*. In this book, they defined the "Peter Principle" as "In a Hierarchy Every Employee Tends to Rise to His [sic] Level of Incompetence."[9] Because Peter and Hull coined the term "Peter Principle," it was up to them to define the term as they saw fit. You cannot argue with this definition; it simply is the definition that was stipulated.

> **stipulative definition**
>
> Definition given to a word or term the first time that word or term is coined by someone.

Theoretical Definitions

Theoretical definitions are used to describe all parts related to a particular type of idea or object. Admittedly, these definitions are frequently ambiguous and difficult to fully comprehend. For example, if you attempted to define the word "peace" in a manner that could be used to describe all aspects of peace, then you would be using a theoretical definition. These definitions are considered theoretical because the definitions attempt to create an all-encompassing theory of the word itself.

> **theoretical definition**
>
> Definition used to describe all parts related to a particular type idea or object.

In an interpersonal communication course, one of our coauthors asked a group of random people online to define the term "falling in love." Here are some of the theoretical definitions they provided:

I think falling in love would be the act of feeling attracted to a person, with mutual respect given to each other, a strong desire to be close and near a person,…and more.

Being content with the person you are with and missing them every minute they are gone.

Um…falling in love is finding a guy with lots of credit cards and no balances owing.

Falling in love is when you take away the feeling, the passion, and the romance in a relationship and find out you still care for that person.

Meeting someone who makes your heart sing.

Skydiving for someone's lips.

Definitions are important to provide clarity for your audience. Effective speakers strike a balance between using definitions where they are needed to increase audience understanding and leaving out definitions of terms that the audience is likely to know. For example, you may need to define what a "claw hammer" is when speaking to a group of Cub Scouts learning about basic tools, but you would appear foolish—or even condescending—if you defined it in a speech to a group of carpenters who use claw hammers every day. On the other hand, just assuming that others know the terms you are using can lead to ineffective communication as well. Medical doctors are often criticized for using technical terms while talking to their patients without taking time to define those terms. Patients may then walk away not really understanding what their health situation is or what needs to be done about it.

2.3 Examples

Another often-used type of support is examples. An example is a specific situation, problem, or story designed to help illustrate a principle, method, or phenomenon. Examples are useful because they can help make an abstract idea more concrete for an audience by providing a specific case. Let's examine four common types of examples used as support: positive, negative, nonexamples, and best examples.

Positive Examples

positive example

Form of example used to clarify or clearly illustrate a principle, method, or phenomenon.

A **positive example** is used to clarify or clearly illustrate a principle, method, or phenomenon. A speaker discussing crisis management could talk about how a local politician handled herself when a local newspaper reported that her husband was having an affair or give an example of a professional baseball player who immediately came clean about steroid use. These examples would provide a positive model for how a corporation in the first instance, and an individual in the second instance, should behave in crisis management. The purpose of a positive example is to show a desirable solution, decision, or course of action.

Negative Examples

negative example

Form of example used to illustrate how people should not behave.

Negative examples, by contrast, are used to illustrate what *not* to do. On the same theme of crisis management, a speaker could discuss the lack of communication from Union Carbide during the 1984 tragedy in Bhopal, India, or the many problems with how the US government responded to Hurricane Katrina in 2005. The purpose of a negative example is to show an undesirable solution, decision, or course of action.

Nonexamples

A **nonexample** is used to explain what something is *not*. On the subject of crisis management, you might mention a press release for a new Adobe Acrobat software upgrade as an example of corporate communication that is not crisis management. The press release nonexample helps the audience differentiate between crisis management and other forms of corporate communication.

nonexample
Form of example used to explain what something is not.

Best Examples

The final type of example is called the **best example** because it is held up as the "best" way someone should behave within a specific context. On the crisis management theme, a speaker could show a clip of an effective CEO speaking during a press conference to show how one should behave both verbally and nonverbally during a crisis. While positive examples show appropriate ways to behave, best examples illustrate the best way to behave in a specific context.

best example
Form of example used to explain the best way someone should behave within a specific context.

Although examples can be very effective at helping an audience to understand abstract or unfamiliar concepts, they do have one major drawback: some audience members may dismiss them as unusual cases that do not represent what happens most of the time. For example, some opponents of wearing seat belts claim that *not* wearing your seat belt can help you be thrown from a car and save you from fire or other hazards in the wrecked automobile. Even if a speaker has a specific example of an accident where this was true, many audience members would see this example as a rare case and thus not view it as strong support.

Simply finding an example to use, then, is not enough. An effective speaker needs to consider how the audience will respond to the example and how the example fits with what else the audience knows, as discussed under the heading of accuracy earlier in this chapter.

2.4   Narratives

A fourth form of support are **narratives**, or stories that help an audience understand the speaker's message. Narratives are similar to examples except that narratives are generally longer and take on the form of a story with a clear arc (beginning, middle, and end). People like stories. In fact, narratives are so important that communication scholar Walter Fisher believes humans are innately storytelling animals, so appealing to people through stories is a great way to support one's speech.[10]

narrative
An illustrative story or extended example with a clear beginning, middle, and end.

However, you have an ethical responsibility as a speaker to clearly identify whether the narrative you are sharing is real or hypothetical. In 1981, *Washington Post* reporter Janet Cooke was awarded a Pulitzer Prize for her story of an eight-year-old heroin addict.[11] After acknowledging that her story was a fake, she lost her job and the prize was rescinded.[12] In 2009, Louisiana Governor Bobby Jindal gave a nationally televised speech where he recounted a story of his interaction with a local sheriff in getting help for Hurricane Katrina victims. His story was later found to be false; Jindal admitted that he had heard the sheriff tell the story after it happened but he had not really been present at the time.[13]

Obviously, we are advocating that you select narratives that are truthful when you use this form of support in a speech. Clella Jaffe explains that narratives are a fundamental part of public speaking and that narratives can be used for support in all three general purposes of speaking: informative, persuasive, and entertaining. [14]

Informative Narratives

Jaffe defines **informative narratives** as those that provide information or explanations about a speaker's topic.[15] Informative narratives can help audiences understand nature and natural phenomena, for example. Often the most complicated science and mathematical issues in our world can be understood through the use of story. While many people may not know all the mathematics behind gravity, most of us have grown up with the story of how Sir Isaac Newton was hit on the head by an apple and developed the theory of gravity. Even if the story is not precisely accurate, it serves as a way to help people grasp the basic concept of gravity.

informative narrative
Type of narrative used to provide information or explanations about a speaker's topic.

Persuasive Narratives

Persuasive narratives are stories used to persuade people to accept or reject a specific attitude, value, belief, or behavior. Religious texts are filled with persuasive narratives designed to teach followers various attitudes, values, beliefs, and behaviors. Parables or fables are designed to teach people basic lessons about life. For example, read the following fable from Aesop (http://www.aesopfables.com): "One winter a farmer found a snake stiff and frozen with cold. He had compassion on it, and taking it up, placed it in his bosom. The Snake was quickly revived by the warmth, and resuming its natural instincts, bit its benefactor, inflicting on him a mortal wound. 'Oh,' cried the Farmer with his last breath,

persuasive narrative
Type of narrative used to persuade people to accept or reject a specific attitude, value, belief, or behavior.

'I am rightly served for pitying a scoundrel.'" This persuasive narrative is designed to warn people that just because you help someone in need doesn't mean the other person will respond in kind.

Entertaining Narratives

Entertaining narratives are stories designed purely to delight an audience and transport them from their daily concerns. Some professional speakers make a very good career by telling their own stories of success or how they overcame life's adversities. Comedians such as Jeff Foxworthy tell stories that are ostensibly about their own lives in a manner designed to make the audience laugh. While entertaining narratives may be a lot of fun, people should use them sparingly as support for a more serious topic or for a traditional informative or persuasive speech.

2.5   Testimony

Another form of support you may employ during a speech is testimony. When we use the word "testimony" in this text, we are specifically referring to expert opinion or direct accounts of witnesses to provide support for your speech. Notice that within this definition, we refer to both expert and eyewitness testimony.

Expert Testimony

Expert testimony accompanies the discussion we had earlier in this chapter related to what qualifies someone as an expert. In essence, **expert testimony** expresses the attitudes, values, beliefs, or behaviors recommended by someone who is an acknowledged expert on a topic. For example, imagine that you're going to give a speech on why physical education should be mandatory for all grades K–12 in public schools. During the course of your research, you come across *The Surgeon General's Vision for a Fit and Healthy Nation* (http://www.surgeongeneral.gov/library/obesityvision/obesityvision2010.pdf). You might decide to cite information from within the report written by US Surgeon General Dr. Regina Benjamin about her strategies for combating the problem of childhood obesity within the United States. If so, you are using the words from Dr. Benjamin, as a noted expert on the subject, to support your speech's basic premise. Her expertise is being used to give credibility to your claims.

Eyewitness Testimony

Eyewitness testimony, on the other hand, is given by someone who has direct contact with the phenomenon of your speech topic. Imagine that you are giving a speech on the effects of the 2010 "Deepwater Horizon" disaster in the Gulf of Mexico. Perhaps one of your friends happened to be on a flight that passed over the Gulf of Mexico and the pilot pointed out where the platform was. You could tell your listeners about your friend's testimony of what she saw as she was flying over the spill.

However, using eyewitness testimony as support can be a little tricky because you are relying on someone's firsthand account, and firsthand accounts may not always be reliable. As such, you evaluate the credibility of your witness and the recency of the testimony.

To evaluate your witness's credibility, you should first consider how you received the testimony. Did you ask the person for the testimony, or did he or she give you the information without being asked? Second, consider whether your witness has anything to gain from his or her testimony. Basically, you want to know that your witness isn't biased.

Second, consider whether your witness' account was recent or something that happened some time ago. With a situation like the BP oil spill, the date when the spill was seen from the air makes a big difference. If the witness saw the oil spill when the oil was still localized, he or she could not have seen the eventual scope of the disaster.

Overall, the more detail you can give about the witness and when the witness made his or her observation, the more useful that witness testimony will be when attempting to create a solid argument. However, never rely completely on eyewitness testimony because this form of support is not always the most reliable and may still be perceived as biased by a segment of your audience.

2.6   Analogies

An analogy is a figure of speech that compares two ideas or objects, showing how they are similar in some way. Analogies, for public speaking purposes, can also be based in logic. The logical notion of analogies starts with the idea that two ideas or objects are similar, and because of this similarity, the two ideas or objects must be similar in other ways as well. There are two different types of analogies that speakers can employ: figurative and literal.

Figurative Analogies

Figurative analogies compare two ideas or objects from two different classes. For the purposes of understanding analogies, a "class" refers to a group that has common attributes, characteristics, qualities, or traits. For example, you can compare a new airplane to an eagle. In this case, airplanes and eagles clearly are not the same type of objects. While both may have the ability to fly, airplanes are made by humans and eagles exist in nature.

Alternatively, you could attempt to compare ideas such as the struggle of The Church of Reality (http://www.churchofreality.org/wisdom/welcome_home/, a group that sees the use of marijuana as a religious sacrament) to the struggle of the civil rights movement. Is a church's attempt to get marijuana legalized truly the same as the 1960s civil rights movement? Probably not, in most people's view, as fighting for human rights is not typically seen as equivalent to being able to use a controlled substance.

Figurative analogies are innately problematic because people often hear them and immediately dismiss them as far-fetched. While figurative analogies may be very vivid and help a listener create a mental picture, they do not really help a listener determine the validity of the information being presented. Furthermore, speakers often overly rely on figurative analogies when they really don't have any other solid evidence. Overall, while figurative analogies may be useful, we recommend solidifying them with other, more tangible support.

figurative analogy

Comparison between two ideas or objects from two different classes.

Literal Analogies

Literal analogies, on the other hand, compare two objects or ideas that clearly belong to the same class. The goal of the literal analogy is to demonstrate that the two objects or ideas are similar; therefore, they should have further similarities that support your argument. For example, maybe you're giving a speech on a new fast-food brand that you think will be a great investment. You could easily compare that new fast-food brand to preexisting brands like McDonald's, Subway, or Taco Bell. If you can show that the new start-up brand functions similarly to other brands, you can use that logic to suggest that the new brand will also have the same kind of success as the existing brands.

When using literal analogies related to ideas, make sure that the ideas are closely related and can be viewed as similar. For example, take the Church of Reality discussed in Section 2. You could compare the Church of Reality's use of marijuana to the Native American Church's legal exemption to use peyote in its religious practices. In this instance, comparing two different religious groups' use of illegal drugs and demonstrating that one has legal exemption supports the idea that the other should have an exemption, too.

As with figurative analogies, make sure that the audience can see a reasonable connection between the two ideas or objects being compared. If your audience sees your new fast-food brand as very different from McDonald's or Subway, then they will not accept your analogy. You are basically asking your audience to confirm the logic of your comparison, so if they don't see the comparison as valid, it won't help to support your message.

literal analogy

Comparison between two objects or ideas that clearly belong to the same class.

KEY TAKEAWAYS

- Speakers often use facts and statistics to reinforce or demonstrate information. Unfortunately, many speakers and audience members do not have a strong mathematical background, so it is important to understand the statistics used and communicate this information to the audience.

- Speakers use definitions—which may be lexical, persuasive, stipulative, or theoretical—to clarify their messages. Lexical definitions state how a word is used within a given language. Persuasive definitions are devised to express a word or term in a specific persuasive manner. Stipulative definitions are created when a word or term is coined. Theoretical definitions attempt to describe all parts related to a particular type of idea or object.

- Examples—positive, negative, non, and best—help the audience grasp a concept. Positive examples are used to clarify or clearly illustrate a principle, method, or phenomenon. Negative examples show how not to behave in a specific situation. Nonexamples are used to express what something is not. Best examples show the best way someone should behave in a situation.

- Narratives can be used in all three general purposes of speaking: informative, persuasive, and entertaining. Informative narratives provide information or explanations about a speaker's topic. Persuasive narratives are stories a speaker can use to get his or her audience to accept or reject a specific attitude, value, belief, or behavior. Entertaining narratives are stories that are designed purely to delight an audience. Speakers have an ethical obligation to let the audience know whether a narrative is true or hypothetical.

- Expert testimony is an account given by someone who is a recognized expert on a given topic. Eyewitness testimony is an account given by an individual who has had firsthand experience with a specific phenomenon or idea. Explaining the context of the testimony is important so your audience can evaluate the likelihood that the testimony is accurate, current, and unbiased.

- Analogies, both figurative and literal, can help audiences understand unfamiliar concepts. Figurative analogies compare two ideas or objects from two different classes. Conversely, literal analogies compare two objects or ideas that clearly belong to the same class. Speakers using analogies need to make sure that the audience will be able to see the similarity between the objects or ideas being compared.

EXERCISES

1. Look at the speech you are currently preparing for your public speaking class. What types of support are you using? Could you enhance the credibility of your speech by using other types of support? If so, what types of support do you think you are lacking?

2. Find and analyze a newspaper op-ed piece or letter to the editor that takes a position on an issue. Which types of support does the writer use? How effective and convincing do you think the use of support is? Why?

3. You've been asked to give a speech on child labor within the United States. Provide a list of possible examples you could use in your speech. You should have one from each of the four categories: positive, negative, non, and best.

4. Of the three types of narratives (informative, persuasive, and entertaining), which one would you recommend to a friend who is giving a sales presentation. Why?

3.   USING SUPPORT AND CREATING ARGUMENTS

LEARNING OBJECTIVES

1. Explain how to distinguish between useful and nonuseful forms of support.
2. Understand the five ways support is used within a speech.
3. Describe the purpose of a reverse outline.
4. Clarify why it is important to use support for every claim made within a speech.
5. Evaluate the three-step process for using support within a speech.

Supporting one's ideas with a range of facts and statistics, definitions, examples, narratives, testimony, and analogies can make the difference between a boring speech your audience will soon forget and one that has a lasting effect on their lives.

Although the research process is designed to help you find effective support, you still need to think through how you will use the support you have accumulated. In this section, we will examine how to use support effectively in one's speech, first by examining the types of support one needs in a speech and then by seeing how support can be used to enhance one's argument.

3.1   Understanding Arguments

You may associate the word "argument" with a situation in which two people are having some kind of conflict. But in this context we are using a definition for the word **argument** that goes back to the ancient Greeks, who saw arguments as a set of logical premises leading to a clear conclusion. While we lack the time for an entire treatise on the nature and study of arguments, we do want to highlight some of the basic principles in argumentation.

First, all arguments are based on a series of statements that are divided into two basic categories: premises and conclusions. A **premise** is a statement that is designed to provide support or evidence, whereas the **conclusion** is a statement that can be clearly drawn from the provided premises. Let's look at an example and then explain this in more detail:

Premise 1: Eating fast food has been linked to childhood obesity.

Premise 2: Childhood obesity is clearly linked to early onset type 2 diabetes, which can have many negative health ramifications.

Conclusion: Therefore, for children to avoid developing early onset type 2 diabetes, they must have their fast-food intake limited.

In this example, the first two statements are premises linking fast food to childhood obesity to diabetes. Once we've made this logical connection, we can then provide a logical conclusion that one important way of preventing type 2 diabetes is to limit, if not eliminate, fast food from children's diets. While this may not necessary be a popular notion for many people, the argument itself is logically sound.

How, then, does this ultimately matter for you and your future public speaking endeavors? Well, a great deal of persuasive speaking is built on creating arguments that your listeners can understand and that will eventually influence their ideas or behaviors. In essence, creating strong arguments is a fundamental part of public speaking.

Now, in the example above, we are clearly missing one important part of the argument process—support or evidence. So far we have presented two premises that many people may believe, but we need support or evidence for those premises if we are going to persuade people who do not already believe those statements. As such, when creating logical arguments (unless you are a noted expert on a subject), you must provide support to ensure that your arguments will be seen as credible. And that is what we will discuss next.

3.2   Sifting Through Your Support

When researching a topic, you're going to find a range of different types of supporting evidence. You may find examples of all six types of support: facts and statistics, definitions, examples, narratives, testimony, and analogies. Sooner or later, you are going to have to make some decisions as to which pieces of support you will use and which you won't. While there is no one way to select your support, here are some helpful suggestions.

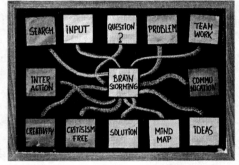

© Thinkstock

argument

A set of logical premises leading to a clear conclusion.

premise

Part of an argument represented by a statement or series of statements designed to provide support or evidence for a conclusion.

conclusion

Part of an argument represented that can be clearly or logically drawn from the provided premises.

Use a Variety of Support Types

One of the most important parts of using support is variety. Nothing will kill a speech faster than if you use the same type of support over and over again. Try to use as much support as needed to make your point without going overboard. You might decide to begin with a couple of definitions and rely on a gripping piece of eyewitness testimony as your other major support. Or you might use a combination of facts, examples, and narratives. In another case, statistics and examples might be most effective. Audience members are likely to have different preferences for support; some may like statistics while others really find narratives compelling. By using a variety of forms of support, you are likely to appeal to a broader range of audience members and thus effectively adapt to your audience. Even if your audience members prefer a specific form of support, providing multiple types of support is important to keep them interested. To use an analogy, even people who love ice cream would get tired of it if they ate only ice cream every day for a week, so variety is important.

Choose Appropriate Forms of Support

Depending on the type of speech you are giving, your speech's context, and your audience, different types of evidence may or may not be appropriate. While speeches using precise lexical definitions may be useful for the courtroom, they may not be useful in an after-dinner speech to entertain. At the same time, entertaining narratives may be great for a speech whose general purpose is to entertain, but may decrease a speaker's credibility when attempting to persuade an audience about a serious topic.

Check for Relevance

Another consideration about potential support is whether or not it is relevant. Each piece of supporting material you select needs to support the specific purpose of your speech. You may find the coolest quotation, but if that quotation doesn't really help your core argument in your speech, you need to leave it out. If you start using too many irrelevant support sources, your audience will quickly catch on and your credibility will drop through the floor.

Your support materials should be relevant not only to your topic but also to your audience. If you are giving a speech to an audience of sixty-year-olds, you may be able to begin with "Think back to where you were when you heard that President Kennedy had been shot," but this would be meaningless with an audience of twenty-five-year-olds. Similarly, references to music download sites or the latest popular band may not be effective with audiences who are not interested in music.

Don't Go Overboard

In addition to being relevant, supporting materials need to help you support your speech's specific purpose without interfering with your speech. You may find three different sources that support your speech's purpose in the same way. If that happens, you shouldn't include all three forms of support. Instead, pick the form of support that is the most beneficial for your speech. Remember, the goal is to support your speech, not to have the support become your speech.

Don't Manipulate Your Support

support-manipulation

The unethical practice of finding and using support designed to enhance one's argument in a devious manner.

The last factor related to shifting through your support involves a very important ethical area called **support-manipulation**. Often speakers will attempt to find support that says exactly what they want it to say despite the fact that the overwhelming majority of evidence says the exact opposite. When you go out of your way to pull the wool over your audience's eyes, you are being unethical and not treating your audience with respect. Here are some very important guidelines to consider to avoiding support-manipulation:

- Do not overlook significant factors or individuals related to your topic.
- Do not ignore evidence that does not support your speech's specific purpose.
- Do not jump to conclusions that are simply not justified based on the supporting evidence you have.
- Do not use evidence to support faulty logic.
- Do not use out-of-date evidence that is no longer supported.
- Do not use evidence out of its original context.
- Do not knowingly use evidence from a source that is clearly biased.
- Make sure you clearly cite all your supporting evidence within your speech.

3.3   Using Support within Your Speech

Now that we've described ways to sift through your evidence, it's important to discuss how to use your evidence within your speech. In the previous sections of this chapter, we've talked about the various types of support you can use (facts and statistics, definitions, examples, narratives, testimonies, and analogies). In this section, we're going to examine how these types of evidence are actually used within a speech. Then we will discuss ways to think through the support you need for a speech and also how to actually use support while speaking.

Forms of Speech Support

Let's begin by examining the forms that support can take in a speech: quotations, paraphrases, summaries, numerical support, and pictographic support.

Quotations

The first common form of support utilized in a speech is direct quotation. **Direct quotations** occur when Speaker A uses the exact wording by another speaker or writer within his or her new speech. Quotations are very helpful and can definitely provide you a tool for supporting your speech's specific purpose. Here are five tips for using quotations within a speech:

direct quotation
Repeating the exact wording of another speaker or writer within a speech.

1. Use a direct quotation if the original author's words are witty, engaging, distinct, or particularly vivid.
2. Use a direct quotation if you want to highlight a specific expert and his or her expertise within your speech.
3. Use a direct quotation if you are going to specifically analyze something that is said within the quotation. If your analysis depends on the exact wording of the quotation, then it is important to use the quotation.
4. Keep quotations to a minimum. One of the biggest mistakes some speakers make is just stringing together a series of quotations and calling it a speech. Remember, a speech is your unique insight into a topic, not just a series of quotations.
5. Keep quotations short. Long quotations can lose an audience, and the connection between your support and your argument can get lost.

Paraphrases

The second form support takes on during a speech is paraphrasing. **Paraphrasing** involves taking the general idea or theme from another speaker or author and condensing the idea or theme in your own words. As we described in Chapter 7, a mistake that some speakers make is dropping a couple of words or rearranging some words within a direct quotation and thinking that is a paraphrase. When paraphrasing you need to understand the other speaker or author's ideas well enough to relate them without looking back at the original. Here are four tips for using paraphrases in your speeches:

paraphrase
Taking the central idea or theme from another speaker or author and adapting it in one's own words.

1. Paraphrase when you can say it more concisely than the original speaker or author.
2. Paraphrase when the exact wording from the original speaker or author won't improve your audience's understanding of the support.
3. Paraphrase when you want to adapt an example, analogy, or narrative by another speaker or author to make its relevance more evident.
4. Paraphrase information that is not likely to be questioned by your audience. If you think your audience may question your support, then relying on a direct quotation may be more effective.

Summaries

Whereas quotations and paraphrases are taking a whole text and singling out a couple of lines or a section, a **summary** involves condensing or encapsulating the entire text as a form of support. Summaries are helpful when you want to clearly spell out the intent behind a speaker's or author's text. Here are three suggestions for using summaries within your speech.

summary
An encapsulation or condensation of the entire text from another speaker or author.

1. Summarize when you need another speaker or author's complete argument to understand the argument within your speech.
2. Summarize when explaining possible counterarguments to the one posed within your speech.
3. Summarize when you need to cite a number of different sources effectively and efficiently to support a specific argument.

Numerical Support

numerical support

The use of numbers, data, or statistics within a speech to support a point.

Speakers often have a need to use **numerical support**, or citing data and numbers within a speech. The most common reason for using numerical support comes when a speaker needs to cite statistics. When using data to support your speech, you need to make sure that your audience can accurately interpret the numbers in the same way you are doing. Here are three tips for using numerical support:

1. Clearly state the numbers used and where they came from.
2. Make sure you explain what the numbers mean and how you think they should be interpreted.
3. If the numbers are overly complicated or if you use a variety of numbers within a speech, consider turning this support into a visual aid to enhance your audience's understanding of the numerical support.

Pictographic Support

pictographic support

Photographic, diagrammatic, or other visual representation of an object or process.

The last form of support commonly used in speeches we label pictographic support, but it is more commonly referred to as visual aids. **Pictographic support** is any drawn or visual representation of an object or process. For the purposes of this chapter, we call visual aids pictographic support in order to stress that we are using images as a form of support taken from a source. For example, if you're giving a speech on how to swing a golf club, you could bring in a golf club and demonstrate exactly how to use the golf club. While the golf club in this instance is a visual aid, it is not pictographic support. If you showed a diagram illustrating the steps for an effective golf swing, the diagram is an example of pictographic support. So while all forms of pictographic support are visual aids, not all visual aids are pictographic support. Here are five suggestions for effectively using pictographic support in your speech.

1. Use pictographic support when it would be easier and shorter than orally explaining an object or process.
2. Use pictographic support when you really want to emphasize the importance of the support. Audiences recall information more readily when they both see and hear it than if they see or hear the information.
3. Make sure that pictographic support is aesthetically pleasing. See Chapter 15 on using visual aids for more ideas on how to make visual aids aesthetically pleasing.
4. Pictographic support should be easy to understand, and it should take less time to use than words alone.
5. Make sure everyone in your audience can easily see your pictographic support. If listeners cannot see it, then it will not help them understand how it is supposed to help your speech's specific purpose.

Is Your Support Adequate?

Now that we've examined the ways to use support in your speech, how do you know if you have enough support?

Use a Reverse Outline

reverse outline

Tool used to determine the adequacy of support by starting with a speaker's conclusion and logically working backward through the speech to determine if the support provided is appropriate and comprehensive.

One recommendation we have for selecting the appropriate support for your speech is what we call a reverse outline. A **reverse outline** is a tool you can use to determine the adequacy of your speech's support by starting with your conclusion and logically working backward through your speech to determine if the support you provided is appropriate and comprehensive. In essence, we recommend that you think of your speech in terms of the conclusion first and then work your way backward showing how you get to the conclusion. By forcing yourself to think about logic in reverse, you're more likely to find missteps along the way. This technique is not only helpful for analyzing the overall flow of your speech, but it can also let you see if different sections of your speech are not completely supported individually.

Support Your Claims

When selecting the different types of support for your speech, you need to make sure that every claim you make within the speech can be supported within the speech. For example, if you state, "The majority of Americans want immigration reform," you need to make sure that you have a source that actually says this. As noted at the beginning of this chapter, too often people make claims within a speech that they have no support for whatsoever. When you go through your speech, you need to make sure that each and every claim that you make is adequately supported by the evidence you have selected to use within the speech.

Oral Presentation

Finally, after you have selected and evaluated your forms of support, it is time to plan how you will present your support orally within your speech. How will you present the information to make it effective? To help you think about using support, we recommend a three-step process: setup, execution, and analysis.

Setup

The first step in using support within a speech is what we call the setup. The **setup** is a sentence or phrase in which you explain to your audience where the information you are using came from. Note that if you found the information on a website, it is not sufficient to merely give your audience the URL. Depending on the source of your support, all the following information could be useful: name of source, location of source, date of source, name of author, and identification of author. First, you need to tell your audience the name of your source. Whether you are using a song or an article from a magazine, you need to tell your audience the name of the person who wrote it and its title. Second, if your source comes from a larger work, you need to include the location of the source. For example, a single article (name of source) may come from a magazine (the location). Third, you need to specify the date of the source. Depending on the type of source you are using, you may need to provide just a year or the day and month as well. You should provide as much information on the date as is provided on the copyright information page of the source.

Thus far we've talked only about the information you need to provide specifically about the source; let's now switch gears and talk about the author. When discussing the author, you need to clearly explain not only who the author is but also why the author is an expert (if appropriate). Some sources are written by authors who are not experts, so you really don't need to explain their expertise. In other cases, your audience will already know why the source is an expert, so there is less need to explain why the source is an expert. For example, if giving a speech on current politics in the United States, you probably do not need to explain the expertise of Barack Obama or John Boehner. However, when you don't provide information on an author's expertise and your audience does not already know why the source is an expert, your audience will question the validity of your support.

Now that we've explained the basic information necessary for using support within a speech, here are two different examples:

1. According to Melanie Smithfield in an article titled "Do It Right, or Do It Now," published in the June 18, 2009, issue of *Time Magazine*…

2. According to Roland Smith, a legendary civil rights activist and former chair of the Civil Rights Defense League, in his 2001 book *The Path of Peace*…

In the first example we have an author who wrote an article in a magazine, and in the second one we have an author of a book. In both cases, we provided the information that was necessary to understand where the source was located. The more information we can provide our audiences about our support, the more information our audiences have to evaluate the strength of our arguments.

Execution

Once we have set up the support, the second part of using support is what we call execution. The **execution** of support involves actually reading a quotation, paraphrasing a speaker or author's words, summarizing a speaker or author's ideas, providing numerical support, or showing pictographic support. Effective execution should be seamless and flow easily within the context of your speech. While you want your evidence to make an impact, you also don't want it to seem overly disjointed. One mistake that some novice public speakers make is that when they start providing evidence, their whole performance changes and the use of evidence looks and sounds awkward. Make sure you practice the execution of your evidence when you rehearse your speech.

Analysis

The final stage of using support effectively is the one which many speakers forget: **analysis** of the support. Too often speakers use support without ever explaining to an audience how they should interpret it. While we don't want to "talk down" to our listeners, audiences often need to be shown the connection between the support provided and the argument made. Here are three basic steps you can take to ensure your audience will make the connection between your support and your argument:

1. Summarize the support in your own words (unless you started with a summary).

2. Specifically tell your audience how the support relates to the argument.

3. Draw a sensible conclusion based on your support. We cannot leave an audience hanging, so drawing a conclusion helps complete the support package.

setup

Step in the oral presentation of support process in which the speaker explains to the audience where the information being used came from.

execution

Step in the oral presentation of support process in which the speaker delivers a quotation, paraphrase, or summary; provides numerical support; or shows pictographic support.

analysis

Step in the oral presentation of support process in which the speaker explains to the audience how they should interpret the support provided.

KEY TAKEAWAYS

- Systematically think through the support you have accumulated through your research. Examine the accumulated support to ensure that a variety of forms of support are used. Choose appropriate forms of support depending on the speech context or audience. Make sure all the support is relevant to the specific purpose of your speech and to your audience. Don't go overboard using so much support that the audience is overwhelmed. Lastly, don't manipulate supporting materials.

- Speakers ultimately turn support materials into one of five formats. Quotations are used to take another speaker or author's ideas and relay them verbatim. Paraphrases take a small portion of a source and use one's own words to simplify and clarify the central idea. Summaries are used to condense an entire source into a short explanation of the source's central idea. Numerical support is used to quantify information from a source. Pictographic support helps audience members both see and hear the idea being expressed by a source.

- Use a reverse outline to ensure that all the main ideas are thoroughly supported. Start with the basic conclusion and then work backward to ensure that the argument is supported at every point of the speech.

- Every claim within a speech should be supported. While some experts can get away with not supporting every claim, nonexperts must show they have done their homework.

- To present support in a speech, use a three-step process: setup, execution, and analysis. The setup explains who the speaker or author is and provides the name of the source and other relevant bibliographic information to the audience. The execution is the actual delivery of the support. Lastly, a speaker needs to provide analysis explaining how an audience should interpret the support provided.

EXERCISES

1. Choose and analyze a speech from the top one hundred speeches given during the twentieth century (http://www.americanrhetoric.com/top100speechesall.html). How does this speaker go through the three-step process for using support?

2. Think about your upcoming speech and audience. What forms of support could you use to enhance your speech? Why did you select those options? Could you use other options?

3. As you prepare your next speech, script out how you will use the three-step process for ensuring that all your support is used effectively.

4. CHAPTER EXERCISES

SPEAKING ETHICALLY

While preparing a speech on the Department of Homeland Security (DHS), Aban runs across a website that has a lot of useful information. The website has numerous articles and links that all discuss the importance of the different functions of the DHS. Being a good speaker, Aban delves into the website to determine the credibility of the information being provided.

Aban quickly realizes that the group sponsoring the website is a fringe-militia group that believes no immigrants should be allowed into the United States. While the information Aban is interested has nothing to do with immigration, he wonders if all the information provided on the website has been distorted to support the organization's basic cause.

1. Should Aban use the useful information about DHS even though the other information on the website is from an extremist group?

2. Are all sources on the extremist group's website automatically suspect because of the group's stated anti-immigration stance?

3. Is it ethical for Aban to use any of the information from this website?

4. If Aban was a friend of yours and he showed you the website, how would you tell him to proceed?

END-OF-CHAPTER ASSESSMENT

1. Which of the following is *not* a potential source of bias that a speaker or author may have?

    a. organizations to which the speaker or author belongs

    b. political affiliations of the speaker or author

    c. financial interests of the speaker or author

    d. information that is widely cited and supported by other sources

    e. information that is only found on the speaker's or author's website

2. During a speech, Juanita says the following: "In his book *The Dilbert Principle*, Scott Adams defines the Dilbert principle as the idea 'that companies tend to systematically promote their least-competent employees to management (generally middle management), in order to limit the amount of damage they are capable of doing.'" What type of definition is Juanita using?

    a. lexical

    b. persuasive

    c. précising

    d. stipulative

    e. theoretical

3. Edward was delivering a speech on using the Internet for job hunting. In his speech he uses the example of his friend Barry, who was able to network using LinkedIn and other social networking sites to find his dream job. What type of example has Edward used?

    a. positive

    b. negative

    c. non

    d. circular

    e. best

4. Which of the following is *not* a potential form of support manipulation?

    a. overlooking significant factors or individuals related to your topic

    b. ignoring evidence that does not support your speech's specific purpose

    c. using evidence in its original context

    d. using evidence to support faulty logic

    e. using evidence from clearly biased sources

5. During her speech about rodents, Anna shows a series of slides explaining the lifecycle of chipmunks. What form of support has Anna used within her speech?

    a. pictographic

    b. quotation

    c. paraphrase

    d. numerical

    e. summary

ANSWER KEY

1. d
2. d
3. e
4. c
5. a

ENDNOTES

1. Malthus, T. R. (1798). *An essay on the principle of population as it affects the future improvement of society, with remarks on the speculations of Mr. Godwin, M. Condorcet, and other writers.* London, England: J. Johnson, in St. Paul's Churchyard.

2. See, for example, Lizotte, K. (2007). *The expert's edge: Become the go-to authority people turn to every time.* New York, NY: McGraw-Hill.

3. Weinstein, B. D. (1993). What is an expert? *Theoretical Medicine, 14,* 57–93.

4. Germain, M. L. (2006). *Development and preliminary validation of a psychometric measure of expertise: The generalized expertise measure (GEM).* (Unpublished doctoral dissertation). Barry University, Florida.

5. Quart, A. (2010, July/August). The trouble with experts: The web allows us to question authority in new ways. *Columbia Journalism Review.* Retrieved from http://www.cjr.org

6. ScienceBlogs LLC (n.d.). Who (or what) is Orac? [Web log post]. Retrieved from http://scienceblogs.com/insolence/; see also http://scienceblogs.com/insolence/medicine/autism

7. Twain, M. (1924). *Autobiography* (Vol. 1). New York, NY: Harper & Bros., p. 538.

8. Luntz, F. (2007). *Words that work: It's not what you say, it's what people hear.* New York, NY: Hyperion.

9. Peter, L. J., & Hull, R. (1969). *The Peter principle: Why things always go wrong.* New York, NY: William Morrow & Company, p. 15.

10. Fisher, W. R. (1987). *Human communication as narration: Toward a philosophy of reason, value, and action.* Columbia, SC: University of South Carolina Press.

11. Cooke, J. (1980, September 28). Jimmy's world. *The Washington Post,* p. A1.

12. Green, B. (1981, April 19). The confession: At the end, there were the questions, then the tears. *The Washington Post,* p. A14.

13. Finch, S. (2009, Feb 27). Bobby Jindal's fishy Katrina story. *Daily Kos.* Retrieved from http://www.dailykos.com/story/2009/02/27/702671/-Bobby-Jindals-Fishy-Katrina-Story

14. Jaffe, C. (2010). *Public speaking: Concepts and skills for a diverse society* (6th ed.). Boston, MA: Cengage.

15. Jaffe, C. (2010). *Public speaking: Concepts and skills for a diverse society* (6th ed.). Boston, MA: Cengage.

CHAPTER 9
Introductions Matter: How to Begin a Speech Effectively

One of the most common complaints novice public speakers have is that they simply don't know how to start a speech. Many times speakers get ideas for how to begin their speeches as they go through the process of researching and organizing ideas. In this chapter, we will explore why introductions are important and various ways speakers can create memorable introductions. There may not be any one "best" way to start a speech, but we can provide some helpful guidelines that will make starting a speech much easier.

© Thinkstock

1. THE IMPORTANCE OF AN INTRODUCTION

LEARNING OBJECTIVES

1. Explain the general length of an introduction.
2. List and explain the five basic functions of an introduction.
3. Understand how to use three factors of credibility in an introduction.

The introduction for a speech is generally only 10 to 15 percent of the entire time the speaker will spend speaking. This means that if your speech is to be five minutes long, your introduction should be no more than forty-five seconds. If your speech is to be ten minutes long, then your introduction should be no more than a minute and a half. Unfortunately, that 10 to 15 percent of your speech can either make your audience interested in what you have to say or cause them to tune out before you've really gotten started. Overall, a good introduction should serve five functions. Let's examine each of these.

© Thinkstock

1.1 Gain Audience Attention and Interest

The first major purpose of an introduction is to gain your audience's attention and make them interested in what you have to say. One of the biggest mistakes that novice speakers make is to assume that people will naturally listen because the speaker is speaking. While many audiences may be polite and not talk while you're speaking, actually getting them to listen to what you are saying is a completely different challenge. Let's face it—we've all tuned someone out at some point because we weren't interested in what they had to say. If you do not get the audience's attention at the outset, it will only become more difficult to do so as you continue speaking. We'll talk about some strategies for grabbing an audience's attention later on in this chapter.

1.2 State the Purpose of Your Speech

The second major function of an introduction is to reveal the purpose of your speech to your audience. Have you ever sat through a speech wondering what the basic point was? Have you ever come away after a speech and had no idea what the speaker was talking about? An introduction is important because it forces the speaker to be mindfully aware of explaining the topic of the speech to the audience. If the speaker doesn't know what her or his topic is and cannot convey that topic to the audience, then we've got really big problems! Robert Cavett, the founder of the National Speaker's Association, used the analogy of a preacher giving a sermon when he noted, "When it's foggy in the pulpit, it's cloudy in the pews."

As we discussed in Chapter 6, the specific purpose is the one idea you want your audience to remember when you are finished with your speech. Your specific purpose is the rudder that guides your research, organization, and development of main points. The more clearly focused your purpose is, the easier your task will be in developing your speech. In addition, a clear purpose provides the audience with a single, simple idea to remember even if they daydream during the body of your speech. To develop a specific purpose, you should complete the following sentence: "I want my audience to understand that…" Notice that your specific speech purpose is phrased in terms of expected audience responses, not in terms of your own perspective.

1.3 Establish Credibility

One of the most researched areas within the field of communication has been Aristotle's concept of *ethos* or credibility. First, and foremost, the concept of credibility must be understood as a perception of receivers. You may be the most competent, caring, and trustworthy speaker in the world on a given topic, but if your audience does not perceive you as credible, then your expertise and passion will not matter. As public speakers, we need to make sure that we explain to our audiences why we are credible speakers on a given topic.

James C. McCroskey and Jason J. Teven have conducted extensive research on credibility and have determined that an individual's credibility is composed of three factors: competence, trustworthiness, and caring/goodwill.[1] **Competence** is the degree to which a speaker is perceived to be knowledgeable or expert in a given subject by an audience member. Some individuals are given expert status because of positions they hold in society. For example, Dr. Regina Benjamin, the US Surgeon General, is expected to be competent in matters related to health and wellness as a result of being the United States' top physician.

competence

The degree to which an audience member perceives a speaker as being knowledgeable or expert on a given topic.

FIGURE 9.1 Regina Benjamin

Source: Photo by Lawrence Jackson, White House photographer, http://www.whitehouse.gov/assets/images/surgeon_general-0075.jpg.

trustworthiness

The degree to which an audience member perceives a speaker as being honest.

But what if you do not possess a fancy title that lends itself to established competence? You need to explain to the audience why you are competent to speak on your topic. Keep in mind that even well-known speakers are not perceived as universally credible. US Surgeon General Regina Benjamin may be seen as competent on health and wellness issues, but may not be seen as a competent speaker on trends in Latin American music or different ways to cook summer squash. Like well-known speakers, you will need to establish your credibility on each topic you address, so establishing your competence about the energy efficiency of furnace systems during your informative speech does not automatically mean you will be seen as competent on the topic of organ donation for your persuasive speech.

The second factor of credibility noted by McCroskey and Teven is **trustworthiness**, or the degree to which an audience member perceives a speaker as honest. Nothing will turn an audience against a speaker faster than if the audience believes the speaker is lying. When an audience does not perceive a speaker as trustworthy, the information coming out of the speaker's mouth is automatically perceived as deceitful. The speaker could be 100 percent honest, but the audience will still find the information suspect. For example, in the summer of 2009, many Democratic members of Congress attempted to hold public town-hall meetings about health care. For a range of reasons, many of the people who attended these town-hall meetings refused to let their elected officials actually speak because the audiences were convinced that the Congressmen and Congresswomen were lying.

In these situations, where a speaker is in front of a very hostile audience, there is little a speaker can do to reestablish that sense of trustworthiness. These public town-hall meetings became screaming matches between the riled-up audiences and the congressional representatives. Some police departments actually ended up having to escort the representatives from the buildings because they feared for their safety. Check out this video from CNN.com to see what some of these events actually looked like: http://www.cnn.com/video/#/video/bestoftv/2009/08/07/ldt.sylvester.town.hall.cnn?iref=videosearch. We hope that you will not be in physical danger when you speak to your classmates or in other settings, but these incidents serve to underscore how important speaker trustworthiness is across speaking contexts.

Caring/goodwill is the final factor of credibility noted by McCroskey and Teven. **Caring/goodwill** refers to the degree to which an audience member perceives a speaker as caring about the audience member. As noted by Wrench, McCroskey, and Richmond, "If a receiver does not believe that a source has the best intentions in mind for the receiver, the receiver will not see the source as credible. Simply put, we are going to listen to people who we think truly care for us and are looking out for our welfare."[2] As a speaker, then, you need to establish that your information is being presented because you care about your audience and are not just trying to manipulate them. We should note that research has indicated that caring/goodwill is the most important factor of credibility. This means that if an audience believes that a speaker truly cares about the audience's best interests, the audience may overlook some competence and trust issues.

> **caring/goodwill**
>
> The degree to which an audience member believes that a speaker has the audience member's best interests at heart.

1.4   Provide Reasons to Listen

The fourth major function of an introduction is to establish a connection between the speaker and the audience, and one of the most effective means of establishing a connection with your audience is to provide them with reasons why they should listen to your speech. The idea of establishing a connection is an extension of the notion of caring/goodwill. In the chapters on Language and Speech Delivery, we'll spend a lot more time talking about how you can establish a good relationship with your audience. However, this relationship starts the moment you step to the front of the room to start speaking.

Instead of assuming the audience will make their own connections to your material, you should explicitly state how your information might be useful to your audience. Tell them directly how they might use your information themselves. It is not enough for you alone to be interested in your topic. You need to build a bridge to the audience by explicitly connecting your topic to their possible needs.

1.5   Preview Main Ideas

The last major function of an introduction is to preview the main ideas that your speech will discuss. A preview establishes the direction your speech will take. We sometimes call this process signposting because you're establishing signs for audience members to look for while you're speaking. In the most basic speech format, speakers generally have three to five major points they plan on making. During the preview, a speaker outlines what these points will be, which demonstrates to the audience that the speaker is organized.

A study by Baker found that individuals who were unorganized while speaking were perceived as less credible than those individuals who were organized.[3] Having a solid preview of the information contained within one's speech and then following that preview will definitely help a speaker's credibility. It also helps your audience keep track of where you are if they momentarily daydream or get distracted.

KEY TAKEAWAYS

- Introductions are only 10–15 percent of one's speech, so speakers need to make sure they think through the entire introduction to ensure that they will capture an audience. During an introduction, speakers attempt to impart the general and specific purpose of a speech while making their audience members interested in the speech topic, establishing their own credibility, and providing the audience with a preview of the speech structure.
- A speaker's perceived credibility is a combination of competence, trustworthiness, and caring/goodwill. Research has shown that caring/goodwill is probably the most important factor of credibility because audiences want to know that a speaker has their best interests at heart. At the same time, speakers should strive to be both competent and honest while speaking.

EXERCISES

1. What are the five basic functions of an introduction? Discuss with your classmates which purpose you think is the most important. Why?
2. Why is establishing a relationship with one's audience important? How do you plan on establishing a relationship with your audience during your next speech?
3. Of the three factors of credibility, which do you think is going to be hardest to establish with your peers during your next speech? Why? What can you do to enhance your peers' perception of your credibility?

2.   THE ATTENTION-GETTER: THE FIRST STEP OF AN INTRODUCTION

LEARNING OBJECTIVES

1. Understand the different tools speakers can use to gain their audience's attention.
2. Name some common mistakes speakers make in trying to gain attention.

© Thinkstock

attention-getter

The device a speaker uses at the beginning of a speech to capture an audience's interest and make them interested in the speech's topic.

As you know by now, a good introduction will capture an audience's attention, while a bad introduction can turn an audience against a speaker. An **attention-getter** is the device a speaker uses at the beginning of a speech to capture an audience's interest and make them interested in the speech's topic. Typically, there are four things to consider in choosing a specific attention-getting device:

1. Appropriateness or relevance to audience
2. Purpose of speech
3. Topic
4. Occasion

First, when selecting an attention-getting device, you want to make sure that the option you choose is actually appropriate and relevant to your specific audience. Different audiences will have different backgrounds and knowledge, so you should use your audience analysis to determine whether specific information you plan on using would be appropriate for a specific audience. For example, if you're giving a speech on family units to a group of individuals over the age of sixty-five, starting your speech with a reference to the television show *Gossip Girl* may not be the best idea because the television show may not be relevant to that audience.

Second, you need to consider the basic purpose of your speech. As discussed earlier in this text, there are three basic purposes you can have for giving a speech: to inform, to persuade, and to entertain. When selecting an attention-getter, you want to make sure that you select one that corresponds with your basic purpose. If your goal is to entertain an audience, then starting a speech with a quotation about how many people are dying in Africa each day from malnutrition may not be the best way to get your audience's attention. Remember, one of the basic goals of an introduction is to prepare your audience for your speech. If your attention-getter differs drastically in tone from the rest of your speech (e.g., dying in Africa when you want your audience to laugh), the disjointedness may cause your audience to become confused or tune you out completely.

Your third basic consideration when picking an attention-getting device is your speech topic. Ideally, your attention-getting device should have a relevant connection to your speech. Imagine if a speaker pulled condoms out of his pocket, yelled "Free sex!" and threw the condoms at the audience in the beginning of a speech about the economy. While this may clearly get the audience's attention, this isn't really a good way to prepare an audience for a speech about bull and bear markets. Not every attention-getter is appropriate for a given topic. Instead, a speaker could start this speech by explaining that "according to a 2004 episode of 60 Minutes, adults in the United States spend approximately $10 billion annually on adult entertainment, which is roughly the equivalent to the amounts they spend attending professional sporting events, buying music, or going out to the movies."[4] Notice how effective the shocking statistic is in clearly introducing the monetary value of the adult entertainment industry.

The last consideration when picking an attention-getting device involves the speech occasion. Different occasions will necessitate different tones, or particular styles or manners of speaking. For example, a persuasive speech about death and dying shouldn't be happy and hilarious. An informative speech on the benefits of laughing shouldn't be dull, dreary, and depressing. When selecting an attention-getter, you want to make sure that the attention-getter sets the tone for the speech.

Now that we've explored the four major considerations you must think of when selecting an attention-getter, let's look at a range of different attention-getters you may employ. Miller (1946)[5] discovered that speakers tend to use one of eleven attention-getting devices when starting a speech. The rest of this section is going to examine these eleven attention-getting devices.

2.1   Reference to Subject

The first attention-getting method to consider is to tell your audience the subject of your speech. This device is probably the most direct, but it may also be the least interesting of the possible attention-getters. Here's an example:

> *We are surrounded by statistical information in today's world, so understanding statistics is becoming paramount to citizenship in the twenty-first century.*

This sentence explicitly tells an audience that the speech they are about to hear is about the importance of understanding statistics. While this isn't the most entertaining or interesting attention-getter, it is very clear and direct.

2.2   Reference to Audience

The second attention-getting device to consider is a direct reference to the audience. In this case, the speaker has a clear understanding of the audience and points out that there is something unique about the audience that should make them interested in the speech's content. Here's an example:

© *Thinkstock*

> *As human resource professionals, you and I know the importance of talent management. In today's competitive world, we need to invest in getting and keeping the best talent for our organizations to succeed.*

In this example, the speaker reminds the audience of their shared status as human resource professionals and uses the common ground to acknowledge the importance of talent management in human resources.

2.3   Quotation

Another way to capture your listeners' attention is to use the words of another person that relate directly to your topic. Maybe you've found a really great quotation in one of the articles or books you read while researching your speech. If not, you can also use a number of sources that compile useful quotations from noted individuals. Probably the most famous quotation book of all time is *Bartlett's Familiar Quotations* (http://www.bartleby.com/100), now in its seventeenth edition. Here are some other websites that contain useful databases of quotations for almost any topic:

- http://www.quotationspage.com
- http://www.bartleby.com/quotations
- http://www.quotationreference.com
- http://www.moviequotes.com
- http://www.quotesandsayings.com
- http://www.quoteland.com

Quotations are a great way to start a speech, so let's look at an example that could be used for a speech on deception:

> *Oliver Goldsmith, a sixteenth-century writer, poet, and physician, once noted that "the true use of speech is not so much to express our wants as to conceal them."*

2.4   Reference to Current Events

Referring to a current news event that relates to your topic is often an effective way to capture attention, as it immediately makes the audience aware of how relevant the topic is in today's world. For example, consider this attention-getter for a persuasive speech on frivolous lawsuits:

> *On January 10, 2007, Scott Anthony Gomez Jr. and a fellow inmate escaped from a Pueblo, Colorado, jail. During their escape the duo attempted to rappel from the roof of the jail using a makeshift ladder of bed sheets. During Gomez's attempt to scale the building, he slipped, fell forty feet, and injured his back. After being quickly apprehended, Gomez filed a lawsuit against the jail for making it too easy for him to escape.*

In this case, the speaker is highlighting a news event that illustrates what a frivolous lawsuit is, setting up the speech topic of a need for change in how such lawsuits are handled.

2.5   Historical Reference

You may also capture your listeners' attention by referring to a historical event related to your topic. Obviously, this strategy is closely related to the previous one, except that instead of a recent news event you are reaching further back in history to find a relevant reference. For example, if you are giving a speech on the Iraq War that began in 2003, you could refer back to the Vietnam War as way of making a comparison:

> *During the 1960s and '70s, the United States intervened in the civil strife between North and South Vietnam. The result was a long-running war of attrition in which many American lives were lost and the country of Vietnam suffered tremendous damage and destruction. Today, we see a similar war being waged in Iraq. American lives are being lost, and stability has not yet returned to the region.*

In this example, the speaker is evoking the audience's memories of the Vietnam War to raise awareness of similarities to the war in Iraq.

2.6   Anecdote

anecdote

A brief account or story of an interesting or humorous event.

Another device you can use to start a speech is to tell an anecdote related to the speech's topic. An **anecdote** is a brief account or story of an interesting or humorous event. Notice the emphasis here is on the word "brief." A common mistake speakers make when telling an anecdote is to make the anecdote too long. Remember, your entire introduction should only be 10 to 15 percent of your speech, so your attention-getter must be very short.

One type of anecdote is a real story that emphasizes a speech's basic message. For example, here is an anecdote a speaker could use to begin a speech on how disconnected people are from the real world because of technology:

> *In July 2009, a high school girl named Alexa Longueira was walking along a main boulevard near her home on Staten Island, New York, typing in a message on her cell phone. Not paying attention to the world around her, she took a step and fell right into an open manhole.[6]*

parable or fable

An allegorical anecdote designed to teach general life lessons.

A second type of anecdote is a parable or fable. A **parable or fable** is an allegorical anecdote designed to teach general life lessons. The most widely known parables for most Americans are those given in the Bible and the best-known fables are Aesop's Fables (http://www.aesopfables.com). For the same speech on how disconnected people are with the real world because of technology, the speaker could have used the Fable of The Boy and the Filberts:

The ancient Greek writer Aesop told a fable about a boy who put his hand into a pitcher of filberts. The boy grabbed as many of the delicious nuts as he possibly could. But when he tried to pull them out, his hand wouldn't fit through the neck of the pitcher because he was grasping so many filberts. Instead of dropping some of them so that his hand would fit, he burst into tears and cried about his predicament. The moral of the story? "Don't try to do too much at once."[7]

After recounting this anecdote, the speaker could easily relate the fable to the notion that the technology in our society leads us to try to do too many things at once.

While parables and fables are short and entertaining, their application to your speech topic should be clear. We'll talk about this idea in more detail later in this chapter when we discuss how to link your attention-getter explicitly to your topic.

2.7   Startling Statement

The eighth device you can use to start a speech is to surprise your audience with startling information about your topic. Often, startling statements come in the form of statistics and strange facts. The goal of a good startling statistic is that it surprises the audience and gets them engaged in your topic. For example, if you're giving a speech about oil conservation, you could start by saying, "A Boeing 747 airliner holds 57,285 gallons of fuel." You could start a speech on the psychology of dreams by noting, "The average person has over 1,460 dreams a year." A strange fact, on the other hand, is a statement that does not involve numbers but is equally surprising to most audiences. For example, you could start a speech on the gambling industry by saying, "There are no clocks in any casinos in Las Vegas." You could start a speech on the Harlem Globetrotters by saying, "In 2000, Pope John Paul II became the most famous honorary member of the Harlem Globetrotters." All four of these examples came from a great website for strange facts (http://www.strangefacts.com).

Although startling statements are fun, it is important to use them ethically. First, make sure that your startling statement is factual. The Internet is full of startling statements and claims that are simply not factual, so when you find a statement you'd like to use, you have an ethical duty to ascertain its truth before you use it. Second, make sure that your startling statement is relevant to your speech and not just thrown in for shock value. We've all heard startling claims made in the media that are clearly made for purposes of shock or fear mongering. As speakers, we have an ethical obligation to avoid playing on people's emotions in this way.

2.8   Question

Another strategy for getting your audience's attention is to ask them a question. There are two types of questions commonly used as attention-getters: response questions and rhetorical questions. A **response question** is a question that the audience is expected to answer in some manner. For example, you could ask your audience, "Please raise your hand if you have ever thought about backpacking in Europe" or "Have you ever voted for the Electoral College? If so, stand up." In both of these cases, the speaker wants her or his audience to respond. A **rhetorical question**, on the other hand, is a question to which no actual reply is expected. For example, a speaker talking about the importance of HIV testing could start by asking the audience, "I have two questions that I'd like you to think about. How many students on this campus have had sexual intercourse? Of those who have had sex, how many have been tested for HIV?" In this case, the speaker does not expect the audience to give an estimate of the numbers of students that fit into each category but rather to think about the questions as the speech goes on.

response question

A question that the audience is expected to answer in some manner.

rhetorical question

A question for which no actual response is expected.

2.9   Humor

Humor is another effective method for gaining an audience's attention. Humor is an amazing tool when used properly. We cannot begin to explain all the amazing facets of humor within this text, but we can say that humor is a great way of focusing an audience on what you are saying. However, humor is a double-edged sword. If you do not wield the sword carefully, you can turn your audience against you very quickly. When using humor, you really need to know your audience and understand what they will find humorous. One of the biggest mistakes a speaker can make is to use some form of humor that the audience either doesn't find funny or finds offensive. Think about how incompetent the character of Michael Scott seems on the television program *The Office*, in large part because of his ineffective use of humor. We always recommend that you test out humor of any kind on a sample of potential audience members prior to actually using it during a speech.

© Thinkstock

Now that we've warned you about the perils of using humor, let's talk about how to use humor as an attention-getter. Humor can be incorporated into several of the attention-getting devices mentioned. You could use a humorous anecdote, quotation, or current event. As with other attention-getting devices, you need to make sure your humor is relevant to your topic, as one of the biggest mistakes some novices make when using humor is to add humor that really doesn't support the overall goal of the speech. So when looking for humorous attention-getters you want to make sure that the humor is nonoffensive to your audiences and relevant to your speech. For example, here's a humorous quotation from Nicolas Chamfort, a French author during the sixteenth century, "The only thing that stops God from sending another flood is that the first one was useless." While this quotation could be great for some audiences, other audiences may find this humorous quotation offensive (e.g., religious audiences). The Chamfort quotation could be great for a speech on the ills of modern society, but probably not for a speech on the state of modern religious conflict. You want to make sure that the leap from your attention-getter to your topic isn't too complicated for your audience, or the attention-getter will backfire.

2.10   Personal Reference

The tenth device you may consider to start a speech is to refer to a story about yourself that is relevant for your topic. Some of the best speeches are ones that come from personal knowledge and experience. If you are an expert or have firsthand experience related to your topic, sharing this information with the audience is a great way to show that you are credible during your attention-getter. For example, if you had a gastric bypass surgery and you wanted to give an informative speech about the procedure, you could introduce your speech in this way:

> *In the fall of 2008, I decided that it was time that I took my life into my own hands. After suffering for years with the disease of obesity, I decided to take a leap of faith and get a gastric bypass in an attempt to finally beat the disease.*

If you use a personal example, don't get carried away with the focus on yourself and your own life. Your speech topic is the purpose of the attention-getter, not the other way around. Another pitfall in using a personal example is that it may be too personal for you to maintain your composure. For example, a student once started a speech about her grandmother by stating, "My grandmother died of cancer at 3:30 this morning." The student then proceeded to cry nonstop for ten minutes. While this is an extreme example, we strongly recommend that you avoid any material that could get you overly choked up while speaking. When speakers have an emotional breakdown during their speech, audience members stop listening to the message and become very uncomfortable.

2.11   Reference to Occasion

The last device we mention for starting a speech is to refer directly to the speaking occasion. This attention-getter is only useful if the speech is being delivered for a specific occasion. Many toasts, for example, start with the following statement: "Today we are here to honor X." In this case, the "X" could be a retirement, a marriage, a graduation, or any number of other special occasions. Because of its specific nature, this attention-getter is the least likely to be used for speeches being delivered for college courses.

KEY TAKEAWAYS

- In developing the introduction to your speech, begin by deciding upon a statement to capture the audience's attention.
- Attention-getters can include references to the audience, quotations, references to current events, historical references, anecdotes, startling statements, questions, humor, personal references, and references to the occasion.

3. PUTTING IT TOGETHER: STEPS TO COMPLETE YOUR INTRODUCTION

LEARNING OBJECTIVES

1. Clearly identify why an audience should listen to a speaker.
2. Discuss how you can build your credibility during a speech.
3. Understand how to write a clear thesis statement.
4. Design an effective preview of your speech's content for your audience.

Once you have captured your audience's attention, it's important to make the rest of your introduction interesting, and use it to lay out the rest of the speech. In this section, we are going to explore the five remaining parts of an effective introduction: linking to your topic, reasons to listen, stating credibility, thesis statement, and preview.

3.1 Link to Topic

© Thinkstock

After the attention-getter, the second major part of an introduction is called the link to topic. The link to topic is the shortest part of an introduction and occurs when a speaker demonstrates how an attention-getting device relates to the topic of a speech. Often the attention-getter and the link to topic are very clear. For example, if you look at the attention-getting device example under historical reference above, you'll see that the first sentence brings up the history of the Vietnam War and then shows us how that war can help us understand the Iraq War. In this case, the attention-getter clearly flows directly to the topic. However, some attention-getters need further explanation to get to the topic of the speech. For example, both of the anecdote examples (the girl falling into the manhole while texting and the boy and the filberts) need further explanation to connect clearly to the speech topic (i.e., problems of multitasking in today's society).

Let's look at the first anecdote example to demonstrate how we could go from the attention-getter to the topic.

> *In July 2009, a high school girl named Alexa Longueira was walking along a main boulevard near her home on Staten Island, New York, typing in a message on her cell phone. Not paying attention to the world around her, she took a step and fell right into an open manhole. This anecdote illustrates the problem that many people are facing in today's world. We are so wired into our technology that we forget to see what's going on around us—like a big hole in front of us.*

In this example, the third sentence here explains that the attention-getter was an anecdote that illustrates a real issue. The fourth sentence then introduces the actual topic of the speech.

Let's now examine how we can make the transition from the parable or fable attention-getter to the topic:

The ancient Greek writer Aesop told a fable about a boy who put his hand into a pitcher of filberts. The boy grabbed as many of the delicious nuts as he possibly could. But when he tried to pull them out, his hand wouldn't fit through the neck of the pitcher because he was grasping so many filberts. Instead of dropping some of them so that his hand would fit, he burst into tears and cried about his predicament. The moral of the story? "Don't try to do too much at once." In today's world, many of us are us are just like the boy putting his hand into the pitcher. We are constantly trying to grab so much or do so much that it prevents us from accomplishing our goals. I would like to show you three simple techniques to manage your time so that you don't try to pull too many filberts from your pitcher.

In this example, we added three new sentences to the attention-getter to connect it to the speech topic.

3.2   Reasons to Listen

Once you have linked an attention-getter to the topic of your speech, you need to explain to your audience why your topic is important. We call this the "why should I care?" part of your speech because it tells your audience why the topic is directly important to them. Sometimes you can include the significance of your topic in the same sentence as your link to the topic, but other times you may need to spell out in one or two sentences why your specific topic is important.

People in today's world are very busy, and they do not like their time wasted. Nothing is worse than having to sit through a speech that has nothing to do with you. Imagine sitting through a speech about a new software package you don't own and you will never hear of again. How would you react to the speaker? Most of us would be pretty annoyed at having had our time wasted in this way. Obviously, this particular speaker didn't do a great job of analyzing her or his audience if the audience isn't going to use the software package—but even when speaking on a topic that is highly relevant to the audience, speakers often totally forget to explain how and why it is important.

3.3   Appearing Credible

The next part of a speech is not so much a specific "part" as an important characteristic that needs to be pervasive throughout your introduction and your entire speech. As a speaker, you want to be seen as credible (competent, trustworthy, and caring/having goodwill). As mentioned earlier in this chapter, credibility is ultimately a perception that is made by your audience. While your audience determines whether they perceive you as competent, trustworthy, and caring/having goodwill, there are some strategies you can employ to make yourself appear more credible.

First, to make yourself appear competent, you can either clearly explain to your audience why you are competent about a given subject or demonstrate your competence by showing that you have thoroughly researched a topic by including relevant references within your introduction. The first method of demonstrating competence—saying it directly—is only effective if you are actually a competent person on a given subject. If you are an undergraduate student and you are delivering a speech about the importance of string theory in physics, unless you are a prodigy of some kind, you are probably not a recognized expert on the subject. Conversely, if your number one hobby in life is collecting memorabilia about the Three Stooges, then you may be an expert about the Three Stooges. However, you would need to explain to your audience your passion for collecting Three Stooges memorabilia and how this has made you an expert on the topic.

If, on the other hand, you are not actually a recognized expert on a topic, you need to demonstrate that you have done your homework to become more knowledgeable than your audience about your topic. The easiest way to demonstrate your competence is through the use of appropriate references from leading thinkers and researchers on your topic. When you demonstrate to your audience that you have done your homework, they are more likely to view you as competent.

The second characteristic of credibility, trustworthiness, is a little more complicated than competence, for it ultimately relies on audience perceptions. One way to increase the likelihood that a speaker will be perceived as trustworthy is to use reputable sources. If you're quoting Dr. John Smith, you need to explain who Dr. John Smith is so your audience will see the quotation as being more trustworthy. As speakers we can easily manipulate our sources into appearing more credible than they actually are, which would be unethical. When you are honest about your sources with your audience, they will trust you and your information more so than when you are ambiguous. The worst thing you can do is to out-and-out lie about information during your speech. Not only is lying highly unethical, but if you are caught lying, your audience will deem you untrustworthy and perceive everything you are saying as untrustworthy. Many speakers have attempted to lie to an audience because it will serve their own purposes or even because they believe their message is in their audience's best interest, but lying is one of the fastest ways to turn off an audience and get them to distrust both the speaker and the message.

The third characteristic of credibility to establish during the introduction is the sense of caring/goodwill. While some unethical speakers can attempt to manipulate an audience's perception that the speaker cares, ethical speakers truly do care about their audiences and have their audience's best interests in mind while speaking. Often speakers must speak in front of audiences that may be hostile toward the speaker's message. In these cases, it is very important for the speaker to explain that he or she really does believe her or his message is in the audience's best interest. One way to show that you have your audience's best interests in mind is to acknowledge disagreement from the start:

> *Today I'm going to talk about why I believe we should enforce stricter immigration laws in the United States. I realize that many of you will disagree with me on this topic. I used to believe that open immigration was a necessity for the United States to survive and thrive, but after researching this topic, I've changed my mind. While I may not change all of your minds today, I do ask that you listen with an open mind, set your personal feelings on this topic aside, and judge my arguments on their merits.*

While clearly not all audience members will be open or receptive to opening their minds and listening to your arguments, by establishing that there is known disagreement, you are telling the audience that you understand their possible views and are not trying to attack their intellect or their opinions.

3.4   Thesis Statement

A **thesis statement** is a short, declarative sentence that states the purpose, intent, or main idea of a speech. A strong, clear thesis statement is very valuable within an introduction because it lays out the basic goal of the entire speech. We strongly believe that it is worthwhile to invest some time in framing and writing a good thesis statement. You may even want to write your thesis statement before you even begin conducting research for your speech. While you may end up rewriting your thesis statement later, having a clear idea of your purpose, intent, or main idea before you start searching for research will help you focus on the most appropriate material. To help us understand thesis statements, we will first explore their basic functions and then discuss how to write a thesis statement.

> **thesis statement**
>
> A short, declarative sentence that states the purpose, intent, or main idea of a speech.

Basic Functions of a Thesis Statement

A thesis statement helps your audience by letting them know "in a nutshell" what you are going to talk about. With a good thesis statement you will fulfill four basic functions: you express your specific purpose, provide a way to organize your main points, make your research more effective, and enhance your delivery.

Express Your Specific Purpose

To orient your audience, you need to be as clear as possible about your meaning. A strong thesis will prepare your audience effectively for the points that will follow. Here are two examples:

1. "Today, I want to discuss academic cheating." (weak example)
2. "Today, I will clarify exactly what plagiarism is and give examples of its different types so that you can see how it leads to a loss of creative learning interaction." (strong example)

The weak statement will probably give the impression that you have no clear position about your topic because you haven't said what that position is. Additionally, the term "academic cheating" can refer to many behaviors—acquiring test questions ahead of time, copying answers, changing grades, or allowing others to do your coursework—so the specific topic of the speech is still not clear to the audience.

The strong statement not only specifies plagiarism but also states your specific concern (loss of creative learning interaction).

Provide a Way to Organize Your Main Points

A thesis statement should appear, almost verbatim, toward the end of the introduction to a speech. A thesis statement helps the audience get ready to listen to the arrangement of points that follow. Many speakers say that if they can create a strong thesis sentence, the rest of the speech tends to develop with relative ease. On the other hand, when the thesis statement is not very clear, creating a speech is an up-hill battle.

When your thesis statement is sufficiently clear and decisive, you will know where you stand about your topic and where you intend to go with your speech. Having a clear thesis statement is especially important if you know a great deal about your topic or you have strong feelings about it. If this is the case for you, you need to know exactly what you are planning on talking about in order to fit within specified time limitations. Knowing where you are and where you are going is the entire point in establishing a thesis statement; it makes your speech much easier to prepare and to present.

Let's say you have a fairly strong thesis statement, and that you've already brainstormed a list of information that you know about the topic. Chances are your list is too long and has no focus. Using your thesis statement, you can select only the information that (1) is directly related to the thesis and (2) can be arranged in a sequence that will make sense to the audience and will support the thesis. In essence, a strong thesis statement helps you keep useful information and weed out less useful information.

Make Your Research More Effective

If you begin your research with only a general topic in mind, you run the risk of spending hours reading mountains of excellent literature about your topic. However, mountains of literature do not always make coherent speeches. You may have little or no idea of how to tie your research all together, or even whether you should tie it together. If, on the other hand, you conduct your research with a clear thesis statement in mind, you will be better able to zero in only on material that directly relates to your chosen thesis statement. Let's look at an example that illustrates this point:

> *Many traffic accidents involve drivers older than fifty-five.*

While this statement may be true, you could find industrial, medical, insurance literature that can drone on *ad infinitum* about the details of all such accidents in just one year. Instead, focusing your thesis statement will help you narrow the scope of information you will be searching for while gathering information. Here's an example of a more focused thesis statement:

> *Three factors contribute to most accidents involving drivers over fifty-five years of age: failing eyesight, slower reflexes, and rapidly changing traffic conditions.*

This framing is somewhat better. This thesis statement at least provides three possible main points and some keywords for your electronic catalog search. However, if you want your audience to understand the context of older people at the wheel, consider something like:

> *Mature drivers over fifty-five years of age must cope with more challenging driving conditions than existed only one generation ago: more traffic moving at higher speeds, the increased imperative for quick driving decisions, and rapidly changing ramp and cloverleaf systems. Because of these challenges, I want my audience to believe that drivers over the age of sixty-five should be required to pass a driving test every five years.*

This framing of the thesis provides some interesting choices. First, several terms need to be defined, and these definitions might function surprisingly well in setting the tone of the speech. Your definitions of words like "generation," "quick driving decisions," and "cloverleaf systems" could jolt your audience out of assumptions they have taken for granted as truth.

Second, the framing of the thesis provides you with a way to describe the specific changes as they have occurred between, say, 1970 and 2010. How much, and in what ways, have the volume and speed of traffic changed? Why are quick decisions more critical now? What is a "cloverleaf," and how does any driver deal cognitively with exiting in the direction seemingly opposite to the desired one? Questions like this, suggested by your own thesis statement, can lead to a strong, memorable speech.

Enhance Your Delivery

When your thesis is not clear to you, your listeners will be even more clueless than you are—but if you have a good clear thesis statement, your speech becomes clear to your listeners. When you stand in front of your audience presenting your introduction, you can vocally emphasize the essence of your speech, expressed as your thesis statement. Many speakers pause for a half second, lower their vocal pitch slightly, slow down a little, and deliberately present the thesis statement, the one sentence that encapsulates its purpose. When this is done effectively, the purpose, intent, or main idea of a speech is driven home for an audience.

How to Write a Thesis Statement

Now that we've looked at why a thesis statement is crucial in a speech, let's switch gears and talk about how we go about writing a solid thesis statement. A thesis statement is related to the general and specific purposes of a speech as we discussed them in Chapter 6.

Choose Your Topic

The first step in writing a good thesis statement was originally discussed in Chapter 6 when we discussed how to find topics. Once you have a general topic, you are ready to go to the second step of creating a thesis statement.

Narrow Your Topic

One of the hardest parts of writing a thesis statement is narrowing a speech from a broad topic to one that can be easily covered during a five- to ten-minute speech. While five to ten minutes may sound like a long time to new public speakers, the time flies by very quickly when you are speaking. You can easily run out of time if your topic is too broad. To ascertain if your topic is narrow enough for a specific time frame, ask yourself three questions.

First, is your thesis statement narrow or is it a broad overgeneralization of a topic? An overgeneralization occurs when we classify everyone in a specific group as having a specific characteristic. For example, a speaker's thesis statement that "all members of the National Council of La Raza are militant" is an overgeneralization of all members of the organization. Furthermore, a speaker would have to correctly demonstrate that all members of the organization are militant for the thesis statement to be proven, which is a very difficult task since the National Council of La Raza consists of millions of Hispanic Americans. A more appropriate thesis related to this topic could be, "Since the creation of the National Council of La Raza [NCLR] in 1968, the NCLR has become increasingly militant in addressing the causes of Hispanics in the United States."

The second question to ask yourself when narrowing a topic is whether your speech's topic is one clear topic or multiple topics: A strong thesis statement consists of only a single topic. The following is an example of a thesis statement that contains too many topics: "Medical marijuana, prostitution, and gay marriage should all be legalized in the United States." Not only are all three fairly broad, but you also have three completely unrelated topics thrown into a single thesis statement. Instead of a thesis statement that has multiple topics, limit yourself to only one topic. Here's an example of a thesis statement examining only one topic: "Today we're going to examine the legalization and regulation of the oldest profession in the state of Nevada." In this case, we're focusing our topic to how one state has handled the legalization and regulation of prostitution.

The last question a speaker should ask when making sure a topic is sufficiently narrow is whether the topic has direction. If your basic topic is too broad, you will never have a solid thesis statement or a coherent speech. For example, if you start off with the topic "Barack Obama is a role model for everyone," what do you mean by this statement? Do you think President Obama is a role model because of his dedication to civic service? Do you think he's a role model because he's a good basketball player? Do you think he's a good role model because he's an excellent public speaker? When your topic is too broad, almost anything can become part of the topic. This ultimately leads to a lack of direction and coherence within the speech itself. To make a cleaner topic, a speaker needs to narrow her or his topic to one specific area. For example, you may want to examine why President Obama is a good speaker.

Put Your Topic into a Sentence

Once you've narrowed your topic to something that is reasonably manageable given the constraints placed on your speech, you can then formalize that topic as a complete sentence. For example, you could turn the topic of President Obama's public speaking skills into the following sentence: "Because of his unique sense of lyricism and his well-developed presentational skills, President Barack Obama is a modern symbol of the power of public speaking." Once you have a clear topic sentence, you can start tweaking the thesis statement to help set up the purpose of your speech.

Add Your Argument, Viewpoint, or Opinion

This function only applies if you are giving a speech to persuade. If your topic is informative, your job is to make sure that the thesis statement is nonargumentative and focuses on facts. For example, in the preceding thesis statement we have a couple of opinion-oriented terms that should be avoided for informative speeches: "unique sense," "well-developed," and "power." All three of these terms are laced with an individual's opinion, which is fine for a persuasive speech but not for an informative speech. For informative speeches, the goal of a thesis statement is to explain what the speech will be informing the audience about, not attempting to add the speaker's opinion about the speech's topic. For an informative speech, you could rewrite the thesis statement to read, "This speech is going to analyze Barack Obama's use of lyricism in his speech, 'A World That Stands as One,' delivered July 2008 in Berlin."

On the other hand, if your topic is persuasive, you want to make sure that your argument, viewpoint, or opinion is clearly indicated within the thesis statement. If you are going to argue that Barack Obama is a great speaker, then you should set up this argument within your thesis statement.

Use the Thesis Checklist

Once you have written a first draft of your thesis statement, you're probably going to end up revising your thesis statement a number of times prior to delivering your actual speech. A thesis statement is something that is constantly tweaked until the speech is given. As your speech develops, often your thesis will need to be rewritten to whatever direction the speech itself has taken. We often start with a speech going in one direction, and find out through our research that we should have gone in a different direction. When you think you finally have a thesis statement that is good to go for your speech, take a second and make sure it adheres to the criteria shown in Table 9.1

TABLE 9.1 Thesis Checklist

Instructions: For each of the following questions, check either "yes" or "no."	Yes	No
1. Does your thesis clearly reflect the topic of your speech?		
2. Can you adequately cover the topic indicated in your thesis within the time you have for your speech?		
3. Is your thesis statement simple?		
4. Is your thesis statement direct?		
5. Does your thesis statement gain an audience's interest?		
6. Is your thesis statement easy to understand?		
Persuasive Speeches		
7. Does your thesis statement introduce a clear argument?		
8. Does your thesis statement clearly indicate what your audience should do, how your audience should think, or how your audience should feel?		
Scoring: For a strong thesis statement, all your answers should have been "yes."		

3.5 Preview of Speech

The final part of an introduction contains a preview of the major points to be covered within your speech. I'm sure we've all seen signs that have three cities listed on them with the mileage to reach each city. This mileage sign is an indication of what is to come. A preview works the same way. A preview foreshadows what the main body points will be in the speech. For example, to preview a speech on bullying in the workplace, one could say, "To understand the nature of bullying in the modern workplace, I will first define what workplace bullying is and the types of bullying, I will then discuss the common characteristics of both workplace bullies and their targets, and lastly, I will explore some possible solutions to workplace bullying." In this case, each of the phrases mentioned in the preview would be a single distinct point made in the speech itself. In other words, the first major body point in this speech would examine what workplace bullying is and the types of bullying; the second major body point in this speech would discuss the common characteristics of both workplace bullies and their targets; and lastly, the third body point in this speech would explore some possible solutions to workplace bullying.

KEY TAKEAWAYS

- Linking the attention-getter to the speech topic is essential so that you maintain audience attention and so that the relevance of the attention-getter is clear to your audience.
- Establishing how your speech topic is relevant and important shows the audience why they should listen to your speech.
- To be an effective speaker, you should convey all three components of credibility, competence, trustworthiness, and caring/goodwill, by the content and delivery of your introduction.
- A clear thesis statement is essential to provide structure for a speaker and clarity for an audience.
- An effective preview identifies the specific main points that will be present in the speech body.

EXERCISES

1. Make a list of the attention-getting devices you might use to give a speech on the importance of recycling. Which do you think would be most effective? Why?
2. Create a thesis statement for a speech related to the topic of collegiate athletics. Make sure that your thesis statement is narrow enough to be adequately covered in a five- to six-minute speech.
3. Discuss with a partner three possible body points you could utilize for the speech on the topic of volunteerism.
4. Fill out the introduction worksheet to help work through your introduction for your next speech. Please make sure that you answer all the questions clearly and concisely.

4.   ANALYZING AN INTRODUCTION

LEARNING OBJECTIVES

1. See what a full introduction section looks like.
2. Distinguish among the six parts of an introduction.

Thus far, this chapter has focused on how to create a clear introduction. We discussed why introductions are important and the six important functions of effective introductions. In this section we're going to examine an actual introduction to a speech. Before we start analyzing the introduction, please read the introduction paragraph that follows.

© Thinkstock

Smart Dust Introduction

In 2002, the famed science fiction writer Michael Crichton released his book Prey, which was about a swarm of nanomachines that were feeding off living tissue. The nanomachines were solar-powered, self-sufficient, and intelligent. Most disturbingly, the nanomachines could work together as a swarm as it overtook and killed its prey in its need for new resources. The technology for this level of sophistication in nanotechnology is surprisingly more science fact than science fiction. In 2000, three professors of Electrical Engineering and Computer Science at the University of California at Berkeley, Professors Kahn, Katz, and Pister, hypothesized in the Journal of Communications and Networks that wireless networks of tiny microelectromechanical sensors, or MEMS: sensors, robots, or devices could detect phenomena including light, temperature, or vibration. By 2004, Fortune Magazine listed "smart dust" as the first in their "Top 10 Tech Trends to Bet On." Thus far researchers have hypothesized that smart dust could be used for everything from tracking patients in hospitals to early warnings of natural disasters and as a defense against bioterrorism. Today I'm going to explain what smart dust is and the various applications smart dust has in the near future. To help us understand the small of it all, we will first examine what smart dust is and how it works, we will then examine some military applications of smart dust, and we will end by discussing some nonmilitary applications of smart dust.

Now that you've had a chance to read the introduction to the speech on smart dust, read it over a second time and look for the six parts of the speech introduction as discussed earlier in this chapter. Once you're done analyzing this introduction, Table 9.2 shows you how the speech was broken down into the various parts of an introduction.

TABLE 9.2 Smart Dust Introduction

Part of Introduction	Analysis
In 2002, famed science fiction writer, Michael Crichton, released his book *Prey*, which was about a swarm of nanomachines that were feeding off living tissue. The nanomachines were solar-powered, self-sufficient, and intelligent. Most disturbingly, the nanomachines could work together as a swarm as it over took and killed its prey in its need for new resources.	**Attention-Getter** This attention-getter is using an anecdote derived from a best-selling novel.
The technology for this level of sophistication in nanotechnology is surprisingly more science fact than science fiction. In 2000, three professors of Electrical Engineering and Computer Science at the University of California at Berkeley, professors Kahn, Katz, and Pister, hypothesized in the *Journal of Communications and Networks* that wireless networks of tiny microelectromechanical sensors, or MEMS: sensors, robots, or devices could detect phenomena including light, temperature, or vibration.	**Link to Topic** This link to topic shows how the book *Prey* is actually very close to what scientists are attempting to accomplish.
By 2004, *Fortune Magazine* listed "smart dust" as the first in their "Top 10 Tech Trends to Bet On." Thus far researchers have hypothesized that smart dust could be used for everything from tracking patients in hospitals to early warnings of natural disasters and as a defense against bioterrorism.	**Reasons to Listen** In this section, the speaker indicates that business professionals have already recognized smart dust as a good economic investment with various applications.
"Professors Kahn, Katz, and Pister hypothesized in the *Journal of Communications and Networks*" "By 2004 *Fortune Magazine* listed"	**Espousal of Credibility** Notice the inclusion of research from both the *Journal of Communications and Networks* and *Fortune Magazine*. This is an attempt to indicate that the speaker has conducted research on the subject.
Today I'm going to explain what smart dust is and the various applications smart dust has in the near future.	**Thesis Statement** This thesis statement clearly indicates that this is an informative speech because it does not attempt to build an argument or share a specific opinion.
To help us understand the small of it all, we will first examine what smart dust is and how it works, we will then examine some military applications of smart dust, and we will end by discussing some nonmilitary applications of smart dust.	**Preview** This preview clearly indicates three body points that will be discussed in the speech.

Need More Speech Examples?

The following YouTube videos will show you a wide range of different speeches. While watching these videos, ask yourself the following questions: How have they utilized various attention-getting devices? Have they clearly used all aspects of an introduction? Do they have a strong thesis and preview? How could you have made the introduction stronger?

Animal Experimentation

http://www.youtube.com/watch?v=c4yYDt4di0o

Life after Having a Child

http://www.youtube.com/watch?v=e7-DhSLsk1U

Pros and Cons of Cholesterol

http://www.youtube.com/watch?v=k7VIOs6aiAc

On Being a Hero

http://www.youtube.com/watch?v=KYtm8uEo5vU

LASIK Eye Surgery

http://www.youtube.com/watch?v=Z0YWy8CXoYk

5. CHAPTER EXERCISES

SPEAKING ETHICALLY

Imagine that you are preparing a speech on the benefits of a new drug, and you find a direct quotation that clearly establishes your argument. Unfortunately, you soon realize that the source of your quotation is actually a lobbyist who works for the pharmaceutical company that manufactures the drug. You really want to use this quotation as your attention-getter, but you realize that the source is clearly biased. Which of the following options do you think is the most ethical? Why?

1. Disregard the quotation and find another way to start your speech.
2. Use the quotation, but acknowledge that the source comes from a paid lobbyist of the pharmaceutical company who manufactures the drug.
3. Use the quotation and just give the name of the source. If your audience is interested in your topic, they'll do their own research and make informed decisions for themselves.

END-OF-CHAPTER ASSESSMENT

1. During a keynote presentation, the speaker mentions that she is the head of neurology at a major medical center. The speaker then goes on to discuss why wearing helmets is important for bicyclists of all ages. What factor of credibility has the speaker attempted to establish?

    a. competence

    b. caring/goodwill

    c. extroversion

    d. trustworthiness

    e. character

2. A kid perched on the roof of his house one day notices a wolf walking by. The kid yells at the wolf, "Evil, vile creature! Why have you come near honest folks' homes?" The wolf quickly replied, "It is easy to be brave from a safe distance." What type of attention-getting device does this represent?

    a. personal reference

    b. fairy tale

    c. personal anecdote

    d. parable or fable

    e. humor

3. During an introduction, a speaker says, "I realize that many of us disagree on the use of corporal punishment in public schools. I just ask that you listen to my arguments with an open mind." Which aspect of credibility is the speaker attempting to enhance?

    a. competence

    b. caring/goodwill

    c. extroversion

    d. trustworthiness

    e. character

4. Which of the following is a function of a thesis statement?

    a. It provides a clear ending point for your speech.

    b. It helps to organize your introduction.

    c. It enhances your language usage.

    d. It expresses the body points in your speech.

    e. It clarifies your perspective about your topic.

5. What part of an introduction does the following sentence represent? "Today we're going to examine the video gaming industry by first discussing the history of video games, then by examining the current trends in video gaming, and lastly, by discussing the future of video games."

    a. attention-getter

    b. link to topic

    c. preview

    d. thesis

    e. significance of topic

ANSWER KEY

1. a
2. d
3. b
4. e
5. c

Introduction Worksheet

Directions: Use this worksheet to map out the introduction to your next speech. A copy of this worksheet suitable for editing in a word processing program can be downloaded from http://www.flatworldknowledge.com/sites/all/files/wrench_1.0-09ws.doc.

1. What is your general purpose? (circle one)

   | To inform | To persuade | To entertain |

2. What is your specific purpose?

   _____
   _____
   _____

3. Which attention-getting device do you plan on using?

   _____
   _____
   _____

4. How will you link your attention-getting device to your actual topic?

   _____
   _____
   _____

5. Why should your audience listen to your speech?

   _____
   _____
   _____

6. How will you establish your credibility during speech?

   a. Competence

      _____
      _____
      _____

   b. Trustworthiness

      _____
      _____
      _____

   c. Caring/goodwill

      _____
      _____
      _____

   d. What is your thesis statement?

      _____
      _____
      _____

7. What are your three main body points?

   a. Body point 1

      _____
      _____
      _____

   b. Body point 2

      _____
      _____
      _____

   c. Body point 3

      _____
      _____
      _____

   d. Write a preview of your three main body points.

      _____

ENDNOTES

1. McCroskey, J. C., & Teven, J. J. (1999). Goodwill: A reexamination of the construct and its measurement. *Communication Monographs, 66*, 90–103.

2. Wrench, J. S., McCroskey, J. C., & Richmond, V. P. (2008). *Human communication in everyday life: Explanations and applications*. Boston, MA: Allyn & Bacon, pp. 33–34.

3. Baker, E. E. (1965). The immediate effects of perceived speaker disorganization on speaker credibility and audience attitude change in persuasive speaking. *Western Speech, 29*, 148–161.

4. Leung, R. (2004, September 5). Porn in the U.S.A.: Steve Kroft reports on a $10 billion industry. Retrieved from http://www.cbsnews.com

5. Miller, E. (1946). Speech introductions and conclusions. *Quarterly Journal of Speech, 32*, 181–183.

6. Whitney, L. (2009, July 13). Don't text while walking? Girl learns the hard way. *CNET News Wireless*. Retrieved from http://news.cnet.com/8301-1035_3-10285466-94.html

7. Aesop (1881). *Aesop's fables*. New York, NY: Wm. L. Allison. Retrieved from http://www.litscape.com/author/Aesop/The_Boy_and_the_Filberts.html

CHAPTER 10
Creating the Body of a Speech

In a series of important and ground-breaking studies conducted during the 1950s and 1960s, researchers started investigating how a speech's organization was related to audience perceptions of those speeches. The first study, conducted by Raymond Smith in 1951, randomly organized the parts of a speech to see how audiences would react. Not surprisingly, when speeches were randomly organized, the audience perceived the speech more negatively than when audiences were presented with a speech with clear, intentional organization. Smith also found that audiences who listened to unorganized speeches were less interested in those speeches than audiences who listened to organized speeches.[1] Thompson furthered this investigation and found that unorganized speeches were also harder for audiences to recall after the speech. Basically, people remember information from speeches that are clearly organized—and forget information from speeches that are poorly organized.[2] A third study by Baker found that when audiences were presented with a disorganized speaker, they were less likely to be persuaded, and saw the disorganized speaker as lacking credibility.[3]

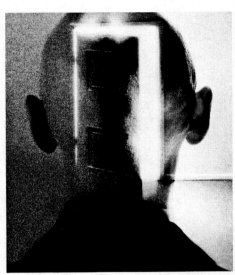

© *Thinkstock*

These three very important studies make the importance of organization very clear. When speakers are not organized they are not perceived as credible and their audiences view the speeches negatively, are less likely to be persuaded, and don't remember specific information from the speeches after the fact.

We start this chapter discussing these studies because we want you to understand the importance of speech organization on real audiences. If you are not organized, your speech will never have its intended effect. In this chapter, we are going to discuss the basics of organizing the body of your speech.

1. DETERMINING YOUR MAIN IDEAS

L E A R N I N G   O B J E C T I V E S

1. Revisit the function of a specific purpose.
2. Understand how to make the transition from a specific purpose to a series of main points.
3. Be able to narrow a speech from all the possible points to the main points.
4. Explain how to prepare meaningful main points.

© *Thinkstock*

When creating a speech, it's important to remember that speeches have three clear parts: an introduction, a body, and a conclusion. The introduction establishes the topic and whets your audience's appetite, and the conclusion wraps everything up at the end of your speech. The real "meat" of your speech happens in the body. In this section, we're going to discuss how to think strategically about the body of your speech.

We like the word *strategic* because it refers to determining what is important or essential to the overall plan or purpose of your speech. Too often, new speakers just throw information together and stand up and start speaking. When that happens, audience members are left confused and the reason for the speech may get lost. To avoid being seen as disorganized, we want you to start thinking critically about the organization of your speech. In this section, we will discuss how to take your speech from a specific purpose to creating the main points of your speech.

1.1   What Is Your Specific Purpose?

Before we discuss how to determine the main points of your speech, we want to revisit your speech's specific purpose, which we discussed in detail in Chapter 6. Recall that a speech can have one of three general purposes: to inform, to persuade, or to entertain. The general purpose refers to the broad goal for creating and delivering the speech. The specific purpose, on the other hand, starts with one of those broad goals (inform, persuade, or entertain) and then further informs the listener about the *who, what, when, where, why,* and *how* of the speech.

The specific purpose is stated as a sentence incorporating the general purpose, the specific audience for the speech, and a prepositional phrase that summarizes the topic. Suppose you are going to give a speech about using open-source software. Here are three examples (each with a different general purpose and a different audience):

General Purpose	To inform
Specific Purpose	To inform a group of school administrators about the various open-source software packages that could be utilized in their school districts
General Purpose	To persuade
Specific Purpose	To persuade a group of college students to make the switch from Microsoft Office to the open-source office suite OpenOffice
General Purpose	To entertain
Specific Purpose	To entertain members of a business organization with a mock eulogy of for-pay software giants as a result of the proliferation of open-source alternatives

In each of these three examples, you'll notice that the general topic is the same—open-source software—but the specific purpose is different because the speech has a different general purpose and a different audience. Before you can think strategically about organizing the body of your speech, you need to know what your specific purpose is. If you have not yet written a specific purpose for your current speech, please go ahead and write one now.

1.2   From Specific Purpose to Main Points

Once you've written down your specific purpose, you can now start thinking about the best way to turn that specific purpose into a series of main points. **Main points** are the key ideas you present to enable your speech to accomplish its specific purpose. In this section, we're going to discuss how to determine your main points and how to organize those main points into a coherent, strategic speech.

How Many Main Points Do I Need?

While there is no magic number for how many main points a speech should have, speech experts generally agree that the fewer the number of main points the better. First and foremost, experts on the subject of memory have consistently shown that people don't tend to remember very much after they listen to a message or leave a conversation.[4] While many different factors can affect a listener's ability to retain information after a speech, how the speech is organized is an important part of that process.[5] For the speeches you will be delivering in a typical public speaking class, you will usually have just two or three main points. If your speech is less than three minutes long, then two main points will probably work best. If your speech is between three and ten minutes in length, then it makes more sense to use three main points.

You may be wondering why we are recommending only two or three main points. The reason comes straight out of the research on listening. According to LeFrancois, people are more likely to remember information that is meaningful, useful, and of interest to them; different or unique; organized; visual; and simple.[6] Two or three main points are much easier for listeners to remember than ten or even five. In addition, if you have two or three main points, you'll be able to develop each one with examples, statistics, or other forms of support. Including support for each point will make your speech more interesting and more memorable for your audience.

Narrowing Down Your Main Points

When you write your specific purpose and review the research you have done on your topic, you will probably find yourself thinking of quite a few points that you'd like to make in your speech. Whether that's the case or not, we recommend taking a few minutes to brainstorm and develop a list of points. In brainstorming, your goal is simply to think of as many different points as you can, not to judge how valuable or important they are. What information does your audience need to know to understand your topic? What information does your speech need to convey to accomplish its specific purpose? Consider the following example:

Specific Purpose	To inform a group of school administrators about the various open-source software packages that could be utilized in their school districts
Brainstorming List of Points	Define open-source software.
	Define educational software.
	List and describe the software commonly used by school districts.
	Explain the advantages of using open-source software.
	Explain the disadvantages of using open-source software.
	Review the history of open-source software.
	Describe the value of open-source software.
	Describe some educational open-source software packages.
	Review the software needs of my specific audience.
	Describe some problems that have occurred with open-source software.

Now that you have brainstormed and developed a list of possible points, how do you go about narrowing them down to just two or three main ones? Remember, your main points are the key ideas that help build your speech. When you look over the preceding list, you can then start to see that many of the points are related to one another. Your goal in narrowing down your main points is to identify which individual, potentially minor points can be combined to make main points. This process is called **chunking** because it involves taking smaller chunks of information and putting them together with like chunks to create more fully developed chunks of information. Before reading our chunking of the preceding list, see if you can determine three large chunks out of the list (note that not all chunks are equal).

main points

The series of key ideas that you develop to help your audience understand your specific purpose.

chunking

The process of taking smaller chunks of information and putting them together with like chunks to create more fully developed, larger chunks of information.

Specific Purpose	To inform a group of school administrators about the various open-source software packages that could be utilized in their school districts
Main Point 1	**School districts use software in their operations.**
	Define educational software.
	List and describe the software commonly used by school districts.
Main Point 2	**What is open-source software?**
	Define open-source software.
	Review the history of open-source software.
	Explain the advantages of using open-source software.
	Describe the value of open-source software.
	Explain the disadvantages of using open-source software.
	Describe some problems that have occurred with open-source software.
Main Point 3	**Name some specific open-source software packages that may be appropriate for these school administrators to consider.**
	Review the software needs of my specific audience.
	Describe some educational open-source software packages.

You may notice that in the preceding list, the number of subpoints under each of the three main points is a little disjointed or the topics don't go together clearly. That's all right. Remember that these are just general ideas at this point. It's also important to remember that there is often more than one way to organize a speech. Some of these points could be left out and others developed more fully, depending on the purpose and audience. We'll develop the preceding main points more fully in a moment.

Helpful Hints for Preparing Your Main Points

Now that we've discussed how to take a specific purpose and turn it into a series of main points, here are some helpful hints for creating your main points.

Uniting Your Main Points

Once you've generated a possible list of main points, you want to ask yourself this question: "When you look at your main points, do they fit together?" For example, if you look at the three preceding main points (school districts use software in their operations; what is open-source software; name some specific open-source software packages that may be appropriate for these school administrators to consider), ask yourself, "Do these main points help my audience understand my specific purpose?"

Suppose you added a fourth main point about open-source software for musicians—would this fourth main point go with the other three? Probably not. While you may have a strong passion for open-source music software, that main point is extraneous information for the speech you are giving. It does not help accomplish your specific purpose, so you'd need to toss it out.

Keeping Your Main Points Separate

The next question to ask yourself about your main points is whether they overlap too much. While some overlap may happen naturally because of the singular nature of a specific topic, the information covered within each main point should be clearly distinct from the other main points. Imagine you're giving a speech with the specific purpose "to inform my audience about the health reasons for eating apples and oranges." You could then have three main points: that eating fruits is healthy, that eating apples is healthy, and that eating oranges is healthy. While the two points related to apples and oranges are clearly distinct, both of those main points would probably overlap too much with the first point "that eating fruits is healthy," so you would probably decide to eliminate the first point and focus on the second and third. On the other hand, you could keep the first point and then develop two new points giving additional support to why people should eat fruit.

Balancing Main Points

One of the biggest mistakes some speakers make is to spend most of their time talking about one of their main points, completely neglecting their other main points. To avoid this mistake, organize your speech so as to spend roughly the same amount of time on each main point. If you find that one of your main points is simply too large, you may need to divide that main point into two main points and consolidate your other main points into a single main point.

Let's see if our preceding example is balanced (school districts use software in their operations; what is open-source software; name some specific open-source software packages that may be appropriate for these school administrators to consider). What do you think? Obviously, the answer depends on how much time a speaker will have to talk about each of these main points. If you have an hour to talk, then you may find that these three main points are balanced. However, you may also find them wildly unbalanced if you only have five minutes to speak because five minutes is not enough time to even explain what open-source software is. If that's the case, then you probably need to rethink your specific purpose to ensure that you can cover the material in the allotted time.

Creating Parallel Structure for Main Points

Another major question to ask yourself about your main points is whether or not they have a parallel structure. By parallel structure, we mean that you should structure your main points so that they all sound similar. When all your main points sound similar, it's simply easier for your audiences to re-member your main points and retain them for later. Let's look at our sample (school districts use soft-ware in their operations; what is open-source software; name some specific open-source software pack-ages that may be appropriate for these school administrators to consider). Notice that the first and third main points are statements, but the second one is a question. Basically, we have an example here of main points that are not parallel in structure. You could fix this in one of two ways. You could make them all questions: what are some common school district software programs; what is open-source software; and what are some specific open-source software packages that may be appropriate for these school administrators to consider. Or you could turn them all into statements: school districts use soft-ware in their operations; define and describe open-source software; name some specific open-source software packages that may be appropriate for these school administrators to consider. Either of these changes will make the grammatical structure of the main points parallel.

Maintaining Logical Flow of Main Points

The last question you want to ask yourself about your main points is whether the main points make sense in the order you've placed them. The next section goes into more detail of common organization-al patterns for speeches, but for now we want you to just think logically about the flow of your main points. When you look at your main points, can you see them as progressive, or does it make sense to talk about one first, another one second, and the final one last? If you look at your order, and it doesn't make sense to you, you probably need to think about the flow of your main points. Often, this process is an art and not a science. But let's look at a couple of examples.

School Dress Codes Example	
Main Point 1	History of school dress codes
Main Point 2	Problems with school dress codes
Main Point 3	Eliminating school dress codes

Rider Law Legislation	
Main Point 1	Why should states have rider laws?
Main Point 2	What are the effects of a lack of rider laws?
Main Point 3	What is rider law legislation?

When you look at these two examples, what are your immediate impressions of the two examples? In the first example, does it make sense to talk about history, and then the problems, and finally how to eliminate school dress codes? Would it make sense to put history as your last main point? Probably not. In this case, the main points are in a logical sequential order. What about the second example? Does it make sense to talk about your solution, then your problem, and then define the solution? Not really! What order do you think these main points should be placed in for a logical flow? Maybe you should explain the problem (lack of rider laws), then define your solution (what is rider law legislation), and then argue for your solution (why states should have rider laws). Notice that in this example you don't even need to know what "rider laws" are to see that the flow didn't make sense.

KEY TAKEAWAYS

- All speeches start with a general purpose and then move to a specific purpose that gives the *who*, *what*, *where*, and *how* for the speech.
- Transitioning from the specific purpose to possible main points means developing a list of potential main points you could discuss. Then you can narrow your focus by looking for similarities among your potential main points and combining ones that are similar.
- Shorter speeches will have two main points while longer speeches will generally have three or more main points. When creating your main points, make sure that they are united, separate, balanced, parallel, and logical.

EXERCISES

1. Generate a specific purpose for your current speech. Conduct a brainstorming activity where you try to think of all the possible points you could possibly make related to your specific purpose. Once you've finished creating this list, see if you can find a meaningful pattern that helps you develop three main points.
2. Pair up with a partner. Take the three main points you developed in the previous exercise, exchange papers with your partner and ask him or her to see whether or not they are united, separate, balanced, parallel, and logical. You do the same for your partner's main points. If they are not, what can you or your partner do to fix your main points?

2. USING COMMON ORGANIZING PATTERNS

LEARNING OBJECTIVES

1. Differentiate among the common speech organizational patterns: categorical/topical, comparison/contrast, spatial, chronological, biographical, causal, problem-cause-solution, and psychological.
2. Understand how to choose the best organizational pattern, or combination of patterns, for a specific speech.

Previously in this chapter we discussed how to make your main points flow logically. This section is going to provide you with a number of organization patterns to help you create a logically organized speech. The first organization pattern we'll discuss is categorical/topical.

2.1 Categorical/Topical

By far the most common pattern for organizing a speech is by categories or topics. The categories function as a way to help the speaker organize the message in a consistent fashion. The goal of a **categorical/topical speech pattern** is to create categories (or chunks) of information that go together to help support your original specific purpose. Let's look at an example.

Specific Purpose	To persuade a group of high school juniors to apply to attend Generic University
Main Points	I. Life in the dorms
	II. Life in the classroom
	III. Life on campus

© Thinkstock

categorical/topical speech pattern

Speech format in which a speaker organizes the information into categories, which helps an audience understand a single topic.

In this case, we have a speaker trying to persuade a group of high school juniors to apply to attend Generic University. To persuade this group, the speaker has divided the information into three basic categories: what it's like to live in the dorms, what classes are like, and what life is like on campus. Almost anyone could take this basic speech and specifically tailor the speech to fit her or his own university or college. The main points in this example could be rearranged and the organizational pattern would still be effective because there is no inherent logic to the sequence of points. Let's look at a second example.

Specific Purpose	To inform a group of college students about the uses and misuses of Internet dating
Main Points	I. Define and describe Internet dating.
	II. Explain some strategies to enhance your Internet dating experience.
	III. List some warning signs to look for in potential online dates.

In this speech, the speaker is talking about how to find others online and date them. Specifically, the speaker starts by explaining what Internet dating is; then the speaker talks about how to make Internet dating better for her or his audience members; and finally, the speaker ends by discussing some negative aspects of Internet dating. Again, notice that the information is chunked into three categories or topics and that the second and third could be reversed and still provide a logical structure for your speech

2.2   Comparison/Contrast

Another method for organizing main points is the **comparison/contrast speech pattern**. While this pattern clearly lends itself easily to two main points, you can also create a third point by giving basic information about what is being compared and what is being contrasted. Let's look at two examples; the first one will be a two-point example and the second a three-point example.

Specific Purpose	To inform a group of physicians about Drug X, a newer drug with similar applications to Drug Y
Main Points	I. Show how Drug X and Drug Y are similar.
	II. Show how Drug X and Drug Y differ.
Specific Purpose	To inform a group of physicians about Drug X, a newer drug with similar applications to Drug Y
Main Points	I. Explain the basic purpose and use of both Drug X and Drug Y.
	II. Show how Drug X and Drug Y are similar.
	III. Show how Drug X and Drug Y differ.

If you were using the comparison/contrast pattern for persuasive purposes, in the preceding examples, you'd want to make sure that when you show how Drug X and Drug Y differ, you clearly state why Drug X is clearly the better choice for physicians to adopt. In essence, you'd want to make sure that when you compare the two drugs, you show that Drug X has all the benefits of Drug Y, but when you contrast the two drugs, you show how Drug X is superior to Drug Y in some way.

2.3   Spatial

The **spatial speech pattern** organizes information according to how things fit together in physical space. This pattern is best used when your main points are oriented to different locations that can exist independently. The basic reason to choose this format is to show that the main points have clear locations. We'll look at two examples here, one involving physical geography and one involving a different spatial order.

Specific Purpose	To inform a group of history students about the states that seceded from the United States during the Civil War
Main Points	I. Locate and describe the Confederate states just below the Mason-Dixon Line (Virginia, North Carolina, and Tennessee).
	II. Locate and describe the Confederate states in the deep South (South Carolina, Georgia, Alabama, Mississippi, and Florida).
	III. Locate and describe the western Confederate states (Louisiana, Arkansas, and Texas).

If you look at a basic map of the United States, you'll notice that these groupings of states were created because of their geographic location to one another. In essence, the states create three spatial territories to explain.

Now let's look at a spatial speech unrelated to geography.

comparison/contrast speech pattern

Speech format in which a speaker selects two objects or ideas and demonstrates how they are similar or how they are different.

spatial speech pattern

Speech format in which a speaker organizes information according to how things fit together in physical space.

Specific Purpose	To explain to a group of college biology students how the urinary system works
Main Points	I. Locate and describe the kidneys and ureters.
	II. Locate and describe the bladder.
	III. Locate and describe the sphincter and urethra.

In this example, we still have three basic spatial areas. If you look at a model of the urinary system, the first step is the kidney, which then takes waste through the ureters to the bladder, which then relies on the sphincter muscle to excrete waste through the urethra. All we've done in this example is create a spatial speech order for discussing how waste is removed from the human body through the urinary system. It is spatial because the organization pattern is determined by the physical location of each body part in relation to the others discussed.

2.4   Chronological

chronological speech pattern

Speech format in which a speaker presents information in the order in which it occurred in time—whether backward or forward.

The **chronological speech pattern** places the main idea in the time order in which items appear—whether backward or forward. Here's a simple example.

Specific Purpose	To inform my audience about the books written by Winston Churchill
Main Points	I. Examine the style and content of Winston Churchill's writings prior to World War II.
	II. Examine the style and content of Winston Churchill's writings during World War II.
	III. Examine the style and content of Winston Churchill's writings after World War II.

In this example, we're looking at the writings of Winston Churchill in relation to World War II (before, during, and after). By placing his writings into these three categories, we develop a system for understanding this material based on Churchill's own life. Note that you could also use reverse chronological order and start with Churchill's writings after World War II, progressing backward to his earliest writings.

2.5   Biographical

biographical speech pattern

Speech format generally used when a speaker wants to describe a person's life.

As you might guess, the **biographical speech pattern** is generally used when a speaker wants to describe a person's life—either a speaker's own life, the life of someone they know personally, or the life of a famous person. By the nature of this speech organizational pattern, these speeches tend to be informative or entertaining; they are usually not persuasive. Let's look at an example.

Specific Purpose	To inform my audience about the early life of Marilyn Manson
Main Points	I. Describe Brian Hugh Warner's early life and the beginning of his feud with Christianity.
	II. Describe Warner's stint as a music journalist in Florida.
	III. Describe Warner's decision to create Marilyn Manson and the Spooky Kids.

In this example, we see how Brian Warner, through three major periods of his life, ultimately became the musician known as Marilyn Manson.

In this example, these three stages are presented in chronological order, but the biographical pattern does not have to be chronological. For example, it could compare and contrast different periods of the subject's life, or it could focus topically on the subject's different accomplishments.

2.6   Causal

causal speech pattern

Speech format that is built upon two main points: cause and effect.

The **causal speech pattern** is used to explain cause-and-effect relationships. When you use a causal speech pattern, your speech will have two basic main points: cause and effect. In the first main point, typically you will talk about the causes of a phenomenon, and in the second main point you will then show how the causes lead to either a specific effect or a small set of effects. Let's look at an example.

Specific Purpose	To inform my audience about the problems associated with drinking among members of Native American tribal groups
Main Points	I. Explain the history and prevalence of drinking alcohol among Native Americans.
	II. Explain the effects that abuse of alcohol has on Native Americans and how this differs from the experience of other populations.

In this case, the first main point is about the history and prevalence of drinking alcohol among Native Americans (the cause). The second point then examines the effects of Native American alcohol consumption and how it differs from other population groups.

However, a causal organizational pattern can also begin with an effect and then explore one or more causes. In the following example, the effect is the number of arrests for domestic violence.

Specific Purpose	To inform local voters about the problem of domestic violence in our city
Main Points	I. Explain that there are significantly more arrests for domestic violence in our city than in cities of comparable size in our state.
	II. List possible causes for the difference, which may be unrelated to the actual amount of domestic violence.

In this example, the possible causes for the difference might include stricter law enforcement, greater likelihood of neighbors reporting an incident, and police training that emphasizes arrests as opposed to other outcomes. Examining these possible causes may suggest that despite the arrest statistic, the actual number of domestic violence incidents in your city may not be greater than in other cities of similar size.

2.7 Problem-Cause-Solution

Another format for organizing distinct main points in a clear manner is the **problem-cause-solution speech pattern**. In this format you describe a problem, identify what you believe is causing the problem, and then recommend a solution to correct the problem.

Specific Purpose	To persuade a civic group to support a citywide curfew for individuals under the age of eighteen
Main Points	I. Demonstrate that vandalism and violence among youth is having a negative effect on our community.
	II. Show how vandalism and violence among youth go up after 10:00 p.m. in our community.
	III. Explain how instituting a mandatory curfew at 10:00 p.m. would reduce vandalism and violence within our community.

In this speech, the speaker wants to persuade people to pass a new curfew for people under eighteen. To help persuade the civic group members, the speaker first shows that vandalism and violence are problems in the community. Once the speaker has shown the problem, the speaker then explains to the audience that the cause of this problem is youth outside after 10:00 p.m. Lastly, the speaker provides the mandatory 10:00 p.m. curfew as a solution to the vandalism and violence problem within the community. The problem-cause-solution format for speeches generally lends itself to persuasive topics because the speaker is asking an audience to believe in and adopt a specific solution.

2.8 Psychological

A further way to organize your main ideas within a speech is through a **psychological speech pattern** in which "a" leads to "b" and "b" leads to "c." This speech format is designed to follow a logical argument, so this format lends itself to persuasive speeches very easily. Let's look at an example.

Specific Purpose	To persuade a group of nurses to use humor in healing the person
Main Points	I. How laughing affects the body
	II. How the bodily effects can help healing
	III. Strategies for using humor in healing

In this speech, the speaker starts by discussing how humor affects the body. If a patient is exposed to humor (a), then the patient's body actually physiologically responds in ways that help healing (b—e.g.,

problem-cause-solution speech pattern

Speech format in which a speaker discusses what a problem is, what the speaker believes is causing the problem, and then what the solution should be to correct the problem.

psychological speech pattern

Speech format built on basic logic in which "a" leads to "b" and "b" leads to "c."

reduces stress, decreases blood pressure, bolsters one's immune system, etc.). Because of these benefits, nurses should engage in humor use that helps with healing (c).

2.9 Selecting an Organizational Pattern

Each of the preceding organizational patterns is potentially useful for organizing the main points of your speech. However, not all organizational patterns work for all speeches. For example, as we mentioned earlier, the biographical pattern is useful when you are telling the story of someone's life. Some other patterns, particularly comparison/contrast, problem-cause-solution, and psychological, are well suited for persuasive speaking. Your challenge is to choose the best pattern for the particular speech you are giving.

You will want to be aware that it is also possible to combine two or more organizational patterns to meet the goals of a specific speech. For example, you might wish to discuss a problem and then compare/contrast several different possible solutions for the audience. Such a speech would thus be combining elements of the comparison/contrast and problem-cause-solution patterns. When considering which organizational pattern to use, you need to keep in mind your specific purpose as well as your audience and the actual speech material itself to decide which pattern you think will work best.

KEY TAKEAWAY

- Speakers can use a variety of different organizational patterns, including categorical/topical, comparison/contrast, spatial, chronological, biographical, causal, problem-cause-solution, and psychological. Ultimately, speakers must really think about which organizational pattern best suits a specific speech topic.

EXERCISES

1. Imagine that you are giving an informative speech about your favorite book. Which organizational pattern do you think would be most useful? Why? Would your answer be different if your speech goal were persuasive? Why or why not?

2. Working on your own or with a partner, develop three main points for a speech designed to persuade college students to attend your university. Work through the preceding organizational patterns and see which ones would be possible choices for your speech. Which organizational pattern seems to be the best choice? Why?

3. Use one of the common organizational patterns to create three main points for your next speech.

3.   KEEPING YOUR SPEECH MOVING

Have you ever been listening to a speech or a lecture and found yourself thinking, "I am so lost!" or "Where the heck is this speaker going?" Chances are one of the reasons you weren't sure what the speaker was talking about was that the speaker didn't effectively keep the speech moving. When we are reading and encounter something we don't understand, we have the ability to reread the paragraph and try to make sense of what we're trying to read. Unfortunately, we are not that lucky when it comes to listening to a speaker. We cannot pick up our universal remote and rewind the person. For this reason, speakers need to really think about how they keep a speech moving so that audience members are easily able to keep up with the speech. In this section, we're going to look at four specific techniques speakers can use that make following a speech much easier for an audience: transitions, internal previews, internal summaries, and signposts.

3.1   Transitions between Main Points

A **transition** is a phrase or sentence that indicates that a speaker is moving from one main point to another main point in a speech. Basically, a transition is a sentence where the speaker summarizes what was said in one point and previews what is going to be discussed in the next point. Let's look at some examples:

© Thinkstock

transition

A phrase or sentence that indicates that a speaker is moving from one main point to another main point in a speech.

- Now that we've seen the problems caused by lack of adolescent curfew laws, let's examine how curfew laws could benefit our community.
- Thus far we've examined the history and prevalence of alcohol abuse among Native Americans, but it is the impact that this abuse has on the health of Native Americans that is of the greatest concern.
- Now that we've thoroughly examined how these two medications are similar to one another, we can consider the many clear differences between the two medications.
- Although he was one of the most prolific writers in Great Britain prior to World War II, Winston Churchill continued to publish during the war years as well.

You'll notice that in each of these transition examples, the beginning phrase of the sentence indicates the conclusion of a period of time (now that, thus far). Table 10.1 contains a variety of transition words that will be useful when keeping your speech moving.

TABLE 10.1 Transition Words

Addition	also, again, as well as, besides, coupled with, following this, further, furthermore, in addition, in the same way, additionally, likewise, moreover, similarly
Consequence	accordingly, as a result, consequently, for this reason, for this purpose, hence, otherwise, so then, subsequently, therefore, thus, thereupon, wherefore
Generalizing	as a rule, as usual, for the most part, generally, generally speaking, ordinarily, usually
Exemplifying	chiefly, especially, for instance, in particular, markedly, namely, particularly, including, specifically, such as
Illustration	for example, for instance, for one thing, as an illustration, illustrated with, as an example, in this case
Emphasis	above all, chiefly, with attention to, especially, particularly, singularly
Similarity	comparatively, coupled with, correspondingly, identically, likewise, similar, moreover, together with
Exception	aside from, barring, besides, except, excepting, excluding, exclusive of, other than, outside of, save
Restatement	in essence, in other words, namely, that is, that is to say, in short, in brief, to put it differently
Contrast and Comparison	contrast, by the same token, conversely, instead, likewise, on one hand, on the other hand, on the contrary, nevertheless, rather, similarly, yet, but, however, still, nevertheless, in contrast
Sequence	at first, first of all, to begin with, in the first place, at the same time, for now, for the time being, the next step, in time, in turn, later on, meanwhile, next, then, soon, the meantime, later, while, earlier, simultaneously, afterward, in conclusion, with this in mind
Common Sequence Patterns	first, second, third…
	generally, furthermore, finally
	in the first place, also, lastly
	in the first place, pursuing this further, finally
	to be sure, additionally, lastly
	in the first place, just in the same way, finally
	basically, similarly, as well
Summarizing	after all, all in all, all things considered, briefly, by and large, in any case, in any event, in brief, in conclusion, on the whole, in short, in summary, in the final analysis, in the long run, on balance, to sum up, to summarize, finally
Diversion	by the way, incidentally
Direction	here, there, over there, beyond, nearly, opposite, under, above, to the left, to the right, in the distance
Location	above, behind, by, near, throughout, across, below, down, off, to the right, against, beneath, in back of, onto, under, along, beside, in front of, on top of, among, between, inside, outside, around, beyond, into, over

Beyond transitions, there are several other techniques that you can use to clarify your speech organization for your audience. The next sections address several of these techniques, including internal previews, internal summaries, and signposts.

3.2 Internal Previews

An **internal preview** is a phrase or sentence that gives an audience an idea of what is to come within a section of a speech. An internal preview works similarly to the preview that a speaker gives at the end of a speech introduction, quickly outlining what he or she is going to talk about (i.e., the speech's three main body points). In an internal preview, the speaker highlights what he or she is going to discuss within a specific main point during a speech.

Ausubel was the first person to examine the effect that internal previews had on retention of oral information.[7] Basically, when a speaker clearly informs an audience what he or she is going to be talking about in a clear and organized manner, the audience listens for those main points, which leads to higher retention of the speaker's message. Let's look at a sample internal preview:

> *To help us further understand why recycling is important, we will first explain the positive benefits of recycling and then explore how recycling can help our community.*

When an audience hears that you will be exploring two different ideas within this main point, they are ready to listen for those main points as you talk about them. In essence, you're helping your audience keep up with your speech.

Rather than being given alone, internal previews often come after a speaker has transitioned to that main topic area. Using the previous internal preview, let's see it along with the transition to that main point.

> *Now that we've explored the effect that a lack of consistent recycling has on our community, let's explore the importance of recycling for our community (transition). To help us further understand why recycling is important, we will first explain the positive benefits of recycling and then explore how recycling can help our community (internal preview).*

While internal previews are definitely helpful, you do not need to include one for every main point of your speech. In fact, we recommend that you use internal previews sparingly to highlight only main points containing relatively complex information.

3.3   Internal Summaries

Whereas an internal preview helps an audience know what you are going to talk about within a main point at the beginning, an **internal summary** is delivered to remind an audience of what they just heard within the speech. In general, internal summaries are best used when the information within a specific main point of a speech was complicated. To write your own internal summaries, look at the summarizing transition words in Table 10.1 Let's look at an example.

internal summary
A phrase or sentence that reaffirms to an audience the information that was just delivered within the speech.

> *To sum up, school bullying is a definite problem. Bullying in schools has been shown to be detrimental to the victim's grades, the victim's scores on standardized tests, and the victim's future educational outlook.*

In this example, the speaker was probably talking about the impact that bullying has on an individual victim educationally. Of course, an internal summary can also be a great way to lead into a transition to the next point of a speech.

> *In this section, we have explored how bullying in schools has been shown to be detrimental to the victim's grades, the victim's scores on standardized tests, and the victim's future educational outlook (internal summary). Therefore, schools need to implement campus-wide, comprehensive antibullying programs (transition).*

While not sounding like the more traditional transition, this internal summary helps readers summarize the content of that main point. The sentence that follows then leads to the next major part of the speech, which is going to discuss the importance of antibullying programs.

3.4   Signposts

Have you ever been on a road trip and watched the green rectangular mile signs pass you by? Fifty miles to go. Twenty-five miles to go. One mile to go. Signposts within a speech function the same way. A **signpost** is a guide a speaker gives her or his audience to help the audience keep up with the content of a speech. If you look at Table 10.1 and look at the "common sequence patterns," you'll see a series of possible signpost options. In essence, we use these short phrases at the beginning of a piece of information to help our audience members keep up with what we're discussing. For example, if you were giving a speech whose main point was about the three functions of credibility, you could use internal signposts like this:

signpost
A guide a speaker gives her or his audience to help the audience keep up with the content of a speech.

- The first function of credibility is competence.
- The second function of credibility is trustworthiness.
- The final function of credibility is caring/goodwill.

Signposts are simply meant to help your audience keep up with your speech, so the more simplistic your signposts are, the easier it is for your audience to follow.

In addition to helping audience members keep up with a speech, signposts can also be used to highlight specific information the speaker thinks is important. Where the other signposts were designed to show the way (like highway markers), signposts that call attention to specific pieces of information are more like billboards. Words and phrases that are useful for highlighting information can be found in Table 10.1 under the category "emphasis." All these words are designed to help you call attention to what you are saying so that the audience will also recognize the importance of the information.

KEY TAKEAWAYS

- Transitions are very important because they help an audience stay on top of the information that is being presented to them. Without transitions, audiences are often left lost and the ultimate goal of the speech is not accomplished.
- Specific transition words, like those found in Table 10.1, can be useful in constructing effective transitions.
- In addition to major transitions between the main points of a speech, speakers can utilize internal previews, internal summaries, and signposts to help focus audience members on the information contained within a speech.

EXERCISES

1. Using the main points you created earlier in this chapter, create clear transitions between each main point. Look at the possible transition words in Table 10.1 See which words are best suited for your speech. Try your transitions out on a friend or classmate to see if the transition makes sense to other people.
2. Take your most complicated main point and create an internal preview for that main point and then end the point with an internal summary.
3. Think about your current speech. Where can you use signposts to help focus your audience's attention? Try at least two different ways of phrasing your signposts and then decide which one is better to use.

4. ANALYZING A SPEECH BODY

LEARNING OBJECTIVE

1. See what a full speech body looks like in order to identify major components of the speech body.

Thus far this chapter has focused on how you go about creating main points and organizing the body of your speech. In this section we're going to examine the three main points of an actual speech. Before we start analyzing the introduction, please read the paragraphs that follow.

© Thinkstock

Smart Dust Speech Body

To help us understand smart dust, we will begin by first examining what smart dust is. Dr. Kris Pister, a professor in the robotics lab at the University of California at Berkeley, originally conceived the idea of smart dust in 1998 as part of a project funded by the Defense Advanced Research Projects Agency (DARPA). According to a 2001 article written by Bret Warneke, Matt Last, Brian Liebowitz, and Kris Pister titled "Smart Dust: Communicating with a Cubic-Millimeter Computer" published in Computer, Pister's goal was to build a device that contained a built-in sensor, communication device, and a small computer that could be integrated into a cubic millimeter package. For comparison purposes, Doug Steel, in a 2005 white paper titled "Smart Dust" written for C. T. Bauer College of Business at the University of Houston, noted that a single grain of rice has a volume of five cubic millimeters. Each individual piece of dust, called a mote, would then have the ability to interact with other motes and supercomputers. As Steve Lohr wrote in the January 30, 2010, edition of the New York Times in an article titled "Smart Dust? Not Quite, but We're Getting There," smart dust could eventually consist of "tiny digital sensors, strewn around the globe, gathering all sorts of information and communicating with powerful computer networks to monitor, measure, and understand the physical world in new ways."

Now that we've examined what smart dust is, let's switch gears and talk about some of the military applications for smart dust. Because smart dust was originally conceptualized under a grant from DARPA, military uses of smart dust have been widely theorized and examined. According to the Smart Dust website, smart dust could eventually be used for "battlefield surveillance, treaty monitoring, transportation monitoring, scud hunting" and other clear military applications. Probably the number one benefit of smart dust in the military environment is its surveillance abilities. Major Scott Dickson in a Blue Horizons Paper written for the Center for Strategy and Technology for the United States Air Force Air War College, sees smart dust as helping the military in battlespace awareness, homeland security, and weapons of mass destruction (WMD) identification. Furthermore, Major Dickson also believes it may be possible to create smart dust that has the ability to defeat communications jamming equipment created by foreign governments, which could help the US military to not only communicate among itself, but could also increase communications with civilians in military combat zones. On a much larger scale, smart dust could even help the US military and NASA protect the earth. According to a 2010 article written by Jessica Griggs in New Scientist, one of the first benefits of smart dust could be an early defense warning for space storms and other debris that could be catastrophic.

Now that we've explored some of the military benefits of smart dust, let's switch gears and see how smart dust may be able to have an impact on our daily lives. According to the smart dust project website, smart dust could quickly become a part of our daily lives. Everything from pasting smart dust particles to our finger tips to create a virtual computer keyboard to inventory control to product quality control have been discussed as possible applications for smart dust. Steve Lohr in his 2010 New York Times article wrote, "The applications for sensor-based computing, experts say, include buildings that manage their own energy use, bridges that sense motion and metal fatigue to tell engineers they need repairs, cars that track traffic patterns and report potholes, and fruit and vegetable shipments that tell grocers when they ripen and begin to spoil." Medically, according to the smart dust project website, smart dust could help disabled individuals interface with computers. Theoretically, we could all be injected with smart dust, which relays information to our physicians and detects adverse changes to our body instantly. Smart dust could detect the microscopic formations of cancer cells or alert us when we've been infected by a bacteria or virus, which could speed up treatment and prolong all of our lives.

Now that you've had a chance to read the body of the speech on smart dust, take a second and attempt to conduct your own analysis of the speech's body. What are the main points? Do you think the main points make sense? What organizational pattern is used? Are there clear transitions? What other techniques are used to keep the speech moving? Is evidence used to support the speech? Once you're done analyzing the speech body, look at Table 10.2, which presents our basic analysis of the speech's body.

TABLE 10.2 Smart Dust Speech Body Analysis

First Main Point	Analysis
To help us understand smart dust, we will begin by first examining what smart dust is. Dr. Kris Pister, a professor in the robotics lab at the University of California at Berkeley, originally conceived the idea of smart dust in 1998 as part of a project funded by the Defense Advanced Research Projects Agency (DARPA). According to a 2001 article written by Bret Warneke, Matt Last, Brian Liebowitz, and Kris Pister titled "Smart Dust: Communicating with a Cubic-Millimeter Computer" published in *Computer*, Pister's goal was to build a device that contained a built-in sensor, communication device, and a small computer that could be integrated into a cubic millimeter package. For comparison purposes, Doug Steel, in a 2005 white paper titled "Smart Dust" written for C. T. Bauer College of Business at the University of Houston, noted that a single grain of rice has a volume of five cubic millimeters. Each individual piece of dust, called a mote, would then have the ability to interact with other motes and supercomputers. As Steve Lohr wrote in the January 30, 2010, edition of the *New York Times* in an article titled "Smart Dust? Not Quite, but We're Getting There," smart dust could eventually consist of "tiny digital sensors, strewn around the globe, gathering all sorts of information and communicating with powerful computer networks to monitor, measure, and understand the physical world in new ways."	Notice this transition from the introduction to the first main point.

Second Main Point	Analysis
Now that we've examined what smart dust is, let's switch gears and talk about some of the military applications for smart dust. Because smart dust was originally conceptualized under a grant from DARPA, military uses of smart dust have been widely theorized and examined. According to the Smart Dust website, smart dust could eventually be used for "battlefield surveillance, treaty monitoring, transportation monitoring, scud hunting" and other clear military applications. Probably the number one benefit of smart dust in the military environment is its surveillance abilities. Major Scott Dickson in a Blue Horizons Paper written for the Center for Strategy and Technology for the United States Air Force Air War College, sees smart dust as helping the military in battlespace awareness, homeland security, and weapons of mass destruction (WMD) identification. Furthermore, Major Dickson also believes it may be possible to create smart dust that has the ability to defeat communications jamming equipment created by foreign governments, which could help the US military not only communicate among itself, but could also increase communications with civilians in military combat zones. On a much larger scale, smart dust could even help the US military and NASA protect the earth. According to a 2010 article written by Jessica Griggs in *New Scientist*, one of the first benefits of smart dust could be an early defense warning for space storms and other debris that could be catastrophic.	This transition is designed to move from the first main point to the second main point. Also notice that this speech is designed with a categorical/topic speech pattern.

Third Main Point	Analysis
Now that we've explored some of the military benefits of smart dust, let's switch gears and see how smart dust may be able to have an impact on our daily lives. According to the smart dust project website, smart dust could quickly become a part of our daily lives. Everything from pasting smart dust particles to our finger tips to create a virtual computer keyboard to inventory control to product quality control have been discussed as possible applications for smart dust. Steve Lohr in his 2010 *New York Times* article wrote, "The applications for sensor-based computing, experts say, include buildings that manage their own energy use, bridges that sense motion and metal fatigue to tell engineers they need repairs, cars that track traffic patterns and report potholes, and fruit and vegetable shipments that tell grocers when they ripen and begin to spoil." Medically, according to the smart dust project website, smart dust could help disabled individuals interface with computers. Theoretically, we could all be injected with smart dust, which relays information to our physicians and detects adverse changes to our body instantly. Smart dust could detect the microscopic formations of cancer cells or alert us when we've been infected by a bacteria or virus, which could speed up treatment and prolong all of our lives.	This is a third transition sentence.

5. CHAPTER EXERCISES

Johanna was in the midst of preparing her speech. She'd done the research and found a number of great sources for her speech. The specific purpose of her speech was to persuade a group of wildlife experts to step up their help for saving the water channel between the islands of Maui and Lanai, an area where humpback whales migrate during the winter to give birth.

Johanna had a very strong first point and a strong third point, but she just couldn't shake the fact that her middle point really was underdeveloped and not as strong as the other two. In fact, the middle point was originally going to be her last point, but when her research went bust she ultimately downgraded the point and sandwiched it in between the other two. Now that she looked at her second point, she realized that the sources weren't credible and the point should probably be dropped.

In the back of Johanna's head, she heard that small voice reminding her of the fact that most audiences don't remember the middle of the speech, so it really won't matter anyway.

1. Is it unethical to use a main point that you know is underdeveloped?

2. Should a speaker ever purposefully put less credible information in the middle of a speech, knowing that people are less likely to remember that information?

3. If you were Johanna, what would you do?

END-OF-CHAPTER ASSESSMENT

1. Juan is finishing writing his specific purpose. He brainstorms about his specific purpose and finally settles on three topics he plans on talking about during his speech. What are these three topics called?

    a. specific topics

    b. main points

    c. generalized topics

    d. specific points

    e. main topics

2. Which speech format does the following outline represent?

Specific Purpose	To inform my audience about the life of Paris Hilton
Main Points	I. Describe Paris Hilton's life before she became famous.
	II. Describe Paris Hilton's first job as a model working for Donald Trump.
	III. Describe Paris Hilton's transition from model to media personality.

    a. atopical

    b. categorical/topical

    c. biographical

    d. spatial

    e. psychological

3. Which speech format does the following outline represent?

Specific Purpose	To persuade my audience to invest in VetoMax
Main Points	I. Tell the history of VetoMax.
	II. Explain the VetoMax advantage.
	III. Describe the VetoMax pledge to investors.

    a. atopical

    b. categorical/topical

    c. biographical

    d. spatial

    e. psychological

4. Bobby is creating a speech related to the Hawaiian islands. He plans on talking about each of the islands in order from southeast to northwest. Which speech format is probably the most effective for Bobby's speech?

    a. atopical

    b. categorical/topical

    c. biographical

    d. spatial

    e. psychological

5. What is a phrase or sentence that indicates that a speaker is moving from one main point in a speech to another main point in a speech?

    a. transition

    b. guidepost

    c. internal preview

    d. internal summary

    e. thesis statement

ENDNOTES

1. Smith, R. G. (1951). An experimental study of the effects of speech organization upon attitudes of college students. *Speech Monographs, 18*, 292–301.

2. Thompson, E. C. (1960). An experimental investigation of the relative effectiveness of organizational structure in oral communication. *Southern Speech Journal, 26*, 59–69.

3. Baker, E. E. (1965). The immediate effects of perceived speaker disorganization on speaker credibility and audience attitude change in persuasive speaking. *Western Speech, 29*, 148–161.

4. Bostrom, R. N., & Waldhart, E. S. (1988). Memory models and the measurement of listening. *Communication Education, 37*, 1–13.

5. Dunham, J. R. (1964). *Voice contrast and repetition in speech retention* (Doctoral dissertation). Retrieved from: http://etd.lib.ttu.edu/theses; Smith, R. G. (1951). An experimental study of the effects of speech organization upon attitudes of college students. *Speech Monographs, 18*, 292–301; Thompson, E. C. (1960). An experimental investigation of the relative effectiveness of organizational structure in oral communication. *Southern Speech Journal, 26*, 59–69.

6. LeFrancois, G. R. (1999). *Psychology for teaching* (10th ed.). Belmont, CA: Wadsworth.

7. Ausubel, D. P. (1968). *Educational psychology*. New York, NY: Holt, Rinehart, & Winston.

C H A P T E R 1 1
Concluding with Power

ALMOST TO THE FINISH LINE

When reading a great novel, many people just can't wait to get to the end of the book. Some people will actually jump ahead hundreds of pages and read the last chapter just to see what happens. Humans have an innate desire to "get to the end." Imagine reading a novel and finding that the author just stopped writing five or six chapters from the end—how satisfied would you be with that author? In the same way, when a speaker doesn't think through her or his conclusion properly, audience members are often left just as dissatisfied. In other words, conclusions are really important!

© Thinkstock

1. WHY CONCLUSIONS MATTER

L E A R N I N G   O B J E C T I V E S

1. Understand the basic benefits of a strong conclusion.
2. Explain the serial position effect and its importance on public speaking.

As public speaking professors and authors, we have seen many students give otherwise good speeches that seem to fall apart at the end. We've seen students end their three main points by saying things such as "OK, I'm done"; "Thank God that's over!"; or "Thanks. Now what? Do I just sit down?" It's understandable to feel relief at the end of a speech, but remember that as a speaker, your conclusion is the last chance you have to drive home your ideas. When a speaker opts to end the speech with an ineffective conclusion—or no conclusion at all—the speech loses the energy that's been created, and the audience is left confused and disappointed. Instead of falling prey to emotional exhaustion, remind yourself to keep your energy up as you approach the end of your speech, and plan ahead so that your conclusion will be an effective one.

© Thinkstock

Of course, a good conclusion will not rescue a poorly prepared speech. Thinking again of the chapters in a novel, if one bypasses all the content in the middle, the ending often isn't very meaningful or helpful. So to take advantage of the advice in this chapter, you need to keep in mind the importance of developing a speech with an effective introduction and an effective body; if you have these elements, you will have the foundation you need to be able to conclude effectively. Just as a good introduction helps bring an audience member into the world of your speech, and a good speech body holds the audience in that world, a good conclusion helps bring that audience member back to the reality outside of your speech.

In this section, we're going to examine the functions fulfilled by the conclusion of a speech. A strong conclusion serves to signal the end of the speech and to help your listeners remember your speech.

1.1 Signals the End

The first thing a good conclusion can do is to signal the end of a speech. You may be thinking that showing an audience that you're about to stop speaking is a "no brainer," but many speakers really don't prepare their audience for the end. When a speaker just suddenly stops speaking, the audience is left confused and disappointed. Instead, we want to make sure that audiences are left knowledgeable and satisfied with our speeches. In Section 2, we'll explain in great detail about how to ensure that you signal the end of your speech in a manner that is both effective and powerful.

1.2 Aids Audience's Memory of Your Speech

serial position effect

The notion that when items are presented in a linear fashion people remember the items at the beginning of the list and at the end of the list.

primacy

Information that is presented first.

recency

Information that is presented last.

The second reason for a good conclusion stems out of some very interesting research reported by the German psychologist Hermann Ebbinghaus back in 1885 in his book *Memory: A Contribution to Experimental Psychology*.[1] Ebbinghaus proposed that humans remember information in a linear fashion, which he called the **serial position effect**. He found an individual's ability to remember information in a list (e.g., a grocery list, a chores list, or a to-do list) depends on the location of an item on the list. Specifically, he found that items toward the top of the list and items toward the bottom of the list tended to have the highest recall rates. The serial position effect basically finds that information at the beginning of a list (**primacy**) and information at the end of the list (**recency**) are easier to recall than information in the middle of the list.

So what does this have to do with conclusions? A lot! Ray Ehrensberger wanted to test Ebbinghaus' serial position effect in public speaking. Ehrensberger created an experiment that rearranged the ordering of a speech to determine the recall of information.[2] Ehrensberger's study reaffirmed the importance of primacy and recency when listening to speeches. In fact, Ehrensberger found that the information delivered during the conclusion (recency) had the highest level of recall overall.

KEY TAKEAWAYS

- A strong conclusion is very important because it's a speaker's final chance to really explain the importance of her or his message and allows the speaker to both signal the end of the speech and help the audience to remember the main ideas. As such, speakers need to thoroughly examine how they will conclude their speeches with power.
- The serial position effect is the idea that people remember ideas that are stated either first (primacy) or last (recency) in a list the most. It is important to speech conclusions because restating your main ideas helps you to take advantage of the recency effect and helps your audience remember your ideas.

EXERCISES

1. Think about a recent speech you heard either in class or elsewhere. Did the speaker have a strong conclusion? List the elements of the conclusion that were particularly effective and ineffective. Identify two ways you could have made the speaker's conclusion stronger.
2. After listening to a speech or class lecture, close your eyes and say aloud the main points you remember from the presentation. Does your memory follow what you would expect according to the serial position effect?

2.   STEPS OF A CONCLUSION

LEARNING OBJECTIVES

1. Examine the three steps of an effective conclusion: restatement of the thesis, review of the main points, and concluding device.
2. Differentiate among Miller's (1946) ten concluding devices.

In Section 1, we discussed the importance a conclusion has on a speech. In this section, we're going to examine the three steps in building an effective conclusion.

2.1   Restatement of the Thesis

© Thinkstock

Restating a thesis statement is the first step in a powerful conclusion. As we explained in Chapter 9, a thesis statement is a short, declarative sentence that states the purpose, intent, or main idea of a speech. When we restate the thesis statement at the conclusion of our speech, we're attempting to reemphasize what the overarching main idea of the speech has been. Suppose your thesis statement was, "I will analyze Barack Obama's use of lyricism in his July 2008 speech, 'A World That Stands as One.'" You could restate the thesis in this fashion at the conclusion of your speech: "In the past few minutes, I have analyzed Barack Obama's use of lyricism in his July 2008 speech, 'A World That Stands as One.'" Notice the shift in tense: the statement has gone from the future tense (this is what I will speak about) to the past tense (this is what I have spoken about). Restating the thesis in your conclusion reminds the audience of the major purpose or goal of your speech, helping them remember it better.

2.2   Review of Main Points

After restating the speech's thesis, the second step in a powerful conclusion is to review the main points from your speech. One of the biggest differences between written and oral communication is the necessity of repetition in oral communication. When we preview our main points in the introduction, effectively discuss and make transitions to our main points during the body of the speech, and finally, review the main points in the conclusion, we increase the likelihood that the audience will retain our main points after the speech is over.

In the introduction of a speech, we deliver a *preview* of our main body points, and in the conclusion we deliver a *review*. Let's look at a sample preview:

> In order to understand the field of gender and communication, I will first differentiate between the terms biological sex and gender. I will then explain the history of gender research in communication. Lastly, I will examine a series of important findings related to gender and communication.

In this preview, we have three clear main points. Let's see how we can review them at the conclusion of our speech:

> Today, we have differentiated between the terms biological sex and gender, examined the history of gender research in communication, and analyzed a series of research findings on the topic.

> In the past few minutes, I have explained the difference between the terms "biological sex" and "gender," discussed the rise of gender research in the field of communication, and examined a series of groundbreaking studies in the field.

Notice that both of these conclusions review the main points originally set forth. Both variations are equally effective reviews of the main points, but you might like the linguistic turn of one over the other.

Remember, while there is a lot of science to help us understand public speaking, there's also a lot of art as well, so you are always encouraged to choose the wording that you think will be most effective for your audience.

2.3 Concluding Device

concluding device

The device a speaker uses at the end of a speech to ensure that the audience is left with a mental picture predetermined by the speaker.

The final part of a powerful conclusion is the concluding device. A **concluding device** is essentially the final thought you want your audience members to have when you stop speaking. It also provides a definitive sense of closure to your speech. One of the authors of this text often makes an analogy between a gymnastics dismount and the concluding device in a speech. Just as a gymnast dismounting the parallel bars or balance beam wants to stick the landing and avoid taking two or three steps, a speaker wants to "stick" the ending of the presentation by ending with a concluding device instead of with, "Well, umm, I guess I'm done." Miller observed that speakers tend to use one of ten concluding devices when ending a speech.[3] The rest of this section is going to examine these ten concluding devices.

Conclude with a Challenge

challenge

Call to engage in some kind of activity that requires a contest or special effort.

The first way that Miller found that some speakers end their speeches is with a challenge. A **challenge** is a call to engage in some kind of activity that requires a contest or special effort. In a speech on the necessity of fund-raising, a speaker could conclude by challenging the audience to raise 10 percent more than their original projections. In a speech on eating more vegetables, you could challenge your audience to increase their current intake of vegetables by two portions daily. In both of these challenges, audience members are being asked to go out of their way to do something different that involves effort on their part.

Conclude with a Quotation

A second way you can conclude a speech is by reciting a quotation relevant to the speech topic. When using a quotation, you need to think about whether your goal is to end on a persuasive note or an informative note. Some quotations will have a clear call to action, while other quotations summarize or provoke thought. For example, let's say you are delivering an informative speech about dissident writers in the former Soviet Union. You could end by citing this quotation from Alexander Solzhenitsyn: "A great writer is, so to speak, a second government in his country. And for that reason no regime has ever loved great writers."[4] Notice that this quotation underscores the idea of writers as dissidents, but it doesn't ask listeners to put forth effort to engage in any specific thought process or behavior. If, on the other hand, you were delivering a persuasive speech urging your audience to participate in a very risky political demonstration, you might use this quotation from Martin Luther King Jr.: "If a man hasn't discovered something that he will die for, he isn't fit to live."[5] In this case, the quotation leaves the audience with the message that great risks are worth taking, that they make our lives worthwhile, and that the right thing to do is to go ahead and take that great risk.

Conclude with a Summary

When a speaker ends with a summary, he or she is simply elongating the review of the main points. While this may not be the most exciting concluding device, it can be useful for information that was highly technical or complex or for speeches lasting longer than thirty minutes. Typically, for short speeches (like those in your class), this summary device should be avoided.

Conclude by Visualizing the Future

The purpose of a conclusion that refers to the future is to help your audience imagine the future you believe can occur. If you are giving a speech on the development of video games for learning, you could conclude by depicting the classroom of the future where video games are perceived as true learning tools and how those tools could be utilized. More often, speakers use visualization of the future to depict how society would be, or how individual listeners' lives would be different, if the speaker's persuasive attempt worked. For example, if a speaker proposes that a solution to illiteracy is hiring more reading specialists in public schools, the speaker could ask her or his audience to imagine a world without illiteracy. In this use of visualization, the goal is to persuade people to adopt the speaker's point of view. By showing that the speaker's vision of the future is a positive one, the conclusion should help to persuade the audience to help create this future.

Conclude with an Appeal for Action

Probably the most common persuasive concluding device is the appeal for action or the call to action. In essence, the **appeal for action** occurs when a speaker asks her or his audience to engage in a specific behavior or change in thinking. When a speaker concludes by asking the audience "to do" or "to think" in a specific manner, the speaker wants to see an actual change. Whether the speaker appeals for people to eat more fruit, buy a car, vote for a candidate, oppose the death penalty, or sing more in the shower, the speaker is asking the audience to engage in action.

One specific type of appeal for action is the **immediate call to action**. Whereas some appeals ask for people to engage in behavior in the future, the immediate call to action asks people to engage in behavior right now. If a speaker wants to see a new traffic light placed at a dangerous intersection, he or she may conclude by asking all the audience members to sign a digital petition right then and there, using a computer the speaker has made available (http://www.petitiononline.com). Here are some more examples of immediate calls to action:

- In a speech on eating more vegetables, pass out raw veggies and dip at the conclusion of the speech.
- In a speech on petitioning a lawmaker for a new law, provide audience members with a prewritten e-mail they can send to the lawmaker.
- In a speech on the importance of using hand sanitizer, hand out little bottles of hand sanitizer and show audience members how to correctly apply the sanitizer.
- In a speech asking for donations for a charity, send a box around the room asking for donations.

These are just a handful of different examples we've actually seen students use in our classrooms to elicit an immediate change in behavior. These immediate calls to action may not lead to long-term change, but they can be very effective at increasing the likelihood that an audience will change behavior in the short term.

Conclude by Inspiration

By definition, the word **inspire** means to affect or arouse someone. Both affect and arouse have strong emotional connotations. The ultimate goal of an inspiration concluding device is similar to an "appeal for action" but the ultimate goal is more lofty or ambiguous; the goal is to stir someone's emotions in a specific manner. Maybe a speaker is giving an informative speech on the prevalence of domestic violence in our society today. That speaker could end the speech by reading Paulette Kelly's powerful poem "I Got Flowers Today." "I Got Flowers Today" is a poem that evokes strong emotions because it's about an abuse victim who received flowers from her abuser every time she was victimized. The poem ends by saying, "I got flowers today... / Today was a special day—it was the day of my funeral / Last night he killed me."[6]

Conclude with Advice

The next concluding device is one that should be used primarily by speakers who are recognized as expert authorities on a given subject. **Advice** is essentially a speaker's opinion about what should or should not be done. The problem with opinions is that everyone has one, and one person's opinion is not necessarily any more correct than another's. There needs to be a really good reason your opinion—and therefore your advice—should matter to your audience. If, for example, you are an expert in nuclear physics, you might conclude a speech on energy by giving advice about the benefits of nuclear energy.

Conclude by Proposing a Solution

Another way a speaker can conclude a speech powerfully is to offer a solution to the problem discussed within a speech. For example, perhaps a speaker has been discussing the problems associated with the disappearance of art education in the United States. The speaker could then propose a solution of creating more community-based art experiences for school children as a way to fill this gap. Although this can be an effective conclusion, a speaker must ask herself or himself whether the solution should be discussed in more depth as a stand-alone main point within the body of the speech so that audience concerns about the proposed solution may be addressed.

Conclude with a Question

Another way you can end a speech is to ask a rhetorical question that forces the audience to ponder an idea. Maybe you are giving a speech on the importance of the environment, so you end the speech by saying, "Think about your children's future. What kind of world do you want them raised in? A world

appeal for action

When a speaker asks her or his audience to engage in a specific behavior or change in thinking.

immediate call to action

When a speaker asks the audience to engage in a specific behavior immediately following the conclusion of a speech.

inspire

To affect or arouse someone.

advice

A speaker's opinion about what should or should not be done.

that is clean, vibrant, and beautiful—or one that is filled with smog, pollution, filth, and disease?" Notice that you aren't actually asking the audience to verbally or nonverbally answer the question; the goal of this question is to force the audience into thinking about what kind of world they want for their children.

Conclude with a Reference to Audience

The last concluding device discussed by Miller (1946) was a reference to one's audience. This concluding device is when a speaker attempts to answer the basic audience question, "What's in it for me?" The goal of this concluding device is to spell out the direct benefits a behavior or thought change has for audience members. For example, a speaker talking about stress reduction techniques could conclude by clearly listing all the physical health benefits stress reduction offers (e.g., improved reflexes, improved immune system, improved hearing, reduction in blood pressure). In this case, the speaker is clearly spelling out why audience members should care—what's in it for them!

2.4   Informative versus Persuasive Conclusions

As you read through the ten possible ways to conclude a speech, hopefully you noticed that some of the methods are more appropriate for persuasive speeches and others are more appropriate for informative speeches. To help you choose appropriate conclusions for informative, persuasive, or entertaining speeches, we've created a table (Table 11.1) to help you quickly identify appropriate concluding devices.

TABLE 11.1 Your Speech Purpose and Concluding Devices

Types of Concluding Devices	General Purposes of Speeches		
	Informative	Persuasive	Entertaining
Challenge		x	x
Quotation	x	x	x
Summary	x	x	x
Visualizing the Future	x	x	x
Appeal		x	x
Inspirational	x	x	x
Advice		x	x
Proposal of Solution		x	x
Question	x	x	x
Reference to Audience		x	x

KEY TAKEAWAYS

- An effective conclusion contains three basic parts: a restatement of the speech's thesis; a review of the main points discussed within the speech; and a concluding device that helps create a lasting image in audiences' minds.
- Miller (1946) found that speakers tend to use one of ten concluding devices. All of these devices are not appropriate for all speeches, so speakers need to determine which concluding device would have the strongest, most powerful effect for a given audience, purpose, and occasion.

EXERCISES

1. Take the last speech you gave in class and rework the speech's conclusion to reflect the three parts of a conclusion. Now do the same thing with the speech you are currently working on for class.
2. Think about the speech you are currently working on in class. Write out concluding statements using three of the devices discussed in this chapter. Which of the devices would be most useful for your speech? Why?

3. ANALYZING A CONCLUSION

So far this chapter has focused on how to go about creating a clear conclusion. We discussed why conclusions are important, the three steps of effective conclusions, and ten different ways to conclude a speech. In this section, we're going to examine an actual conclusion to a speech. Please read the sample conclusion paragraph for the smart dust speech.

3.1   Sample Conclusion: Smart Dust

© Thinkstock

> Today, we've explored how smart dust may impact all of our lives in the near future by examining what smart dust is, how smart dust could be utilized by the US military, and how smart dust could impact all of our lives sooner rather than later. While smart dust is quickly transforming from science fiction to science fact, experts agree that the full potential of smart dust will probably not occur until 2025. While smart dust is definitely coming, swarms of smart dust eating people as was depicted in Michael Crichton's 2002 novel, Prey, aren't reality. However, as with any technological advance, there are definite ethical considerations and worries to consider. Even Dr. Kris Pister's Smart Dust Project website admits that as smart dust becomes more readily available, one of the trade-offs will be privacy. Pister responds to these critiques by saying, "As an engineer, or a scientist, or a hair stylist, everyone needs to evaluate what they do in terms of its positive and negative effect. If I thought that the negatives of working on this project were larger than or even comparable to the positives, I wouldn't be working on it. As it turns out, I think that the potential benefits of this technology far outweigh the risks to personal privacy."

Now that you've had a chance to read the conclusion to the speech on smart dust, read it a second time and try to find the three parts of an introduction as discussed earlier in this chapter. Once you're finished analyzing this conclusion, take a look at Table 11.2, which shows you how the speech was broken down into the various parts of a conclusion.

TABLE 11.2 Smart Dust Conclusion

Parts of a Conclusion	Analysis
Today we've explored how smart dust may impact all of our lives in the near future by	*Restate Thesis*
	The first part of the conclusion is a restatement of the thesis statement.
examining what smart dust is, how smart dust could be utilized by the US military, and how smart dust could impact all of our lives in the near future.	*Review Main Points*
	Following the thesis statement, the speech briefly reiterates the three main points discussed in the speech.
While smart dust is quickly transferring from science fiction to science fact, experts agree that the full potential of smart dust will probably not occur until 2025. While smart dust is definitely in our near future, swarms of smart dust eating people as was depicted in Michael Crichton's 2002 novel, *Prey*, isn't reality. However, as with any technological advance, there are definite ethical considerations and worries to consider. Even Dr. Kris Pister's Smart Dust Project website admits that as smart dust becomes more readily available, one of the trade-offs will be privacy. Pister responds to these critiques by saying, "As an engineer, or a scientist, or a hair stylist, everyone needs to evaluate what they do in terms of its positive and negative effect. If I thought that the negatives of working on this project were larger than or even comparable to the positives, I wouldn't be working on it. As it turns out, I think that the potential benefits of this technology far outweigh the risks to personal privacy."	*Concluding Device*
	In this concluding device, we see not only a referral to the attention getter (Michael Crichton's book *Prey*), we also see a visualizing of some future oriented factors people need to consider related to smart dust, which is then followed by a direct quotation.
	Notice that in an informative speech this type of conclusion is appropriate because we are trying to inform people about smart dust, but would you want to end a persuasive speech in this fashion? Definitely not!
	However, you could create an entire persuasive speech advocating for smart dust (its many applications are more important than the loss of privacy) or against smart dust (privacy is more important than its many applications).

3.2 Your Turn

Now that you have seen the above analysis of a speech conclusion, we encourage you to do a similar analysis of the conclusions of other speeches. Listen to a speech in your class or online. Does it end with a restatement of the thesis, a review of the main points, and a concluding device? Can you suggest ways to improve the conclusion?

Here is another exercise to try. Consider the specific purpose and three main points of a hypothetical speech. Based on those components, develop a conclusion for that speech.

4. CHAPTER EXERCISES

SPEAKING ETHICALLY

Tika's speech on death camps in Africa was a real flop, and she knew it. The speech was quickly prepared, inadequately researched, and not very logical. Thankfully, Tika knew she had an ace in her back pocket. She planned on ending her speech with a video showing mass graves that she knew would make people sick.

She thought, *Who cares if your speech sucks as long as you get them in the end!*

1. Would you say that Tika's approach to public speaking is ethical? Why or why not?

2. Which type of concluding device is Tika planning to use? Is this device appropriate to her speech? Why or why not? If you conclude it is not appropriate, which devices would be better approaches? Why?

3. Is it ever ethical to rely heavily on an emotional conclusion to persuade one's audience? Why?

END-OF-CHAPTER ASSESSMENT

1. Karla knows that people tend to remember the information at the beginning of a speech and at the end of a speech. What is this process called?

    a. serial position effect
    b. central limit theorem
    c. law of position effect
    d. law of limits theorem
    e. serial limits theorem

2. Which of the following best explains why conclusions are important?

    a. primacy
    b. recency
    c. closing stages
    d. predominance
    e. speech finish

3. What is the device a speaker uses at the end of a speech to ensure that the audience is left with a mental picture predetermined by the speaker?

    a. recency device
    b. predominance device
    c. finishing device
    d. concluding device
    e. finalizing device

4. At the end of her speech, Daniel asks his audience to sign a petition helping a candidate get on the ballot in his state. By having the audience members sign the petition right after the speech, what is Daniel engaging in?

    a. a call to public service
    b. a call to civic duty
    c. a proclamational appeal
    d. an appeal to one's general sense of right and wrong
    e. an immediate call to action

5. Miller's (1946) concluding device "reference to audience" can best be summed up by which phrase?

    a. A good or a bad audience is still receptive.
    b. It's all about me.
    c. Don't forget to love your audience.
    d. What's in it for me?
    e. A suffering audience is a persuaded audience.

ANSWER KEY

1. a
2. b
3. d
4. e
5. d

ENDNOTES

1. Ebbinghaus, H. (1885). *Memory: A contribution to experimental psychology* [Online version]. Retrieved from http://psychclassics.yorku.ca/Ebbinghaus/index.htm

2. Ehrensberger, R. (1945). An experimental study of the relative effectiveness of certain forms of emphasis in public speaking. *Speech Monographs, 12*, 94–111. doi: 10.1080/03637754509390108

3. Miller, E. (1946). Speech introductions and conclusions. *Quarterly Journal of Speech, 32*, 181–183.

4. Solzhenitsyn, A. (1964). *The first circle*. New York: Harper & Row. Cited in Bartlett, J., & Kaplan, J. (Eds.), *Bartlett's familiar quotations* (6th ed.). Boston, MA: Little, Brown & Co., p. 746.

5. King, M. L. (1963, June 23). Speech in Detroit. Cited in Bartlett, J., & Kaplan, J. (Eds.), *Bartlett's familiar quotations* (6th ed.). Boston, MA: Little, Brown & Co., p. 760.

6. Kelly, P. (1994). I got flowers today. In C. J. Palmer & J. Palmer, *Fire from within*. Painted Post, NY: Creative Arts & Science Enterprises.

CHAPTER 12

Outlining

THE FUN OF OUTLINING

Think of an outline as a skeleton you must assemble bone by bone, gradually making it take form into a coherent whole. Or think of it as a puzzle in which you must put all the pieces in their correct places in order to see the full picture. Or think of it as a game of solitaire in which the right cards must follow a legitimate sequence in order for you to win. The more fully you can come to understand the outline as both rule-bound and creative, the more fully you will experience its usefulness and its power to deliver your message in a unified, coherent way.

© *Thinkstock*

This means, of course, that there are no shortcuts, but there are helpful strategies. If you leave a bone out of a skeleton, something will fall apart. By the same token, if you omit a step in reasoning, your speech will be vulnerable to lapses in logic, lapses in the evidence you need to make your case, and the risk of becoming a disjointed, disorienting message. When you are talking informally with friends, your conversation might follow a haphazard course, but a public speech must not do so. Even in conversations with your friends, you might believe they understand what you mean, but they might not. In a prepared speech, you must be attentive to reasoning in logical steps so that your audience understands the meaning you intend to convey. This is where your outline can help you.

1. WHY OUTLINE?

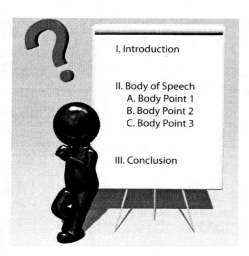

I. Introduction

II. Body of Speech
   A. Body Point 1
   B. Body Point 2
   C. Body Point 3

III. Conclusion

In order for your speech to be as effective as possible, it needs to be organized into logical patterns. Information will need to be presented in a way your audience can understand. This is especially true if you already know a great deal about your topic. You will need to take careful steps to include pertinent information your audience might not know and to explain relationships that might not be evident to them. Using a standard outline format, you can make decisions about your main points, the specific information you will use to support those points, and the language you will use. Without an outline, your message is liable to lose **logical integrity**. It might even deteriorate into a list of bullet points with no apparent connection to each other except the topic, leaving your audience relieved when your speech is finally over.

A full-sentence outline lays a strong foundation for your message. It will call on you to have one clear and **specific purpose** for your message. As we have seen in other chapters of this book, writing your specific purpose in clear language serves you well. It helps you frame a clear, concrete thesis statement. It helps you exclude irrelevant information. It helps you focus only on information that directly bears on your thesis. It reduces the amount of research you must do. It suggests what kind of supporting evidence is needed, so less effort is expended in trying to figure out what to do next. It helps both you and your audience remember the central message of your speech.

Finally, a solid full-sentence outline helps your audience understand your message because they will be able to follow your reasoning. Remember that live audiences for oral communications lack the ability to "rewind" your message to figure out what you said, so it is critically important to help the audience follow your reasoning as it reaches their ears.

Your authors have noted among their past and present students a reluctance to write full-sentence outlines. It's a task too often perceived as busywork, unnecessary, time consuming, and restricted. On one hand, we understand that reluctance. But on the other hand, we find that students who carefully write a full-sentence outline show a stronger tendency to give powerful presentations of excellent messages.

1.1 Tests Scope of Content

When you begin with a clear, concrete thesis statement, it acts as kind of a compass for your outline. Each of the main points should directly **explicate** the **thesis statement**. The test of the scope will be a comparison of each main point to the thesis statement. If you find a poor match, you will know you've wandered outside the scope of the thesis.

Let's say the general purpose of your speech is to inform, and your broad topic area is wind-generated energy. Now you must narrow this to a specific purpose. You have many choices, but let's say your specific purpose is to inform a group of property owners about the economics of wind farms where electrical energy is generated.

---

logical integrity

A characteristic of reasoning in which each claim is carefully supported by an orderly sequence of the right kind of evidence and by the right amount of evidence.

specific purpose

A concrete, narrow purpose. For instance, a general purpose might be to inform the audience about airport security in general. The specific purpose might be to explain the specific reasons for the watch list.

explicate

To provide a detailed explanation.

thesis statement

A short, declarative sentence that states the purpose, intent, or main idea.

Your first main point could be that modern windmills require a very small land base, making the cost of real estate low. This is directly related to economics. All you need is information to support your **claim** that only a small land base is needed.

In your second main point, you might be tempted to claim that windmills don't pollute in the ways other sources do. However, you will quickly note that this claim is unrelated to the thesis. You must resist the temptation to add it. Perhaps in another speech, your thesis will address environmental impact, but in this speech, you must stay within the economic scope. Perhaps you will say that once windmills are in place, they require virtually no maintenance. This claim is related to the thesis. Now all you need is supporting information to support this second claim.

Your third point, the point some audience members will want to hear, is the cost for generating electrical energy with windmills compared with other sources. This is clearly within the scope of energy economics. You should have no difficulty finding **authoritative sources** of information to support that claim.

When you write in outline form, it is much easier to test the scope of your content because you can visually locate specific information very easily and then check it against your thesis statement.

1.2   Tests Logical Relation of Parts

You have many choices for your topic, and therefore, there are many ways your content can be logically organized. In the example above, we simply listed three main points that were important economic considerations about wind farms. Often the main points of a speech can be arranged into a logical pattern; let's take a look at some such patterns.

A chronological pattern arranges main ideas in the order events occur. In some instances, reverse order might make sense. For instance, if your topic is archaeology, you might use the reverse order, describing the newest artifacts first.

A cause-and-effect pattern calls on you to describe a specific situation and explain what the effect is. However, most effects have more than one cause. Even dental cavities have multiple causes: genetics, poor nutrition, teeth too tightly spaced, sugar, ineffective brushing, and so on. If you choose a cause-and-effect pattern, make sure you have enough reliable support to do the topic justice.

A biographical pattern is usually chronological. In describing the events of an individual's life, you will want to choose the three most significant events. Otherwise, the speech will end up as a very lengthy and often pointless time line or bullet point list. For example, Mark Twain had several clear phases in his life. They include his life as a Mississippi riverboat captain, his success as a world-renowned writer and speaker, and his family life. A simple time line would present great difficulty in highlighting the relationships between important events. An outline, however, would help you emphasize the key events that contributed to Mark Twain's extraordinary life.

Although a comparison-contrast pattern appears to dictate just two main points, McCroskey, Wrench, and Richmond explain how a comparison-and-contrast can be structured as a speech with three main points. They say that "you can easily create a third point by giving basic information about what is being compared and what is being contrasted. For example, if you are giving a speech about two different medications, you could start by discussing what the medications' basic purposes are. Then you could talk about the similarities, and then the differences, between the two medications."[1]

Whatever logical pattern you use, if you examine your thesis statement and then look at the three main points in your outline, you should easily be able to see the logical way in which they relate.

1.3   Tests Relevance of Supporting Ideas

When you create an outline, you can clearly see that you need supporting **evidence** for each of your main points. For instance, using the example above, your first main point claims that less land is needed for windmills than for other utilities. Your supporting evidence should be about the amount of acreage required for a windmill and the amount of acreage required for other energy generation sites, such as nuclear power plants or hydroelectric generators. Your sources should come from experts in economics, economic development, or engineering. The evidence might even be expert opinion but not the opinions of ordinary people. The expert opinion will provide stronger support for your point.

Similarly, your second point claims that once a wind turbine is in place, there is virtually no maintenance cost. Your supporting evidence should show how much annual maintenance for a windmill costs and what the costs are for other energy plants. If you used a comparison with nuclear plants to support your first main point, you should do so again for the sake of consistency. It becomes very clear, then, that the third main point about the amount of electricity and its profitability needs authoritative references to compare it to the profit from energy generated at a nuclear power plant. In this third main point, you should make use of just a few well-selected statistics from authoritative sources to show the effectiveness of wind farms compared to the other energy sources you've cited.

claim

A statement that warrants the support of facts from authoritative sources.

authoritative sources

Sources that use factually verifiable observations and data to provide rigorous conclusions that will not collapse under scrutiny.

evidence

Information from an expert source, which is relevant to a main point.

Where do you find the kind of information you would need to support these main points? A reference librarian can quickly guide you to authoritative statistics manuals and help you make use of them.

An important step you will notice is that the full-sentence outline includes its authoritative sources within the text. This is a major departure from the way you've learned to write a research paper. In the research paper, you can add that information to the end of a sentence, leaving the reader to turn to the last page for a fuller citation. In a speech, however, your listeners can't do that. From the beginning of the supporting point, you need to fully cite your source so your audience can assess its importance.

Because this is such a profound change from the academic habits that you're probably used to, you will have to make a concerted effort to overcome the habits of the past and provide the information your listeners need when they need it.

1.4　Test the Balance and Proportion of the Speech

Part of the value of writing a full-sentence outline is the visual space you use for each of your main points. Is each main point of approximately the same importance? Does each main point have the same number of supporting points? If you find that one of your main points has eight supporting points while the others only have three each, you have two choices: either choose the best three from the eight supporting points or strengthen the authoritative support for your other two main points.

Remember that you should use the best supporting evidence you can find even if it means investing more time in your search for knowledge.

1.5　Serves as Notes during the Speech

Although we recommend writing a full-sentence outline during the speech preparation phase, you should also create a shortened outline that you can use as notes allowing for a strong delivery. If you were to use the full-sentence outline when delivering your speech, you would do a great deal of reading, which would limit your ability to give eye contact and use gestures, hurting your connection with your audience. For this reason, we recommend writing a short-phrase outline on 4 × 6 notecards to use when you deliver your speech. The good news is that your three main points suggest how you should prepare your notecards.

Your first 4 × 6 notecard can contain your thesis statement and other key words and phrases that will help you present your introduction. Your second card can contain your first main point, together with key words and phrases to act as a map to follow as you present. If your first main point has an exact quotation you plan to present, you can include that on your card. Your third notecard should be related to your second main point, your fourth card should be about your third main point, and your fifth card should be related to your conclusion. In this way, your five notecards follow the very same organizational pattern as your full outline. In the next section, we will explore more fully how to create a speaking outline.

KEY TAKEAWAYS

- Your outline can help you stay focused on the thesis of your presentation as you prepare your presentation by testing the scope of your content, examining logical relationships between topics, and checking the relevance of supporting ideas.
- Your outline can help you organize your message by making sure that all of your main points are well developed.
- Your outline can help you stay focused during your presentation by forming the foundation for your speaking outline, which lets you connect to your audience and be clear in the message you're presenting.

EXERCISES

1. In one sentence, write a clear, compelling thesis statement about each of the following topics: the effects of schoolyard bullying, the impact of alcohol on brain development, and the impact of the most recent volcano eruption in Iceland. Fully cite the sources where you verify that your thesis statements are actually true.
2. Prepare a full-sentence outline for your next speech assignment. Trade outlines with a classmate and check through the outline for logical sequence of ideas, presence of credible support, proper citation, and clear organization. Give feedback to your partner on areas where he or she has done well and where the outline might be improved.
3. Transfer information from your speech outline to notecards using the guidelines described above. Practice delivering your speech for a small audience (e.g., family member, group of friends or classmates) using first the outline and then the notecards. Ask the audience for feedback comparing your delivery using the two formats.

2. TYPES OF OUTLINES

LEARNING OBJECTIVES

1. Define three types of outlines: working outline, full-sentence outline, and speaking outline.
2. Identify the advantages of using notecards to present your speaking outline.

When we discuss outlining, we are actually focusing on a series of outlines instead of a single one. Outlines are designed to evolve throughout your speech preparation process, so this section will discuss how you progress from a working outline to a full-sentence outline and, finally, a speaking outline. We will also discuss how using notecards for your speaking outline can be helpful to you as a speaker.

2.1 Working Outline

© Thinkstock

A working outline is an outline you use for developing your speech. It undergoes many changes on its way to completion. This is the outline where you lay out the basic structure of your speech. You must have a general and specific purpose; an introduction, including a grabber; and a concrete, specific thesis statement and preview. You also need three main points, a conclusion, and a list of references.

One strategy for beginning your working outline is to begin by typing in your labels for each of the elements. Later you can fill in the content.

When you look ahead to the full-sentence outline, you will notice that each of the three main points moves from the general to the particular. Specifically, each main point is a claim, followed by particular information that supports that claim so that the audience will perceive its validity. For example, for a speech about coal mining safety, your first main point might focus on the idea that coal mining is a hazardous occupation. You might begin by making a very general claim, such as "Coal mining is one of the most hazardous occupations in the United States," and then become more specific by providing statistics, authoritative quotations, or examples to support your primary claim.

A working outline allows you to work out the kinks in your message. For instance, let's say you've made the claim that coal mining is a hazardous occupation but you cannot find authoritative evidence as support. Now you must reexamine that main point to assess its validity. You might have to change that main point in order to be able to support it. If you do so, however, you must make sure the new main point is a logical part of the thesis statement–three main points–conclusion sequence.

The working outline shouldn't be thought of a "rough copy," but as a careful step in the development of your message. It will take time to develop. Here is an example of a working outline:

Name: Anomaly May McGillicuddy

Topic: Smart dust

General Purpose: To inform

Specific Purpose: To inform a group of science students about the potential of smart dust

Main Ideas:

1. Smart dust is an assembly of microcomputers.
2. Smart dust can be used by the military—no, no—smart dust could be an enormous asset in covert military operations. (That's better because it is more clear and precise.)
3. Smart dust could also have applications to daily life.

Introduction: **(Grabber)** (fill in later)

(Thesis Statement) Thus far, researchers hypothesize that smart dust could be used for everything from tracking patients in hospitals to early warnings of natural disasters and defending against bioterrorism.

(Preview) Today, I'm going to explain what smart dust is and the various applications smart dust has in the near future. To help us understand the small of it all, we will first examine what smart dust is and how it works. We will then examine some military applications of smart dust. And we will end by discussing some nonmilitary applications of smart dust.

(Transition) (fill in later)

Main Point I: Dr. Kris Pister, a professor in the robotics lab at the University of California at Berkeley, originally conceived the idea of smart dust in 1998 as part of a project funded by the Defense Advanced Research Projects Agency (DARPA).

   A. (supporting point)
   B. (supporting point)

(Transition) (fill in later)

Main Point II: Because smart dust was originally conceptualized under a grant from DARPA, military uses of smart dust have been widely theorized and examined.

   A. (supporting point)
   B. (supporting point)

(Transition) (fill in later)

Main Point III: According to the smart dust project website, smart dust could quickly become a common part of our daily lives.

   A. (supporting point)
   B. (supporting point)

(Transition) (fill in later)

Conclusion: (Bring your message "full circle" and create a psychologically satisfying closure.)

This stage of preparation turns out to be a good place to go back and examine whether all the main points are directly related to the thesis statement and to each other. If so, your message has a strong potential for unity of focus. But if the relationship of one of the main points is weak, this is the time to strengthen it. It will be more difficult later for two reasons: first, the sheer amount of text on your pages will make the visual task more difficult, and second, it becomes increasingly difficult to change things in which you have a large investment in time and thought.

You can see that this working outline can lay a strong foundation for the rest of your message. Its organization is visually apparent. Once you are confident in the internal unity of your basic message, you can begin filling in the supporting points in descending detail—that is, from the general (main points) to the particular (supporting points) and then to greater detail. The outline makes it visually apparent where information fits. You only need to assess your supporting points to be sure they're authoritative and directly relevant to the main points they should support.

Sometimes transitions seem troublesome, and that's not surprising. We often omit them when we have informal conversations. Our conversation partners understand what we mean because of our gestures and vocal strategies. However, others might not understand what we mean, but think they do, and so we might never know whether they understood us. Even when we include transitions, we don't generally identify them as transitions. In a speech, however, we need to use effective transitions as a gateway from one main point to the next. The listener needs to know when a speaker is moving from one main point to the next.

In the next type of outline, the full-sentence outline, take a look at the transitions and see how they make the listener aware of the shifting focus to the next main point.

2.2 Full-Sentence Outline

Your full-sentence outline should contain full sentences only. There are several reasons why this kind of outline is important. First, you have a full plan of everything you intend to say to your audience, so that you will not have to struggle with wordings or examples. Second, you have a clear idea of how much time it will take to present your speech. Third, it contributes a fundamental ingredient of good preparation, part of your ethical responsibility to your audience. This is how a full-sentence outline looks:

Name: Anomaly May McGillicuddy

Topic: Smart dust

General Purpose: To inform

Specific Purpose: To inform a group of science students about the potential of smart dust.

Main Ideas:

1. Smart dust is an assembly of microcomputers.
2. Smart dust could be an enormous asset in covert military operations.
3. Smart dust could also have applications to daily life.

Introduction: **(Grabber)** In 2002, famed science fiction writer, Michael Crichton, released his book *Prey*, which was about a swarm of nanomachines that were feeding off living tissue. The nanomachines were solar powered, self-sufficient, and intelligent. Most disturbingly, the nanomachines could work together as a swarm as it took over and killed its prey in its need for new resources. The technology for this level of sophistication in nanotechnology is surprisingly more science fact than science fiction. In 2000, three professors of electrical engineering and computer Science at the University of California at Berkeley, Kahn, Katz, and Pister, hypothesized in the *Journal of Communications and Networks* that wireless networks of tiny microelectromechanical sensors, or MEMS; robots; or devices could detect phenomena including light, temperature, or vibration. By 2004, *Fortune Magazine* listed "smart dust" as the first in their "Top 10 Tech Trends to Bet On."

(Thesis Statement) Thus far researchers hypothesized that smart dust could be used for everything from tracking patients in hospitals to early warnings of natural disasters and as a defense against bioterrorism.

(Preview) Today, I'm going to explain what smart dust is and the various applications smart dust has in the near future. To help us understand the small of it all, we will first examine what smart dust is and how it works. We will then examine some military applications of smart dust. And we will end by discussing some nonmilitary applications of smart dust.

(Transition) To help us understand smart dust, we will begin by first examining what smart dust is.

Main Point I: Dr. Kris Pister, a professor in the robotics lab at the University of California at Berkeley, originally conceived the idea of smart dust in 1998 as part of a project funded by the Defense Advanced Research Projects Agency (DARPA).

A. According to a 2001 article written by Bret Warneke, Matt Last, Brian Liebowitz, and Kris Pister titled "Smart Dust: Communicating with a Cubic-Millimeter Computer" published in *Computer*, Pister's goal was to build a device that contained a built-in sensor, communication device, and a small computer that could be integrated into a cubic millimeter package.

B. For comparison purposes, Doug Steel, in a 2005 white paper titled "Smart Dust" written for C. T. Bauer College of Business at the University of Houston, noted that a single grain of rice has a volume of five cubic millimeters.

   1. Each individual piece of dust, called a mote, would then have the ability to interact with other motes and supercomputers.

   2. As Steve Lohr wrote in the January 30, 2010, edition of the *New York Times* in an article titled "Smart Dust? Not Quite, But We're Getting There," smart dust could eventually consist of "Tiny digital sensors, strewn around the glove, gathering all sorts of information and communicating with powerful computer networks to monitor, measure, and understand the physical world in new ways."

(Transition) Now that we've examined what smart dust is, let's switch gears and talk about some of the military applications for smart dust.

Main Point II: Because smart dust was originally conceptualized under a grant from DARPA, military uses of smart dust have been widely theorized and examined.

    A. According to the smart dust website, smart dust could eventually be used for "battlefield surveillance, treaty monitoring, transportation monitoring, scud hunting" and other clear military applications.

        1. Probably the number one benefit of smart dust in the military environment is its surveillance abilities.

            a. Major Scott Dickson, in a Blue Horizons paper written for the US Air Force Center for Strategy and Technology's Air War College, sees smart dust as helping the military in battlespace awareness, homeland security, and weapons of mass destruction (WMD) identification.

            b. Furthermore, Major Dickson also believes it may be possible to create smart dust that has the ability to defeat communications jamming equipment created by foreign governments, which could help the US military not only communicate among itself, but could also increase communications with civilians in military combat zones.

    B. According to a 2010 article written by Jessica Griggs in new *Scientist*, one of the first benefits of smart dust could be an early defense warning for space storms and other debris that could be catastrophic.

(Transition) Now that we've explored some of the military benefits of smart dust, let's switch gears and see how smart dust may be able to have an impact on our daily lives.

Main Point III: According to the smart dust project website, smart dust could quickly become a common part of our daily lives.

    A. Everything from pasting smart dust particles to our finger tips to create a virtual computer keyboard to inventory control to product quality control have been discussed as possible applications for smart dust.

        1. Steve Lohr, in his 2010 *New York Times* article, wrote, "The applications for sensor-based computing, experts say, include buildings that manage their own energy use, bridges that sense motion and metal fatigue to tell engineers they need repairs, cars that track traffic patterns and report potholes, and fruit and vegetable shipments that tell grocers when they ripen and begin to spoil."

    B. Medically, according to the smart dust website, smart dust could help disabled individuals interface with computers.

        1. Theoretically, we could all be injected with smart dust, which relays information to our physicians and detects adverse changes to our body instantly.

        2. Smart dust could detect the microscopic formations of center cells or alert us when we've been infected by a bacterium or virus, which could speed up treatment and prolong all of our lives.

(Transition) Today, we've explored what smart dust is, how smart dust could be utilized by the US military, and how smart dust could impact all of our lives in the near future.

Conclusion: While smart dust is quickly transferring from science fiction to science fact, experts agree that the full potential of smart dust will probably not occur until 2025. Smart dust is definitely in our near future, but swarms of smart dust eating people as was depicted in Michael Crichton's 2002 novel, *Prey*, isn't reality. However, as with any technological advance, there are definite ethical considerations and worries related to smart dust. Even Dr. Kris Pister's smart dust project website admits that as smart dust becomes more readily available, one of the trade-offs will be privacy. Pister responds to these critiques by saying, "As an engineer, or a scientist, or a hair stylist, everyone needs to evaluate what they do in terms of its positive and negative effect. If I thought that the negatives of working on this project were greater than or even comparable to the positives, I wouldn't be working on it. As it turns out, I think that the potential benefits of this technology far outweigh the risks to personal privacy."

References

Crichton, M. (2002). *Prey*. New York, NY: Harper Collins.

Dickson, S. (2007, April). *Enabling battlespace persistent surveillance: the firm, function, and future of smart dust* (Blue Horizons Paper, Center for Strategy and Technology, USAF Air War College). Retrieved from USAF Air War College website: http://www.au.af.mil/au/awc/awcgate/cst/bh_dickson.pdf

Griggs, J. (2010, February 6). Smart dust to provide solar early warning defense. *New Scientist, 205*(2746), 22.

Kahn, J. M., Katz, R. H., & Pister, K. S. J. (2000). Emerging challenges: Mobile networking for "smart dust." *Journal of Communications and Networks, 2*, 188–196.

Lohr, S. (2010, January 30). Smart dust? Not quite, but we're getting there. *New York Times*. Retrieved from *http://www.nytimes.com*

Pister, K., Kahn, J., & Boser, B. (n.d.). Smart dust: Autonomous sensing and communication at the cubic millimeter. Retrieved from *http://robotics.eecs.berkeley.edu/~pister/SmartDust*

Steel, D. (2005, March). Smart dust: UH ISRC technology briefing. Retrieved from *http://www.uhisrc.com*

Vogelstein, F., Boyle, M., Lewis, P., Kirkpatrick, D., Lashinsky, A.,…Chen, C. (2004, February 23). 10 tech trends to bet on. *Fortune, 149*(4), 74–88.

Warneke, B., Last, M., Liebowitz, B., & Pister, K. S. J. (2001). Smart dust: Communicating with a cubic millimeter computer. *Computer, 31*, 44–51.

When you prepare your full-sentence outline carefully, it may take as much as 1 ½ hours to complete the first part of the outline from your name at the top through the introduction. When you've completed that part, take a break and do something else. When you return to the outline, you should be able to complete your draft in another 1 ½ hours. After that, you only need to do a detailed check for completeness, accuracy, relevance, balance, omitted words, and consistency. If you find errors, instead of being frustrated, be glad you can catch these errors *before* you're standing up in front of your audience.

You will notice that the various parts of your speech, for instance, the transition and main points, are labeled. There are compelling reasons for these labels. First, as you develop your message, you will sometimes find it necessary to go back and look at your wording in another part of the outline. Your labels help you find particular passages easily. Second, the labels work as a checklist so that you can make sure you've included everything you intended to. Third, it helps you prepare your speaking outline.

You'll also notice the full references at the end of the outline. They match the citations within the outline. Sometimes while preparing a speech, a speaker finds it important to go back to an original source to be sure the message will be accurate. If you type in your references as you develop your speech rather than afterward, they will be a convenience to you if they are complete and accurate.

Don't think of the references as busywork or drudgery. Although they're more time consuming than text, they are good practice for the more advanced academic work you will do in the immediate future.

2.3   Speaking Outline

Your full-sentence outline prepares you to present a clear and well-organized message, but your speaking outline will include far less detail. Whenever possible, you will use key words and phrases, but in some instances, an extended quotation will need to be fully written on your speaking outline.

Resist the temptation to use your full-sentence outline as your speaking outline. The temptation is real for at least two reasons. First, once you feel that you've carefully crafted every sequence of words in your speech, you might not want to sacrifice quality when you shift to vocal presentation. Second, if you feel anxiety about how well you will do in front of an audience, you may want to use your full-sentence outline as a "safety net." In our experience, however, if you have your full-sentence outline with you, you will end up reading, rather than speaking, to your audience. The subject of reading to your audience will be taken up in Chapter 14 on speech delivery. For now, it is enough to know you shouldn't read, but instead, use carefully prepared notecards.

Your speech has five main components: introduction, main point one, main point two, main point three, and the conclusion. Therefore we strongly recommend the use of five notecards: one for each of those five components. There are extenuating circumstances that might call for additional cards, but begin with five cards only.

How will five notecards suffice in helping you produce a complete, rich delivery? Why can't you use the full-sentence outline you labored so hard to write? First, the presence of your full-sentence outline will make it appear that you don't know the content of your speech. Second, the temptation to read the speech directly from the full-sentence outline is nearly overwhelming; even if you resist this temptation, you will find yourself struggling to remember the words on the page rather than speaking extemporaneously. Third, sheets of paper are noisier and more awkward than cards. Fourth, it's easier to lose your place using the full outline. Finally, cards just look better. Carefully prepared cards, together with practice, will help you more than you might think.

Plan to use five cards. Use 4 × 6 cards. The smaller 3 × 5 cards are too small to provide space for a visually organized set of notes. With five cards, you will have one card for the introduction, one card for each of the three main points, and one card for the conclusion. You should number your cards and write on one side only. Numbering is helpful if you happen to drop your cards, and writing on only one side means that the audience is not distracted by your handwritten notes and reminders to yourself while you are speaking. Each card should contain key words and key phrases but not full sentences.

Some speeches will include direct or extended quotations from expert sources. Some of these quotations might be highly technical or difficult to memorize for other reasons, but they must be presented correctly. This is a circumstance in which you could include an extra card in the sequence of notecards. This is the one time you may read fully from a card. If your quotation is important and the exact wording is crucial, your audience will understand that.

How will notecards be sufficient? When they are carefully written, your practice will reveal that they will work. If, during practice, you find that one of your cards doesn't work well enough, you can rewrite that card.

Using a set of carefully prepared, sparingly worded cards will help you resist the temptation to rely on overhead transparencies or PowerPoint slides to get you through the presentation. Although they will never provide the exact word sequence of your full-sentence outline, they should keep you organized during the speech.

The "trick" to selecting the phrases and quotations for your cards is to identify the labels that will trigger a recall sequence. For instance, if the phrase "more science fact" brings to mind the connection to science fiction and the differences between the real developments and the fictive events of Crichton's novel *Prey*, that phrase on your card will support you through a fairly extended part of your introduction.

You must discover what works for you and then select those words that tend to jog your recall. Having identified what works, make a preliminary set of no more than five cards written on one side only, and practice with them. Revise and refine them as you would an outline.

The following is a hypothetical set of cards for the smart dust speech:

Card 1.

Introduction: 2002, *Prey*, swarm nanomachines feed on living tissue.

Kahn, Katz, and Pister, U C Berkeley engineering and computer sci. profs. hyp.

Microelectromechanical (MEMS) devices could detect light, temp, or vib.

Thesis Statement: Researchers hyp that s.d. could track patients, warn of natural disaster, act as defense against bioterrorism.

Prev.: What smart dust is and how it works, military aps, nonmilitary aps.

Transition: To help understand, first, what smart dust is.

Card 2.

I. Dr. Kris Pister, prof robotics lab UC Berkeley conceived the idea in 1998 in a proj. Defense Advanced Research Projects Agency (DARPA).

    A. 2001 article by Bret Warneke et al titled "Smart Dust: Communicating with a Cubic-Millimeter Computer" publ. in *Computer*, Pister wanted sensors, comm. devices, and computer in a cubic millimeter package.

    B. Doug Steel of CT Bauer College of Bus at Houston noted grain of rice = 5 cm.

        1. Each mote could interact w/ others.

        2. (see extended quotation, next card)

Card 3.

Quotation: Steve Lohr, NYT Jan 30 2005, "Smart Dust? Not Quite, but We're Getting There." Smart dust could eventually consist of "Tiny digital sensors, strewn around the globe, gathering all sorts of information and communicating with powerful computer networks to monitor, measure, and understand the physical world in new ways."

Card 4.

II. Orig conceptualized under DARPA, military uses theor. and examined.

    A. Smart Dust website, battlefield surveill., treaty monitor., transp. monitor., + scud hunting.

        1. benefit, surveill.

            a. Maj. Scott Dickson, Blue Horizons Paper for Ctr for Strat and Tech for USAF air war college, sees s.d. as help for battlespace awareness, homeland security, and WMD ID.

            b. could also defeat comm. jamming equipt by communicating among itself and w/ civilians in combat zones.

    B. 2010 article Jessica Griggs *New Scientist*, early defense, storms and debris.

Transition: Switch gears to daily lives.

Card 5.

III. s.d. project website: s.d. could become common in daily life.

    A. Pasting particles for virtual computer keyboard to inventory control poss.

        1. Steve Lohr, 2010, NYT, "The applications for sensor-based computing, experts say, include buildings that manage their own energy use, bridges that sense motion and metal fatigue to tell engineers they need repairs, cars that track traffic patterns and report potholes, and fruit and vegetable shipments that tell grocers when they ripen and begin to spoil."

    B. Medically, accdng to SD project website, help disabled.

        1. interface w/ computers

        2. injected, cd. relay info to docs and detect body changes instantly

            a. cancer cells, bacteria or virus, speed up treatment, and so on.

Transition: We expl. What SD is, how SD cd be used military, and how SD cd impact our lives.

Card 6.

Conclusion: Transf fiction to fact, experts agree potential 2025. Michael Crichton's Prey isn't reality, but in developing SD as fact, there are ethical considerations. Pister: privacy.

Dr. Kris Pister: "As an engineer, or a scientist, or a hair stylist, everyone needs to evaluate what they do in terms of its positive and negative effect. If I thought that the negatives of working on this project were larger or even comparable to the positives, I wouldn't be working on it. As it turns out, I think that the potential benefits of this technology far far outweigh the risks to personal privacy."

Using a set of cards similar to this could help you get through an impressive set of specialized information. But what if you lose your place during a speech? With a set of cards, it will take less time to refind it than with a full-sentence outline. You will not be rustling sheets of paper, and because your cards are written on one side only, you can keep them in order without flipping them back and forth to check both sides.

What if you go blank? Take a few seconds to recall what you've said and how it leads to your next points. There may be several seconds of silence in the middle of your speech, and it may seem like minutes to you, but you can regain your footing most easily with a small set of well-prepared cards.

Under no circumstances should you ever attempt to put your entire speech on cards in little tiny writing. You will end up reading a sequence of words to your audience instead of telling them your message.

KEY TAKEAWAYS

- Working outlines help you with speech logic, development, and planning.
- The full-sentence outline develops the full detail of the message.
- The speaking outline helps you stay organized in front of the audience without reading to them.
- Using notecards for your speaking outline helps with delivery and makes it easier to find information if you lose your place or draw a blank.

1. With respect to your speech topic, what words need to be defined?
2. Define what you mean by the terms you will use.
3. How does your definition compare with those of experts?

3. USING OUTLINING FOR SUCCESS

LEARNING OBJECTIVE

1. Understand five basic principles of outline creation.

As with any part of the speech process, there are some pretty commonly agreed upon principles for creating an outline. Now that we've examined the basics of outline creation, there are some important factors to consider when creating a logical and coherent outline: singularity, consistency, adequacy, uniformity, and parallelism.

3.1 Singularity

For the sake of clarity, make sure your thesis statement expresses one idea only. Only in this way will it be optimally useful to you as you build your outline. If you have narrowed your topic skillfully, you can readily focus the thesis statement as one central point. For instance, if you have a thesis statement that says the Second Amendment protects gun ownership rights but most people are unaware of the responsibility involved, you have a thesis statement focusing on two different issues. Which focus will you follow? It's crucial to choose just one, saving the other perhaps for a different speech.

The same holds true for your three main points: they should each express one clear idea. For the sake of your audience, maintain clarity. If many different ideas are required in order to build a complete message, you can handle them in separate sentences with the use of such transitions as "at the same time," "alternately," "in response to that event," or some other transition that clarifies the relationship between two separate ideas.

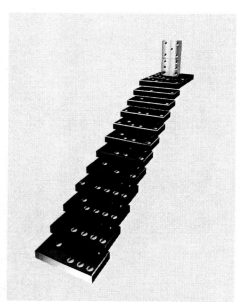

© Thinkstock

3.2 Consistency

The entire point of framing a thesis with one clear focus is to help you maintain consistency throughout your speech. Beyond the grammatical requirements of subject-verb agreement, you will want to maintain a consistent approach. For instance, unless your speech has a chronological structure that begins in the past and ends in the future, you should choose a tense, past or present, to use throughout the speech. Similarly, you should choose language and use it consistently. For instance, use humanity instead of mankind or humans, and use that term throughout.

Similarly, define your terms and use those terms only to designate the meanings in your definition. To do otherwise could result in equivocation and confusion. For instance, if you use the word "right" in two or three different senses, you should change your language. The word "right" can be applicable to your *right* to a good education; the ethical difference between *right* and wrong; and the status of a statement as *right*, or accurate and correct. By the same token, in a health care setting, saying that a medical test had a positive outcome can be confusing. Does the patient test positive for the presence of disease, or does the test reveal some good news? If you find yourself using the same word to mean different things, you will need to spend extra time in your speech explaining these meanings very clearly—or avoid the problem by making other word choices.

3.3   Adequacy

To make sure your audience will understand your speech, you must set aside the assumption that what is obvious to you is also obvious to your audience. Therefore, pay attention to adequacy in two ways: definitions of terms and support for your main points.

You should use concrete language as much as you can. For instance, if you use the word "community," you're using an abstract term that can mean many things. You might be referring to a suburban neighborhood; to a cultural group, such as the Jewish community; to an institutional setting that includes an academic community; or to a general sense of overarching mainstream community standards for what materials should or should not be broadcast on television, for instance. You may not find any definition of "community" that conveys your meaning. Therefore, you will need to define for your audience what *you* mean by "community."

Adequacy is also a concern when you use evidence to support your main points. Evidence of the right kind and the right weight are needed. For instance, if you make a substantial claim, such as a claim that all printed news sources will be obsolete within ten years, you need expert sources. This means you need at least two well-known experts from the institutions that provide news (newspapers, television news, or news radio). They should be credible sources, not sources with extreme views whose contact with reality is questioned. This will give you the right kind of evidence, and a large enough amount of evidence.

3.4   Uniformity

A full-sentence outline readily shows whether you are giving "equal time" to each of your three main points. For example, are you providing three pieces of evidence to support each main point? It should also show whether each main point is directly related to the thesis statement.

3.5   Parallelism

Parallelism refers to the idea that the three main points follow the same structure or make use of the same kind of language. For instance, in the sample outline we used previously, you see that each of the main points emphasizes the topic, smart dust.

Parallelism also allows you to check for inconsistencies and self-contradictory statements. For instance, does anything within main point two contradict anything in main point one? Examining your text for this purpose can strengthen the clarity of your message. For instance, if in main point one you claim that computer crime leaves an electronic trail, but in main point two you claim that hackers often get away with their crimes, you have some explaining to do. If an electronic trail can readily lead to the discovery of the electronic felon, how or why do they get away with it? The answer might be that cyber-crime does not fall within the jurisdiction of any law enforcement agency or that the law lags behind technology. Perhaps there are other reasons as well, and you must make sure you don't leave your audience confused. If you confuse them, you will sound confused, and you will lose credibility. There is no doubt that a full-sentence outline provides the most useful opportunity to examine your message for the details that either clarify or undermine your message.

Finally, your conclusion should do two things. First, it should come "full circle" in order to show the audience that you have covered all the territory you laid out in your preview. Second, it should provide satisfying, decisive, psychological closure. In other words, your audience should know when your speech is over. You should not trail off. You should not have to say, "That's it." Your audience should not have to wait to see whether you're going to say anything else. At the right time, they should feel certain that the speech is over and that they can clap.

KEY TAKEAWAY

- For an outline to be useful, it's important to follow five basic principles: singularity, consistency, adequacy, uniformity, and parallelism.

1. Look at an outline you've created for your public speaking course. Did you follow the five basic rules of outlining? How could you have changed your outline to follow those five basic principles?

2. Write an outline for your next speech in your course, paying special attention to the structure of the outline to ensure that none of the principles of outlining are violated.

4. CHAPTER EXERCISES

SPEAKING ETHICALLY

George needs to turn in an outline for the speech he is assigned to deliver. The speech itself is two weeks away, but the outline is due today. George has already written the entire speech, and he does not see why he should spend time deleting parts of it to transform it into an outline. He knows exactly what he's going to say when he gives the speech. Then he discovers that the word-processing program in his computer can create an outline version of a document. Aha! Technology to the rescue! George happily turns in the computer-generated outline, feeling confident that never again will he have to hassle with writing an outline himself.

1. Do you think George's use of a computer-generated outline fulfills the purpose of creating an outline for a speech? Why or why not?

2. Do you think George's professor will be able to tell that the outline was created by a word-processing program?

END-OF-CHAPTER ASSESSMENT

1. Joe is beginning to prepare his speech and has constructed a brief outline that sketches out his thesis and main points but does not yet have a fully developed conclusion or transitions. Which type of outline has Joe constructed?

   a. speaking outline

   b. full-sentence outline

   c. opening outline

   d. working outline

   e. transitory outline

2. Brenda has prepared her speaking outline on a set of six notecards, so she believes she is finished preparing for her speech. You tell her that simply preparing the speaking outline is not enough; she needs to practice using her notecards as well. Why is this the case?

   a. She should get used to how the notecards feel in her hand.

   b. She needs to make sure the information on the cards will work as a memory cue for her.

   c. She needs to know whether her audience prefers white or colored notecards.

   d. You think she needs to add more notecards.

   e. She needs to memorize all the quotations she is using.

ANSWER KEY

1. d
2. b

ENDNOTES

1. McCroskey, J. C., Wrench, J. S., & Richmond, V. P., (2003). *Principles of public speaking.*
   Indianapolis, IN: The College Network.

The Importance of Language

LANGUAGE MATTERS

Ask any professional speaker or speech writer, and they will tell you that language matters. In fact, some of the most important and memorable lines in American history came from speeches given by American presidents:

It is true that you may fool all the people some of the time; you can even fool some of the people all the time; but you can't fool all of the people all the time.[1]

   - Abraham Lincoln

Speak softly and carry a big stick.[2]

   - Theodore Roosevelt

The only thing we have to fear is fear itself.[3]

   - Franklin Delano Roosevelt

Ask not what your country can do for you; ask what you can do for your country.[4]

   - John F. Kennedy

© *Thinkstock*

We lose ourselves when we compromise the very ideals that we fight to defend. And we honor those ideals by upholding them not when it's easy, but when it is hard.[5]

   - Barack Obama

You don't have to be a president or a famous speaker to use language effectively. So in this chapter, we're going to explore the importance of language. First, we will discuss the difference between oral and written language, then we will talk about some basic guidelines for using language, and lastly, we'll look at six key elements of language.

1. ORAL VERSUS WRITTEN LANGUAGE

LEARNING OBJECTIVES

1. Understand the importance of language.
2. Explain the difference between denotative and connotative definitions.
3. Understand how denotative and connotative definitions can lead to misunderstandings.
4. Differentiate between oral and written language.

© Thinkstock

When we use the word "language," we are referring to the words you choose to use in your speech—so by definition, our focus is on spoken language. Spoken language has always existed prior to written language. Wrench, McCroskey, and Richmond suggested that if you think about the human history of language as a twelve-inch ruler, written language or recorded language has only existed for the "last quarter of an inch."[6] Furthermore, of the more than six thousand languages that are spoken around the world today, only a minority of them actually use a written alphabet.[7] To help us understand the importance of language, we will first look at the basic functions of language and then delve into the differences between oral and written language.

1.1 Basic Functions of Language

language

Any formal system of gestures, signs, sounds, or symbols, used or conceived as a means of communicating thought.

Language is any formal system of gestures, signs, sounds, and symbols used or conceived as a means of communicating thought. As mentioned above, there are over six thousand language schemes currently in use around the world. The language spoken by the greatest number of people on the planet is Mandarin; other widely spoken languages are English, Spanish, and Arabic.[8] Language is ultimately important because it is the primary means through which humans have the ability to communicate and interact with one another. Some linguists go so far as to suggest that the acquisition of language skills is the primary advancement that enabled our prehistoric ancestors to flourish and succeed over other hominid species.[9]

In today's world, effective use of language helps us in our interpersonal relationships at home and at work. Using language effectively also will improve your ability to be an effective public speaker. Because language is an important aspect of public speaking that many students don't spend enough time developing, we encourage you to take advantage of this chapter.

One of the first components necessary for understanding language is to understand how we assign meaning to words. Words consist of sounds (oral) and shapes (written) that have agreed-upon meanings based in concepts, ideas, and memories. When we write the word "blue," we may be referring to a portion of the visual spectrum dominated by energy with a wavelength of roughly 440–490 nanometers. You could also say that the color in question is an equal mixture of both red and green light. While both of these are technically correct ways to interpret the word "blue," we're pretty sure that neither of these definitions is how you thought about the word. When hearing the word "blue," you may have thought of your favorite color, the color of the sky on a spring day, or the color of a really ugly car you saw in the parking lot. When people think about language, there are two different types of meanings that people must be aware of: denotative and connotative.

Denotative Meaning

denotative meaning

The common agreed-upon meaning of a word that is often found in dictionaries.

Denotative meaning is the specific meaning associated with a word. We sometimes refer to denotative meanings as dictionary definitions. The definitions provided above for the word "blue" are examples of definitions that might be found in a dictionary. The first dictionary was written by Robert Cawdry in 1604 and was called *Table Alphabeticall*. This dictionary of the English language consisted of three thousand commonly spoken English words. Today, the *Oxford English Dictionary* contains more than 200,000 words.[10]

Connotative Meaning

connotative meaning

An individual's perception suggested by or associated with a word.

Connotative meaning is the idea suggested by or associated with a word. In addition to the examples above, the word "blue" can evoke many other ideas:

- State of depression (feeling blue)
- Indication of winning (a blue ribbon)

- Side during the Civil War (blues vs. grays)
- Sudden event (out of the blue)

We also associate the color blue with the sky and the ocean. Maybe your school's colors or those of your archrival include blue. There are also various forms of blue: aquamarine, baby blue, navy blue, royal blue, and so on.

Some miscommunication can occur over denotative meanings of words. For example, one of the authors of this book recently received a flyer for a tennis center open house. The expressed goal was to introduce children to the game of tennis. At the bottom of the flyer, people were encouraged to bring their own racquets if they had them but that "a limited number of racquets will be available." It turned out that the denotative meaning of the final phrase was interpreted in multiple ways: some parents attending the event perceived it to mean that loaner racquets would be available for use during the open house event, but the people running the open house intended it to mean that parents could purchase racquets onsite. The confusion over denotative meaning probably hurt the tennis center, as some parents left the event feeling they had been misled by the flyer.

Although denotatively based misunderstanding such as this one do happen, the majority of communication problems involving language occur because of differing connotative meanings. You may be trying to persuade your audience to support public funding for a new professional football stadium in your city, but if mentioning the team's or owner's name creates negative connotations in the minds of audience members, you will not be very persuasive. The potential for misunderstanding based in connotative meaning is an additional reason why audience analysis, discussed earlier in this book, is critically important. By conducting effective audience analysis, you can know in advance how your audience might respond to the connotations of the words and ideas you present. Connotative meanings can not only differ between individuals interacting at the same time but also differ greatly across time periods and cultures. Ultimately, speakers should attempt to have a working knowledge of how their audiences could potentially interpret words and ideas to minimize the chance of miscommunication.

1.2   Twelve Ways Oral and Written Language Differ

A second important aspect to understand about language is that oral language (used in public speaking) and written language (used for texts) does not function the same way. Try a brief experiment. Take a textbook, maybe even this one, and read it out loud. When the text is read aloud, does it sound conversational? Probably not. Public speaking, on the other hand, should sound like a conversation. McCroskey, Wrench, and Richmond highlighted the following twelve differences that exist between oral and written language:

1. Oral language has a smaller variety of words.
2. Oral language has words with fewer syllables.
3. Oral language has shorter sentences.
4. Oral language has more self-reference words (*I, me, mine*).
5. Oral language has fewer quantifying terms or precise numerical words.
6. Oral language has more pseudoquantifying terms (*many, few, some*).
7. Oral language has more extreme and superlative words (*none, all, every, always, never*).
8. Oral language has more qualifying statements (clauses beginning with *unless* and *except*).
9. Oral language has more repetition of words and syllables.
10. Oral language uses more contractions.
11. Oral language has more interjections ("Wow!," "Really?," "No!," "You're kidding!").
12. Oral language has more colloquial and nonstandard words.[11]

These differences exist primarily because people listen to and read information differently. First, when you read information, if you don't grasp content the first time, you have the ability to reread a section. When we are listening to information, we do not have the ability to "rewind" life and relisten to the information. Second, when you read information, if you do not understand a concept, you can look up the concept in a dictionary or online and gain the knowledge easily. However, we do not always have the ability to walk around with the Internet and look up concepts we don't understand. Therefore, oral communication should be simple enough to be easily understood in the moment by a specific audience, without additional study or information.

EXERCISES

1. Find a magazine article and examine its language choices. Which uses of language could be misunderstood as a result of a reader's connotative application of meaning?
2. Think of a situation in your own life where denotative or connotative meanings led to a conflict. Why do you think you and the other person had different associations of meaning?
3. Read a short newspaper article. Take that written article and translate it into language that would be orally appropriate. What changes did you make to adjust the newspaper article from written to oral language? Orally present the revised article to a classmate or friend. Were you successful in adapting your language to oral style?

2. USING LANGUAGE EFFECTIVELY

LEARNING OBJECTIVES

1. Explain what it means to use appropriate language.
2. Explain what is meant by vivid language.
3. Define inclusive language and explain why using it is important for public speakers.
4. Explain the importance of using familiar language in public speaking.

When considering how to use language effectively in your speech, consider the degree to which the language is appropriate, vivid, inclusive, and familiar. The next sections define each of these aspects of language and discuss why each is important in public speaking.

2.1 Use Appropriate Language

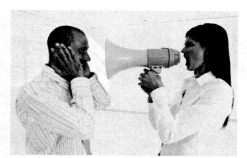

© Thinkstock

As with anything in life, there are positive and negative ways of using language. One of the first concepts a speaker needs to think about when looking at language use is appropriateness. By appropriate, we mean whether the language is suitable or fitting for ourselves, as the speaker; our audience; the speaking context; and the speech itself.

Appropriate for the Speaker

One of the first questions to ask yourself is whether the language you plan on using in a speech fits with your own speaking pattern. Not all language choices are appropriate for all speakers. The language you select should be suitable for you, not someone else. If you're a first-year college student, there's no need to force yourself to sound like an astrophysicist even if you are giving a speech on new planets. One of the biggest mistakes novice speakers make is thinking that they have to use million-dollar words because it makes them sound smarter. Actually, million-dollar words don't tend to function well in oral communication to begin with, so using them will probably make you uncomfortable as a speaker. Also, it may be difficult for you or the audience to understand the nuances of meaning when you use such words, so using them can increase the risk of denotative or connotative misunderstandings.

Appropriate for the Audience

The second aspect of appropriateness asks whether the language you are choosing is appropriate for your specific audience. Let's say that you're an engineering student. If you're giving a presentation in an engineering class, you can use language that other engineering students will know. On the other hand, if you use that engineering vocabulary in a public speaking class, many audience members will not understand you. As another example, if you are speaking about the Great Depression to an audience of young adults, you can't assume they will know the meaning of terms like "New Deal" and "WPA," which would be familiar to an audience of senior citizens. In other chapters of this book, we have explained the importance of audience analysis; once again, audience analysis is a key factor in choosing the language to use in a speech.

Appropriate for the Context

The next question about appropriateness is whether the language you will use is suitable or fitting for the context itself. The language you may employ if you're addressing a student assembly in a high school auditorium will differ from the language you would use at a business meeting in a hotel ballroom. If you're giving a speech at an outdoor rally, you cannot use the same language you would use in a classroom. Recall that the speaking context includes the occasion, the time of day, the mood of the audience, and other factors in addition to the physical location. Take the entire speaking context into consideration when you make the language choices for your speech.

Appropriate for the Topic

The fourth and final question about the appropriateness of language involves whether the language is appropriate for your specific topic. If you are speaking about the early years of The Walt Disney Company, would you want to refer to Walt Disney as a "thaumaturgic" individual (i.e., one who works wonders or miracles)? While the word "thaumaturgic" may be accurate, is it the most appropriate for the topic at hand? As another example, if your speech topic is the dual residence model of string theory, it makes sense to expect that you will use more sophisticated language than if your topic was a basic introduction to the physics of, say, sound or light waves.

2.2   Use Vivid Language

After appropriateness, the second main guideline for using language is to use vivid language. **Vivid language** helps your listeners create strong, distinct, clear, and memorable mental images. Good vivid language usage helps an audience member truly understand and imagine what a speaker is saying. Two common ways to make your speaking more vivid are through the use of imagery and rhythm.

Imagery

Imagery is the use of language to represent objects, actions, or ideas. The goal of imagery is to help an audience member create a mental picture of what a speaker is saying. A speaker who uses imagery successfully will tap into one or more of the audience's five basic senses (hearing, taste, touch, smell, and sight). Three common tools of imagery are concreteness, simile, and metaphor.

Concreteness

When we use language that is **concrete**, we attempt to help our audiences see specific realities or actual instances instead of abstract theories and ideas. The goal of concreteness is to help you, as a speaker, show your audience something instead of just telling them. Imagine you've decided to give a speech on the importance of freedom. You could easily stand up and talk about the philosophical work of Rudolf Steiner, who divided the ideas of freedom into freedom of thought and freedom of action. If you're like us, even reading that sentence can make you want to go to sleep. Instead of defining what those terms mean and discussing the philosophical merits of Steiner, you could use real examples where people's freedom to think or freedom to behave has been stifled. For example, you could talk about how Afghani women under Taliban rule have been denied access to education, and how those seeking education have risked public flogging and even execution.[12] You could further illustrate how Afghani women under the Taliban are forced to adhere to rigid interpretations of Islamic law that functionally limit their behavior. As illustrations of the two freedoms discussed by Steiner, these examples make things more concrete for audience members and thus easier to remember. Ultimately, the goal of concreteness is to show an audience something instead of talking about it abstractly.

vivid language

Language that helps a listener create strong, distinct, or clearly perceptible mental images.

imagery

The use of language to represent objects, actions, or ideas.

concreteness

Language that helps an audience see specific realities or actual instances instead of abstract theories and ideas.

Simile

simile

Figure of speech in which two unlike things are explicitly compared using "like" or "as."

The second form of imagery is **simile**. As you probably learned in English courses, a simile is a figure of speech in which two unlike things are explicitly compared. Both aspects being compared within a simile are able to remain separate within the comparison. The following are some examples:

- The thunderous applause was *like* a party among the gods.
- After the revelation, she was as angry *as* a raccoon caught in a cage.
- Love is *like* a battlefield.

When we look at these two examples, you'll see that two words have been italicized: "like" and "as." All similes contain either "like" or "as" within the comparison. Speakers use similes to help an audience understand a specific characteristic being described within the speech. In the first example, we are connecting the type of applause being heard to something supernatural, so we can imagine that the applause was huge and enormous. Now think how you would envision the event if the simile likened the applause to a mime convention—your mental picture changes dramatically, doesn't it?

To effectively use similes within your speech, first look for instances where you may already be finding yourself using the words "like" or "as"—for example, "his breath smelled like a fishing boat on a hot summer day." Second, when you find situations where you are comparing two things using "like" or "as," examine what it is that you are actually comparing. For example, maybe you're comparing someone's breath to the odor of a fishing vessel. Lastly, once you see what two ideas you are comparing, check the mental picture for yourself. Are you getting the kind of mental image you desire? Is the image too strong? Is the image too weak? You can always alter the image to make it stronger or weaker depending on what your aim is.

Metaphor

metaphor

Figure of speech where a term or phrase is applied to something in a nonliteral way to suggest a resemblance.

The other commonly used form of imagery is the **metaphor**, or a figure of speech where a term or phrase is applied to something in a nonliteral way to suggest a resemblance. In the case of a metaphor, one of the comparison items is said to *be* the other (even though this is realistically not possible). Let's look at a few examples:

- Love is a *battlefield*.
- Upon hearing the charges, the accused *clammed up* and refused to speak without a lawyer.
- Every year a new *crop* of activists are *born*.

In these examples, the comparison word has been italicized. Let's think through each of these examples. In the first one, the comparison is the same as one of our simile examples except that the word "like" is omitted—instead of being *like* a battlefield, the metaphor states that love *is* a battlefield, and it is understood that the speaker does not mean the comparison literally. In the second example, the accused "clams up," which means that the accused refused to talk in the same way a clam's shell is closed. In the third example, we refer to activists as "crops" that arise anew with each growing season, and we use "born" figuratively to indicate that they come into being—even though it is understood that they are not newborn infants at the time when they become activists.

To use a metaphor effectively, first determine what you are trying to describe. For example, maybe you are talking about a college catalog that offers a wide variety of courses. Second, identify what it is that you want to say about the object you are trying to describe. Depending on whether you want your audience to think of the catalog as good or bad, you'll use different words to describe it. Lastly, identify the other object you want to compare the first one to, which should mirror the intentions in the second step. Let's look at two possible metaphors:

1. Students *groped* their way through the *maze* of courses in the catalog.
2. Students *feasted on* the *abundance* of courses in the catalog.

While both of these examples evoke comparisons with the course catalog, the first example is clearly more negative and the second is more positive.

One mistake people often make in using metaphors is to make two incompatible comparisons in the same sentence or line of thought. Here is an example:

- "That's awfully thin gruel for the right wing to hang their hats on."[13]

This is known as a mixed metaphor, and it often has an incongruous or even hilarious effect. Unless you are aiming to entertain your audience with fractured use of language, be careful to avoid mixed metaphors.

Rhythm

Our second guideline for effective language in a speech is to use rhythm. When most people think of rhythm, they immediately think about music. What they may not realize is that language is inherently musical; at least it can be. **Rhythm** refers to the patterned, recurring variance of elements of sound or speech. Whether someone is striking a drum with a stick or standing in front of a group speaking, rhythm is an important aspect of human communication. Think about your favorite public speaker. If you analyze his or her speaking pattern, you'll notice that there is a certain cadence to the speech. While much of this cadence is a result of the nonverbal components of speaking, some of the cadence comes from the language that is chosen as well. Let's examine four types of rhythmic language: parallelism, repetition, alliteration, and assonance.

rhythm
The patterned, recurring variance of elements of sound or speech.

Parallelism

When listing items in a sequence, audiences will respond more strongly when those ideas are presented in a grammatically parallel fashion, which is referred to as **parallelism**. For example, look at the following two examples and determine which one sounds better to you:

1. "Give me liberty or I'd rather die."
2. "Give me liberty or give me death."

Technically, you're saying the same thing in both, but the second one has better rhythm, and this rhythm comes from the parallel construction of "give me." The lack of parallelism in the first example makes the sentence sound disjointed and ineffective.

parallelism
Presenting ideas in a grammatically parallel fashion.

Repetition

As we mentioned earlier in this chapter, one of the major differences between oral and written language is the use of **repetition**. Because speeches are communicated orally, audience members need to hear the core of the message repeated consistently. Repetition as a linguistic device is designed to help audiences become familiar with a short piece of the speech as they hear it over and over again. By repeating a phrase during a speech, you create a specific rhythm. Probably the most famous and memorable use of repetition within a speech is Martin Luther King Jr.'s use of "I have a dream" in his speech at the Lincoln Memorial on August 1963 during the March on Washington for Jobs and Freedom. In that speech, Martin Luther King Jr. repeated the phrase "I have a dream" eight times to great effect.

repetition
The oral linguistic device where key words or phrases are repeated in an attempt to help audience members recall the words or phrases after the speech.

Alliteration

Another type of rhythmic language is **alliteration**, or repeating two or more words in a series that begin with the same consonant. In the *Harry Potter* novel series, the author uses alliteration to name the four wizards who founded Hogwarts School for Witchcraft and Wizardry: Godric Gryffindor, Helga Hufflepuff, Rowena Ravenclaw, and Salazar Slytherin. There are two basic types of alliteration: immediate juxtaposition and nonimmediate juxtaposition. *Immediate juxtaposition* occurs when the consonants clearly follow one after the other—as we see in the *Harry Potter* example. *Nonimmediate juxtaposition* occurs when the consonants are repeated in nonadjacent words (e.g., "It is the poison that we must purge from our politics, the wall that we must tear down before the hour grows too late").[14] Sometimes you can actually use examples of both immediate and nonimmediate juxtaposition within a single speech. The following example is from Bill Clinton's acceptance speech at the 1992 Democratic National Convention: "Somewhere at this very moment, a child is being born in America. Let it be our cause to give that child a happy home, a healthy family, and a hopeful future."[15]

alliteration
The repeating of two or more words in a series with the same consonant.

Assonance

Assonance is similar to alliteration, but instead of relying on consonants, assonance gets its rhythm from repeating the same vowel sounds with different consonants in the stressed syllables. The phrase "how now brown cow," which elocution students traditionally used to learn to pronounce rounded vowel sounds, is an example of assonance. While rhymes like "free as a breeze," "mad as a hatter," and "no pain, no gain" are examples of assonance, speakers should be wary of relying on assonance because when it is overused it can quickly turn into bad poetry.

assonance
Form of rhyming pattern where the same vowel sounds are used with different consonants in the stressed syllables.

2.3 Use Inclusive Language

inclusive language

Language that avoids placing any one group of people above or below other groups while speaking.

Language can either inspire your listeners or turn them off very quickly. One of the fastest ways to alienate an audience is through the use of noninclusive language. **Inclusive language** is language that avoids placing any one group of people above or below other groups while speaking. Let's look at some common problem areas related to language about gender, ethnicity, sexual orientation, and disabilities.

Gender-Specific Language

The first common form of noninclusive language is language that privileges one of the sexes over the other. There are three common problem areas that speakers run into while speaking: using "he" as generic, using "man" to mean all humans, and gender typing jobs.

Generic "He"

The generic "he" happens when a speaker labels all people within a group as "he" when in reality there is a mixed sex group involved. Consider the statement, "Every morning when an officer of the law puts on his badge, he risks his life to serve and protect his fellow citizens." In this case, we have a police officer that is labeled as male four different times in one sentence. Obviously, both male and female police officers risk their lives when they put on their badges. A better way to word the sentence would be, "Every morning when officers of the law put on their badges, they risk their lives to serve and protect their fellow citizens." Notice that in the better sentence, we made the subject plural ("officers") and used neutral pronouns ("they" and "their") to avoid the generic "he."

Use of "Man"

Traditionally, speakers of English have used terms like "man," "mankind," and (in casual contexts) "guys" when referring to both females and males. In the second half of the twentieth century, as society became more aware of gender bias in language, organizations like the National Council of Teachers of English developed guidelines for nonsexist language.[16] For example, instead of using the word "man," you could refer to the "human race." Instead of saying, "hey, guys," you could say, "OK, everyone." By using gender-fair language you will be able to convey your meaning just as well, and you won't risk alienating half of your audience.

Gender-Typed Jobs

The last common area where speakers get into trouble with gender and language has to do with job titles. It is not unusual for people to assume, for example, that doctors are male and nurses are female. As a result, they may say "she is a woman doctor" or "he is a male nurse" when mentioning someone's occupation, perhaps not realizing that the statements "she is a doctor" and "he is a nurse" already inform the listener as to the sex of the person holding that job. Speakers sometimes also use a gender-specific pronoun to refer to an occupation that has both males and females. Table 13.1 lists some common gender-specific jobs titles along with more inclusive versions of those job titles.

TABLE 13.1 Gender Type Jobs

Exclusive Language	Inclusive Language
Policeman	Police officer
Businessman	Businessperson
Fireman	Firefighter
Stewardess	Flight attendant
Waiters	Wait staff / servers
Mailman	Letter carrier / postal worker
Barmaid	Bartender

Ethnic Identity

ethnic identity

A group an individual identifies with based on a common culture that is real or assumed.

Another type of inclusive language relates to the categories used to highlight an individual's ethnic identity. **Ethnic identity** refers to a group an individual identifies with based on a common culture. For example, within the United States we have numerous ethnic groups, including Italian Americans, Irish Americans, Japanese Americans, Vietnamese Americans, Cuban Americans, and Mexican Americans. As with the earlier example of "male nurse," avoid statements such as "The committee is made up of four women and a Vietnamese man." Instead, say, "The committee is made up of four women and a man" or, if race and ethnicity are central to the discussion, "The committee is made up of three European American women, an Israeli American woman, a Brazilian American woman, and a

Vietnamese American man." In recent years, there has been a trend toward steering inclusive language away from broad terms like "Asians" and "Hispanics" because these terms are not considered precise labels for the groups they actually represent. If you want to be safe, the best thing you can do is ask a couple of people who belong to an ethnic group how they prefer to label themselves.

Sexual Orientation

Another area that can cause some problems is referred to as heterosexism. **Heterosexism** occurs when a speaker presumes that everyone in an audience is heterosexual or that opposite-sex relationships are the only norm. For example, a speaker might begin a speech by saying, "I am going to talk about the legal obligations you will have with your future husband or wife." While this speech starts with the notion that everyone plans on getting married, which isn't the case, it also assumes that everyone will label their significant others as either "husbands" or "wives." Although some members of the gay, lesbian, bisexual, and transgender/transexual community will use these terms, others prefer for more gender neutral terms like "spouse" and "partner." Moreover, legal obligations for same-sex couples may be very different from those for heterosexual couples. Notice also that we have used the phrase "members of the gay, lesbian, bisexual, and transgender/transexual community" instead of the more clinical-sounding term "homosexual."

heterosexism

The presumption that everyone in an audience is heterosexual or that opposite-sex relationships are the only norm.

Disability

The last category of exclusive versus inclusive language that causes problems for some speakers relates to individuals with physical or mental disabilities. Table 13.2 provides some other examples of exclusive versus inclusive language.

TABLE 13.2 Inclusive Language for Disabilities

Exclusive Language	Inclusive Language
Handicapped People	People with disabilities
Insane Person	Person with a psychiatric disability (or label the psychiatric diagnosis, e.g. "person with schizophrenia")
Person in a wheelchair	Person who uses a wheelchair
Crippled	Person with a physical disability
Special needs program	Accessible needs program
Mentally retarded	Person with an intellectual disability

2.4 Use Familiar Language

The last category related to using language appropriately simply asks you to use language that is familiar both to yourself and to your audience. If you are not comfortable with the language you are using, then you are going to be more nervous speaking, which will definitely have an impact on how your audience receives your speech. You may have a hard time speaking genuinely and sincerely if you use unfamiliar language, and this can impair your credibility. Furthermore, you want to make sure that the language you are using is familiar to your audience. If your audience cannot understand what you are saying, you will not have an effective speech.

KEY TAKEAWAYS

- Using appropriate language means that a speaker's language is suitable or fitting for themselves, as the speaker; our audience; the speaking context; and the speech itself.
- Vivid language helps listeners create mental images. It involves both imagery (e.g., concreteness, simile, and metaphor) and rhythm (e.g., parallelism, repetition, alliteration, and assonance).
- Inclusive language avoids placing any one group of people above or below other groups while speaking. As such, speakers need to think about how they refer to various groups within society.
- Using familiar language is important for a speaker because familiar language will make a speaker more comfortable, which will improve audience perceptions of the speech.

3. SIX ELEMENTS OF LANGUAGE

LEARNING OBJECTIVES

1. Understand the six elements of language important for public speakers.
2. Utilize the six elements of language in your own public speeches.

Language is a very important aspect of anyone's public speaking performance. Whether a speaker uses lots of complicated words or words most people have in their vocabularies, language will determine how an audience experiences the speech. To help you think through your language choices, we are going to talk about six important elements of language and how they affect audience perceptions.

3.1 Clarity

The first important element of language is **clarity**, or the use of language to make sure the audience understands a speaker's ideas in the way the speaker intended. While language, or verbal communication, is only one channel we can use to transmit information, it is a channel that can lend itself to numerous problems. For example, as discussed earlier, if people have different connotative definitions for words, the audience can miss the intended meaning of a message.

Imagine you're listening to a speaker talking and he or she uses the phrase, "Older female relative who became aerodynamic venison road kill," or "Obese personification fabricated of compressed mounds of minute crystals." If you're like most people, these two phrases just went right over your head. We'll give you a hint, these are two common Christmas songs. The first phrase refers to "Grandma Got Run Over by a Reindeer," and the second one is "Frosty the Snowman." Notice that in both of these cases, the made-up title with all the polysyllabic words is far less clear than the commonly known one. While you are probably unlikely to deliberately distort the clarity of your speech by choosing such outlandish words to express simple thoughts, the point we are illustrating is that clear language makes a big difference in how well a message can be understood.

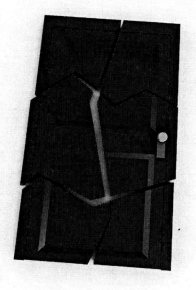

© Thinkstock

clarity

The use of language to make sure a speaker's ideas are understood by an audience, mirroring a speaker's intent.

economy

The use of only those words necessary to accurately express your idea.

3.2 Economy

Another common mistake among new public speakers is thinking that more words are more impressive. In fact, the opposite is true. When people ramble on and on without actually making a point, audiences become bored and distracted. To avoid this problem, we recommend word **economy**, or the use of only those words necessary to accurately express your idea. If the fundamental idea you are trying to say is, "that stinks," then saying something like "while the overall outcome may be undesirable and definitely not recommended" becomes overkill. We do have one caveat here: you want to make sure that your language isn't so basic that it turns off your audience. If you are speaking to adults and use vocabulary appropriate for school children, you'll end up offending your audience. So while economy is definitely important, you don't want to become so overly basic that you are perceived as "talking down" to your audience.

3.3   Obscenity

Obscenity, or indecent language, consists of curse words or pornographic references. While it may be fun to use obscene language in casual conversations with your friends, we cannot recommend using obscene language while delivering a speech. Even if you're giving a speech related to an obscene word, you must be careful with your use of the word itself. Whether we agree with societal perceptions of obscenity, going out of our way to use obscenity will end up focusing the audience on the obscenity and not on our message.

obscenity
Language that contains curse words or pornographic references.

3.4   Obscure Language/Jargon

Obscure language and jargon are two terms that closely relate to each other. **Obscure language** refers to language choices that are not typically understood or known by most of your audience. Imagine you're listening to a speech and the speaker says, "Today I've given you a plethora of ideas for greening your workplace." While you may think the word "plethora" is commonly known, we can assure you that many people have no idea that plethora means many or an abundance of something. Similarly, you may think most people know what it means to "green" a workplace, but in fact many people do not know that it means to make the workplace more environmentally friendly, or to reduce its impact on the environment. In the case of this example, plethora simply means the speaker has given many ideas for greening the workplace. You can still use the word "plethora," but you should include a definition so that you're sure all of your audience will understand.

obscure language
Language choices that are not typically understood or known by most of your audience.

Jargon, on the other hand, refers to language that is commonly used by a highly specialized group, trade, or profession. For example there is legal jargon, or the language commonly used by and understood by lawyers. There is also medical jargon, or the language commonly used by and understood by health care practitioners. Every group, trade, or profession will have its own specific jargon. The problem that occurs for many speakers is not realizing that jargon is group, trade, or profession specific and not universal. One common form of jargon is the acronym, a word formed by taking the first letters or groups of letters of words, such as NASDAQ (National Association of Securities Dealers Automated Quotations), PET (positron emission tomography) scan, or IHOP (International House of Pancakes). Another form of jargon is initialism, formed by pronouncing the initials rather than the name of an organization or other entity. For example, CDC stands for the Centers for Disease Control and Prevention, fMRI stands for Functional Magnetic Resonance Imaging, and B of A stands for Bank of America. In political discussions, you may come across various CFRs, or Codes of Federal Regulations. If you are going to use a specific acronym or initialism within your speech, you need to explain it the first time you use it. For example, you could say,

jargon
Language that is commonly used by a highly specialized group, trade, or profession.

> *According to the United States Code of Federal Regulations, or CFR, employment discrimination in the Department of Homeland Security is not allowed based on biological sex, religion, sexual orientation, or race. Furthermore, the US CFR does not permit discrimination in receiving contracts based on biological sex, religion, sexual orientation, or race.*

By defining the jargon upon first mention, we are subsequently able to use the jargon because we can be certain the audience now understands the term.

3.5   Power

Power is an individual's ability to influence another person to think or behave in a manner the other person would not have otherwise done. DeVito examined how language can be used to help people gain power over others or lose power over others[17] . Table 13.3 provides examples of both powerful language and powerless language a speaker can use during a speech. Powerless language should generally be avoided in public speaking because it can damage audience perceptions of the speaker's credibility.

power
An individual's ability to get another person to think or behave in a manner the other person would not have done otherwise.

TABLE 13.3 Powerful and Powerless Language

Language Strategy	Definition	Example
Powerful Language		
Direct Requests	Asking the audience to engage in a specific behavior.	"At the conclusion of today's speech, I want you to go out and buy a bottle of hand sanitizer and start using it to protect your life."
Bargaining	An agreement that affects both parties of a situation.	"If you vote for me, I promise to make sure that our schools get the funding they so desperately need."
Ingratiation	Attempting to bring oneself into the favor or good graces of an audience.	"Because you are all smart and talented people, I know that you will see why we need to cut government spending."
Powerless Language		
Hesitations	Language that makes the speaker sound unprepared or uncertain.	"Well, as best I was able to find out, or I should say, from what little material I was able to dig up, I kind of think that this is a pretty interesting topic."
Intensifiers	Overemphasizing all aspects of the speech.	"Great! Fantastic! This topic is absolutely amazing and fabulous!"
Disqualifiers	Attempts to downplay one's qualifications and competence about a specific topic.	"I'm not really an expert on this topic, and I'm not very good at doing research, but here goes nothing."
Tag Questions	A question added to the end of a phrase seeking the audience's consent for what was said.	"This is a very important behavior, isn't it?" or "You really should do this, don't you think?"
Self-Critical Statements	Downplaying one's own abilities and making one's lack of confidence public.	"I have to tell you that I'm not a great public speaker, but I'll go ahead and give it a try."
Hedges	Modifiers used to indicate that one isn't completely sure of the statement just made.	"I really believe this may be true, sort of." "Maybe my conclusion is a good idea. Possibly not."
Verbal Surrogates	Utterances used to fill space while speaking; filler words.	"I was, like, err, going to, uhhh, say something, um, important, like, about this."

3.6 Variety

variety

A speaker's ability to use and implement a range of different language choices.

The last important aspect of language is **variety**, or a speaker's ability to use and implement a range of different language choices. In many ways, variety encompasses all the characteristics of language previously discussed in this chapter. Often speakers find one language device and then beat it into the ground like a railroad spike. Unfortunately, when a speaker starts using the same language device too often, the language device will start to lose the power that it may have had. For this reason, we recommend that you always think about the language you plan on using in a speech and make sure that you use a range of language choices.

KEY TAKEAWAYS

- Public speakers need to make sure that they are very aware of their language. Six common language issues that impact public speakers are clarity, economy, obscenity, obscure language/jargon, power, and variety.
- When public speakers prepare their speeches, they need to make sure that their speeches contain clear language, use as few words as possible to get their point across, avoid obscenity, be careful with obscure language/jargon, use powerful language, and include variety.

1. Find a passage in a specialized book or upper-level textbook that expresses a complex idea. Rewrite the passage so that it is clear and avoids jargon. Test out your explanation by seeing if the message is clear to someone unfamiliar with the topic and by seeing if it is an accurate revision to someone who is very familiar with the topic.

2. Find a written copy of a speech at least one page in length (Vital Speeches of the Day is an excellent source for this exercise). Summarize the speech accurately and completely in one paragraph. Then reduce your summary to twenty words. How did you go about changing your language for greater economy of word use?

4. CHAPTER EXERCISES

SPEAKING ETHICALLY

Jonathan knows he hasn't really prepared for his speech very well. Instead of going to the library, he went to a party over the weekend. Instead of finding supporting evidence, he went to the movies with his best friend.

Two days before he's going to give his speech, Jonathan decides that he won't even bother with the library. Instead, he opts to just write out a quick speech and fill it with lots of "flowery" language. He creates a number of interesting similes and metaphors. He makes sure that his speech has a fun rhythm to it and has some great instances of alliteration.

Upon finishing his preparation, Jonathan thinks to himself, *Well, the speech may have no content, but no one will really notice.*

1. Is it ever ethical to be devoid of content and opt instead for colorful language?

2. Should language ever be a substitute for strong arguments?

3. If you were a friend of Jonathan's, how would you explain to him that his behavior was unethical?

END-OF-CHAPTER ASSESSMENT

1. Which of the following is an accurate statement about oral language?

    a. Oral language has more words than written language.

    b. Oral language has longer sentences than written language.

    c. Oral language has more qualifying statements than written language.

    d. Oral language uses fewer interjections than written language.

    e. Oral language has fewer quantifying terms than written language.

2. Jenny was conversing with Darlene about her pet rabbit. Jenny grew up in the country and remembers raising rabbits for food for her pet snake, whereas Darlene remembers having pet rabbits her whole life. How are the two differing in their understanding of the word "rabbit?"

    a. Jenny and Darlene have different metaphors for the word "rabbit."

    b. Jenny and Darlene have different assonance for the word "rabbit."

    c. Jenny and Darlene have different denotative meanings for the word "rabbit."

    d. Jenny and Darlene have the same perception of the word "rabbit."

    e. Jenny and Darlene have different connotative meanings for the word "rabbit."

3. Which of the following is *not* an example of inclusive language?

    a. person with disability

    b. Italian American

    c. lesbian woman

    d. handicapped person

    e. bartender

4. During a speech on the history of Colorado, Alban said, "The early pioneers came to Colorado by covered wagon, which traveled at a snail's pace." This phrase contains which form of language?

    a. simile

    b. metaphor

    c. assonance

    d. inclusive language

    e. immediate juxtaposition

5. Which of the following phrases is an example of the powerless form of language known as a hesitation?

    a. "Well, umm, you know that I, err, wish I could go on the trip with you."

    b. "Well, I may not be a specialist, but I'll be glad to help."

    c. "I'm really not a pianist, but I can play a few songs."

    d. "I may be completely off track, but here goes nothing."

    e. "I think that is a great idea, don't you think so?"

ANSWER KEY

1. d
2. e
3. d
4. b
5. a

ENDNOTES

1. McClure, A. K. (1904). *Lincoln's yarns and stories: A complete collection of the funny and witty anecdotes that made Abraham Lincoln famous as America's greatest story teller.* Philadelphia, PA: The J. C. Winston Company. Quoted in Bartlett, J. (1992). *Bartlett's familiar quotations* (J. Kaplan, Ed.) (16th ed.). Boston, MA: Little, Brown, & Company, p. 451.

2. Roosevelt, T. (1901, September 2). Speech at Minnesota State Fair. Quoted in Bartlett, J. (1992). *Bartlett's familiar quotations* (J. Kaplan, Ed.) (16th ed.). Boston, MA: Little, Brown, & Company, p. 575.

3. Roosevelt, F. D. (1933, March 4). Quoted in Bartlett, J. (1992). *Bartlett's familiar quotations* (J. Kaplan, Ed.) (16th ed.). Boston, MA: Little, Brown, & Company, p. 648.

4. Kennedy, J. F. (1961, January 20). Inaugural address. Quoted in Bartlett, J. (1992). *Bartlett's familiar quotations* (J. Kaplan, Ed.) (16th ed.). Boston, MA: Little, Brown, & Company, p. 741.

5. Obama, B. (2009, December 10). Remarks at the acceptance of the Nobel Peace Prize. Retrieved from http://www.whitehouse.gov/the-press-office/remarks-president-acceptance-nobel-peace-prize

6. Wrench, J. S., McCroskey, J. C., & Richmond, V. P. (2008). *Human communication in everyday life: Explanations and applications.* Boston, MA: Allyn & Bacon, p. 304.

7. Lewis, M. P. (2009). *Ethnologue* (16th ed.). Retrieved from http://www.ethnologue.com/ethno_docs/distribution.asp?by=size

8. Lewis, M. P. (2009). *Ethnologue* (16th ed.). Retrieved from http://www.ethnologue.com/ethno_docs/distribution.asp?by=size

9. Mayell, H. (2003, February). When did "modern" behavior emerge in humans? *National Geographic News.* Retrieved from http://news.nationalgeographic.com/news/2003/02/0220_030220_humanorigins2.html

10. Oxford University Press. (2011). How many words are there in the English language? Retrieved from http://oxforddictionaries.com/page/howmanywords

11. McCroskey, J. C., Wrench, J. S., & Richmond, V. P. (2003). *Principles of public speaking.* Indianapolis, IN: The College Network.

12. Iacopino, V., & Rasekh, Z. (1998). *The Taliban's war on women: A health and human rights crisis in Afghanistan.* Boston, MA: Physicians for Human Rights.

13. Nordquist, R. (2009). *Mixed metaphor.* Retrieved from About.com at http://grammar.about.com/od/mo/g/mixmetterm.htm

14. Obama, B. (2008, January 20). The great need of the hour. Remarks delivered at Ebenezer Baptist Church, Atlanta. Retrieved from http://www.realclearpolitics.com/articles/2008/01/the_great_need_of_the_hour.html

15. Clinton, W. J. (2005). *My life.* New York, NY: Vintage Books, p. 421.

16. National Council of Teachers of English (2002). *Guidelines for gender-fair use of language.* Retrieved from http://www.ncte.org/positions/statements/genderfairuseoflang

17. DeVito, J. A. (2009). *The interpersonal communication book* (12th ed.). Boston, MA: Allyn & Bacon.

CHAPTER 14
Delivering the Speech

How we deliver a speech is just as important, if not more so, than the basic message we are trying to convey to an audience. But if you have worked hard on preparing the verbal part of your speech, you may feel that delivery is just an "extra" that should not require much time or effort. After all, your speech is carefully planned, researched, and polished. It is committed safely to paper and hard drive. It's a carefully constructed, logically crafted, ethical message. The words alone should engage your audience's attention and interest—right?

© Thinkstock

After all the work of building such a message, you might wish that you could simply read it to the audience. However, this is the case in only a few kinds of circumstances: when the message is highly technical, complex, and extremely important (as in a new medical discovery); when international protocols and etiquette are crucially important and the world is listening; or when the speaker is representing a high-ranking person, such as a president or a king, who is unable to be present. For the purposes of your public speaking class, you will not be encouraged to read your speech. Instead, you will be asked to give an extemporaneous presentation. We will examine what that means.

The nonverbal part of your speech is a presentation of yourself as well as your message. Through the use of eye contact, vocal expression, body posture, gestures, and facial display, you enhance your message and invite your audience to give their serious attention to it, and to you. Your credibility, your sincerity, and your knowledge of your speech become apparent through your nonverbal behaviors.

The interplay between the verbal and nonverbal components of your speech can either bring the message vividly to life or confuse or bore the audience. Therefore, it is best that you neither overdramatize your speech delivery behaviors nor downplay them. This is a balance achieved through rehearsal, trial and error, and experience.

In this chapter, we are going to examine effective strategies for delivering a speech. To help you enhance your delivery, we will begin by exploring the four basic methods of speech delivery. Second, we will discuss how to prepare your delivery for different environments. Third, we will talk about how to effectively use notes to enhance your delivery. Finally, we will examine characteristics of good delivery and give some strategies for practicing effectively for the day when you will deliver your speech.

1. FOUR METHODS OF DELIVERY

LEARNING OBJECTIVES

1. Differentiate among the four methods of speech delivery.
2. Understand when to use each of the four methods of speech delivery.

© *Thinkstock*

The easiest approach to speech delivery is not always the best. Substantial work goes into the careful preparation of an interesting and ethical message, so it is understandable that students may have the impulse to avoid "messing it up" by simply reading it word for word. But students who do this miss out on one of the major reasons for studying public speaking: to learn ways to "connect" with one's audience and to increase one's confidence in doing so. You already know how to read, and you already know how to talk. But public speaking is neither reading nor talking.

Speaking in public has more formality than talking. During a speech, you should present yourself professionally. This doesn't mean you must wear a suit or "dress up" (unless your instructor asks you to), but it does mean making yourself presentable by being well groomed and wearing clean, appropriate clothes. It also means being prepared to use language correctly and appropriately for the audience and the topic, to make eye contact with your audience, and to look like you know your topic very well.

While speaking has more formality than talking, it has less formality than reading. Speaking allows for meaningful pauses, eye contact, small changes in word order, and vocal emphasis. Reading is a more or less exact replication of words on paper without the use of any nonverbal interpretation. Speaking, as you will realize if you think about excellent speakers you have seen and heard, provides a more animated message.

The next sections introduce four methods of delivery that can help you balance between too much and too little formality when giving a public speech.

1.1 Impromptu Speaking

impromptu speaking

The presentation of a short message without advance preparation.

Impromptu speaking is the presentation of a short message without advance preparation. Impromptu speeches often occur when someone is asked to "say a few words" or give a toast on a special occasion. You have probably done impromptu speaking many times in informal, conversational settings. Self-introductions in group settings are examples of impromptu speaking: "Hi, my name is Steve, and I'm a volunteer with the Homes for the Brave program." Another example of impromptu speaking occurs when you answer a question such as, "What did you think of the documentary?"

The advantage of this kind of speaking is that it's spontaneous and responsive in an animated group context. The disadvantage is that the speaker is given little or no time to contemplate the central theme of his or her message. As a result, the message may be disorganized and difficult for listeners to follow.

Here is a step-by-step guide that may be useful if you are called upon to give an impromptu speech in public.

- Take a moment to collect your thoughts and plan the main point you want to make.
- Thank the person for inviting you to speak.
- Deliver your message, making your main point as briefly as you can while still covering it adequately and at a pace your listeners can follow.
- Thank the person again for the opportunity to speak.
- Stop talking.

As you can see, impromptu speeches are generally most successful when they are brief and focus on a single point.

1.2   Extemporaneous Speaking

Extemporaneous speaking is the presentation of a carefully planned and rehearsed speech, spoken in a conversational manner using brief notes. By using notes rather than a full manuscript, the extemporaneous speaker can establish and maintain eye contact with the audience and assess how well they are understanding the speech as it progresses. The opportunity to assess is also an opportunity to re-state more clearly any idea or concept that the audience seems to have trouble grasping.

For instance, suppose you are speaking about workplace safety and you use the term "sleep deprivation." If you notice your audience's eyes glazing over, this might not be a result of their own sleep deprivation, but rather an indication of their uncertainty about what you mean. If this happens, you can add a short explanation; for example, "sleep deprivation is sleep loss serious enough to threaten one's cognition, hand-to-eye coordination, judgment, and emotional health." You might also (or instead) provide a concrete example to illustrate the idea. Then you can resume your message, having clarified an important concept.

Speaking extemporaneously has some advantages. It promotes the likelihood that you, the speaker, will be perceived as knowledgeable and credible. In addition, your audience is likely to pay better attention to the message because it is engaging both verbally and nonverbally. The disadvantage of extemporaneous speaking is that it requires a great deal of preparation for both the verbal and the nonverbal components of the speech. Adequate preparation cannot be achieved the day before you're scheduled to speak.

Because extemporaneous speaking is the style used in the great majority of public speaking situations, most of the information in this chapter is targeted to this kind of speaking.

extemporaneous speaking

The presentation of a carefully planned and rehearsed speech using brief notes, spoken in a conversational manner.

1.3   Speaking from a Manuscript

Manuscript speaking is the word-for-word iteration of a written message. In a manuscript speech, the speaker maintains his or her attention on the printed page except when using visual aids.

The advantage to reading from a manuscript is the exact repetition of original words. As we mentioned at the beginning of this chapter, in some circumstances this can be extremely important. For example, reading a statement about your organization's legal responsibilities to customers may require that the original words be exact. In reading one word at a time, in order, the only errors would typically be mispronunciation of a word or stumbling over complex sentence structure.

However, there are costs involved in manuscript speaking. First, it's typically an uninteresting way to present. Unless the speaker has rehearsed the reading as a complete performance animated with vocal expression and gestures (as poets do in a poetry slam and actors do in a reader's theater), the presentation tends to be dull. Keeping one's eyes glued to the script precludes eye contact with the audience. For this kind of "straight" manuscript speech to hold audience attention, the audience must be already interested in the message before the delivery begins.

It is worth noting that professional speakers, actors, news reporters, and politicians often read from an autocue device, such as a TelePrompTer, especially when appearing on television, where eye contact with the camera is crucial. With practice, a speaker can achieve a conversational tone and give the impression of speaking extemporaneously while using an autocue device. However, success in this medium depends on two factors: (1) the speaker is already an accomplished public speaker who has learned to use a conversational tone while delivering a prepared script, and (2) the speech is written in a style that sounds conversational.

manuscript speaking

The word-for-word iteration of a written message.

1.4   Speaking from Memory

Memorized speaking is the rote recitation of a written message that the speaker has committed to memory. Actors, of course, recite from memory whenever they perform from a script in a stage play, television program, or movie scene. When it comes to speeches, memorization can be useful when the message needs to be exact and the speaker doesn't want to be confined by notes.

The advantage to memorization is that it enables the speaker to maintain eye contact with the audience throughout the speech. Being free of notes means that you can move freely around the stage and use your hands to make gestures. If your speech uses visual aids, this freedom is even more of an advantage. However, there are some real and potential costs. First, unless you also plan and memorize every **vocal cue** (the subtle but meaningful variations in speech delivery, which can include the use of pitch, tone, volume, and pace), gesture, and facial expression, your presentation will be flat and uninteresting, and even the most fascinating topic will suffer. You might end up speaking in a monotone or a sing-song repetitive delivery pattern. You might also present your speech in a rapid "machine-gun" style that fails to emphasize the most important points. Second, if you lose your place and start trying

memorized speaking

The rote recitation of a memorized written message.

vocal cue

The subtle but meaningful variations in speech delivery, which can include the use of pitch, tone, volume, and pace.

to ad lib, the contrast in your style of delivery will alert your audience that something is wrong. More frighteningly, if you go completely blank during the presentation, it will be extremely difficult to find your place and keep going.

KEY TAKEAWAYS

- There are four main kinds of speech delivery: impromptu, extemporaneous, manuscript, and memorized.
- Impromptu speaking involves delivering a message on the spur of the moment, as when someone is asked to "say a few words."
- Extemporaneous speaking consists of delivering a speech in a conversational fashion using notes. This is the style most speeches call for.
- Manuscript speaking consists of reading a fully scripted speech. It is useful when a message needs to be delivered in precise words.
- Memorized speaking consists of reciting a scripted speech from memory. Memorization allows the speaker to be free of notes.

EXERCISES

1. Find a short newspaper story. Read it out loud to a classroom partner. Then, using only one notecard, tell the classroom partner in your own words what the story said. Listen to your partner's observations about the differences in your delivery.
2. In a group of four or five students, ask each student to give a one-minute impromptu speech answering the question, "What is the most important personal quality for academic success?"
3. Watch the evening news. Observe the differences between news anchors using a TelePrompTer and interviewees who are using no notes of any kind. What differences do you observe?

2. SPEAKING CONTEXTS THAT AFFECT DELIVERY

LEARNING OBJECTIVES

1. Understand how the physical setting of a speech is an element that calls for preparation.
2. Examine some tips and strategies for common speaking situations.

© Thinkstock

The Reverend Dr. Martin Luther King Jr. gave his famous "I Have a Dream" speech on the steps of the Lincoln Memorial at a gigantic civil rights rally on an August afternoon in 1963. His lectern was bristling with microphones placed there for news coverage and for recording the historic event. His audience, estimated to number a quarter of a million people, extended as far as the eye could see. He was the last speaker of the day, delivering his speech after more than a dozen civil rights leaders and world-famous performers such as Joan Baez, Mahalia Jackson, and Charlton Heston had occupied the stage.[1] King gave us his speech in the assertive ringing tones of inspired vision. Nothing less would have worked that day.

Most of us will never speak to so many people at once. Even an appearance on television will probably command a much smaller audience than the crowd that heard King's speech. Even though you don't expect an audience of such size or a setting of such symbolic importance, you should still be prepared to adapt to the setting in which you will speak.

Our audiences, circumstances, and physical contexts for public speaking will vary. At some point in your life you may run for public office or rise to a leadership role in a business or volunteer organization. Or you may be responsible for informing coworkers about a new policy, regulation, or opportunity. You may be asked to deliver remarks in the context of a worship service, wedding, or funeral. You may be asked to introduce a keynote speaker or simply to make an important announcement in some context. Sometimes you will speak in a familiar environment, while at other times you may be faced with an unfamiliar location and very little time to get used to speaking with a microphone. These are contexts and situations we address in the following subsections.

2.1   Using Lecterns

A **lectern** is a small raised surface, usually with a slanted top, where a speaker can place notes during a speech. While a lectern adds a measure of formality to the speaking situation, it allows speakers the freedom to do two things: to come out from behind the lectern to establish more immediate contact with the audience and to use both hands for gestures.

However, for new speakers who feel anxious, it is all too tempting to grip the edges of the lectern with both hands for security. You might even wish you could hide behind it. Be aware of these temptations so you can manage them effectively and present yourself to your audience in a manner they will perceive as confident. One way to achieve this is by limiting your use of the lectern to simply a place to rest your notes. Try stepping to the side or front of the lectern when speaking with free hands, only occasionally standing at the lectern to consult your notes. This will enhance your eye contact as well as free up your hands for gesturing.

lectern
A small raised surface, usually with a slanted top, where a speaker can place his or her notes during a speech.

2.2   Speaking in a Small or Large Physical Space

If you are accustomed to being in a classroom of a certain size, you will need to make adjustments when speaking in a smaller or larger space than what you are used to.

A large auditorium can be intimidating, especially for speakers who feel shy and "exposed" when facing an audience. However, the maxim that "proper preparation prevents poor performance" is just as true here as anywhere. If you have prepared and practiced well, you can approach a large-venue speaking engagement with confidence. In terms of practical adjustments, be aware that your voice is likely to echo, so you will want to speak more slowly than usual and make use of pauses to mark the ends of phrases and sentences. Similarly, your facial expressions and gestures should be larger so that they are visible from farther away. If you are using visual aids, they need to be large enough to be visible from the back of the auditorium.

Limited space is not as disconcerting for most speakers as enormous space, but it has the advantage of minimizing the tendency to pace back and forth while you speak. We have all seen dramatic soliloquies in the movies and plays where an actor makes use of the space on the stage, but this is generally not a good strategy for a speech. A small space also calls for more careful management of notecards and visual aids, as your audience will be able to see up close what you are doing with your hands. Do your best to minimize fumbling, including setting up in advance or arriving early to decide how to organize your materials in the physical space. We will discuss visual aids further in Chapter 15.

2.3   Speaking Outdoors

Outdoor settings can be charming, but they are prone to distractions. If you're giving a speech in a setting that is picturesquely beautiful, it may be difficult to maintain the audience's attention. If you know this ahead of time, you might plan your speech to focus more on mood than information and perhaps to make reference to the lovely view.

More typically, outdoor speech venues can pose challenges with weather, sun glare, and uninvited guests, such as ants and pigeons. If the venue is located near a busy highway, it might be difficult to make yourself heard over the ambient noise. You might lack the usual accommodations, such as a lectern or table. Whatever the situation, you will need to use your best efforts to project your voice clearly without sounding like you're yelling.

2.4   Using a Microphone

Most people today are familiar with microphones that are built into video recorders and other electronic devices, but they may be new at using a microphone to deliver a speech. One overall principle to remember is that a microphone only amplifies, it does not clarify. If you are not enunciating clearly, the microphone will merely enable your audience to hear amplified mumbling.

Microphones come in a wide range of styles and sizes. Generally, the easiest microphone to use is the clip-on style worn on the front of your shirt. If you look closely at many television personalities and news anchors, you will notice these tiny microphones clipped to their clothing. They require very little adaptation. You simply have to avoid looking down—at your notes, for instance—because your voice will be amplified when you do so.

Lectern and handheld microphones require more adaptation. If they're too close to your mouth, they can screech. If they're too far away, they might not pick up your voice. Some microphones are directional, meaning that they are only effective when you speak directly into them. If there is any opportunity to do so, ask for tips about how to use a particular microphone and practice with it for a few minutes while you have someone listen from a middle row in the audience and signal whether you can be heard well. The best plan, of course, would be to have access to the microphone for practice ahead of the speaking date.

Often a microphone is provided when it isn't necessary. If the room is small or the audience is close to you, do not feel obligated to use the microphone. Sometimes an amplified voice can feel less natural and less compelling than a direct voice. However, if you forgo the microphone, make sure to speak loudly enough for all audience members to hear you—not just those in front.

2.5 Audience Size

A small audience is an opportunity for a more intimate, minimally formal tone. If your audience has only eight to twelve people, you can generate greater audience contact. Make use of all the preparation you have done. You do not have to revamp your speech just because the audience is small. When the presentation is over, there will most likely be opportunities to answer questions and have individual contact with your listeners.

Your classroom audience may be as many as twenty to thirty students. The format for an audience of this size is still formal but conversational. Depending on how your instructor structures the class, you may or may not be asked to leave time after your speech for questions and answers.

Some audiences are much larger. If you have an audience that fills an auditorium, or if you have an auditorium with only a few people in it, you still have a clearly formal task, and you should be guided as much as possible by your preparation.

KEY TAKEAWAYS

- Not every speaking setting happens in a classroom. As such, different environments call for speakers to think through their basic speaking strategies.
- Speakers need to be prepared to deal with five common challenges in speaking contexts: using a lectern, large or small space, speaking in the outdoors, using a microphone, and audience size.

EXERCISES

1. Get permission from your instructor and announce a campus event to the class. Make sure your details are complete and accurate. How does your physical space affect the way you present the information?
2. Watch a speech that takes place indoors or outside. How do you think this speech would be different if the speech occurred in the other location? What changes would you recommend for the speaker?
3. If you were suddenly asked to give your next classroom speech in front of two hundred of your peers, how would adjust your speech? Why?

3. USING NOTES EFFECTIVELY

LEARNING OBJECTIVES

1. Know how to use notecards to free you from your manuscript.
2. Know how to use notecards to stay organized while you make audience contact.
3. Understand how to develop effective notecards for a speech.

It's a great deal of work to prepare a good speech, and you want to present it effectively so that your audience will benefit as much as possible. We've already said that extemporaneous speaking provides the best opportunity for speaker-audience contact and that speaking extemporaneously means you do not have your full manuscript or outline with you. Instead, you will use notecards. The cards should have notes, not the full text of your speech. This can also be done with an autocue device—the TelePrompTer does not have to provide a full word-for-word script.

© Thinkstock

We have developed a system for creating highly effective notecards. Our system has been used effectively both in public speaking courses and in freshman composition courses. Surprisingly, the system consists of only five cards. For many people, this does not sound like nearly enough cards. We would make the case that you can do a good job with five cards, and we have seen many students do just that.

3.1 The Purpose of Speaker Notes

Using notes adds to your credibility as a speaker. If you depend on a full manuscript to get through your delivery, your listeners might believe you don't know the content of your speech. Second, the temptation to read the entire speech directly from a manuscript, even if you're only carrying it as a safety net, is nearly overwhelming. Third, well-prepared cards are more gracefully handled than sheets of paper, and they don't rattle if your hands tremble from nervousness. Finally, cards look better than sheets of paper. Five carefully prepared cards, together with practice, will help you more than you might think.

3.2 Key Tips for Using Notes

Plan on using just five cards, written on one side only. Get 4 × 6 cards. Use one card for the introduction, one card for each of your three main points, and one card for the conclusion.

Include Only Key Words

Your cards should include key words and phrases, not full sentences. The words and phrases should be arranged in order so that you can stay organized and avoid forgetting important points.

One exception to the key word guideline would be an extended or highly technical quotation from an authoritative source. If it is critically important to present an exact quotation, you may add one additional card that will contain the quotation together with its citation. If you plan to use such a quotation, make sure it has central importance in your speech.

Hold Your Notes Naturally

Notes are a normal part of giving a presentation. You do not need to conceal them from the audience; in fact, trying to hide and use your notes at the same time tends to be very awkward and distracting. Some instructors recommend that you avoid gesturing with your notes on the grounds that nervous shaking is more noticeable if you are holding your notes in your hand. If this is the case for you, practice gesturing with your free hand, or put your cards down if you need to use both hands. Other instructors recommend treating notecards as a natural extension of your hand, as they believe it is distracting to put your notes down and pick them up again. Whichever "rule" you follow, remember that the goal is for your use of notecards to contribute to your overall appearance of confidence and credibility.

Prepare Notecards to Trigger Recall

The "trick" to selecting the words to write on your cards is to identify the keywords that will trigger a recall sequence. For instance, if the word "Fukushima" brings to mind the nuclear power plant meltdown that followed the earthquake and tsunami that hit Japan in 2011, then that one word on your notecard should propel you through a sizable sequence of points and details. Once you have delivered that material, perhaps you'll glance at your card again to remind yourself of the key word or phrase that comes next.

You must discover what works for you and then select those words that tend to jog your recall. Having identified what works, make a preliminary set of five cards, written on one side only. Number the cards, and practice with them. Revise and refine them the way you would an outline. If you must, rewrite an entire card to make it work better, and test it the next time you practice.

Always practice with your notecards—and with any visual aids you plan to use. Practicing is also the best way to find out what kinds of things might go wrong with your notes in the presented speech and what steps you should take to make things go smoothly.

Write in Large Letters

You should be able to read something on your card by glancing, not peering at it. A few key words and phrases, written in large, bold print with plenty of white space between them, will help you. If the lighting in your speech location is likely to have glare, be sure to write your notes in ink, as pencil can be hard to read in poor lighting.

3.3 Using Notecards Effectively

If you use as much care in developing your five notecards as you do your speech, they should serve you well. If you lose your place or go blank during the speech, you will only need a few seconds to find where you were and get going again. For instance, if you know that you presented the introduction and the first main point, which centers on the Emancipation Proclamation, you can readily go to your second card and remind yourself that your next main point is about the Thirteenth Amendment to the US Constitution.

In addition, the use of your notecards allows you to depart from the exact prepared wordings in your manuscript. In your recovery from losing your place, you can transpose a word or phrase to make your recovery graceful. It allows you to avoid feeling pressured to say every single word in your manuscript.

Under no circumstances should you ever attempt to put your entire speech on cards in little tiny writing. You will end up reading words to your audience instead of telling them your meaning, and the visual aspect of your speech will be spoiled by your need to squint to read your cards.

KEY TAKEAWAYS

- Good notecards keep you from reading to your audience.
- Good notecards are carefully based on key words and phrases to promote recall.
- Good notecards should enhance your relationship with listeners.

EXERCISES

1. Using the introduction to your speech, create a 4 × 6 notecard that includes the grabber, the thesis statement, and the preview. Test it by standing as you would during a speech and using it to guide you.

2. Answer these questions: Is it absolutely crucial to utter every word on your outline? Are there some words or phrases that are crucially important? How can you use your notecards to focus on the most important ideas?

3. Select key terms from your speech that you believe will trigger your recall of the sequence of main ideas in your speech. Use them as the basis of your next four notecards. Test the cards by practicing with them to see whether your selected terms are the ones you should use.

4. PRACTICING FOR SUCCESSFUL SPEECH DELIVERY

LEARNING OBJECTIVES

1. Explain why having a strong conversational quality is important for effective public speaking.
2. Explain the importance of eye contact in public speaking.
3. Define vocalics and differentiate among the different factors of vocalics.
4. Explain effective physical manipulation during a speech.
5. Understand how to practice effectively for good speech delivery.

There is no foolproof recipe for good delivery. Each of us is unique, and we each embody different experiences and interests. This means each person has an approach, or a style, that is effective for her or him. This further means that anxiety can accompany even the most carefully researched and interesting message. Even when we know our messages are strong and well-articulated on paper, it is difficult to know for sure that our presentation will also be good.

© *Thinkstock*

We are still obligated to do our best out of respect for the audience and their needs. Fortunately, there are some tools that can be helpful to you even the very first time you present a speech. You will continue developing your skills each time you put them to use and can experiment to find out which combination of delivery elements is most effective for you.

4.1   What Is Good Delivery?

The more you care about your topic, the greater your motivation to present it well. Good delivery is a process of presenting a clear, coherent message in an interesting way. Communication scholar Stephen E. Lucas tells us:

> Good delivery...conveys the speaker's ideas clearly, interestingly, and without distracting the audience. Most audiences prefer delivery that combines a certain degree of formality with the best attributes of good conversation—directness, spontaneity, animation, vocal and facial expressiveness, and a lively sense of communication. [2]

Many writers on the nonverbal aspects of delivery have cited the findings of psychologist Albert Mehrabian, asserting that the bulk of an audience's understanding of your message is based on nonverbal communication. Specifically, Mehrabian is often credited with finding that when audiences decoded a speaker's meaning, the speaker's face conveyed 55 percent of the information, the vocalics conveyed 38 percent, and the words conveyed just 7 percent.[3] Although numerous scholars, including Mehrabian himself, have stated that his findings are often misinterpreted,[4] scholars and speech instructors do agree that nonverbal communication and speech delivery are extremely important to effective public speaking.

In this section of the chapter, we will explain six elements of good delivery: conversational style, conversational quality, eye contact, vocalics, physical manipulation, and variety. And since delivery is only as good as the practice that goes into it, we conclude with some tips for effective use of your practice time.

Conversational Style

Conversational style is a speaker's ability to sound expressive and to be perceived by the audience as natural. It's a style that approaches the way you normally express yourself in a much smaller group than your classroom audience. This means that you want to avoid having your presentation come across as didactic or overly exaggerated. You might not feel natural while you're using a conversational style, but for the sake of audience preference and receptiveness, you should do your best to appear natural. It might be helpful to remember that the two most important elements of the speech are the message and the audience. You are the conduit with the important role of putting the two together in an effective way. Your audience should be thinking about the message, not the delivery.

conversational style

A speaker's ability to sound expressive and be perceived by the audience as natural.

Stephen E. Lucas defines **conversational quality** as the idea that "no matter how many times a speech has been rehearsed, it still *sounds* spontaneous" [emphasis in original].[5] No one wants to hear a speech that is so well rehearsed that it sounds fake or robotic. One of the hardest parts of public speaking is rehearsing to the point where it can appear to your audience that the thoughts are magically coming to you while you're speaking, but in reality you've spent a great deal of time thinking through each idea. When you can sound conversational, people pay attention.

Eye Contact

Eye contact is a speaker's ability to have visual contact with everyone in the audience. Your audience should feel that you're speaking to them, not simply uttering main and supporting points. If you are new to public speaking, you may find it intimidating to look audience members in the eye, but if you think about speakers you have seen who did not maintain eye contact, you'll realize why this aspect of speech delivery is important. Without eye contact, the audience begins to feel invisible and unimportant, as if the speaker is just speaking to hear her or his own voice. Eye contact lets your audience feel that your attention is on them, not solely on the cards in front of you.

Sustained eye contact with your audience is one of the most important tools toward effective delivery. O'Hair, Stewart, and Rubenstein note that eye contact is mandatory for speakers to establish a good relationship with an audience.[6] Whether a speaker is speaking before a group of five or five hundred, the appearance of eye contact is an important way to bring an audience into your speech.

Eye contact can be a powerful tool. It is not simply a sign of sincerity, a sign of being well prepared and knowledgeable, or a sign of confidence; it also has the power to convey meanings. Arthur Koch tells us that all facial expressions "can communicate a wide range of emotions, including sadness, compassion, concern, anger, annoyance, fear, joy, and happiness."[7]

If you find the gaze of your audience too intimidating, you might feel tempted to resort to "faking" eye contact with them by looking at the wall just above their heads or by sweeping your gaze around the room instead of making actual eye contact with individuals in your audience until it becomes easier to provide real contact. The problem with fake eye contact is that it tends to look mechanical. Another problem with fake attention is that you lose the opportunity to assess the audience's understanding of your message. Still, fake eye contact is somewhat better than gripping your cards and staring at them and only occasionally glancing quickly and shallowly at the audience.

This is not to say that you may never look at your notecards. On the contrary, one of the skills in extemporaneous speaking is the ability to alternate one's gaze between the audience and one's notes. Rehearsing your presentation in front of a few friends should help you develop the ability to maintain eye contact with your audience while referring to your notes. When you are giving a speech that is well prepared and well rehearsed, you will only need to look at your notes occasionally. This is an ability that will develop even further with practice. Your public speaking course is your best chance to get that practice.

Effective Use of Vocalics

Vocalics, also known as paralanguage, is the subfield of nonverbal communication that examines how we use our voices to communicate orally. This means that you speak loudly enough for all audience members (even those in the back of the room) to hear you clearly, and that you enunciate clearly enough to be understood by all audience members (even those who may have a hearing impairment or who may be English-language learners). If you tend to be soft-spoken, you will need to practice using a louder volume level that may feel unnatural to you at first. For all speakers, good vocalic technique is best achieved by facing the audience with your chin up and your eyes away from your notecards and by setting your voice at a moderate speed. Effective use of vocalics also means that you make use of appropriate pitch, pauses, vocal variety, and correct pronunciation.

If you are an English-language learner and feel apprehensive about giving a speech in English, there are two things to remember: first, you can meet with a reference librarian to learn the correct pronunciations of any English words you are unsure of; and second, the fact that you have an accent means you speak more languages than most Americans, which is an accomplishment to be proud of.

If you are one of the many people with a stutter or other speech challenge, you undoubtedly already know that there are numerous techniques for reducing stuttering and improving speech fluency and that there is no one agreed-upon "cure." The Academy Award–winning movie *The King's Speech* did much to increase public awareness of what a person with a stutter goes through when it comes to public speaking. It also prompted some well-known individuals who stutter, such as television news reporter John Stossel, to go public about their stuttering.[8] If you have decided to study public speaking in spite of a speech challenge, we commend you for your efforts and encourage you to work with your speech instructor to make whatever adaptations work best for you.

Volume

Volume refers to the loudness or softness of a speaker's voice. As mentioned, public speakers need to speak loudly enough to be heard by everyone in the audience. In addition, volume is often needed to overcome ambient noise, such as the hum of an air conditioner or the dull roar of traffic passing by. In addition, you can use volume strategically to emphasize the most important points in your speech. Select these points carefully; if you emphasize everything, nothing will seem important. You also want to be sure to adjust your volume to the physical setting of the presentation. If you are in a large auditorium and your audience is several yards away, you will need to speak louder. If you are in a smaller space, with the audience a few feet away, you want to avoid overwhelming your audience with shouting or speaking too loudly.

volume
The loudness or softness of a speaker's voice.

Rate

Rate is the speed at which a person speaks. To keep your speech delivery interesting, your rate should vary. If you are speaking extemporaneously, your rate will naturally fluctuate. If you're reading, your delivery is less likely to vary. Because rate is an important tool in enhancing the meanings in your speech, you do not want to give a monotone drone or a rapid "machine-gun" style delivery. Your rate should be appropriate for your topic and your points. A rapid, lively rate can communicate such meanings as enthusiasm, urgency, or humor. A slower, moderated rate can convey respect, seriousness, or careful reasoning. By varying rapid and slower rates within a single speech, you can emphasize your main points and keep your audience interested.

rate
The fastness or slowness of a person's speech delivery.

Pitch

Pitch refers to the highness or lowness of a speaker's voice. Some speakers have deep voices and others have high voices. As with one's singing voice range, the pitch of one's speaking voice is determined to a large extent by physiology (specifically, the length of one's vocal folds, or cords, and the size of one's vocal tract). We all have a normal speaking pitch where our voice is naturally settled, the pitch where we are most comfortable speaking, and most teachers advise speaking at the pitch that feels natural to you.

pitch
The highness or lowness of a speaker's voice.

While our voices may be generally comfortable at a specific pitch level, we all have the ability to modulate, or move, our pitch up or down. In fact, we do this all the time. When we change the pitch of our voices, we are using **inflections**. Just as you can use volume strategically, you can also use pitch inflections to make your delivery more interesting and emphatic. If you ordinarily speak with a soprano voice, you may want to drop your voice to a slightly lower range to call attention to a particular point. How we use inflections can even change the entire meaning of what we are saying. For example, try saying the sentence "I love public speaking" with a higher pitch on one of the words—first raise the pitch on "I," then say it again with the pitch raised on "love," and so on. "*I* love public speaking" conveys a different meaning from "I love *public* speaking," doesn't it?

inflections
Changes in the pitch of a speaker's voice.

There are some speakers who don't change their pitch at all while speaking, which is called **monotone**. While very few people are completely monotone, some speakers slip into monotone patterns because of nerves. One way to ascertain whether you sound monotone is to record your voice and see how you sound. If you notice that your voice doesn't fluctuate very much, you will need to be intentional in altering your pitch to ensure that the emphasis of your speech isn't completely lost on your audience.

monotone
The vocal quality of staying at a constant pitch level without inflections.

Finally, resist the habit of pitching your voice "up" at the ends of sentences. It makes them sound like questions instead of statements. This habit can be disorienting and distracting, interfering with the audience's ability to focus entirely on the message. The speaker sounds uncertain or sounds as though he or she is seeking the understanding or approval of the listener. It hurts the speaker's credibility and it needs to be avoided.

The effective use of pitch is one of the keys to an interesting delivery that will hold your audience's attention.

Pauses

Pauses are brief breaks in a speaker's delivery that can show emphasis and enhance the clarity of a message. In terms of timing, the effective use of pauses is one of the most important skills to develop. Some speakers become uncomfortable very quickly with the "dead air" that the pause causes. And if the speaker is uncomfortable, the discomfort can transmit itself to the audience. That doesn't mean you should avoid using pauses; your ability to use them confidently will increase with practice. Some of the best comedians use the well-timed pause to powerful and hilarious effect. Although your speech will not be a comedy routine, pauses are still useful for emphasis, especially when combined with a lowered pitch and rate to emphasize the important point you do not want your audience to miss.

pauses
Brief breaks in a speaker's deliver designed to show emphasis.

Vocal Variety

Vocal variety has to do with changes in the vocalics we have just discussed: volume, pitch, rate, and pauses. No one wants to hear the same volume, pitch, rate, or use of pauses over and over again in a speech. Your audience should never be able to detect that you're about to slow down or your voice is going to get deeper because you're making an important point. When you think about how you sound in a normal conversation, your use of volume, pitch, rate, and pauses are all done spontaneously. If you try to overrehearse your vocalics, your speech will end up sounding artificial. Vocal variety should flow naturally from your wish to speak with expression. In that way, it will animate your speech and invite your listeners to understand your topic the way you do.

Pronunciation

The last major category related to vocalics is **pronunciation**, or the conventional patterns of speech used to form a word. Word pronunciation is important for two reasons: first, mispronouncing a word your audience is familiar with will harm your credibility as a speaker; and second, mispronouncing a word they are unfamiliar with can confuse and even misinform them. If there is any possibility at all that you don't know the correct pronunciation of a word, find out. Many online dictionaries, such as the Wiktionary (http://wiktionary.org), provide free sound files illustrating the pronunciation of words.

Many have commented on the mispronunciation of words such as "nuclear" and "cavalry" by highly educated public speakers, including US presidents. There have been classroom examples as well. For instance, a student giving a speech on the Greek philosopher Socrates mispronounced his name at least eight times during her speech. This mispronunciation created a situation of great awkwardness and anxiety for the audience. Everyone felt embarrassed and the teacher, opting not to humiliate the student in front of the class, could not say anything out loud, instead providing a private written comment at the end of class.

One important aspect of pronunciation is **articulation**, or the ability to clearly pronounce each of a succession of syllables used to make up a word. Some people have difficulty articulating because of physiological problems that can be treated by trained speech therapists, but other people have articulation problems because they come from a cultural milieu where a dialect other than standard American English is the norm. Speech therapists, who generally guide their clients toward standard American English, use the acronym SODA when helping people learn how to more effectively articulate: **substitutions, omissions, distortions**, and **additions**.

- **Substitutions** occur when a speaker replaces one consonant or vowel with another consonant (*water* becomes *wudda*; *ask* becomes *ax*; *mouth* becomes *mouf*).

- **Omissions** occur when a speaker drops a consonant or vowel within a word (*Internet* becomes *Innet*; *mesmerized* becomes *memerized*; *probably* becomes *prolly*).

- **Distortions** occur when a speaker articulates a word with nasal or slurring sounds (*pencil* sounds like *mencil*; *precipitation* sounds like *persination*; *second* sounds like *slecond*).

- **Additions** occur when a speaker adds consonants or vowels to words that are not there (*anyway* becomes *anyways*; *athletic* becomes *athaletic*; *black* becomes *buhlack*; *interpret* becomes *interpretate*).

Another aspect of pronunciation in public speaking is avoiding the use of **verbal surrogates** or "filler" words used as placeholders for actual words (like *er, um, uh*, etc.). You might be able to get away with saying "um" as many as two or three times in your speech before it becomes distracting, but the same cannot be said of "like." We know of a student who trained herself to avoid saying "like." As soon as the first speech was assigned, she began wearing a rubber band on her left wrist. Each time she caught herself saying "like," she snapped herself with the rubber band. It hurt. Very quickly, she found that she could stop inflicting the snap on herself, and she had successfully confronted an unprofessional verbal habit.

Effective Physical Manipulation

In addition to using our voices effectively, a key to effective public speaking is **physical manipulation**, or the use of the body to emphasize meanings or convey meanings during a speech. While we will not attempt to give an entire discourse on nonverbal communication, we will discuss a few basic aspects of physical manipulation: posture, body movement, facial expressions, and dress. These aspects add up to the overall physical dimension of your speech, which we call self-presentation.

physical manipulation
The use of the body to emphasize meanings or convey meanings during a speech.

Posture

"Stand up tall!" I'm sure we've all heard this statement from a parent or a teacher at some point in our lives. The fact is, posture is actually quite important. When you stand up straight, you communicate to your audience, without saying a word, that you hold a position of power and take your position seriously. If however, you are slouching, hunched over, or leaning on something, you could be perceived as ill prepared, anxious, lacking in credibility, or not serious about your responsibilities as a speaker. While speakers often assume more casual posture as a presentation continues (especially if it is a long one, such as a ninety-minute class lecture), it is always wise to start by standing up straight and putting your best foot forward. Remember, you only get one shot at making a first impression, and your body's orientation is one of the first pieces of information audiences use to make that impression.

Body Movement

Unless you are stuck behind a podium because of the need to use a nonmovable microphone, you should never stand in one place during a speech. However, movement during a speech should also not resemble pacing. One of our authors once saw a speaker who would walk around a small table where her speaking notes were located. She would walk around the table once, toss her chalk twice, and then repeat the process. Instead of listening to what the speaker was saying, everyone became transfixed by her walk-and-chalk-toss pattern. As speakers, we must be mindful of how we go about moving while speaking. One common method for easily integrating some movement into your speech is to take a few steps any time you transition from one idea to the next. By only moving at transition points, not only do you help focus your audience's attention on the transition from one idea to the next, but you also are able to increase your nonverbal immediacy by getting closer to different segments of your audience.

Body movement also includes gestures. These should be neither overdramatic nor subdued. At one extreme, arm-waving and fist-pounding will distract from your message and reduce your credibility. At the other extreme, refraining from the use of gestures is the waste of an opportunity to suggest emphasis, enthusiasm, or other personal connection with your topic.

There are many ways to use gestures. The most obvious are hand gestures, which should be used in moderation at carefully selected times in the speech. If you overuse gestures, they lose meaning. Many late-night comedy parodies of political leaders include patterned, overused gestures or other delivery habits associated with a particular speaker. However, the well-placed use of simple, natural gestures to indicate emphasis, direction, size is usually effective. Normally, a gesture with one hand is enough. Rather than trying to have a gesture for every sentence, use just a few well-planned gestures. It is often more effective to make a gesture and hold it for a few moments than to begin waving your hands and arms around in a series of gestures.

Finally, just as you should avoid pacing, you will also want to avoid other distracting movements when you are speaking. Many speakers have unconscious mannerisms such as twirling their hair, putting their hands in and out of their pockets, jingling their keys, licking their lips, or clicking a pen while speaking. As with other aspects of speech delivery, practicing in front of others will help you become conscious of such distractions and plan ways to avoid doing them.

Facial Expressions

Faces are amazing things and convey so much information. As speakers, we must be acutely aware of what our face looks like while speaking. While many of us do not look forward to seeing ourselves on videotape, often the only way you can critically evaluate what your face is doing while you are speaking is to watch a recording of your speech. If video is not available, you can practice speaking in front of a mirror.

There are two extremes you want to avoid: no facial expression and overanimated facial expressions. First, you do not want to have a completely blank face while speaking. Some people just do not show much emotion with their faces naturally, but this blankness is often increased when the speaker is nervous. Audiences will react negatively to the message of such a speaker because they will sense that something is amiss. If a speaker is talking about the joys of Disney World and his face doesn't show any excitement, the audience is going to be turned off to the speaker and his message. On the other extreme end is the speaker whose face looks like that of an exaggerated cartoon character. Instead, your goal is to show a variety of appropriate facial expressions while speaking.

Like vocalics and gestures, facial expression can be used strategically to enhance meaning. A smile or pleasant facial expression is generally appropriate at the beginning of a speech to indicate your wish for a good transaction with your audience. However, you should not smile throughout a speech on drug addiction, poverty, or the oil spill in the Gulf of Mexico. An inappropriate smile creates confusion about your meaning and may make your audience feel uncomfortable. On the other hand, a serious scowl might look hostile or threatening to audience members and become a distraction from the message. If you keep the meaning of your speech foremost in your mind, you will more readily find the balance in facial expression.

Another common problem some new speakers have is showing only one expression. One of our coauthors competed in speech in college. After one of his speeches (about how people die on amusement park rides), one of his judges pulled him aside and informed him that his speech was "creepy." Apparently, while speaking about death, our coauthor smiled the entire time. The incongruity between the speech on death and dying and the coauthor's smile just left the judge a little creeped out. If you are excited in a part of your speech, you should show excitement on your face. On the other hand, if you are at a serious part of your speech, your facial expressions should be serious.

Dress

While there are no clear-cut guidelines for how you should dress for every speech you'll give, dress is still a very important part of how others will perceive you (again, it's all about the first impression). If you want to be taken seriously, you must present yourself seriously. While we do not advocate dressing up in a suit every time you give a speech, there are definitely times when wearing a suit is appropriate.

One general rule you can use for determining dress is the "step-above rule," which states that you should dress one step above your audience. If your audience is going to be dressed casually in shorts and jeans, then wear nice casual clothing such as a pair of neatly pressed slacks and a collared shirt or blouse. If, however, your audience is going to be wearing "business casual" attire, then you should probably wear a sport coat, a dress, or a suit. The goal of the step-above rule is to establish yourself as someone to be taken seriously. On the other hand, if you dress two steps above your audience, you may put too much distance between yourself and your audience, coming across as overly formal or even arrogant.

Another general rule for dressing is to avoid distractions in your appearance. Overly tight or revealing garments, over-the-top hairstyles or makeup, jangling jewelry, or a display of tattoos and piercings can serve to draw your audience's attention away from your speech. Remembering that your message is the most important aspect of your speech, keep that message in mind when you choose your clothing and accessories.

Self-Presentation

When you present your speech, you are also presenting yourself. Self-presentation, sometimes also referred to as poise or stage presence, is determined by how you look, how you stand, how you walk to the lectern, and how you use your voice and gestures. Your self-presentation can either enhance your message or detract from it. Worse, a poor self-presentation can turn a good, well-prepared speech into a forgettable waste of time. You want your self-presentation to support your credibility and improve the likelihood that the audience will listen with interest.

Your personal appearance should reflect the careful preparation of your speech. Your personal appearance is the first thing your audience will see, and from it, they will make inferences about the speech you're about to present.

Variety

One of the biggest mistakes novice public speakers make is to use the same gesture over and over again during a speech. While you don't want your gestures to look fake, you should be careful to include a variety of different nonverbal components while speaking. You should make sure that your face, body, and words are all working in conjunction with each other to support your message.

4.2 Practice Effectively

You might get away with presenting a hastily practiced speech, but the speech will not be as good as it could be. In order to develop your best speech delivery, you need to practice—and use your practice time effectively. Practicing does not mean reading over your notes, mentally running through your speech, or even speaking your speech aloud over and over. Instead, you need to practice with the goal of identifying the weaknesses in your delivery, improving upon them, and building good speech delivery habits.

When you practice your speech, place both your feet in full, firm contact with the floor to keep your body from swaying side to side. Some new public speakers find that they don't know what to do with their hands during the speech. Your practice sessions should help you get comfortable. When you're not gesturing, you can rest your free hand lightly on a lectern or simply allow it to hang at your side. Since this is not a familiar posture for most people, it might feel awkward, but in your practice sessions, you can begin getting used to it.

Seek Input from Others

Because we can't see ourselves as others see us, one of the best ways to improve your delivery is to seek constructive criticism from others. This, of course, is an aspect of your public speaking course, as you will receive evaluations from your instructor and possibly from your fellow students. However, by practicing in front of others before it is time to present your speech, you can anticipate and correct problems so that you can receive a better evaluation when you give the speech "for real."

Ask your practice observers to be honest about the aspects of your delivery that could be better. Sometimes students create study groups just for this purpose. When you create a study group of classroom peers, everyone has an understanding of the entire creative process, and their feedback will thus be more useful to you than the feedback you might get from someone who has never taken the course or given a speech.

If your practice observers seem reluctant to offer useful criticisms, ask questions. How was your eye contact? Could they hear you? Was your voice well modulated? Did you mispronounce any words? How was your posture? Were your gestures effective? Did you have any mannerisms that you should learn to avoid? Because peers are sometimes reluctant to say things that could sound critical, direct questions are often a useful way to help them speak up.

If you learn from these practice sessions that your voice tends to drop at the ends of sentences, make a conscious effort to support your voice as you conclude each main point. If you learn that you have a habit of clicking a pen, make sure you don't have a pen with you when you speak or that you keep it in your pocket. If your practice observers mention that you tend to hide your hands in the sleeves of your shirt or jacket, next time wear short sleeves or roll your sleeves up before beginning your speech. If you learn through practice that you tend to sway or rock while you speak, you can consciously practice and build the habit of *not* swaying.

When it is your turn to give feedback to others in your group, assume that they are as interested in doing well as you are. Give feedback in the spirit of helping their speeches be as good as possible.

Use Audio and/or Video to Record Yourself

Technology has made it easier than ever to record yourself and others using the proliferation of electronic devices people are likely to own. Video, of course, allows you the advantage of being able to see yourself as others see you, while audio allows you to concentrate on the audible aspects of your delivery. As we mentioned earlier in the chapter, if neither video nor audio is available, you can always observe yourself by practicing your delivery in front of a mirror.

After you have recorded yourself, it may seem obvious that you should watch and listen to the recording. This can be intimidating, as you may fear that your performance anxiety will be so obvious that everyone will notice it in the recording. But students are often pleasantly surprised when they watch and listen to their recordings, as even students with very high anxiety may find out that they "come across" in a speech much better than they expected.

A recording can also be a very effective diagnostic device. Sometimes students believe they are making strong contact with their audiences, but their cards contain so many notes that they succumb to the temptation of reading. By finding out from the video that you misjudged your eye contact, you can be motivated to rewrite your notecards in a way that doesn't provide the opportunity to do so much reading.

It is most likely that in viewing your recording, you will benefit from discovering your strengths and finding weak areas you can strengthen.

Good Delivery Is a Habit

Luckily, public speaking is an activity that, when done conscientiously, strengthens with practice. As you become aware of the areas where your delivery has room for improvement, you will begin developing a keen sense of what "works" and what audiences respond to.

It is advisable to practice out loud in front of other people several times, spreading your rehearsals out over several days. To do this kind of practice, of course, you need to have your speech be finalized well ahead of the date when you are going to give it. During these practice sessions, you can time your speech to make sure it lasts the appropriate length of time. A friend of ours was the second student on the program in an event where each student's presentation was to last thirty to forty-five minutes. After the first student had been speaking for seventy-five minutes, the professor in charge asked, "Can we speed this up?" The student said yes, and proceeded to continue speaking for another seventy-five minutes before finally concluding his portion of the program. Although we might fault the professor for not "pulling the plug," clearly the student had not timed his speech in advance.

Your practice sessions will also enable you to make adjustments to your notecards to make them more effective in supporting your contact with your audience. This kind of practice is not just a strategy for beginners; it is practiced by many highly placed public figures with extensive experience in public speaking.

Your public speaking course is one of the best opportunities you will have to manage your performance anxiety, build your confidence in speaking extemporaneously, develop your vocal skills, and become adept at self-presentation. The habits you can develop through targeted practice are to build continuously on your strengths and to challenge yourself to find new areas for improving your delivery. By taking advantage of these opportunities, you will gain the ability to present a speech effectively whenever you may be called upon to speak publicly.

KEY TAKEAWAYS

- Conversational style is a speaker's ability to sound expressive while being perceived by the audience as natural. Conversational quality is a speaker's ability to prepare a speech and rehearse a speech but still sound spontaneous when delivering it.
- Eye contact helps capture and maintain an audience's interest while contributing to the speaker's credibility.
- Vocalics are the nonverbal components of the verbal message. There are six important vocalic components for a speaker to be aware of: volume (loudness or softness), pitch (highness or lowness), rate (fastness or slowness), pauses (use of breaks to add emphasis), vocal variety (use of a range of vocalic strategies), and pronunciation (using conventional patterns of speech formation).
- Physical manipulation is the use of one's body to add meaning and emphasis to a speech. As such, excessive or nonexistent physical manipulation can detract from a speaker's speech.
- Good delivery is a habit that is built through effective practice.

EXERCISES

1. Find a speech online and examine the speaker's overall presentation. How good was the speaker's delivery? Make a list of the aspects of delivery in this chapter and evaluate the speaker according to the list. In what areas might the speaker improve?
2. Record a practice session of your speech. Write a self-critique, answering the following questions: What surprised you the most? What is an area of strength upon which you can build? What is *one* area for improvement?

5. CHAPTER EXERCISES

SPEAKING ETHICALLY

Sam wanted to present a speech on medical errors. He has procrastinated. Two days before the speech, he realized that no matter how hard he worked, his speech would be weak, and he could not do it justice. Instead of choosing a less technical topic or narrowing to one specific kind of medical mistake, he decided to push through it. He could make up for the scant and superficial content by wearing hospital scrubs, borrowed from his brother-in-law, and by sliding his glasses down his nose to make it easier to see his notecards and to match the stereotype of a health care provider.

1. Did Sam treat the audience with respect?
2. Name several things Sam should have done differently.
3. What would you do if you were Sam's instructor?

END-OF-CHAPTER ASSESSMENT

1. According to Albert Mehrabian, which is the correct breakdown for how humans interpret a speaker's message?

     a. 55 percent face, 38 percent vocalics, and 7 percent words

     b. 93 percent face, 7 percent vocalics, and 0 percent words

     c. 40 percent face, 40 percent vocalics, and 20 percent words

     d. 7 percent face, 55 percent vocalics, and 38 percent words

     e. 38 percent face, 7 percent vocalics, and 55 percent words

2. Darlene is preparing a speech for her public speaking class. She goes to the library and does her research. She then prepares a basic outline and creates five notecards with basic ideas to use during her speech. What type of delivery is Darlene using?

     a. impromptu

     b. extemporaneous

     c. manuscript

     d. memorized

     e. elocutionist

3. Which form of vocalics is concerned with the highness or lowness of someone's speech?

     a. pitch

     b. rate

     c. volume

     d. pauses

     e. pronunciation

4. In his speech on landscape architecture, Jimmy uses the word "yaad" instead of the word "yard." What type of articulation problem does Jimmy exhibit?

     a. substitution

     b. omission

     c. distortion

     d. addition

     e. surrogate

5. Which of the following is a recommendation for creating and using notes during a speech?

     a. Include only key words to trigger your memory.

     b. Read from your notes as much as possible.

     c. Never show your notes to your audience.

     d. Write in small letters on your notes so that your audience can't see them.

     e. Do not rehearse with your notes or your delivery will become "stale."

6. Effective speech delivery can be summed up in which term?

     a. vocalics

     b. physical manipulation

     c. self-presentation

     d. conversational quality

     e. paralanguage

ANSWER KEY

1. a

2. b

3. a

4. a

5. a

6. c

ENDNOTES

1. Ross, S. (2007). Civil rights march on Washington. *Infoplease*. Retrieved from http://www.infoplease.com/spot/marchonwashington.html

2. Lucas, S. E. (2009). *The art of public speaking* (9th ed.). Boston, MA: McGraw-Hill, p. 244.

3. Mehrabian, A. (1972). *Nonverbal communication*. Chicago, IL: Aldine-Atherton.

4. Mitchell, O. (n.d.). Mehrabian and nonverbal communication [Web log post]. Retrieved from http://www.speakingaboutpresenting.com/presentation-myths/mehrabian-nonverbal-communication-research

5. Lucas, S. E. (2009). *The art of public speaking* (9th ed.). Boston, MA: McGraw-Hill, p. 247.

6. O'Hair, D., Stewart, R., & Rubenstein, H. (2001). *A speaker's guidebook: Text and reference*. Boston, MA: Bedford/St. Martin's.

7. Koch, A. (2010). *Speaking with a purpose* (8th ed.). Boston, MA: Allyn & Bacon, p. 233.

8. Stossel, J. (2011, March 2). An Academy Award–winning movie, stuttering and me [Web log post]. Retrieved from http://www.humanevents.com/article.php?id=42081

Presentation Aids: Design and Usage

WHAT ARE PRESENTATION AIDS?

When you give a speech, you are presenting much more than just a collection of words and ideas. Because you are speaking "live and in person," your audience members will experience your speech through all five of their senses: hearing, vision, smell, taste, and touch. In some speaking situations, the speaker appeals only to the sense of hearing, more or less ignoring the other senses except to avoid visual distractions by dressing and presenting himself or herself in an appropriate manner. But the speaking event can be greatly enriched by appeals to the other senses. This is the role of presentation aids.

Presentation aids, sometimes also called sensory aids, are the resources beyond the speech itself that a speaker uses to enhance the message conveyed to the audience. The type of presentation aids that speakers most typically make use of are visual aids: pictures, diagrams, charts and graphs, maps, and the like. Audible aids include musical excerpts, audio speech excerpts, and sound effects. A speaker may also use fragrance samples or a food samples as olfactory or gustatory aids. Finally, presentation aids can be three-dimensional objects, animals, and people; they can unfold over a period of time, as in the case of a how-to demonstration.

As you can see, the range of possible presentation aids is almost infinite. However, all presentation aids have one thing in common: To be effective, each presentation aid a speaker uses must be a direct, uncluttered example of a specific element of the speech. It is understandable that someone presenting a speech about Abraham Lincoln might want to include a picture of him, but because most people already know what Lincoln looked like, the picture would not contribute much to the message (unless, perhaps, the message was specifically about the changes in Lincoln's appearance during his time in office). Other visual artifacts are more likely to deliver information more directly relevant to the speech—a diagram of the interior of Ford's Theater where Lincoln was assassinated, a facsimile of the messy and much-edited Gettysburg Address, or a photograph of the Lincoln family, for example. The key is that each presentation aid must directly express an idea in your speech.

Moreover, presentation aids must be used at the time when you are presenting the specific ideas related to the aid. For example, if you are speaking about coral reefs and one of your supporting points is about the location of the world's major reefs, it will make sense to display a map of these reefs while you're talking about location. If you display it while you are explaining what coral actually is, or describing the kinds of fish that feed on a reef, the map will not serve as a useful visual aid—in fact, it's likely to be a distraction.

Presentation aids must also be easy to use. At a conference on organic farming, your author watched as the facilitator opened the orientation session by creating a *conceptual map* of our concerns, using a large newsprint pad on an easel. In his shirt pocket were wide-tipped felt markers in several colors. As he was using the black marker to write the word "pollution," he dropped the cap on the floor, and it rolled a few inches under the easel. When he

presentation aids
The resources beyond the speech itself that a speaker uses to enhance the message conveyed to the audience.

bent over to pick up the cap, all the other markers fell out of his pocket. They rolled about too, and when he tried to retrieve them, he bumped the easel, leading the easel and newsprint pad to tumble over on top of him. The audience responded with amusement and thundering applause, but the serious tone of his speech was ruined. The next two days of the conference were punctuated with allusions to the unforgettable orientation speech. This is not how you will want your speech to be remembered.

To be effective, presentation aids must also be easy for the listeners to see and understand. In this chapter, we will present some principles and strategies to help you incorporate hardworking, effective presentation aids into your speech. We will begin by discussing the functions that good presentation aids fulfill. Next, we will explore some of the many types of presentation aids and how best to design and utilize them. We will also describe various media that can be used for presentation aids. We will conclude with tips for successful preparation and use of presentation aids in a speech.

1. FUNCTIONS OF PRESENTATION AIDS

LEARNING OBJECTIVES

1. List four reasons why presentation aids are important in public speaking.
2. Explain two ways in which presentation aids can increase audience understanding of a message.

Why should you use presentation aids? If you have prepared and rehearsed your speech adequately, shouldn't a good speech with a good delivery be enough to stand on its own? While it is true that impressive presentation aids will not rescue a poor speech, it is also important to recognize that a good speech can often be made even better by the strategic use of presentation aids.

Presentation aids can fulfill several functions: they can serve to improve your audience's understanding of the information you are conveying, enhance audience memory and retention of the message, add variety and interest to your speech, and enhance your credibility as a speaker. Let's examine each of these functions.

1.1 Improving Audience Understanding

Human communication is a complex process that often leads to misunderstandings. If you are like most people, you can easily remember incidents when you misunderstood a message or when someone else misunderstood what you said to them. Misunderstandings happen in public speaking just as they do in everyday conversations.

One reason for misunderstandings is the fact that perception and interpretation are highly complex individual processes. Most of us have seen the image in which, depending on your perception, you see either the outline of a vase or the facial profiles of two people facing each other. This shows how interpretations can differ, and it means that your presentations must be based on careful thought and preparation to maximize the likelihood that your listeners will understand your presentations as you intend them to.

As a speaker, one of your basic goals is to help your audience understand your message. To reduce misunderstanding, presentation aids can be used to clarify or to emphasize.

Clarifying

clarify

To make clear so that the audience understands your meanings the way you intend.

Clarification is important in a speech because if some of the information you convey is unclear, your listeners will come away puzzled or possibly even misled. Presentation aids can help **clarify** a message if the information is complex or if the point being made is a visual one.

If your speech is about the impact of the Coriolis effect on tropical storms, for instance, you will have great difficulty clarifying it without a diagram because the process is a complex one. The diagram in Figure 15.1 would be effective because it shows the audience the interaction between equatorial wind patterns and wind patterns moving in other directions. The diagram allows the audience to process the information in two ways: through your verbal explanation and through the visual elements of the diagram.

Figure 15.2 is another example of a diagram that maps out the process of human communication. In this image you clearly have a speaker and an audience (albeit slightly abstract), with the labels of source, channel, message, receivers, and feedback to illustrate the basic linear model of human communication.

FIGURE 15.1 Coriolis Effect

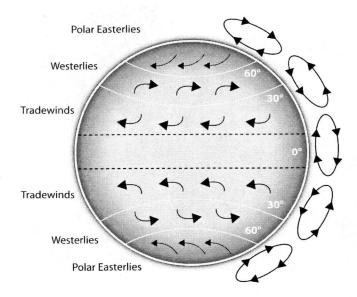

FIGURE 15.2 Model of Communication

FIGURE 15.3 Petroglyph

Another aspect of clarifying occurs when a speaker wants to visually help audience members understand a visual concept. For example, if a speaker is talking about the importance of petroglyphs in Native American culture, just describing the petroglyphs won't completely help your audience to visualize what they look like. Instead, showing an example of a petroglyph, as in Figure 15.3, can more easily help your audience form a clear mental image of your intended meaning.

Emphasizing

When you use a presentational aid for **emphasis**, you impress your listeners with the importance of an idea. In a speech on water conservation, you might try to show the environmental proportions of the resource. When you use a conceptual drawing like the one in Figure 15.4, you show that if the world water supply were equal to ten gallons, only ten drops would be available and potable for human or household consumption. This drawing is effective because it emphasizes the scarcity of useful water and thus draws attention to this important information in your speech.

emphasize

To impress the importance or to repeat the verbal message in visual form.

FIGURE 15.4 Planetary Water Supply

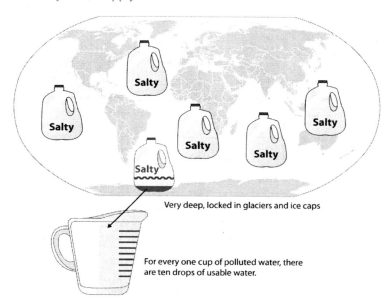

Very deep, locked in glaciers and ice caps

For every one cup of polluted water, there are ten drops of usable water.

FIGURE 15.5 Chinese Lettering Amplified

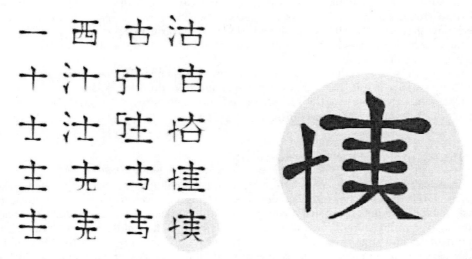

Source: Image courtesy of Wikimedia, http://commons.wikimedia.org/wiki/File:Acupuncture_chart_300px.jpg.

Another way of emphasizing that can be done visually is to zoom in on a specific aspect of interest within your speech. In Figure 15.5, we see a visual aid used in a speech on the importance of various parts of Chinese characters. On the left side of the visual aid, we see how the characters all fit together, with an emphasized version of a single character on the right.

1.2   Aiding Retention and Recall

The second function that presentation aids can serve is to increase the audience's chances of remembering your speech. A 1996 article by the US Department of Labor summarized research on how people learn and remember. The authors found that "83% of human learning occurs visually, and the remaining 17% through the other senses—11% through hearing, 3.5% through smell, 1% through taste, and 1.5% through touch."[1] Most of how people learn is through seeing things, so the visual component of learning is very important. The article goes on to note that information stored in long-term memory is also affected by how we originally learn the material. In a study of memory, learners were asked to recall information after a three day period. The researchers found that they retained 10 percent of what they heard from an oral presentation, 35 percent from a visual presentation, and 65 percent from a visual and oral presentation.[2] It's amazing to see how the combined effect of both the visual and oral components can contribute to long-term memory.

For this reason, exposure to a visual image can serve as a memory aid to your listeners. When your graphic images deliver information effectively and when your listeners understand them clearly, audience members are likely to remember your message long after your speech is over.

Moreover, people often are able to remember information that is presented in sequential steps more easily than if that information is presented in an unorganized pattern. When you use a presentation aid to display the organization of your speech, you will help your listeners to observe, follow, and remember the sequence of information you conveyed to them. This is why some instructors display a lecture outline for their students to follow during class.

An added plus of using presentation aids is that they can boost your memory while you are speaking. Using your presentation aids while you rehearse your speech will familiarize you with the association between a given place in your speech and the presentation aid that accompanies that material. For example, if you are giving an informative speech about diamonds, you might plan to display a sequence of slides illustrating the most popular diamond shapes: brilliant, marquise, emerald, and so on. As you finish describing one shape and advance to the next slide, seeing the next diamond shape will help you remember the information about it that you are going to deliver.

1.3   Adding Variety and Interest

A third function of presentation aids is simply to make your speech more interesting. While it is true that a good speech and a well-rehearsed delivery will already include variety in several aspects of the presentation, in many cases, a speech can be made even more interesting by the use of well-chosen presentation aids.

For example, you may have prepared a very good speech to inform a group of gardeners about several new varieties of roses suitable for growing in your local area. Although your listeners will undoubtedly understand and remember your message very well without any presentation aids, wouldn't your speech have greater impact if you accompanied your remarks with a picture of each rose? You can imagine that your audience would be even more enthralled if you had the ability to display an actual flower of each variety in a bud vase.

Similarly, if you were speaking to a group of gourmet cooks about Indian spices, you might want to provide tiny samples of spices that they could smell and taste during your speech. Taste researcher Linda Bartoshuk has given presentations in which audience members receive small pieces of fruit and are asked to taste them at certain points during the speech.[3]

1.4 Enhancing a Speaker's Credibility

Presentation aids alone will not be enough to create a professional image. As we mentioned earlier, impressive presentation aids will not rescue a poor speech. However, even if you give a good speech, you run the risk of appearing unprofessional if your presentation aids are poorly executed. This means that in addition to containing important information, your presentation aids must be clear, clean, uncluttered, organized, and large enough for the audience to see and interpret correctly. Misspellings and poorly designed presentation aids can damage your credibility as a speaker. Conversely, a high quality presentation will contribute to your professional image. In addition, make sure that you give proper credit to the source of any presentation aids that you take from other sources. Using a statistical chart or a map without proper credit will detract from your credibility, just as using a quotation in your speech without credit would.

If you focus your efforts on producing presentation aids that contribute effectively to your meaning, that look professional, and that are handled well, your audience will most likely appreciate your efforts and pay close attention to your message. That attention will help them learn or understand your topic in a new way and will thus help the audience see you as a knowledgeable, competent, credible speaker.

KEY TAKEAWAYS

- Presentation aids should help audiences more thoroughly understand a speaker's basic message.
- There are four basic reasons to use presentation aids. First, they increase audience understanding of a speaker's message. Second, they help audiences retain and recall a speaker's message after the fact. Third, they make a speech more interesting by adding variety. Lastly, by making a speaker's overall speech more polished, presentation aids can increase an audience's perception of the speaker's credibility.
- Presentation aids help an audience more clearly understand a speaker's message in two ways: they help clarify and they help emphasize. Presentation aids can help the audience to understand complex ideas or processes and can also show which ideas are most important in the speech.

EXERCISES

1. Look at the outline you have prepared for a classroom speech. Where in the speech would it be appropriate to use presentation aids? Why would presentation aids help at the points you identify?
2. Presentational slides from speeches are sometimes available online. Search for and evaluate three sets of presentation slides you find online. Identify three ways that the slides could be improved to be more effective presentation aids.

2. TYPES OF PRESENTATION AIDS

As we saw in the case of the orientation presentation at the organic farming conference, using presentation aids can be risky. However, with a little forethought and adequate practice, you can choose presentation aids that enhance your message and boost your professional appearance in front of an audience.

One principle to keep in mind is to use only as many presentation aids as necessary to present your message or to fulfill your classroom assignment. Although the maxim "less is more" may sound like a cliché, it really does apply in this instance. The number and the technical sophistication of your presentation aids should never overshadow your speech.

Another important consideration is technology. Keep your presentation aids within the limits of the working technology available to you. Whether or not your classroom technology works on the day of your speech, you will still have to present. What will you do if the computer file containing your slides is corrupted? What will you do if the easel is broken? What if you had counted on stacking your visuals on a table that disappears right when you need it? You must be prepared to adapt to an uncomfortable and scary situation. This is why we urge students to go to the classroom at least fifteen minutes ahead of time to test the equipment and ascertain the condition of things they're planning to use. As the speaker, you are responsible for arranging the things you need to make your presentation aids work as intended. Carry a roll of duct tape so you can display your poster even if the easel is gone. Find an extra chair if your table has disappeared. Test the computer setup, and have an alternative plan prepared in case there is some glitch that prevents your computer-based presentation aids from being usable. The more sophisticated the equipment is, the more you should be prepared with an alternative, even in a "smart classroom."

More important than the method of delivery is the audience's ability to see and understand the presentation aid. It must deliver clear information, and it must not distract from the message. Avoid overly elaborate presentation aids because they can distract the audience's attention from your message. Instead, simplify as much as possible, emphasizing the information you want your audience to understand.

Another thing to remember is that presentation aids do not "speak for themselves." When you display a visual aid, you should explain what it shows, pointing out and naming the most important features. If you use an audio aid such as a musical excerpt, you need to tell your audience what to listen for. Similarly, if you use a video clip, it is up to you as the speaker to point out the characteristics in the video that support the point you are making.

Although there are many useful presentation tools, you should not attempt to use every one of these tools in a single speech. Your presentation aids should be designed to look like a coherent set. For instance, if you decide to use three slides and a poster, all four of these visual aids should make use of the same type font and basic design.

Now that we've explored some basic hints for preparing visual aids, let's look at the most common types of visual aids: charts, graphs, representations, objects/models, and people.

2.1 Charts

A **chart** is commonly defined as a graphical representation of data (often numerical) or a sketch representing an ordered process. Whether you create your charts or do research to find charts that already exist, it is important for them to exactly match the specific purpose in your speech. Figure 15.6 shows two charts related to acupuncture. Although both charts are good, they are not equal. One chart might be useful in a speech about the history and development of acupuncture, while the other chart would be more useful for showing the locations of meridians, or the lines along which energy is thought to flow, and the acupuncture points.

chart

A graphical representation of data (often numerical) or a sketch representing an ordered process.

FIGURE 15.6 Acupuncture Charts

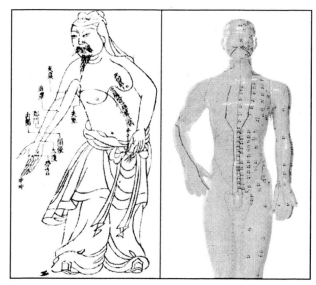

Source: Image on the left from Wikimedia, http://commons.wikimedia.org/wiki/File:Acupuncture_chart_300px.jpg. Image on the right © Thinkstock.

In the rest of this section, we're going to explore three common types of charts: statistical charts, sequence-of-steps chart, and decision trees.

Statistical Charts

FIGURE 15.7 Birth Weight Chi-Square

Congenital Anomalies	Relative Risk	Nunmber of Smokers N = 1,943	Number of Nonsmokers N = 16,073	95% CI	*p*-Value
Cardiovascular System	1.56	43	217	1.12–2.19	*p* < .01
Skeletal System	1.11	19	139	0.68–1.82	NS
Hematologic System	1.39	20	121	0.86–2.25	NS
Nervous System	1.30	4	25	0.91–1.86	NS
Pulmonary System	1.25	7	39	0.55–2.84	NS
Gastrointestinal System	0.54	1	17	0.07–4.11	NS

Source: Woods, S. E., & Raju, U. (2001). Maternal smoking and the risk of congenital birth defects: A cohort study. Journal of the American Board of Family Practitioners, 14, 330–334.

For most audiences, statistical presentations must be kept as simple as possible, and they must be explained. The statistical chart shown in Figure 15.7 is from a study examining the effects of maternal smoking on a range of congenital birth defects. Unless you are familiar with statistics, this chart may be very confusing. When visually displaying information from a quantitative study, you need to make sure that you understand the material and can successfully and simply explain how one should interpret the data. If you are unsure about the data yourself, then you should probably not use this type of information. This is surely an example of a visual aid that, although it delivers a limited kind of information, does not speak for itself.

Sequence-of-Steps Charts

FIGURE 15.8   Steps in Cell Reproduction

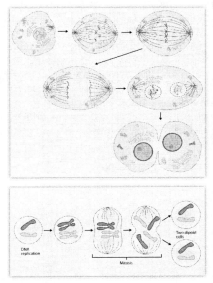

Source: Images courtesy of LadyofHats, http://commons.wikimedia.org/wiki/File:MITOSIS_cells_secuence.svg, and the National Institutes of Health,

http://commons.wikimedia.org/wiki/File:MajorEventsInMitosis.jpg.

Charts are also useful when you are trying to explain a process that involves several steps. The two visual aids in Figure 15.8 both depict the process of cell division called mitosis using a sequence-of-steps chart, but they each deliver different information. The first chart lacks labels to indicate the different phases of cell division. Although the first chart may have more color and look more polished, the missing information may confuse your audience. In the second chart, each phase is labeled with a brief explanation of what is happening, which can help your audience understand the process.

Decision Trees

FIGURE 15.9   To Play or Not to Play

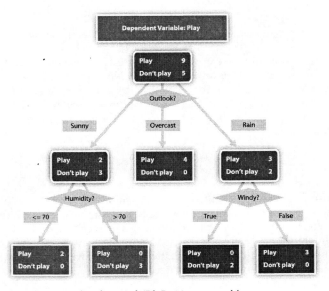

Source: Image courtesy of T-kita, http://commons.wikimedia.org/wiki/File:Decision_tree_model.png.

Decision trees are useful for showing the relationships between ideas. The example in Figure 15.9 shows how a decision tree could be used to determine the appropriate weather for playing baseball. As with the other types of charts, you want to be sure that the information in the chart is relevant to the purpose of your speech and that each question and decision is clearly labeled.

2.2   Graphs

Strictly speaking, a graph may be considered a type of chart, but graphs are so widely used that we will discuss them separately. A **graph** is a pictorial representation of the relationships of quantitative data using dots, lines, bars, pie slices, and the like. Graphs show the variation in one variable in comparison with that of one or more other variables. Where a statistical chart may report the mean ages of individuals entering college, a graph would show how the mean age changes over time. A statistical chart may report the amount of computers sold in the United States, while a graph will show the breakdown of those computers by operating systems such as Windows, Macintosh, and Linux. Public speakers can show graphs using a range of different formats. Some of those formats are specialized for various professional fields. Very complex graphs often contain too much information that is not related to the purpose of a student's speech. If the graph is cluttered, it becomes difficult to comprehend.

In this section, we're going to analyze the common graphs speakers utilize in their speeches: line graphs, bar graphs, and pie graphs.

Line Graph

FIGURE 15.10 Enron's Stock Price

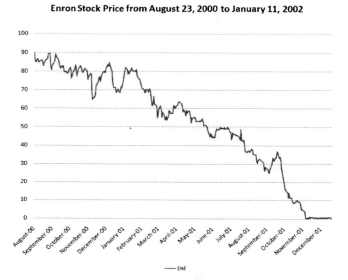

Enron Stock Price from August 23, 2000 to January 11, 2002

Source: Image courtesy of Nehrams 2020, http://commons.wikimedia.org/wiki/File:EnronStockPriceAug00Jan02.jpg.

A line graph is designed to show trends over time. In Figure 15.10, we see a line graph depicting the fall of Enron's stock price from August 2000 to January 2002. Notice that although it has some steep rises, the line has an overall downward trend clearly depicting the plummeting of Enron's stock price. Showing such a line graph helps the audience see the relationships between the numbers, and audiences can understand the information by seeing the graph much more easily than they could if the speaker just read the numbers aloud.

Bar Graph

Bar graphs are useful for showing the differences between quantities. They can be used for population demographics, fuel costs, math ability in different grades, and many other kinds of data.

The graph in Figure 15.11 is well designed. It is relatively simple and is carefully labeled, making it easy for you to guide your audience through the quantities of each type of death. The bar graph is designed to show the difference between suicides and homicides across various age groups. When you look at the data, the first grouping clearly shows that eighteen- to twenty-four-year-olds are more likely to die because of a homicide than any of the other age groups.

FIGURE 15.11 Suicide vs. Homicide

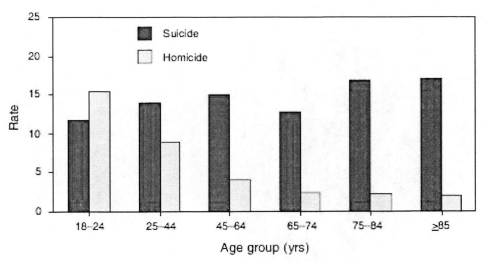

Source: Image courtesy of Centers for Disease Control and Prevention, http://commons.wikimedia.org/wiki/File:Homicide_suicide_USA.gif.

The graph in Figure 15.12 is a complicated bar graph depicting the disparity between the haves and the have nots within the United States. On the left hand side of the graph you can see that the Top 20% of people within the United States account for 84.7% of all of the wealth and 50.1% of all of the income. On the other hand, those in the bottom 40% account for only 0.2% of the wealth and 12.1% of the actual income.

FIGURE 15.12 Distribution of Income and Wealth in the United States

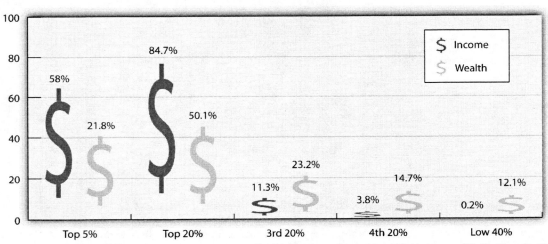

Source: Wolff, E. N. (2007). Recent trends in household wealth in the United States: Rising debt and the middle-class squeeze (Working Paper No. 502). Retrieved from the Levy Economics Institute of Bard College website: http://www.levy.org/pubs/wp_502.pdf

While the graph is very well designed, it presents a great deal of information. In a written publication, readers will have time to sit and analyze the graph, but in a speaking situation, audience members need to be able to understand the information in a graph very quickly. For that reason, this graph is probably not as effective for speeches as the one in Figure 15.11.

Pie Graph

Pie graphs should be simplified as much as possible without eliminating important information. As with other graphs, the sections of the pie need to be plotted proportionally. In the pie graph shown in Figure 15.13, we see a clear and proportional chart that has been color-coded. Color-coding is useful when it's difficult to fit the explanations in the actual sections of the graph; in that case, you need to include a legend, or key, to indicate what the colors in the graph mean. In this graph, audience members can see very quickly that falls are the primary reason children receive concussions.

FIGURE 15.13 Causes of Concussions in Children

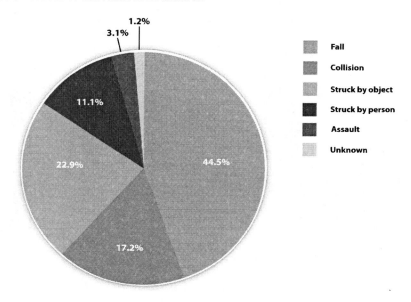

FIGURE 15.14 World Populations

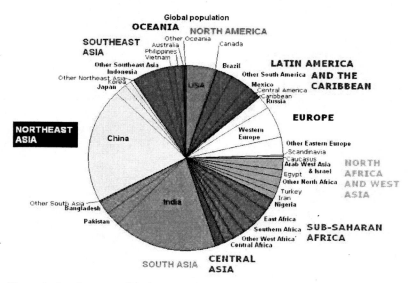

Source: Image courtesy of Brutannica, http://commons.wikimedia.org/wiki/File:World_population_pie_chart.JPG.

The pie graph in Figure 15.14 is jumbled, illegible, confusing, and overwhelming in every way. The use of color coding doesn't help. Overall, this graph simply contains too much information and is more likely to confuse an audience than help them understand something.

2.3 Representations

representation

A presentation aid designed to represent a real process or object.

In the world of presentation aids, **representations** is the word used to classify a group of aids designed to represent real processes or objects. Often, speakers want to visually demonstrate something that they cannot physically bring with them to the speech. Maybe you're giving a speech on the human brain, and you just don't have access to a cadaver's brain. Instead of bringing in a real brain, you could use a picture of a brain or an image that represents the human brain. In this section we're going to explore four common representations: diagrams, maps, photographs, and video or recordings.

Diagrams

Diagrams are drawings or sketches that outline and explain the parts of an object, process, or phenomenon that cannot be readily seen. Like graphs, diagrams can be considered a type of chart, as in the case of organization charts and process flow charts.

FIGURE 15.15 The Human Eye

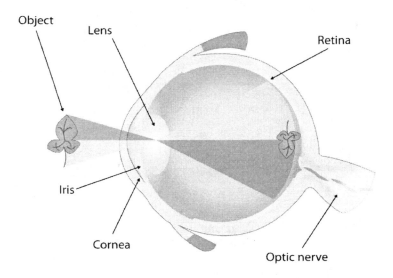

When you use a diagram, be sure to explain each part of the phenomenon, paying special attention to elements that are complicated or prone to misunderstanding. In the example shown in Figure 15.15, you might wish to highlight that the light stimulus is reversed when it is processed through the brain or that the optic nerve is not a single stalk as many people think.

Maps

Maps are extremely useful if the information is clear and limited. There are all kinds of maps, including population, weather, ocean current, political, and economic maps, but you should be able to find the right kind for the purpose of your speech. Choose a map that emphasizes the information you need to deliver.

The map shown in Figure 15.16 is simple, showing clearly the geographic location of Nigeria. This can be extremely valuable for some audiences who might not be able to name and locate countries on the continent of Africa.

FIGURE 15.16 African Map with Nigerian Emphasis

FIGURE 15.17 Rhode Island Map

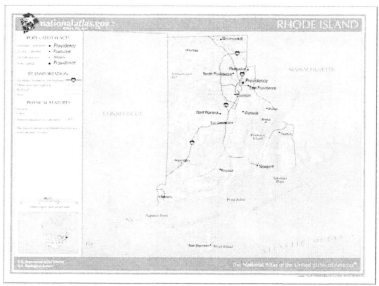

Source: Map courtesy of the National Atlas of the United States.

Figure 15.17 is a map of the state of Rhode Island, and it emphasizes the complicated configuration of islands and waterways that characterize this state's geography. Although the map does not list the names of the islands, it is helpful in orienting the audience to the direction and distance of the islands to other geographic features, such as the city of Providence and the Atlantic Ocean.

Photographs and Drawings

FIGURE 15.18 Wigwam Picture

© *Thinkstock*

FIGURE 15.19 Ship's Rigging

Source: Image courtesy of Mathieu Dréo, http://commons.wikimedia.org/wiki/File:Tall_ship_rigging_in_amsterdam_close.jpg.

Sometimes a photograph or a drawing is the best way to show an unfamiliar but important detail. Figure 15.18 is a photograph of a wigwam, a wigwam was a living dwelling used by Native Americans in the North East. In this photograph you can see the curved birchbark exterior, which makes this dwelling ideal for a variety of weather conditions. The photograph of the tall ship in Figure 15.19 emphasizes the sheer amount and complexity of the ship's rigging.

Video or Audio Recordings

Another very useful type of presentation aid is a video or audio recording. Whether it is a short video from a website such as YouTube or Vimeo, a segment from a song, or a piece of a podcast, a well-chosen video or audio recording may be a good choice to enhance your speech.

Imagine, for example, that you're giving a speech on how "Lap-Band" surgeries help people lose weight. One of the sections of your speech could explain how the Lap-Band works, so you could easily show the following forty-three-second video to demonstrate the medical part of the surgery (http://www.youtube.com/watch?v=KPuThbFMxGg). Maybe you want to include a recording of a real patient explaining why he or she decided to get the Lap-Band. Then you could include a podcast like this one from the Medical University of South Carolina (http://medicaluniversc.http.internapcdn.net/medicaluniversc_vitalstream_com/podcasts/2007/1_Treado_June_22_final.mp3).

There is one major caveat to using audio and video clips during a speech: do not forget that they are supposed to be aids to your speech, not the speech itself! In addition, be sure to avoid these three mistakes that speakers often make when using audio and video clips:

1. Avoid choosing clips that are too long for the overall length of the speech. If you are giving a five-minute speech, then any audio or video clip you use should be under thirty seconds in length.

2. Don't fail to practice with the audio or video equipment prior to speaking. If you are unfamiliar with the equipment, you'll look foolish trying to figure out how it works. This fiddling around will not only take your audience out of your speech but also have a negative impact on your credibility.

3. Don't fail to cue the clip to the appropriate place prior to beginning your speech. We cannot tell you the number of times we've seen students spend valuable speech time trying to find a clip on YouTube or a DVD. You need to make sure your clip is ready to go before you start speaking.

2.4   Objects or Models

Objects and models are another form of presentation aid that can be very helpful in getting your audience to understand your message. **Objects** refer to anything you could hold up and talk about during your speech. If you're talking about the importance of not using plastic water bottles, you might hold up a plastic water bottle and a stainless steel water bottle as examples. If you're talking about the percussion family of musical instruments and you own (and can play) several different percussion instruments, you can show your audience in person what they look like and how they sound.

object

A tangible, physical item a speaker could hold up and talk about during a speech.

model

A three-dimensional re-creation of a physical object.

Models, on the other hand, are re-creations of physical objects that you cannot have readily available with you during a speech. If you're giving a speech on heart murmurs, you may be able to show how heart murmurs work by holding up a model of the human heart.

2.5 People and Animals

The next category of presentation aids are people and animals. We can often use ourselves or other people to adequately demonstrate an idea during our speeches.

Animals as Presentation Aids

When giving a speech on a topic relating to animals, it is often tempting to bring an animal to serve as your presentation aid. While this can sometimes add a very engaging dimension to the speech, it carries some serious risks that you need to consider.

The first risk is that animal behavior tends to be unpredictable. You may think this won't be a problem if your presentation aid animal is a small enough to be kept confined throughout your speech—for example, a goldfish in a bowl or a lizard or bird in a cage. However, even caged animals can be very distracting to your audience if they run about, chirp, or exhibit other agitated behavior. The chances are great that an animal will react to the stress of an unfamiliar situation by displaying behavior that does not contribute positively to your speech.

The second risk is that some audience members may respond negatively to a live animal. In addition to common fears and aversions to animals like snakes, spiders, and mice, many people have allergies to various animals.

The third risk is that some locations may have regulations about bringing animals onto the premises. If animals are allowed, the person bringing the animal may be required to bring a veterinary certificate or may be legally responsible for any damage caused by the animal.

For these reasons, before you decide to use an animal as a presentation aid, ask yourself if you could make your point equally well with a picture, model, diagram, or other representation of the animal in question.

Speaker as Presentation Aid

Speakers can often use their own bodies to demonstrate facets of a speech. If your speech is about ballroom dancing or ballet, you might use your body to demonstrate the basic moves in the cha-cha or the five basic ballet positions.

Other People as Presentation Aids

In many speeches, it can be cumbersome and distracting for the speaker to use her or his own body to illustrate a point. In such cases, the best solution is to ask someone else to serve as your presentation aid.

You should arrange ahead of time for a person (or persons) to be an effective aid—do not assume that an audience member will volunteer on the spot. If you plan to demonstrate how to immobilize a broken bone, your volunteer must know ahead of time that you will touch him or her as much as necessary to splint their foot. You must also make certain that they will arrive dressed presentably and that they will not draw attention away from your message through their appearance or behavior.

The transaction between you and your human presentation aid must be appropriate, especially if you are going to demonstrate something like a dance step. Use your absolute best judgment about behavior, and make sure that your human presentation aid understands this dimension of the task.

KEY TAKEAWAYS

- Various types of charts can aid audience understanding of a speaker's message. Statistical charts help audiences see and interpret numerical information. Sequence-of-steps charts show how a process occurs. Decision trees help audience members see how a specific decision can be made in a logical fashion.
- Line graphs, bar graphs, and pie graphs are commonly used by speakers to help present numerical information. The information presented on a graph should be clean and easily understandable from a distance.
- Representations are presentation aids designed to represent a real process or object. Commonly used representations in public speaking include diagrams, maps, photographs, and video or audio recordings.
- Objects are physical items that can be held up and used during a speech. Models, on the other hand, refer to tangible items that can be held during a speech, but are not the actual object but rather a facsimile of it.
- Speakers often will use their own bodies or the bodies of other people to help them illustrate a part of a speech. When using another person, it is very important to coach that person prior to the speech to ensure that he or she will not upstage the speaker. Using animals as presentation aids is generally not recommended.

EXERCISES

1. Watch the video on gshep1's YouTube channel from Booher Consultants at http://www.youtube.com/user/gshep1. How many mistakes can you identify that this speaker makes in using presentation aids?
2. Find a speech on YouTube and see what types of presentation aids the speaker uses. Does the speaker select appropriate aids? How could you have made them better? Were there any missing presentation aids that should have been in the speech?
3. Create a chart representing the speech creation process. Try using either a sequence-of-steps chart or a decision tree.
4. Think about your next speech. What presentation aids can you use in your speech to enhance your audience's understanding?

3. MEDIA TO USE FOR PRESENTATION AIDS

LEARNING OBJECTIVES

1. Understand the range of media choices for presentation aids.
2. Identify advantages and disadvantages of different presentation aid media.
3. Explain the role of careful planning and good execution when using presentation aids.

The venue of your speech should suggest the appropriate selection of presentation aids. In your classroom, you have several choices, including some that omit technology. If you are speaking in a large auditorium, you will almost certainly need to use technology to project text and images on a large screen.

Many students feel that they lack the artistic skills to render their own graphics, so they opt to use copyright-free graphics on their presentation aids. You may do this as long as you use images that are created in a consistent style. For instance, you should not combine realistic renderings with cartoons unless there is a clear and compelling reason to do so. Being selective in this way will result in a sequence of presentation aids that look like a coherent set, thereby enhancing your professionalism.

In keeping with careful choices and effective design, we also have to do a good job in executing presentation aids. They should never look hastily made, dirty, battered, or disorganized. They do not have to be fancy, but they do need to look professional. In this section we will discuss the major types of media that can be used for presentation aids, which include computer-based media, audiovisual media, and low-tech media.

3.1 Computer-Based Media

In most careers in business, industry, and other professions for which students are preparing themselves, computer-based presentation aids are the norm today. Whether the context is a weekly department meeting in a small conference room or an annual convention in a huge amphitheater, speakers are expected to be comfortable with using PowerPoint or other similar software to create and display presentation aids.

If your public speaking course meets in a smart classroom, you have probably had the opportunity to see the computer system in action. Many such systems today are nimble and easy to use. Still, "easy" is a relative term. Don't take for granted someone else's advice that "it's really self-explanatory"—instead, make sure to practice ahead of time. It is also wise to be prepared for technical problems, which can happen to even the most sophisticated computer users. When Steve Jobs, CEO of Apple and cofounder of Pixar, introduced a new iPhone 4 in June, 2010, his own visual presentation froze.[4] The irony of a high-tech guru's technology not working at a public presentation did not escape the notice of news organizations.

The world was first introduced to computer presentations back in the 1970s, but these software packages were expensive and needed highly trained technicians to operate the programs. Today, there are a number of **presentation software** programs that are free or relatively inexpensive and that can be learned quickly by nonspecialists. Table 15.1 lists several of these.

presentation software

Software packages that enable a speaker to visually show material through the use of a computer and projector.

TABLE 15.1 Presentation Software Packages

Name	Website	Price
280 Slides	http://280slides.com	Free
Adobe Acrobat Presenter	http://www.adobe.com/products/presenter/features	$
Ajax Presents	http://www.ajaxpresents.com	Free
Brainshark	http://www.brainshark.com	$
Google Presentations	http://docs.google.com/support/bin/static.py?page=guide.cs&guide=19431	Free
Harvard Graphics	http://www.harvardgraphics.com	$
Keynote	http://www.apple.com/iwork/keynote	$
OpenOffice Impress	http://www.openoffice.org/product/impress.html	Free
PowerPoint	http://office.microsoft.com/en-us/powerpoint	$
PrezentIt	http://prezentit.com	Free
Prezi	http://prezi.com	Free/$
SlideRocket	http://www.sliderocket.com	$
ThinkFree Show	http://member.thinkfree.com	Free
Zoho Show	http://show.zoho.com	Free

In addition to becoming more readily accessible, presentation software has become more flexible over the years. As recently as the mid-2000s, critics such as the eminent graphic expert and NASA consultant Edward Tufte charged that PowerPoint's tendency to force the user to put a certain number of bullet points on each slide in a certain format was a serious threat to the accurate presentation of data. As Tufte put it, "the rigid slide-by-slide hierarchies, indifferent to content, slice and dice the evidence into arbitrary compartments, producing an anti-narrative with choppy continuity."[5] Tufte argues that poor decision making, such as was involved with the 2003 space shuttle Columbia disaster, may have been related to the shortcomings of such presentation aids in NASA meetings. While more recent versions of PowerPoint and similar programs allow much more creative freedom in designing slides, this freedom comes with a responsibility—the user needs to take responsibility for using the technology to support the speech and not get carried away with the many special effects the software is capable of producing.

What this boils down to is observing the universal principles of good design, which include unity, emphasis or focal point, scale and proportion, balance, and rhythm.[6] As we've mentioned earlier, it's generally best to use a single font for the text on your visuals so that they look like a unified set. In terms of scale or proportion, it is essential to make sure the information is large enough for the audience to see; and since the display size may vary according to the monitor you are using, this is another reason for practicing in advance with the equipment you intend to use. The rhythm of your slide display should be reasonably consistent—you would not want to display a dozen different slides in the first minute of a five-minute presentation and then display only one slide per minute for the rest of the speech.

In addition to presentation software such as PowerPoint, speakers sometimes have access to interactive computer-based presentation aids. These are often called "clickers"—handheld units that audience members hold and that are connected to a monitor to which the speaker has access. These interactive aids are useful for tracking audience responses to questions, and they have the advantage over asking for a show of hands in that they can be anonymous. A number of instructors in various courses use "clickers" in their classrooms.

Using computer-based aids in a speech brings up a few logistical considerations. In some venues, you may need to stand behind a high-tech console to operate the computer. You need to be aware that this will physically isolate you from the audience you with whom you are trying to establish a relationship in your speech. When you stand behind presentation equipment, you may feel really comfortable, but you end up limiting your nonverbal interaction with your audience.

If your classroom is not equipped with a computer and you want to use presentation software media in your speech, you may of course bring your computer, or you may be able to schedule the delivery of a computer cart to your classroom. In either case, check with your instructor about the advance preparations that will be needed. At some schools, there are very few computer carts, so it is important to reserve one well in advance. You will also want to see if you can gain access to one ahead of time to practice and familiarize yourself with the necessary passwords and commands to make your slides run properly. On the day of your speech, be sure to arrive early enough to test out the equipment before class begins.

3.2 Audiovisual Media

Although audio and video clips are often computer-based, they can be (and, in past decades, always were) used without a computer.

Audio presentation aids are useful for illustrating musical themes. For instance, if you're speaking about how the Polish composer Frederick Chopin was inspired by the sounds of nature, you can convey that meaning only through playing an example. If you have a smart classroom, you may be able to use it to play an MP3. Alternatively, you may need to bring your music player. In that case, be sure the speakers in the room are up to the job. The people in the back of the room must be able to hear it, and the speakers must not sound distorted when you turn the volume up.

Video that clarifies, explains, amplifies, emphasizes, or illustrates a key concept in your speech is appropriate, as long as you do not rely on it to do your presentation for you. There are several things you must do. First, identify a specific section of video that delivers meaning. Second, "cue up" the video so that you can just pop it into the player, and it will begin at the right place. Third, tell your audience where the footage comes from. You can tell your audience, for instance, that you are showing them an example from the 1985 BBC documentary titled "In Search of the Trojan War." Fourth, tell your audience why you're showing the footage. For instance, you can tell them, "This is an example of storytelling in the Bardic tradition." You can interrupt or mute the video to make a comment about it, but your total footage should not use more than 20 percent of the time for your speech.

3.3 Low-Tech Media

In some speaking situations, of course, computer technology is not available. Even if you have ready access to technology, there will be contexts where computer-based presentation aids are unnecessary or even counterproductive. And in still other contexts, computer-based media may be accompanied by low-tech presentation aids. One of the advantages of low-tech media is that they are very predictable. There's little that can interfere with using them. Additionally, they can be inexpensive to produce. However, unlike digital media, they can be prone to physical damage in the form of smudges, scratches, dents, and rips. It can be difficult to keep them professional looking if you have to carry them through a rainstorm or blizzard, so you will need to take steps to protect them as you transport them to the speech location. Let's examine some of the low-tech media that you might use with a speech.

Chalk or Dry-Erase Board

If you use a chalkboard or dry-erase board you are not using a **prepared presentation aid**. Your failure to prepare visuals ahead of time can be interpreted in several ways, mostly negative. If other speakers carefully design, produce, and use attractive visual aids, yours will stand out by contrast. You will be seen as the speaker who does not take the time to prepare even a simple aid. Do not use a chalkboard or marker board and pretend it's a prepared presentation aid.

However, numerous speakers do utilize chalk and dry-erase boards effectively. Typically, these speakers use the chalk or dry-erase board for interactive components of a speech. For example, maybe you're giving a speech in front of a group of executives. You may have a PowerPoint all prepared, but at various points in your speech you want to get your audience's responses. Chalk or dry-erase boards are very useful when you want to visually show information that you are receiving from your audience. If you ever use a chalk or dry-erase board, follow these three simple rules:

1. Write large enough so that everyone in the room can see.

prepared presentation aid

A presentation aid designed and created ahead of time to be used as a coherent part of a speech.

2. Print legibly; don't write in cursive script.

3. Write short phrases; don't take time to write complete sentences.

It is also worth mentioning that some classrooms and business conference rooms are equipped with smartboards, or digitally enhanced whiteboards. On a smartboard you can bring up prepared visuals and then modify them as you would a chalk or dry-erase board. The advantage is that you can keep a digital record of what was written for future reference. However, as with other technology-based media, smartboards may be prone to unexpected technical problems, and they require training and practice to be used properly.

Flipchart

A flipchart is useful when you're trying to convey change over a number of steps. For instance, you could use a prepared flipchart to show dramatic population shifts on maps. In such a case, you should prepare highly visible, identical maps on three of the pages so that only the data will change from page to page. Each page should be neatly titled, and you should actively point out the areas of change on each page. You could also use a flip chart to show stages in the growth and development of the malaria-bearing mosquito. Again, you should label each page, making an effort to give the pages a consistent look.

Organize your flip chart in such a way that you flip pages in one direction only, front to back. It will be difficult to flip large pages without damaging them, and if you also have to "back up" and "skip forward," your presentation will look awkward and disorganized. Pages will get damaged, and your audience will be able to hear each rip.

In addition, most flip charts need to be propped up on an easel of some sort. If you arrive for your speech only to find that the easel in the classroom has disappeared, you will need to rig up another system that allows you to flip the pages.

Poster Board or Foam Board

Foam board consists of a thin sheet of Styrofoam with heavy paper bonded to both surfaces. It is a lightweight, inexpensive foundation for information, and it will stand on its own when placed in an easel without curling under at the bottom edge. Poster board tends to be cheaper than foam board, but it is flimsier, more vulnerable to damage, and can't stand on its own.

If you plan to paste labels or paragraphs of text to foam or poster board, for a professional look you should make sure the color of the poster board matches the color of the paper you will paste on. You will also want to choose a color that allows for easy visual contrast so your audience can see it, and it must be a color that's appropriate for the topic. For instance, hot pink would be the wrong color on a poster for a speech about the Protestant Reformation.

Avoid producing a presentation aid that looks like you simply cut pictures out of magazines and pasted them on. Slapping some text and images on a board looks unprofessional and will not be viewed as credible or effective. Instead, when creating a poster you need to take the time to think about how you are going to lay out your aid and make it look professional. You do not have to spend lots of money to make a very sleek and professional-looking poster.

Some schools also have access to expensive, full-color poster printers where you can create large poster for pasting on a foam board. In the real world of public speaking, most speakers rely on the creation of professional posters using a full-color poster printer. Typically, posters are sketched out and then designed on a computer using a program like Microsoft PowerPoint or Publisher (these both have the option of selecting the size of the printed area).

Handouts

Handouts are appropriate for delivering information that audience members can take away with them. As we will see, handouts require a great deal of management if they are to contribute to your credibility as a speaker.

First, make sure to bring enough copies of the handout for each audience member to get one. Having to share or look on with one's neighbor does not contribute to a professional image. Under no circumstances should you ever provide a single copy of a handout to pass around. There are several reasons this is a bad idea. You will have no control over the speed at which it circulates, or the direction it goes. Moreover, only one listener will be holding it while you're making your point about it and by the time most people see it they will have forgotten why they need to see it. In some case, it might not even reach everybody by the end of your speech. Finally, listeners could still be passing your handout around during the next speaker's speech.

There are three possible times to distribute handouts: before you begin your speech, during the speech, and after your speech is over. Naturally, if you need your listeners to follow along in a handout, you will need to distribute it before your speech begins. If you have access to the room ahead of time, place a copy of the handout on each seat in the audience. If not, ask a volunteer to distribute them as quickly as possible while you prepare to begin speaking. If the handout is a "takeaway," leave it on a table near the door so that those audience members who are interested can take one on their way out; in this case, don't forget to tell them to do so as you conclude your speech. It is almost never appropriate to distribute handouts during your speech, as it is distracting and interrupts the pace of your presentation.

Like other presentation aids, handouts should include only the necessary information to support your points, and that information should be organized in such a way that listeners will be able to understand it. For example, in a speech about how new health care legislation will affect small business owners in your state, a good handout might summarize key effects of the legislation and include the names of state agencies with their web addresses where audience members can request more detailed information.

If your handout is designed for your audience to follow along, you should tell them so. State that you will be referring to specific information during the speech. Then, as you're presenting your speech, ask your audience to look, for example, at the second line in the first cluster of information. Read that line out loud and then go on to explain its meaning.

As with any presentation aid, handouts are not a substitute for a well-prepared speech. Ask yourself what information your audience really needs to be able to take with them and how it can be presented on the page in the most useful and engaging way possible.

KEY TAKEAWAYS

- Speakers in professional contexts are expected to be familiar with presentation software, such as PowerPoint.
- Computer-based media can produce very professional-looking presentation aids, but as with any other media, the universal principles of good design apply.
- Speakers using computer-based media need to practice ahead of time with the computer they intend to use in the speech.
- Each presentation aid vehicle has advantages and disadvantages. As such, speakers need to think through the use of visual aids and select the most appropriate ones for their individual speeches.
- Every presentation aid should be created with careful attention to content and appearance.

EXERCISES

1. What's wrong with this presentation aid?

> Indeed, almost the only measure for success is a competitive one, in the bad sense of that term — a comparison of results in the recitation or in the examination to see which child has succeeded in getting ahead of others in storing up, in accumulating, the maximum of information.
> -- John Dewey
> (*The School and Social Process*)

2. How would you change it?
3. What kind of presentation aids might you use in a speech on the health benefits of laughter? Why might these be good choice?

4. TIPS FOR PREPARING PRESENTATION AIDS

LEARNING OBJECTIVES

1. Understand why it is important to keep presentation aids organized and simple.
2. Explain how to make presentation aids easy to see, hear, and understand.
3. Make sure your presentation aids work together as a cohesive set.

As we've seen earlier in this chapter, impressive presentation aids do not take the place of a well-prepared speech. Although your presentation aids should be able to stand on their own in delivering information, do not count on them to do so. Work toward that goal, but also plan on explaining your presentation aids so that your audience will know why you're using them.

One mistake you should avoid is putting too much information on an aid. You have to narrow the topic of your speech, and likewise, you must narrow the content of your presentation aids to match your speech. Your presentation aids should not represent every idea in your speech. Whatever presentation aids you choose to use, they should fulfill one or more of the functions described at the beginning of this chapter: to clarify or emphasize a point, to enhance retention and recall of your message, to add variety and interest to your speech, and to enhance your credibility as a speaker.

As a practical matter in terms of producing presentation aids, you may not be aware that many college campuses have a copy service or multimedia lab available to students for making copies, enlargements, slides, and other presentation aids. Find out from your instructor or a librarian what the resources on your campus are. In the rest of this section, we will offer some tips for designing good-quality presentation aids.

4.1   Easily Seen or Heard by Your Audience

The first rule of presentation aids is that they must be accessible for every audience member. If those in the back of the room cannot see, hear, or otherwise experience a presentation aid, then it is counterproductive to use it. Graphic elements in your presentation aids must be large enough to read. Audio must be loud enough to hear. If you are passing out samples of a food item for audience members to taste, you must bring enough for everyone.

Do not attempt to show your audience a picture by holding up a book open to the page with the photograph. Nobody will be able to see it. It will be too small for your listeners in the back of the room, and the light will glare off of the glossy paper usually used in books with color pictures so that the listeners in front won't be able to see it either.

Text-based visuals, charts, and graphs need to be executed with strong, clean lines and blocks of color. Weak lines in a graph or illustration do not get stronger with magnification. You must either strengthen those lines by hand or choose another graphic element that has stronger lines. On a poster or a slide, a graphic element should take up about a third of the area. This leaves room for a small amount of text, rendered in a large, simple font. The textual elements should be located closest to the part of your graphic element that they are about.

Carefully limit the amount of text on a presentation aid. If a great deal of text is absolutely necessary, try to divide it between two slides or posters. Many students believe that even small text will magnify amply when it's projected, but we find that this is rarely the case. We can't recommend a specific point size because that refers to the distance between the baselines of two lines of text, not to the size of the type itself.

We recommend two things: First, use a simple, easy-to-read type style. It doesn't have to be utterly devoid of style, but it should be readable and not distracting. Second, we recommend that you print your text in three or four sizes on a sheet of paper. Place the printed sheet on the floor and stand up. When you look at your printed sheet, you should be able to make a choice based on which clusters of type you are able to read from that distance.

4.2   Easily Handled

You should be able to carry your presentation aids into the room by yourself. In addition, you should be skilled in using the equipment you will use to present them. Your presentation aids should not distract you from the delivery of your speech.

4.3   Aesthetically Pleasing

For our purposes, **aesthetics** refers to the beauty or good taste of a presentation aid. Earlier we mentioned the universal principles of good design: unity, emphasis or focal point, scale and proportion, balance, and rhythm. Because of wide differences in taste, not everyone will agree on what is aesthetically pleasing, and you may be someone who does not think of yourself as having much artistic talent. Still, if you keep these principles in mind, they will help you to create attractive, professional-looking visuals.

aesthetics
The beauty or good taste of a presentation aid.

The other aesthetic principle to keep in mind is that your presentation aids are intended to support your speech, not the other way around. The decisions you make in designing your visuals should be dictated by the content of your speech. If you use color, use it for a clear reason. If you use a border, keep it simple. Whatever you do, make certain that your presentation aids will be perceived as carefully planned and executed elements of your speech.

Tips for Text Aids

Use text only when you must. For example, if you're presenting an analysis of the First Amendment, it is permissible to display the text of the First Amendment, but not your entire analysis. The type must be big, simple, and bold. It needs white space around it to separate it from another graphic element or cluster of text that might be on the same presentation aid. When you display text, you must read it out loud before you go on to talk about it. That way, you won't expect your listeners to read one thing while trying to listen to something else. However, under no circumstances should you merely read what's on your text aids and consider that a speech.

Tips for Graphic Aids

If you create your graphic images, you will have control over their size and the visible strength of the lines. However, you might want to show your listeners an illustration that you can't create yourself. For instance, you might want to display a photograph of a portion of the Dead Sea Scrolls. First, find a way to enlarge the photograph. Then, to show integrity, cite your source. You should cite your source with an added caption, and you should also cite the source out loud as you display the graphic, even if your photograph is considered to be in the public domain. The NASA photograph "Spaceship Earth" is such an example. Many people use it without citing the source, but citing the source boosts your credibility as a speaker, and we strongly recommend doing so.

Rules for Computer Presentations

Mark Stoner, a professor in the Department of Communication Studies at California State University, Sacramento, has written a useful assessment of the uses and abuses of PowerPoint. Stoner observes that

> PowerPoint is a hybrid between the visual and the written. When we pay attention to the design of our writing—to whether we are putting key word at the beginning or end of a sentence, for instance—we are likely to communicate more effectively. In the same way, it makes sense to understand the impact that PowerPoint's design has on our ability to communicate ideas to an audience.[7]

While this article is specifically about PowerPoint, Stoner's advice works for all presentation software formats. Presentation aids should deliver information that is important or is difficult to present with spoken words only. Although many speakers attempt to put their entire speech on PowerPoint slides or other visual aids, this is a bad idea for several reasons. First, if you try to put your entire speech on PowerPoint, you will lose contact with your audience. Speakers often end up looking at the projected words or directly at the computer screen instead of at their audience. Second, your vocal delivery is likely to suffer, and you will end up giving a boring reading, not a dynamic speech. Third, you will lose credibility, as your listeners question how well you really know your topic. Fourth, you are not using the presentation aids to clarify or emphasize your message, so all the information may come across as equally important.

No matter what presentation software package you decide to utilize, there are some general guidelines you'll need to follow.

Watch Your Font

One of the biggest mistakes novice users of presentational software make is thinking that if you can read it on the screen, your audience will be able to read it in their seats. While this may be the case if you're in a close, intimate conference room, most of us will be speaking in situations where audience members are fifteen feet away or more. Make sure each slide is legible from the back of the room where you will be speaking.

Don't Write Everything Out

In addition to watching your font size, you also need to watch how you use words on the screen. Do not try to put too much information on a slide. Make sure that your slide has the appropriate information to support the point you are making and no more. We strongly recommend avoiding complete sentences on a slide unless you need to display a very important direct quotation.

Don't Bow Down to the Software

Remember, presentation software is an aid, so it should aid and not hinder your presentation. We have seen too many students who only end up reading the slides right off the screen instead of using the slides to enhance their presentations. When you read your slides right off the projector screen, you're killing your eye contact. As a general word of advice, if you ever find yourself being forced to turn your back to the audience to read the screen, then you are not effectively using the technology. On the flip side, you also shouldn't need to hide behind a computer monitor to see what's being projected.

Slide Color

Color is very important and can definitely make a strong impact on an audience. However, don't go overboard or decide to use unappealing combinations of color. For example, you should never use a light font color (like yellow) on a solid white background because it's hard for the eye to read.

You should also realize that while colors may be rich and vibrant on your computer screen at home, they may be distorted by a different monitor. While we definitely are in favor of experimenting with various color schemes, always check your presentation out on multiple computers to see if the slide color is being distorted in a way that makes it hard to read.

Slide Movement

Everyone who has had an opportunity to experiment with PowerPoint knows that animation in transitions between slides or even on a single slide can be fun, but often people do not realize that too much movement can actually distract audience members. While all presentation software packages offer you very cool slide movements and other bells and whistles, they are not always very helpful for your presentation. If you're going to utilize slide transitions or word animation, stick to only three or four different types of transitions in your whole presentation. Furthermore, do not have more than one type of movement on a given slide. If you're going to have all your text come from the right side of the screen in a bulleted list, make sure that all the items on the bulleted list come from the right side of the screen.

Practice, Practice, Practice

It is vital to practice using the technology. Nothing is worse than watching a speaker stand up and not know how to turn on the computer, access the software, or launch his or her presentation. When you use technology, audiences can quickly see if you know what you are doing, so don't give them the opportunity to devalue your credibility because you can't even get the show going.

4.4   Always Have a Backup Plan

Lastly, always have a backup plan. Unfortunately, things often go wrong. One of the parts of being a professional is keeping the speech moving in spite of unexpected problems. Decide in advance what you will do if things break down or disappear right when you need them. Don't count on your instructor to solve such predicaments; it is your responsibility. If you take this responsibility seriously and check the room where you will be presenting early, you will have time to adapt. If the computer or audiovisual setup does not work on the first try, you will need time to troubleshoot and solve the problem. If an easel is missing, you will need time to experiment with using a lectern or a chair to support your flip chart. If you forgot to bring your violin for a speech about music—don't laugh, this actually happened to a friend of ours!—you will need time to think through how to adapt your speech so that it will still be effective.

KEY TAKEAWAYS

- Presentation aids must be organized and simple. The universal principles of good design can be a useful guide.
- Material in presentation aids must be limited in quantity. Remember, presentation aids are supposed to aid a speech, not become the speech itself.
- Presentation aids must visually look like they were designed as a set. When presentation aids look unprofessional, they can decrease a speaker's credibility.
- Always practice with your presentation aids, and be prepared for unexpected problems.

EXERCISES

1. Examine Figure 15.14 in this chapter. How could you go about making this visual aid more understandable?
2. Create a new presentation aid for a previous speech given in your public speaking class. How could that aid have helped your overall speech?
3. Take some time to explore the presentation software packages discussed in Table 15.1 What do you see as some of the advantages and disadvantages of the different software packages?

5. CHAPTER EXERCISES

SPEAKING ETHICALLY

Janet knew that her argument was really weak. She kept looking at the data trying to find a way around the weakness. Finally, it hit her. She realized that she could hide the weakest part of her argument in a really complex presentation aid. *If the people can't understand it, they can't use it against me*, she thought to herself.

While she was nervous during her presentation, she was confident that no one would notice what she did. Thankfully, at the end of her presentation everyone applauded. During the question and answer period that followed, no one questioned the weak information. In fact, no one seemed to even remember the presentation aid at all.

1. Is hiding weak information in a complex presentation aid ethical?
2. Are complex aids that don't lead to audience understanding ever ethical?
3. If you were Janet's boss and you found out what she had done, would you think she was an unethical person or just a good, albeit manipulative, speaker?

END-OF-CHAPTER ASSESSMENT

1. Polly was in the middle of her speech about the importance of climate change. The presentation aid she shows is a picture outlining where the hole in the earth's ozone is located. What aspect of audience understanding is Polly hoping to impact with her aid?

    a. clarifying

    b. explaining

    c. amplifying

    d. emphasizing

    e. illustrating

2. Benny conducted a simple survey of his fraternity members to see what their thoughts were on instituting a no-hazing policy. During his presentation to the group he used the following aid to discuss his findings. What type of aid is Benny using?

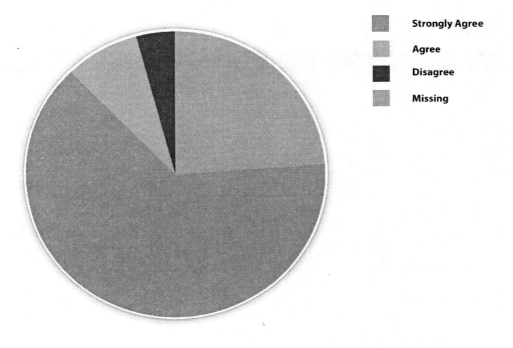

    a. representation

    b. object

    c. graph

    d. decision tree

    e. chart

3. Which form of presentation aids are drawings that outline and explain the parts of an object, process, or phenomenon that cannot be readily seen.

    a. representations

    b. diagrams

    c. objects

    d. charts

    e. graphs

4. Which of the following is *not* true about using black/dry-erase boards as presentation aids?

    a. Don't write in complete sentences.

    b. Never write in cursive.

    c. Write large enough so everyone in the room can see.

    d. Make sure your handwriting is legible.

    e. Black/dry-erase boards are appropriate for every speech context.

5. Which of the following *is* a tip for effectively using presentation aids?

    a. Always pass around presentation aids so your audience can view them up close.

    b. If something happens to your aid, there's no reason to keep going.

    c. Speakers don't need to worry about presentation aid's aesthetics.

    d. Aids need to be large enough to be seen by your entire audience.

    e. Every slide, graphic, and word on a computer presentation should be animated.

ANSWER KEY

1. e
2. c
3. b
4. e
5. d

ENDNOTES

1. United States Department of Labor. (1996). *Presenting effective presentations with visual aids.* Retrieved from http://www.osha.gov

2. Lockard, J., & Sidowski, J. R. (1961). Learning in fourth and sixth graders as a function of sensory mode of stimulus presentation and overt or covert practice. *Journal of Educational Psychology, 52*(5), 262–265. doi: 10.1037/h0043483

3. Association for Psychological Science. (2011, May 28). Miracle fruit and flavor: An experiment performed at APS 2010 [Video file]. Retrieved from http://www.psychologicalscience.org/index.php/publications/observer/obsonline/miracle-fruit-and-flavor-an-experiment-performed-at-aps-2010.html

4. Macworld. (2010, June 7). WWDC: Steve Jobs' iPhone 4 launch glitches [Video file]. Retrieved from http://www.youtube.com/watch?v=yoqh27E6OuU

5. Tufte, E. (2005, September 6). PowerPoint does rocket science—and better techniques for technical reports [Online forum]. Retrieved from http://www.edwardtufte.com/bboard/q-and-a-fetch-msg?msg_id=0001yB&topic_id=1

6. Lauer, D. A., & Pentak, S. (2000). *Design basics* (5th ed.). Fort Worth, TX: Harcourt College Publishers.

7. Stoner, M. (2007). Uncovering the powers within PowerPoint. *Communication Currents, 2*(4). Retrieved from http://www.natcom.org/CommCurrentsArticle.aspx?id=819

CHAPTER 16
Informative Speaking

WELCOME TO INFORMATIVE SPEAKING

An informative speech conveys knowledge, a task that you've engaged in throughout your life. When you give driving directions, you convey knowledge. When you caution someone about crossing the street at a certain intersection, you are describing a dangerous situation. When you steer someone away from using the car pool lane, you are explaining what it's for.

© Thinkstock

When your professors greet you on the first day of a new academic term, they typically hand out a course syllabus, which informs you about the objectives and expectations of the course. Much of the information comes to have greater meaning as you actually encounter your course-work. Why doesn't the professor explain those meanings on the first day? He or she probably does, but in all likelihood, the explanation won't really make sense at the time because you don't yet have the supporting knowledge to put it in context.

However, it is still important that the orientation information be offered. It is likely to answer some specific questions, such as the following: Am I prepared to take this course? Is a textbook required? Will the course involve a great deal of writing? Does the professor have office hours? The answers to these questions should be of central importance to all the students. These orientations are informative because they give important information relevant to the course.

An informative speech does not attempt to convince the audience that one thing is better than another. It does not advocate a course of action. Let's say, for instance, that you have carefully followed the news about BP's Deepwater Horizon oil spill in the Gulf of Mexico. Let's further say that you felt outraged by the sequence of events that led to the spill and, even more so, by its consequences. Consider carefully whether this is a good topic for your informative speech. If your speech describes the process of offshore oil exploration, it will be informative. However, if it expresses your views on what petroleum corporations *should* do to safeguard their personnel and the environment, save that topic for a persuasive speech.

Being honest about your private agenda in choosing a topic is important. It is not always easy to discern a clear line between informative and persuasive speech. Good information has a strong tendency to be persuasive, and persuasion relies on good information. Thus informative and persuasive speaking do overlap. It remains up to you to examine your real motives in choosing your topic. As we have said in various ways, ethical speaking means respecting the intelligence of your audience. If you try to circumvent the purpose of the informative speech in order to plant a persuasive seed, your listeners will notice. Such strategies often come across as dishonest.

1. INFORMATIVE SPEAKING GOALS

© *Thinkstock*

A good informative speech conveys accurate information to the audience in a way that is clear and that keeps the listener interested in the topic. Achieving all three of these goals—accuracy, clarity, and interest—is the key to your effectiveness as a speaker. If information is inaccurate, incomplete, or unclear, it will be of limited usefulness to the audience. There is no topic about which you can give complete information, and therefore, we strongly recommend careful narrowing. With a carefully narrowed topic and purpose, it is possible to give an accurate picture that isn't misleading.

Part of being accurate is making sure that your information is current. Even if you know a great deal about your topic or wrote a good paper on the topic in a high school course, you need to verify the accuracy and completeness of what you know. Most people understand that technology changes rapidly, so you need to update your information almost constantly, but the same is true for topics that, on the surface, may seem to require less updating. For example, the American Civil War occurred 150 years ago, but contemporary research still offers new and emerging theories about the causes of the war and its long-term effects. So even with a topic that seems to be unchanging, you need to carefully check your information to be sure it's accurate and up to date.

In order for your listeners to benefit from your speech, you must convey your ideas in a fashion that your audience can understand. The clarity of your speech relies on logical organization and understandable word choices. You should not assume that something that's obvious to you will also be obvious to the members of your audience. Formulate your work with the objective of being understood in all details, and rehearse your speech in front of peers who will tell you whether the information in your speech makes sense.

In addition to being clear, your speech should be interesting. Your listeners will benefit the most if they can give sustained attention to the speech, and this is unlikely to happen if they are bored. This often means you will decide against using some of the topics you know a great deal about. Suppose, for example, that you had a summer job as a veterinary assistant and learned a great deal about canine parasites. This topic might be very interesting to you, but how interesting will it be to others in your class? In order to make it interesting, you will need to find a way to connect it with their interests and curiosities. Perhaps there are certain canine parasites that also pose risks to humans—this might be a connection that would increase audience interest in your topic.

1.1   Why We Speak to Inform

Informative speaking is a means for the delivery of knowledge. In informative speaking, we avoid expressing opinion.

This doesn't mean you may not speak about controversial topics. However, if you do so, you must deliver a fair statement of each side of the issue in debate. If your speech is about standardized educational testing, you must honestly represent the views both of its proponents and of its critics. You must not take sides, and you must not slant your explanation of the debate in order to influence the opinions of the listeners. You are simply and clearly defining the debate. If you watch the evening news on a major network television (ABC, CBS, or NBC), you will see newscasters who undoubtedly have personal opinions about the news, but are trained to avoid expressing those opinions through the use of loaded words, gestures, facial expressions, or vocal tone. Like those newscasters, you are already educating your listeners simply by informing them. Let them make up their own minds. This is probably the most important reason for informative speaking.

1.2   Making Information Clear and Interesting for the Audience

A clear and interesting speech can make use of description, causal analysis, or categories. With description, you use words to create a picture in the minds of your audience. You can describe physical realities, social realities, emotional experiences, sequences, consequences, or contexts. For instance, you can describe the mindset of the Massachusetts town of Salem during the witch trials. You can also use causal analysis, which focuses on the connections between causes and consequences. For example, in speaking about health care costs, you could explain how a serious illness can put even a well-insured family into bankruptcy. You can also use categories to group things together. For instance, you could say that there are three categories of investment for the future: liquid savings, avoiding debt, and acquiring properties that will increase in value.

There are a number of principles to keep in mind as a speaker to make the information you present clear and interesting for your audience. Let's examine several of them.

Adjust Complexity to the Audience

If your speech is too complex or too simplistic, it will not hold the interest of your listeners. How can you determine the right level of complexity? Your audience analysis is one important way to do this. Will your listeners belong to a given age group, or are they more diverse? Did they all go to public schools in the United States, or are some of your listeners international students? Are they all students majoring in communication studies, or is there a mixture of majors in your audience? The answers to these and other audience analysis questions will help you to gauge what they know and what they are curious about.

Never assume that just because your audience is made up of students, they all share your knowledge set. If you base your speech on an assumption of similar knowledge, you might not make sense to everyone. If, for instance, you're an intercultural communication student discussing **multiple identities**, the psychology students in your audience will most likely reject your message. Similarly, the term "viral" has very different meanings depending on whether it is used with respect to human disease, popular response to a website, or population theory. In using the word "viral," you absolutely must explain specifically what you mean. You should not hurry your explanation of a term that's vulnerable to misinterpretation. Make certain your listeners know what you mean before continuing your speech. Stephen Lucas explains, "You cannot assume they will know what you mean. Rather, you must be sure to explain everything so thoroughly that they cannot help but understand."[1] Define terms to help listeners understand them the way you mean them to. Give explanations that are consistent with your definitions, and show how those ideas apply to your speech topic. In this way, you can avoid many misunderstandings.

Similarly, be very careful about assuming there is anything that "everybody knows." Suppose you've decided to present an informative speech on the survival of the early colonists of New England. You may have learned in elementary school that their survival was attributable, in part, to the assistance of Squanto. Many of your listeners will know which states are in New England, but if there are international students in the audience, they might never have heard of New England. You should clarify the term either by pointing out the region on a map or by stating that it's the six states in the American northeast. Other knowledge gaps can still confound the effectiveness of the speech. For instance, who or what was Squanto? What kind of assistance did the settlers get? Only a few listeners are likely to know that Squanto spoke English and that fact had greatly surprised the settlers when they landed. It was through his knowledge of English that Squanto was able to advise these settlers in survival strategies during that first harsh winter. If you neglect to provide that information, your speech will not be fully informative.

Beyond the opportunity to help improve your delivery, one important outcome of practicing your speech in front of a live audience of a couple of friends or classmates is that you can become aware of terms that are confusing or that you should define for your audience.

Avoid Unnecessary Jargon

If you decide to give an informative speech on a highly specialized topic, limit how much technical language or jargon you use. Loading a speech with specialized language has the potential to be taxing on the listeners. It can become too difficult to "translate" your meanings, and if that happens, you will not effectively deliver information. Even if you define many technical terms, the audience may feel as if they are being bombarded with a set of definitions instead of useful information. Don't treat your speech as a crash course in an entire topic. If you must, introduce one specialized term and carefully define and explain it to the audience. Define it in words, and then use a concrete and relevant example to clarify the meaning.

Some topics, by their very nature, are too technical for a short speech. For example, in a five-minute speech you would be foolish to try to inform your audience about the causes of the Fukushima Daiichi nuclear emergency that occurred in Japan in 2011. Other topics, while technical, can be presented in audience-friendly ways that minimize the use of technical terms. For instance, in a speech about Mount Vesuvius, the volcano that buried the ancient cities of Pompeii and Herculaneum, you can use the term "pyroclastic flow" as long as you take the time to either show or tell what it means.

multiple identities

In communication studies, the idea that everyone has identities connected to family, religion, occupation, cultural origin, gender, and other characteristics.

Create Concrete Images

As a college student, you have had a significant amount of exposure to **abstract** terms. You have become comfortable using and hearing a variety of abstract ideas. However, abstract terms lend themselves to many interpretations. For instance, the abstract term "responsibility" can mean many things. Among other meanings, it can mean duty, task, authority, or blame. Because of the potential for misunderstanding, it is better to use a *concrete* word. For example, instead of saying, "Helen Worth was responsible for the project," you will convey clearer meaning when you say, "Helen Worth was in charge of the project," "Helen Kimes made the project a success," or "Helen Worth was to blame for the failure of the project."

To illustrate the differences between abstract and **concrete** language, let's look at a few pairs of terms:

Abstract	Concrete
transportation	air travel
success	completion of project
discrimination	exclusion of women
athletic	physically fit
profound	knowledgeable

By using an abstraction in a sentence and then comparing the concrete term in the sentence, you will notice the more precise meanings of the concrete terms. Those precise terms are less likely to be misunderstood. In the last pair of terms, "knowledgeable" is listed as a concrete term, but it can also be considered an abstract term. Still, it's likely to be much clearer and more precise than "profound."

Keep Information Limited

When you developed your speech, you carefully narrowed your topic in order to keep information limited yet complete and coherent. If you carefully adhere to your own narrowing, you can keep from going off on tangents or confusing your audience. If you overload your audience with information, they will be unable to follow your narrative. Use the definitions, descriptions, explanations, and examples you need in order to make your meanings clear, but resist the temptation to add **tangential** information merely because you find it interesting.

Link Current Knowledge to New Knowledge

Certain sets of knowledge are common to many people in your classroom audience. For instance, most of them know what Wikipedia is. Many have found it a useful and convenient source of information about topics related to their coursework. Because many Wikipedia entries are lengthy, greatly annotated, and followed by substantial lists of authoritative sources, many students have relied on information acquired from Wikipedia in writing papers to fulfill course requirements. All this is information that virtually every classroom listener is likely to know. This is the current knowledge of your audience.

Because your listeners are already familiar with Wikipedia, you can link important new knowledge to their already-existing knowledge. Wikipedia is an "open source," meaning that anyone can supplement, edit, correct, distort, or otherwise alter the information in Wikipedia. In addition to your listeners' knowledge that a great deal of good information can be found in Wikipedia, they must now know that it isn't authoritative. Some of your listeners may not enjoy hearing this message, so you must find a way to make it acceptable.

One way to make the message acceptable to your listeners is to show what Wikipedia does well. For example, some Wikipedia entries contain many good references at the end. Most of those references are likely to be authoritative, having been written by scholars. In searching for information on a topic, a student can look up one or more of those references in full-text databases or in the library. In this way, Wikipedia can be helpful in steering a student toward the authoritative information they need. Explaining this to your audience will help them accept, rather than reject, the bad news about Wikipedia.

Make It Memorable

If you've already done the preliminary work in choosing a topic, finding an interesting narrowing of that topic, developing and using presentation aids, and working to maintain audience contact, your delivery is likely to be memorable. Now you can turn to your content and find opportunities to make it appropriately vivid. You can do this by using explanations, comparisons, examples, or language.

Let's say that you're preparing a speech on the United States' internment of Japanese American people from the San Francisco Bay area during World War II. Your goal is to paint a memorable image in your listeners' minds. You can do this through a dramatic contrast, before and after. You could say, "In 1941, the Bay area had a vibrant and productive community of Japanese American citizens who went to work every day, opening their shops, typing reports in their offices, and teaching in their classrooms, just as they had been doing for years. But on December 7, 1941, everything changed. Within six months, Bay area residents of Japanese ancestry were gone, transported to internment camps located hundreds of miles from the Pacific coast."

This strategy rests on the ability of the audience to visualize the two contrasting situations. You have alluded to two sets of images that are familiar to most college students, images that they can easily visualize. Once the audience imagination is engaged in visualization, they are likely to remember the speech.

Your task of providing memorable imagery does not stop after the introduction. While maintaining an even-handed approach that does not seek to persuade, you must provide the audience with information about the circumstances that triggered the policy of internment, perhaps by describing the advice that was given to President Roosevelt by his top advisers. You might depict the conditions faced by Japanese Americans during their internment by describing a typical day one of the camps. To conclude your speech on a memorable note, you might name a notable individual—an actor, writer, or politician—who is a survivor of the internment.

Such a strategy might feel unnatural to you. After all, this is not how you talk to your friends or participate in a classroom discussion. Remember, though, that public speaking is not the same as talking. It's prepared and formal. It demands more of you. In a conversation, it might not be important to be memorable; your goal might merely be to maintain friendship. But in a speech, when you expect the audience to pay attention, you must make the speech memorable.

Make It Relevant and Useful

When thinking about your topic, it is always very important to keep your audience members center stage in your mind. For instance, if your speech is about air pollution, ask your audience to imagine feeling the burning of eyes and lungs caused by smog. This is a strategy for making the topic more real to them, since it may have happened to them on a number of occasions; and even if it hasn't, it easily could. If your speech is about Mark Twain, instead of simply saying that he was very famous during his lifetime, remind your audience that he was so prominent that their own great-grandparents likely knew of his work and had strong opinions about it. In so doing, you've connected your topic to their own forebears.

Personalize Your Content

Giving a human face to a topic helps the audience perceive it as interesting. If your topic is related to the Maasai rite of passage into manhood, the prevalence of drug addiction in a particular locale, the development of a professional filmmaker, or the treatment of a disease, putting a human face should not be difficult. To do it, find a case study you can describe within the speech, referring to the human subject by name. This conveys to the audience that these processes happen to real people.

Make sure you use a real case study, though—don't make one up. Using a fictional character without letting your audience know that the example is hypothetical is a betrayal of the listener's trust, and hence, is unethical.

KEY TAKEAWAYS

- One important reason for informative speaking is to provide listeners with information so that they can make up their own minds about an issue.
- Informative speeches must be accurate, clear, and interesting for the listener.
- Strategies to make information clear and interesting to an audience include adjusting the complexity of your information to the audience, avoiding jargon, creating concrete images, limiting information only to what is most relevant, linking information to what the audience already knows, and making information memorable through language or personalization.

2.   TYPES OF INFORMATIVE SPEECHES

© Thinkstock

For some speakers, deciding on a topic is one of the most difficult parts of informative speaking. The following subsections begin by discussing several categories of topics that you might use for an informative presentation. Then we discuss how you might structure your speech to address potential audience difficulties in understanding your topic or information.

2.1   Objects

The term "objects" encompasses many topics we might not ordinarily consider to be "things." It's a category that includes people, institutions, places, substances, and inanimate things. The following are some of these topics:

- Mitochondria
- Dream catchers
- Sharks
- Hubble telescope
- Seattle's Space Needle
- Malta
- Silicon chip
- Spruce Goose
- Medieval armor
- DDT insecticide
- Soy inks
- NAACP

You will find it necessary to narrow your topic about an object because, like any topic, you can't say everything about it in a single speech. In most cases, there are choices about how to narrow the topic. Here are some specific purpose statements that reflect ways of narrowing a few of those topics:

- To inform the audience about the role of soy inks in reducing toxic pollution
- To inform the audience about the current uses of the banned insecticide DDT
- To inform the audience about what we've learned from the Hubble telescope
- To inform the audience about the role of the NAACP in the passage of the Civil Rights Act of 1964
- To describe the significance of the gigantic Spruce Goose, the wooden airplane that launched an airline

These specific purposes reflect a narrow, but interesting, approach to each topic. These purposes are precise, and they should help you maintain your focus on a narrow but deep slice of knowledge.

2.2   People

This category applies both to specific individuals and also to roles. The following are some of these topics:

- Dalai Lamas
- Astronauts
- Tsar Nicholas II
- Modern midwives
- Mata Hari
- Catherine the Great
- Navajo code talkers
- Mahatma Gandhi
- Justice Thurgood Marshall
- Madame Curie
- Leopold Mozart
- Aristotle
- The Hemlock Society
- Sonia Sotomayor
- Jack the Ripper

There is a great deal of information about each one of these examples. In order to narrow the topic or write a thesis statement, it's important to recognize that your speech should not be a biography, or time line, of someone's life. If you attempt to deliver a comprehensive report of every important event and accomplishment related to your subject, then nothing will seem any more important than anything else. To capture and hold your audience's interest, you must narrow to a focus on a feature, event, achievement, or secret about your human topic.

Here are some purpose statements that reflect a process of narrowing:

- To inform the audience about the training program undergone by the first US astronauts to land on the moon
- To inform the audience about how a young Dalai Lama is identified
- To inform the audience about why Gandhi was regarded as a mahatma, or "great heart"
- To inform the audience about the extensive scientific qualifications of modern midwives

Without a limited purpose, you will find, with any of these topics, that there's simply too much to say. Your purpose statement will be a strong decision-making tool about what to include in your speech.

2.3   Events

An event can be something that occurred only once, or an event that is repeated:

- The murder of Emmett Till
- The Iditarod Dogsled Race
- The Industrial Revolution
- The discovery of the smallpox vaccine
- The Bikini Atoll atomic bomb tests
- The Bay of Pigs
- The Super Bowl
- The Academy Awards

Again, we find that any of these topics must be carefully narrowed in order to build a coherent speech. Failure to do so will result in a shallow speech. Here are a few ways to narrow the purpose:

- To explain how the murder of Emmett Till helped energize the civil rights movement
- To describe how the Industrial Revolution affected the lives of ordinary people
- To inform the audience about the purpose of the Iditarod dogsled race

chronological order

Time order; the order in
which events take place.

There are many ways to approach any of these and other topics, but again, you must emphasize an important dimension of the event. Otherwise, you run the risk of producing a time line in which the main point gets lost. In a speech about an event, you may use a **chronological order**, but if you choose to do so, you can't include every detail. The following is an example:

Specific Purpose: To inform the audience about the purpose of the Iditarod dogsled race.

Central Idea: The annual Iditarod commemorates the heroism of Balto, the sled dog that led a dog team carrying medicine 1150 miles to save Nome from an outbreak of diphtheria.

Main Points:

   I. Diphtheria broke out in a remote Alaskan town.

   II. Dogsleds were the only transportation for getting medicine.

   III. The Iditarod Trail was long, rugged, and under siege of severe weather.

   IV. Balto the dog knew where he was going, even when the musher did not.

   V. The annual race commemorates Balto's heroism in saving the lives of the people of Nome.

In this example, you must explain the event. However, another way to approach the same event would describe it. The following is an example:

Specific Purpose: To describe the annual Iditarod Trail Sled Dog Race.

Central Idea: It's a long and dangerous race.

Main Points:

   I. The 1150-mile, ten- to seventeen-day race goes through wilderness with widely spaced checkpoints for rest, first aid, and getting fresh dogs.

   II. A musher, or dogsled driver, must be at least fourteen years old to endure the rigors of severe weather, exhaustion, and loneliness.

   III. A musher is responsible for his or her own food, food for twelve to sixteen dogs, and for making sure they don't get lost.

   IV. Reaching the end of the race without getting lost, even in last place, is considered honorable and heroic.

   V. The expense of participation is greater than the prize awarded to the winner.

By now you can see that there are various ways to approach a topic while avoiding an uninspiring time line. In the example of the Iditarod race, you could alternatively frame it as an Alaskan tourism topic, or you could emphasize the enormous staff involved in first aid, search and rescue, dog care, trail maintenance, event coordination, financial management, and registration.

2.4   Concepts

Concepts are abstract ideas that exist independent of whether they are observed or practiced, such as the example of social equality that follows. Concepts can include hypotheses and theories.

- The glass ceiling
- Ethnocentrism
- Honor codes
- Autism
- Karma
- Wellness
- Fairness theory
- Bioethics
- The American Dream
- Social equality

Here are a few examples of specific purposes developed from the examples:

- To explain why people in all cultures are ethnocentric
- To describe the Hindu concept of karma
- To distinguish the differences between the concepts of wellness and health
- To show the resources available in our local school system for children with autism
- To explain three of Dr. Stephen Suranovic's seven categories of fairness

Here is one possible example of a way to develop one of these topics:

Specific Purpose: To explain why people in all cultures are ethnocentric.
Central Idea: There are benefits to being ethnocentric.
Main Points:

I. Ethnocentrism is the idea that one's own culture is superior to others.

II. Ethnocentrism strongly contributes to positive group identity.

III. Ethnocentrism facilitates the coordination of social activity.

IV. Ethnocentrism contributes to a sense of safety within a group.

V. Ethnocentrism becomes harmful when it creates barriers.

In an example of a concept about which people disagree, you must represent multiple and conflicting views as fully and fairly as possible. For instance:

Specific Purpose: To expose the audience to three different views of the American Dream.
Central Idea: The American Dream is a shared dream, an impossible dream, or a dangerous dream, depending on the perspective of the individual.
Main Points:

I. The concept of the American Dream describes a state of abundant well-being in which an honest and productive American can own a home; bring up a family; work at a permanent, well-paying job with benefits; and retire in security and leisure.

II. Many capitalists support the social pattern of working hard to deserve and acquire the material comforts and security of a comfortable life.

III. Many sociologists argue that the American Dream is far out of reach for the 40 percent of Americans at the bottom of the economic scale.

IV. Many environmentalists argue that the consumption patterns that accompany the American Dream have resulted in the depletion of resources and the pollution of air, water, and soil.

2.5   Processes

If your speech topic is a process, your goal should be to help your audience understand it, or be able to perform it. In either instance, processes involve a predictable series of changes, phases, or steps.

- Soil erosion
- Cell division
- Physical therapy
- Volcanic eruption
- Paper recycling
- Consumer credit evaluations
- Scholarship money searches
- Navy Seal training
- Portfolio building
- The development of Alzheimer's disease

For some topics, you will need presentation aids in order to make your meaning clear to your listeners. Even in cases where you don't absolutely need a presentation aid, one might be useful. For instance, if your topic is evaluating consumer credit, instead of just describing a comparison between two different interest rates applied to the same original amount of debt, it would be helpful to show a graph of the difference. This might also be the sort of topic that would strongly serve the needs of your audience before they find themselves in trouble. Since this will be an informative speech, you must resist the impulse to tell your listeners that one form of borrowing is good and another is bad; you must simply show them the difference in numbers. They can reach their own conclusions.

Organizing your facts is crucially important when discussing a process. Every stage of a process must be clear and understandable. When two or more things occur at the same time, as they might in the development of Alzheimer's disease, it is important to make it clear that several things are occurring at once. For example, as plaque is accumulating in the brain, the patient is likely to begin exhibiting various symptoms.

Here's an example of the initial steps of a speech about a process:

Specific Purpose: To inform the audience about how to build an academic portfolio.
Central Idea: A portfolio represents you and emphasizes your best skills.

Main Points:

I. A portfolio is an organized selection containing the best examples of the skills you can offer an employer.

II. A portfolio should contain samples of a substantial body of written work, print and electronically published pieces, photography, and DVDs of your media productions.

III. A portfolio should be customized for each prospective employer.

IV. The material in your portfolio should be consistent with the skills and experience in your résumé.

In a speech about the process of building a portfolio, there will be many smaller steps to include within each of the main points. For instance, creating separate sections of the portfolio for different types of creative activities, writing a table of contents, labeling and dating your samples, making your samples look attractive and professional, and other steps should be inserted where it makes the most sense, in the most organized places, in order to give your audience the most coherent understanding possible.

You've probably noticed that there are topics that could be appropriate in more than one category. For instance, the 1980 eruption of Mt. St. Helen's could be legitimately handled as an event or as a process. If you approach the eruption as an event, most of the information you include will focus on human responses and the consequences on humans and the landscape. If you approach the eruption as a process, you will be using visual aids and explanations to describe geological changes before and during the eruption. You might also approach this topic from the viewpoint of a person whose life was affected by the eruption. This should remind you that there are many ways to approach most topics, and because of that, your narrowing choices and your purpose will be the important foundation determining the structure of your informative speech.

2.6 Developing Your Topic for the Audience

One issue to consider when preparing an informative speech is how best to present the information to enhance audience learning. Katherine Rowan suggests focusing on areas where your audience may experience confusion and using the likely sources of confusion as a guide for developing the content of your speech. Rowan identifies three sources of audience confusion: difficult concepts or language, difficult-to-envision structures or processes, and ideas that are difficult to understand because they are hard to believe.[2] The following subsections will discuss each of these and will provide strategies for dealing with each of these sources of confusion.

Difficult Concepts or Language

Sometimes audiences may have difficulty understanding information because of the concepts or language used. For example, they may not understand what the term "organic food" means or how it differs from "all-natural" foods. If an audience is likely to experience confusion over a basic concept or term, Rowan suggests using an elucidating explanation composed of four parts. The purpose of such an explanation is to clarify the meaning and use of the concept by focusing on essential features of the concept.

The first part of an elucidating explanation is to provide a typical exemplar, or example that includes all the central features of the concept. If you are talking about what is fruit, an apple or orange would be a typical exemplar.

The second step Rowan suggests is to follow up the typical exemplar with a definition. Fruits might be defined as edible plant structures that contain the seeds of the plant.

After providing a definition, you can move on to the third part of the elucidating explanation: providing a variety of examples and nonexamples. Here is where you might include less typical examples of fruit, such as avocados, squash, or tomatoes, and foods, such as rhubarb, which is often treated as a fruit but is not by definition.

Fourth, Rowan suggests concluding by having the audience practice distinguishing examples from nonexamples. In this way, the audience leaves the speech with a clear understanding of the concept.

Difficult-to-Envision Processes or Structures

A second source of audience difficulty in understanding, according to Rowan, is a process or structure that is complex and difficult to envision. The blood circulation system in the body might be an example of a difficult-to-envision process. To address this type of audience confusion, Rowan suggests a quasi-scientific explanation, which starts by giving a big-picture perspective on the process. Presentation aids or analogies might be helpful in giving an overview of the process. For the circulatory system, you could show a video or diagram of the entire system or make an analogy to a pump. Then you can move to explaining relationships among the components of the process. Be sure when you explain relationships among components that you include transition and linking words like "leads to" and "because" so that your audience understands relationships between concepts. You may remember the childhood song describing the bones in the body with lines such as, "the hip bone's connected to the thigh bone; the thigh bone's connected to the knee bone." Making the connections between components helps the audience to remember and better understand the process.

Difficult to Understand because It's Hard to Believe

A third source of audience confusion, and perhaps the most difficult to address as a speaker, is an idea that's difficult to understand because it's hard to believe. This often happens when people have implicit, but erroneous, theories about how the world works. For example, the idea that science tries to disprove theories is difficult for some people to understand; after all, shouldn't the purpose of science be to prove things? In such a case, Rowan suggests using a transformative explanation. A transformative explanation begins by discussing the audience's implicit theory and showing why it is plausible. Then you move to showing how the implicit theory is limited and conclude by presenting the accepted explanation and why that explanation is better. In the case of scientists disproving theories, you might start by talking about what science has proven (e.g., the causes of malaria, the usefulness of penicillin in treating infection) and why focusing on science as proof is a plausible way of thinking. Then you might show how the science as proof theory is limited by providing examples of ideas that were accepted as "proven" but were later found to be false, such as the belief that diseases are caused by miasma, or "bad air"; or that bloodletting cures diseases by purging the body of "bad humors." You can then conclude by showing how science is an enterprise designed to disprove theories and that all theories are accepted as tentative in light of existing knowledge.

Rowan's framework is helpful because it keeps our focus on the most important element of an informative speech: increasing audience understanding about a topic.

2.7 Ethics

Honesty and credibility must undergird your presentation; otherwise, they betray the trust of your listeners. Therefore, if you choose a topic that turns out to be too difficult, you must decide what will serve the needs and interests of the audience. Shortcuts and oversimplifications are not the answer.

Being ethical often involves a surprising amount of work. In the case of choosing too ambitious a topic, you have some choices:

- Narrow your topic further.
- Narrow your topic in a different way.
- Reconsider your specific purpose.
- Start over with a new topic.

Your goal is to serve the interests and needs of your audience, whoever they are and whether you believe they already know something about your topic.

KEY TAKEAWAYS

- A variety of different topic categories are available for informative speaking.
- One way to develop your topic is to focus on areas that might be confusing to the audience. If the audience is likely to be confused about language or a concept, an elucidating explanation might be helpful. If a process is complex, a quasi-scientific explanation may help. If the audience already has an erroneous implicit idea of how something works then a transformative explanation might be needed.

EXERCISES

1. Choose a topic such as "American Education in the Twenty-First Century." Write a new title for that speech for each of the following audiences: financial managers, first-year college students, parents of high school students, nuns employed in Roman Catholic schools, psychotherapists, and teamsters. Write a specific purpose for the speech for each of these audiences.
2. Think about three potential topics you could use for an informative speech. Identify where the audience might experience confusion with concepts, processes, or preexisting implicit theories. Select one of the topics and outline how you would develop the topic to address the audience's potential confusion.

3.   CHAPTER EXERCISES

Imagine that you have somehow learned a way of bypassing a security system located in many banks. The information you have addresses not only access to the bank itself but also the computers used in the storage of information and the transmission of funds. You are certain that you understand the process well enough to successfully do it. Can you use this as your topic for an informative speech? Explain your answer fully.

Now let's imagine a different topic: You are going to speak about receiving medical care in a hospital emergency room. You intend to describe the long wait, the need for an insurance card, and the many personal details that the patient must give orally to the emergency department receptionist, who sits on the other side of a glass barrier typing the information into a computer. For your introduction, you have created a vivid picture of an emergency room scenario, and you want it to be realistic. Must you say that the scenario is hypothetical rather than actual? Can you say that you witnessed the scenario? Explain your answer. List some alternatives.

E N D - O F - C H A P T E R   A S S E S S M E N T

1. Rob is preparing a speech on the D-day invasion during World War II. By researching in the library and online, he has found a really cool book by a British general published soon after the war and a bunch of old pictures. He thinks this is all he needs as source material. By relying only on potentially outdated sources, Rob is likely to sacrifice which important element of informative speaking?

   a. listener interest
   b. clarity
   c. immediacy
   d. accuracy
   e. transformation

2. Rita is struggling to make her speech on wind energy interesting for the audience. You suggest that she consider including pictures of windmills located a few miles from campus and talk about how those windmills help provide power for the lights and heat in your classroom and across campus. Your suggestion focuses on which technique for making information clear and interesting to your audience?

   a. Personalize the information.
   b. Limit use of jargon.
   c. Narrow the topic.
   d. Adjust the complexity to the audience.
   e. Use abstract language.

3. Brooks is thinking of speaking about the National Baseball Hall of Fame and wants to focus on the big induction weekend at the end of July. Brooks is using which topic category?

   a. people
   b. objects
   c. events
   d. processes
   e. concepts

4. Connie wants to speak about the local school budget. She knows most of her audience thinks that their local property taxes pay for all the educational expenses in the community, but she wants to show them that the state actually pays for more than 30 percent of the costs. According to Rowan, Connie should strongly consider using which type of explanation to develop her topic?

   a. elucidating explanation
   b. quasi-scientific explanation
   c. transformative explanation
   d. concrete explanation
   e. abstract explanation

ANSWER KEY

1. d
2. a
3. c
4. c

ENDNOTES

1. Lucas, Stephen E. (2004). *The art of public speaking*. Boston: McGraw-Hill.

2. Rowan, K. E. (1995). A new pedagogy for explanatory public speaking: Why arrangement should not substitute for invention. *Communication Education, 44,* 236–249.

CHAPTER 17
Persuasive Speaking

FOUNDATIONS OF PERSUASION

Every day we are bombarded by persuasive messages. Some messages are mediated and designed to get us to purchase specific products or vote for specific candidates, while others might come from our loved ones and are designed to get us to help around the house or join the family for game night. Whatever the message being sent, we are constantly being persuaded and persuading others. In this chapter, we are going to focus on persuasive speaking. We will first talk about persuasion as a general concept. We will then examine four different types of persuasive speeches, and finally, we'll look at three organizational patterns that are useful for persuasive speeches.

© Thinkstock

1. PERSUASION: AN OVERVIEW

LEARNING OBJECTIVES

1. Define and explain persuasion.
2. Explain the three theories of persuasion discussed in the text: social judgment theory, cognitive dissonance theory, and the elaboration likelihood model.

In his text *The Dynamics of Persuasion: Communication and Attitudes in the 21st Century*, Richard Perloff noted that the study of persuasion today is extremely important for five basic reasons:

1. The sheer number of persuasive communications has grown exponentially.
2. Persuasive messages travel faster than ever before.
3. Persuasion has become institutionalized.
4. Persuasive communication has become more subtle and devious.
5. Persuasive communication is more complex than ever before.[1]

In essence, the nature of persuasion has changed over the last fifty years as a result of the influx of various types of technology. People are bombarded by persuasive messages in today's world, so thinking about how to create persuasive messages effectively is very important for modern public speakers. A century (or even half a century) ago, public speakers had to contend only with the words printed on paper for attracting and holding an audience's attention. Today, public speakers must contend with laptops, netbooks, iPads, smartphones, billboards, television sets, and many other tools that can send a range of persuasive messages immediately to a target audience. Thankfully, scholars who study persuasion have kept up with the changing times and have found a number of persuasive strategies that help speakers be more persuasive.

© Thinkstock

1.1   What Is Persuasion?

We defined **persuasion** earlier in this text as an attempt to get a person to behave in a manner, or embrace a point of view related to values, attitudes, and beliefs, that he or she would not have done otherwise.

Change Attitudes, Values, and Beliefs

The first type of persuasive public speaking involves a change in someone's attitudes, values, and beliefs. An **attitude** is defined as an individual's general predisposition toward something as being good or bad, right or wrong, or negative or positive. Maybe you believe that local curfew laws for people under twenty-one are a bad idea, so you want to persuade others to adopt a negative attitude toward such laws.

You can also attempt to persuade an individual to change her or his value toward something. **Value** refers to an individual's perception of the usefulness, importance, or worth of something. We can value a college education or technology or freedom. Values, as a general concept, are fairly ambiguous and tend to be very lofty ideas. Ultimately, what we value in life actually motivates us to engage in a range of behaviors. For example, if you value technology, you are more likely to seek out new technology or software on your own. On the contrary, if you do not value technology, you are less likely to seek out new technology or software unless someone, or some circumstance, requires you to.

Lastly, you can attempt to get people to change their personal beliefs. **Beliefs** are propositions or positions that an individual holds as true or false without positive knowledge or proof. Typically, beliefs are divided into two basic categories: core and dispositional. **Core beliefs** are beliefs that people have actively engaged in and created over the course of their lives (e.g., belief in a higher power, belief in extraterrestrial life forms). **Dispositional beliefs**, on the other hand, are beliefs that people have not actively engaged in but rather judgments that they make, based on their knowledge of related subjects, when they encounter a proposition. For example, imagine that you were asked the question, "Can stock cars reach speeds of one thousand miles per hour on a one-mile oval track?" Even though you may never have attended a stock car race or even seen one on television, you can make split-second judgments about your understanding of automobile speeds and say with a fair degree of certainty that you believe stock cars cannot travel at one thousand miles per hour on a one-mile track. We sometimes refer to dispositional beliefs as virtual beliefs.[2]

As we explained in Chapter 6, when it comes to persuading people to alter core and dispositional beliefs, persuading audiences to change core beliefs is more difficult than persuading audiences to change dispositional beliefs. For this reason, you are very unlikely to persuade people to change their deeply held core beliefs about a topic in a five- to ten-minute speech. However, if you give a persuasive speech on a topic related to an audience's dispositional beliefs, you may have a better chance of success. While core beliefs may seem to be exciting and interesting, persuasive topics related to dispositional beliefs are generally better for novice speakers with limited time allotments.

Change Behavior

The second type of persuasive speech is one in which the speaker attempts to persuade an audience to change their behavior. Behaviors come in a wide range of forms, so finding one you think people should start, increase, or decrease shouldn't be difficult at all. Speeches encouraging audiences to vote for a candidate, sign a petition opposing a tuition increase, or drink tap water instead of bottled water are all behavior-oriented persuasive speeches. In all these cases, the goal is to change the behavior of individual listeners.

1.2   Why Persuasion Matters

Frymier and Nadler enumerate three reasons why people should study persuasion.[3] First, when you study and understand persuasion, you will be more successful at persuading others. If you want to be a persuasive public speaker, then you need to have a working understanding of how persuasion functions.

Second, when people understand persuasion, they will be better consumers of information. As previously mentioned, we live in a society where numerous message sources are constantly fighting for our attention. Unfortunately, most people just let messages wash over them like a wave, making little effort to understand or analyze them. As a result, they are more likely to fall for half-truths, illogical arguments, and lies. When you start to understand persuasion, you will have the skill set to actually pick apart the messages being sent to you and see why some of them are good and others are simply not.

---

persuasion

The process an individual goes through attempting to get another person to behave in a manner or embrace a point of view related to values, attitudes, or beliefs that he or she would not have done otherwise.

attitude

An individual's general predisposition toward something as being good or bad, right or wrong, negative or positive, and so on.

value

An individual's perception of the usefulness, importance, or worth of something.

beliefs

Propositions or positions that an individual holds as true or false without positive knowledge or proof.

core beliefs

Beliefs that people have actively engaged in and created over the course of their lives.

dispositional beliefs

Beliefs that people have not actively engaged in; judgments based on related subjects, which people make when they encounter a proposition.

Lastly, when we understand how persuasion functions, we'll have a better grasp of what happens around us in the world. We'll be able to analyze why certain speakers are effective persuaders and others are not. We'll be able to understand why some public speakers can get an audience eating out of their hands, while others flop.

Furthermore, we believe it is an ethical imperative in the twenty-first century to be persuasively literate. We believe that persuasive messages that aim to manipulate, coerce, and intimidate people are unethical, as are messages that distort information. As ethical listeners, we have a responsibility to analyze messages that manipulate, coerce, and/or intimidate people or distort information. We also then have the responsibility to combat these messages with the truth, which will ultimately rely on our own skills and knowledge as effective persuaders.

1.3 Theories of Persuasion

Understanding how people are persuaded is very important to the discussion of public speaking. Thankfully, a number of researchers have created theories that help explain why people are persuaded. While there are numerous theories that help to explain persuasion, we are only going to examine three here: social judgment theory, cognitive dissonance theory, and the elaboration likelihood model.

Social Judgment Theory

Muzafer Sherif and Carl Hovland created social judgment theory in an attempt to determine what types of communicative messages and under what conditions communicated messages will lead to a change in someone's behavior.[4] In essence, Sherif and Hovland found that people's perceptions of attitudes, values, beliefs, and behaviors exist on a continuum including **latitude of rejection**, **latitude of noncommitment**, and **latitude of acceptance** (Figure 17.1).

FIGURE 17.1 Latitudes of Judgments

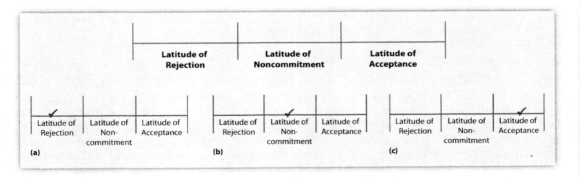

Imagine that you're planning to persuade your peers to major in a foreign language in college. Some of the students in your class are going to disagree with you right off the bat (latitude of rejection, part (a) of Figure 17.1). Other students are going to think majoring in a foreign language is a great idea (latitude of acceptance, part (c) of Figure 17.1). Still others are really going to have no opinion either way (latitude of noncommitment, part (b) of Figure 17.1). Now in each of these different latitudes there is a range of possibilities. For example, one of your listeners may be perfectly willing to accept the idea of minoring in a foreign language, but when asked to major or even double major in a foreign language, he or she may end up in the latitude of noncommitment or even rejection.

Not surprisingly, Sherif and Hovland found that persuasive messages were the most likely to succeed when they fell into an individual's latitude of acceptance. For example, if you are giving your speech on majoring in a foreign language, people who are in favor of majoring in a foreign language are more likely to positively evaluate your message, assimilate your advice into their own ideas, and engage in desired behavior. On the other hand, people who reject your message are more likely to negatively evaluate your message, not assimilate your advice, and not engage in desired behavior.

In an ideal world, we'd always be persuading people who agree with our opinions, but that's not reality. Instead, we often find ourselves in situations where we are trying to persuade others to attitudes, values, beliefs, and behaviors with which they may not agree. To help us persuade others, what we need to think about is the range of possible attitudes, values, beliefs, and behaviors that exist. For example, in our foreign language case, we may see the following possible opinions from our audience members:

1. **Complete agreement.** Let's all major in foreign languages.

2. **Strong agreement.** I won't major in a foreign language, but I will double major in a foreign language.

3. **Agreement in part.** I won't major in a foreign language, but I will minor in a foreign language.

4. **Neutral.** While I think studying a foreign language can be worthwhile, I also think a college education can be complete without it. I really don't feel strongly one way or the other.

5. **Disagreement in part.** I will only take the foreign language classes required by my major.

6. **Strong disagreement.** I don't think I should have to take any foreign language classes.

7. **Complete disagreement.** Majoring in a foreign language is a complete waste of a college education.

These seven possible opinions on the subject do not represent the full spectrum of choices, but give us various degrees of agreement with the general topic. So what does this have to do with persuasion? Well, we're glad you asked. Sherif and Hovland theorized that persuasion was a matter of knowing how great the discrepancy or difference was between the speaker's viewpoint and that of the audience. If the speaker's point of view was similar to that of audience members, then persuasion was more likely. If the discrepancy between the idea proposed by the speaker and the audience's viewpoint is too great, then the likelihood of persuasion decreases dramatically.

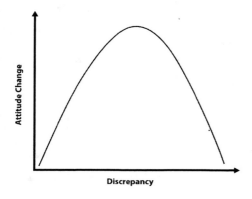

FIGURE 17.2 Discrepancy and Attitude Change

Furthermore, Sherif and Hovland predicted that there was a threshold for most people where attitude change wasn't possible and people slipped from the latitude of acceptance into the latitude of noncommitment or rejection. Figure 17.2 represents this process. All the area covered by the left side of the curve represents options a person would agree with, even if there is an initial discrepancy between the speaker and audience member at the start of the speech. However, there comes a point where the discrepancy between the speaker and audience member becomes too large, which move into the options that will be automatically rejected by the audience member. In essence, it becomes essential for you to know which options you can realistically persuade your audience to and which options will never happen. Maybe there is no way for you to persuade your audience to major or double major in a foreign language, but perhaps you can get them to minor in a foreign language. While you may not be achieving your complete end goal, it's better than getting nowhere at all.

Cognitive Dissonance Theory

In 1957, Leon Festinger proposed another theory for understanding how persuasion functions: cognitive dissonance theory.[5] **Cognitive dissonance** is an aversive motivational state that occurs when an individual entertains two or more contradictory attitudes, values, beliefs, or behaviors simultaneously. For example, maybe you know you should be working on your speech, but you really want to go to a movie with a friend. In this case, practicing your speech and going to the movie are two cognitions that are inconsistent with one another. The goal of persuasion is to induce enough dissonance in listeners that they will change their attitudes, values, beliefs, or behaviors.

cognitive dissonance

An aversive motivational state that occurs when an individual entertains two or more contradictory attitudes, values, beliefs, or behaviors simultaneously.

Frymier and Nadler noted that for cognitive dissonance to work effectively there are three necessary conditions: aversive consequences, freedom of choice, and insufficient external justification.[6] First, for cognitive dissonance to work, there needs to be a strong enough aversive consequence, or punishment, for *not* changing one's attitudes, values, beliefs, or behaviors. For example, maybe you're giving a speech on why people need to eat more apples. If your aversive consequence for not eating apples is that your audience will not get enough fiber, most people will simply not be persuaded, because the punishment isn't severe enough. Instead, for cognitive dissonance to work, the punishment associated with not eating apples needs to be significant enough to change behaviors. If you convince your audience that without enough fiber in their diets they are at higher risk for heart disease or colon cancer, they might fear the aversive consequences enough to change their behavior.

The second condition necessary for cognitive dissonance to work is that people must have a freedom of choice. If listeners feel they are being coerced into doing something, then dissonance will not be aroused. They may alter their behavior in the short term, but as soon as the coercion is gone, the original behavior will reemerge. It's like the person who drives more slowly when a police officer is nearby but ignores speed limits once officers are no longer present. As a speaker, if you want to increase cognitive dissonance, you need to make sure that your audience doesn't feel coerced or manipulated, but rather that they can clearly see that they have a choice of whether to be persuaded.

The final condition necessary for cognitive dissonance to work has to do with external and internal justifications. **External justification** refers to the process of identifying reasons outside of one's own control to support one's behavior, beliefs, and attitudes. **Internal justification** occurs when someone voluntarily changes a behavior, belief, or attitude to reduce cognitive dissonance. When it comes to creating change through persuasion, external justifications are less likely to result in change than internal justifications.[7] Imagine that you're giving a speech with the specific purpose of persuading college students to use condoms whenever they engage in sexual intercourse. Your audience analysis, in the form of an anonymous survey, indicates that a large percentage of your listeners do not consistently use condoms. Which would be the more persuasive argument: (a) "Failure to use condoms inevitably results in unintended pregnancy and sexually transmitted infections, including AIDS"—or (b) "If you think of yourself as a responsible adult, you'll use condoms to protect yourself and your partner"? With the first argument, you have provided external justification for using condoms (i.e., terrible things will happen if you don't use condoms). Listeners who reject this external justification (e.g., who don't believe these dire consequences are inevitable) are unlikely to change their behavior. With the second argument, however, if your listeners think of themselves as responsible adults and they don't consistently use condoms, the conflict between their self-image and their behavior will elicit cognitive dissonance. In order to reduce this cognitive dissonance, they are likely to seek internal justification for the view of themselves as responsible adults by changing their behavior (i.e., using condoms more consistently). In this case, according to cognitive dissonance theory, the second persuasive argument would be the one more likely to lead to a change in behavior.

Elaboration Likelihood Model

The last of the three theories of persuasion discussed here is the elaboration likelihood model created by Petty and Cacioppo.[8] The basic model has a continuum from high elaboration or thought or low elaboration or thought. For the purposes of Petty and Cacioppo's model, the term **elaboration** refers to the amount of thought or cognitive energy someone uses for analyzing the content of a message. High elaboration uses the **central route** and is designed for analyzing the content of a message. As such, when people truly analyze a message, they use cognitive energy to examine the arguments set forth within the message. In an ideal world, everyone would process information through this central route and actually analyze arguments presented to them. Unfortunately, many people often use the **peripheral route** for attending to persuasive messages, which results in low elaboration or thought. Low elaboration occurs when people attend to messages but do not analyze the message or use cognitive energy to ascertain the arguments set forth in a message.

For researchers of persuasion, the question then becomes: how do people select one route or the other when attending to persuasive messages? Petty and Cacioppo noted that there are two basic factors for determining whether someone centrally processes a persuasive message: ability and motivation. First, audience members must be able to process the persuasive message. If the language or message is too complicated, then people will not highly elaborate on it because they will not understand the persuasive message. Motivation, on the other hand, refers to whether the audience member chooses to elaborate on the message. Frymier and Nadler discussed five basic factors that can lead to high elaboration: personal relevance and personal involvement, accountability, personal responsibility, incongruent information, and need for cognition.[9]

Personal Relevance and Personal Involvement

The first reason people are motivated to take the central route or use high elaboration when listening to a persuasive message involves personal relevance and involvement. Personal relevance refers to whether the audience member feels that he or she is actually directly affected by the speech topic. For example, if someone is listening to a speech on why cigarette smoking is harmful, and that listener has never smoked cigarettes, he or she may think the speech topic simply isn't relevant. Obviously, as a speaker you should always think about how your topic is relevant to your listeners and make sure to drive this home throughout your speech. Personal involvement, on the other hand, asks whether the individual is actively engaged with the issue at hand: sends letters of support, gives speeches on the topic, has a bumper sticker, and so forth. If an audience member is an advocate who is constantly denouncing tobacco companies for the harm they do to society, then he or she would be highly involved (i.e., would engage in high elaboration) in a speech that attempts to persuade listeners that smoking is harmful.

Accountability

The second condition under which people are likely to process information using the central route is when they feel that they will be held accountable for the information after the fact. With accountability, there is the perception that someone, or a group of people, will be watching to see if the receiver remembers the information later on. We've all witnessed this phenomenon when one student asks the

---

external justification

The process of identifying reasons outside of one's own control to support one's behavior, beliefs, and attitudes.

internal justification

The process of reducing cognitive dissonance by voluntarily changing a behavior, belief, or attitude.

elaboration

The amount of thought or cognitive energy someone uses for analyzing the content of a message.

central route

Activity of truly analyzing a message using cognitive energy to ascertain the arguments set forth within the message.

peripheral route

Activity of attending to messages but not analyzing them or using cognitive energy to ascertain the arguments set forth in a message.

question "will this be on the test?" If the teacher says "no," you can almost immediately see the glazed eyes in the classroom as students tune out the information. As a speaker, it's often hard to hold your audience accountable for the information given within a speech.

Personal Responsibility

When people feel that they are going to be held responsible, without a clear external accounting, for the evaluation of a message or the outcome of a message, they are more likely to critically think through the message using the central route. For example, maybe you're asked to evaluate fellow students in your public speaking class. Research has shown that if only one or two students are asked to evaluate any one speaker at a time, the quality of the evaluations for that speaker will be better than if everyone in the class is asked to evaluate every speaker. When people feel that their evaluation is important, they take more responsibility and therefore are more critical of the message delivered.

Incongruent Information

Some people are motivated to centrally process information when it does not adhere to their own ideas. Maybe you're a highly progressive liberal, and one of your peers delivers a speech on the importance of the Tea Party movement in American politics. The information presented during the speech will most likely be in direct contrast to your personal ideology, which causes incongruence because the Tea Party ideology is opposed to a progressive liberal ideology. As such, you are more likely to pay attention to the speech, specifically looking for flaws in the speaker's argument.

Need for Cognition

need for cognition

A personality trait characterized by an internal drive or need to engage in critical thinking and information processing.

The final reason some people centrally process information is because they have a personality characteristic called need for cognition. **Need for cognition** refers to a personality trait characterized by an internal drive or need to engage in critical thinking and information processing. People who are high in need for cognition simply enjoy thinking about complex ideas and issues. Even if the idea or issue being presented has no personal relevance, high need for cognition people are more likely to process information using the central route.

KEY TAKEAWAYS

- Persuasion is the use of verbal and nonverbal messages to get a person to behave in a manner or embrace a point of view related to values, attitudes, and beliefs that he or she would not have done otherwise. Studying persuasion is important today because it helps us become more persuasive individuals, become more observant of others' persuasive attempts, and have a more complete understanding of the world around us.
- Social judgment theory says that persuaders need to be aware of an audience's latitudes of acceptance, noncommitment, and rejection in order to effectively persuade an audience. Second, cognitive dissonance theory reasons that people do not like holding to ideas in their heads that are contrary and will do what is necessary to get rid of the dissonance caused by the two contrary ideas. Lastly, the elaboration likelihood model posits that persuaders should attempt to get receivers to think about the arguments being made (going through the central route) rather than having receivers pay attention to nonargument related aspects of the speech.

EXERCISES

1. Imagine you're giving a speech to a group of college fraternity and sorority members about why hazing shouldn't be tolerated. Explain the persuasive process using each of the three theories of persuasion discussed in this chapter.
2. Make a list of strategies that you could employ to ensure that your audience analyzes your message using the central route and not the peripheral route. According to Petty and Cacioppo's (1986) elaboration likelihood model, which of these strategies are most likely to be effective? Why?

2. TYPES OF PERSUASIVE SPEECHES

Obviously, there are many different persuasive speech topics you could select for a public speaking class. Anything from localized claims like changing a specific college or university policy to larger societal claims like adding more enforcement against the trafficking of women and children in the United States could make for an interesting persuasive speech. You'll notice in the previous sentence we referred to the two topics as claims. In this use of the word "claim," we are declaring the goodness or positivity of an attitude, value, belief, or behavior that others may dispute. As a result of the dispute between our perceptions of the goodness of an attitude, value, belief, or behavior and the perceptions of others, we attempt to support the claim we make using some sort of evidence and logic as we attempt to persuade others. There are four common claims that can be made: definitional, factual, policy, and value.

© *Thinkstock*

2.1 Definitional Claims

The first common types of claims that a persuasive speaker can make are definitional or classification claims. **Definitional claims** are claims over the denotation or classification of what something is. In essence, we are trying to argue for what something is or what something is not. Most definitional claims falling to a basic argument formula:

X is (or is not) a **Y** because it has (or does not have) features **A**, **B**, or **C**.

For example, maybe you're trying to persuade your class that while therapeutic massage is often performed on nude clients, it is not a form of prostitution. You could start by explaining what therapeutic massage is and then what prostitution is. You could even look at the legal definition of prostitution and demonstrate to your peers that therapeutic massage does not fall into the legal definition of prostitution because it does not involve the behaviors characterized by that definition.

definitional claim

Persuasive claim about the denotation or classification of what something is.

2.2 Factual Claims

Factual claims set out to argue the truth or falsity of an assertion. Some factual claims are simple to answer: Barack Obama is the first African American President; the tallest man in the world, Robert Wadlow, was eight feet and eleven inches tall; Facebook wasn't profitable until 2009. All these factual claims are well documented by evidence and can be easily supported with a little research.

factual claim

Persuasive claim arguing the truth or falsity of an assertion.

However, many factual claims cannot be answered absolutely. Some factual claims are simply hard to determine the falsity or trueness of because the final answer on the subject has not been discovered (e.g., when is censorship good, what rights should animals have, when does life begin). Probably the most historically interesting and consistent factual claim is the existence of a higher power, God, or other religious deity. The simple fact of the matter is that there is not enough evidence to clearly answer this factual claim in any specific direction, which is where the notion of faith must be involved in this factual claim.

Other factual claims that may not be easily answered using evidence are predictions of what may or may not happen. For example, you could give a speech on the future of climate change or the future of terrorism in the United States. While there may be evidence that something will happen in the future, unless you're a psychic, you don't actually know what will happen in the future.

When thinking of factual claims, it often helps to pretend that you're putting a specific claim on trial and as the speaker your job is to defend your claim as a lawyer would defend a client. Ultimately, your job is to be more persuasive than your audience members who act as both opposition attorneys and judges.

2.3   Policy Claims

The third common claim that is seen in persuasive speeches is the **policy claim**—a statement about the nature of a problem and the solution that should be implemented. Policy claims are probably the most common form of persuasive speaking because we live in a society surrounded by problems and people who have ideas about how to fix these problems. Let's look at a few examples of possible policy claims:

- The United States should stop capital punishment.
- The United States should become independent from the use of foreign oil.
- Human cloning for organ donations should be legal.
- Nonviolent drug offenders should be sent to rehabilitation centers and not prisons.
- The tobacco industry should be required to pay 100 percent of the medical bills for individuals dying of smoking-related cancers.
- The United States needs to invest more in preventing poverty at home and less in feeding the starving around the world.

Each of these claims has a clear perspective that is being advocated. Policy claims will always have a clear and direct opinion for what should occur and what needs to change. When examining policy claims, we generally talk about two different persuasive goals: passive agreement and immediate action.

Gain Passive Agreement

When we attempt to gain the passive agreement of our audiences, our goal is to get our audiences to agree with what we are saying and our specific policy without asking the audience to do anything to en-act the policy. For example, maybe your speech is on why the Federal Communications Commission should regulate violence on television like it does foul language (i.e., no violence until after 9 p.m.). Your goal as a speaker is to get your audience to agree that it is in our best interest as a society to pre-vent violence from being shown on television before 9 p.m., but you are not seeking to have your audi-ence run out and call their senators or congressmen or even sign a petition. Often the first step in larger political change is simply getting a massive number people to agree with your policy perspective.

Let's look at a few more passive agreement claims:

- Racial profiling of individuals suspected of belonging to known terrorist groups is a way to make America safer.
- Requiring American citizens to "show their papers" is a violation of democracy and resembles tactics of Nazi Germany and communist Russia.
- Colleges and universities should voluntarily implement a standardized testing program to ensure student learning outcomes are similar across different institutions.

In each of these claims, the goal is to sway one's audience to a specific attitude, value, or belief, but not necessarily to get the audience to enact any specific behaviors.

Gain Immediate Action

The alternative to passive agreement is immediate action, or persuading your audience to start enga-ging in a specific behavior. Many passive agreement topics can become immediate action-oriented top-ics as soon as you tell your audience what behavior they should engage in (e.g., sign a petition, call a senator, vote). While it is much easier to elicit passive agreement than to get people to do something, you should always try to get your audience to act and do so quickly. A common mistake that speakers make is telling people to enact a behavior that will occur in the future. The longer it takes for people to engage in the action you desire, the less likely it is that your audience will engage in that behavior.

Here are some examples of good claims with immediate calls to action:

- College students should eat more fruit, so I am encouraging everyone to eat the apple I have provided you and start getting more fruit in your diet.
- Teaching a child to read is one way to ensure that the next generation will be stronger than those that have come before us, so please sign up right now to volunteer one hour a week to help teach a child to read.
- The United States should reduce its nuclear arsenal by 20 percent over the next five years. Please sign the letter provided encouraging the president to take this necessary step for global peace. Once you've signed the letter, hand it to me, and I'll fax it to the White House today.

Each of these three examples starts with a basic claim and then tags on an immediate call to action. Re-member, the faster you can get people to engage in a behavior the more likely they actually will.

2.4   Value Claims

The final type of claim is a **value claim**, or a claim where the speaker is advocating a judgment claim about something (e.g., it's good or bad, it's right or wrong, it's beautiful or ugly, moral or immoral).

value claim

Persuasive claim advocating a judgment about something (e.g., it's good or bad, it's right or wrong, it's beautiful or ugly, it's moral or immoral).

Let's look at three value claims. We've italicized the evaluative term in each claim:

- Dating people on the Internet is an *immoral* form of dating.
- SUVs are *gas guzzling monstrosities.*
- It's *unfair* for pregnant women to have special parking spaces at malls, shopping centers, and stores.

Each of these three claims could definitely be made by a speaker and other speakers could say the exact opposite. When making a value claim, it's hard to ascertain why someone has chosen a specific value stance without understanding her or his criteria for making the evaluative statement. For example, if someone finds all forms of technology immoral, then it's really no surprise that he or she would find Internet dating immoral as well. As such, you need to clearly explain your criteria for making the evaluative statement. For example, when we examine the SUV claim, if your criteria for the term "gas guzzling monstrosity" are ecological impact, safety, and gas consumption, then your evaluative statement can be more easily understood and evaluated by your audience. If, however, you state that your criterion is that SUVs are bigger than military vehicles and shouldn't be on the road, then your statement takes on a slightly different meaning. Ultimately, when making a value claim, you need to make sure that you clearly label your evaluative term and provide clear criteria for how you came to that evaluation.

KEY TAKEAWAYS

- There are four types of persuasive claims. Definition claims argue the denotation or classification of what something is. Factual claims argue the truth or falsity about an assertion being made. Policy claims argue the nature of a problem and the solution that should be taken. Lastly, value claims argue a judgment about something (e.g., it's good or bad, it's right or wrong, it's beautiful or ugly, moral or immoral).
- Each of the four claims leads to different types of persuasive speeches. As such, public speakers need to be aware what type of claim they are advocating in order to understand the best methods of persuasion.
- In policy claims, persuaders attempt to convince their audiences to either passively accept or actively act. When persuaders attempt to gain passive agreement from an audience, they hope that an audience will agree with what is said about a specific policy without asking the audience to do anything to enact the policy. Gaining immediate action, on the other hand, occurs when a persuader gets the audience to actively engage in a specific behavior.

EXERCISES

1. Look at the list of the top one hundred speeches in the United States during the twentieth century compiled by Stephen E. Lucas and Martin J. Medhurst (http://www.americanrhetoric.com/top100speechesall.html). Select a speech and examine the speech to determine which type of claim is being made by the speech.
2. Look at the list of the top one hundred speeches in the United States during the twentieth century compiled by Stephen E. Lucas and Martin J. Medhurst and find a policy speech (http://www.americanrhetoric.com/top100speechesall.html). Which type of policy outcome was the speech aimed at achieving—passive agreement or immediate action? What evidence do you have from the speech to support your answer?

3. ORGANIZING PERSUASIVE SPEECHES

LEARNING OBJECTIVES

1. Understand three common organizational patterns for persuasive speeches.
2. Explain the steps utilized in Monroe's motivated sequence.
3. Explain the parts of a problem-cause-solution speech.
4. Explain the process utilized in a comparative advantage persuasive speech.

© Thinkstock

Previously in this text we discussed general guidelines for organizing speeches. In this section, we are going to look at three organizational patterns ideally suited for persuasive speeches: Monroe's motivated sequence, problem-cause-solution, and comparative advantages.

3.1 Monroe's Motivated Sequence

One of the most commonly cited and discussed organizational patterns for persuasive speeches is Alan H. Monroe's motivated sequence. The purpose of Monroe's motivated sequence is to help speakers "sequence supporting materials and motivational appeals to form a useful organizational pattern for speeches as a whole."[10]

While Monroe's motivated sequence is commonly discussed in most public speaking textbooks, we do want to provide one minor caution. Thus far, almost no research has been conducted that has demonstrated that Monroe's motivated sequence is any more persuasive than other structural patterns. In the only study conducted experimentally examining Monroe's motivated sequence, the researchers did not find the method more persuasive, but did note that audience members found the pattern more organized than other methods.[11] We wanted to add this sidenote because we don't want you to think that Monroe's motivated sequence is a kind of magic persuasive bullet; the research simply doesn't support this notion. At the same time, research does support that organized messages are perceived as more persuasive as a whole, so using Monroe's motivated sequence to think through one's persuasive argument could still be very beneficial.

Table 17.1 lists the basic steps of Monroe's motivated sequence and the subsequent reaction a speaker desires from his or her audience.

TABLE 17.1 Monroe's Motivated Sequence

Steps	Audience Response
Attention—Getting Attention	I want to listen to the speaker.
Need—Showing the Need, Describing the Problem	Something needs to be done about the problem.
Satisfaction—Satisfying the Need, Presenting the Solution	In order to satisfy the need or fix the problem this is what I need to do.
Visualization—Visualizing the Results	I can see myself enjoying the benefits of taking action.
Action—Requesting Audience Action or Approval	I will act in a specific way or approve a decision or behavior.

Attention

attention step

First step in Monroe's motivated sequence where a speaker attempts to get his or her audience's attention.

The first step in Monroe's motivated sequence is the **attention step**, in which a speaker attempts to get the audience's attention. To gain an audience's attention, we recommend that you think through three specific parts of the attention step. First, you need to have a strong attention-getting device. As previously discussed in Chapter 9, a strong attention getter at the beginning of your speech is very important. Second, you need to make sure you introduce your topic clearly. If your audience doesn't know what your topic is quickly, they are more likely to stop listening. Lastly, you need to explain to your audience why they should care about your topic.

Needs

In the **need step** of Monroe's motivated sequence, the speaker establishes that there is a specific need or problem. In Monroe's conceptualization of need, he talks about four specific parts of the need: statement, illustration, ramification, and pointing. First, a speaker needs to give a clear and concise statement of the problem. This part of a speech should be crystal clear for an audience. Second, the speaker needs to provide one or more examples to illustrate the need. The illustration is an attempt to make the problem concrete for the audience. Next, a speaker needs to provide some kind of evidence (e.g., statistics, examples, testimony) that shows the ramifications or consequences of the problem. Lastly, a speaker needs to point to the audience and show exactly how the problem relates to them personally.

> **needs step**
> Second step in Monroe's motivated sequence where a speaker establishes that there is a specific need or problem.

Satisfaction

In the third step of Monroe's motivated sequence, the **satisfaction step**, the speaker sets out to satisfy the need or solve the problem. Within this step, Monroe (1935) proposed a five-step plan for satisfying a need:

1. Statement
2. Explanation
3. Theoretical demonstration
4. Reference to practical experience
5. Meeting objections

> **satisfaction step**
> Third step in Monroe's motivated sequence where a speaker sets out to satisfy the need or solve the problem.

First, you need to clearly state the attitude, value, belief, or action you want your audience to accept. The purpose of this statement is to clearly tell your audience what your ultimate goal is.

Second, you want to make sure that you clearly explain to your audience why they should accept the attitude, value, belief, or action you proposed. Just telling your audience they should do something isn't strong enough to actually get them to change. Instead, you really need to provide a solid argument for why they should accept your proposed solution.

Third, you need to show how the solution you have proposed meets the need or problem. Monroe calls this link between your solution and the need a theoretical demonstration because you cannot prove that your solution will work. Instead, you theorize based on research and good judgment that your solution will meet the need or solve the problem.

Fourth, to help with this theoretical demonstration, you need to reference practical experience, which should include examples demonstrating that your proposal has worked elsewhere. Research, statistics, and expert testimony are all great ways of referencing practical experience.

Lastly, Monroe recommends that a speaker respond to possible objections. As a persuasive speaker, one of your jobs is to think through your speech and see what counterarguments could be made against your speech and then rebut those arguments within your speech. When you offer rebuttals for arguments against your speech, it shows your audience that you've done your homework and educated yourself about multiple sides of the issue.

Visualization

The next step of Monroe's motivated sequence is the **visualization step**, in which you ask the audience to visualize a future where the need has been met or the problem solved. In essence, the visualization stage is where a speaker can show the audience why accepting a specific attitude, value, belief, or behavior can positively affect the future. When helping people to picture the future, the more concrete your visualization is, the easier it will be for your audience to see the possible future and be persuaded by it. You also need to make sure that you clearly show how accepting your solution will directly benefit your audience.

According to Monroe, visualization can be conducted in one of three ways: positive, negative, or contrast.[12] The positive method of visualization is where a speaker shows how adopting a proposal leads to a better future (e.g., recycle, and we'll have a cleaner and safer planet). Conversely, the negative method of visualization is where a speaker shows how not adopting the proposal will lead to a worse future (e.g., don't recycle, and our world will become polluted and uninhabitable). Monroe also acknowledged that visualization can include a combination of both positive and negative visualization. In essence, you show your audience both possible outcomes and have them decide which one they would rather have.

> **visualization step**
> Fourth step in Monroe's motivated sequence where a speaker asks his or her audience to visualize a future where the need has been met or the problem solved.

Action

The final step in Monroe's motivated sequence is the **action step**, in which a speaker asks an audience to approve the speaker's proposal. For understanding purposes, we break action into two distinct parts: audience action and approval. Audience action refers to direct physical behaviors a speaker wants from an audience (e.g., flossing their teeth twice a day, signing a petition, wearing seat belts). Approval, on the other hand, involves an audience's consent or agreement with a speaker's proposed attitude, value, or belief.

When preparing an action step, it is important to make sure that the action, whether audience action or approval, is realistic for your audience. Asking your peers in a college classroom to donate one thousand dollars to charity isn't realistic. Asking your peers to donate one dollar is considerably more realistic. In a persuasive speech based on Monroe's motivated sequence, the action step will end with the speech's concluding device. As discussed elsewhere in this text, you need to make sure that you conclude in a vivid way so that the speech ends on a high point and the audience has a sense of energy as well as a sense of closure.

Now that we've walked through Monroe's motivated sequence, let's look at how you could use Monroe's motivated sequence to outline a persuasive speech:

Specific Purpose: To persuade my classroom peers that the United States should have stronger laws governing the use of for-profit medical experiments.

Main Points:

- **Attention:** Want to make nine thousand dollars for just three weeks of work lying around and not doing much? Then be a human guinea pig. Admittedly, you'll have to have a tube down your throat most of those three weeks, but you'll earn three thousand dollars a week.

- **Need:** Every day many uneducated and lower socioeconomic-status citizens are preyed on by medical and pharmaceutical companies for use in for-profit medical and drug experiments. Do you want one of your family members to fall prey to this evil scheme?

- **Satisfaction:** The United States should have stronger laws governing the use of for-profit medical experiments to ensure that uneducated and lower-socioeconomic-status citizens are protected.

- **Visualization:** If we enact tougher experiment oversight, we can ensure that medical and pharmaceutical research is conducted in a way that adheres to basic values of American decency. If we do not enact tougher experiment oversight, we could find ourselves in a world where the lines between research subject, guinea pig, and patient become increasingly blurred.

- **Action:** In order to prevent the atrocities associated with for-profit medical and pharmaceutical experiments, please sign this petition asking the US Department of Health and Human Services to pass stricter regulations on this preying industry that is out of control.

This example shows how you can take a basic speech topic and use Monroe's motivated sequence to clearly and easily outline your speech efficiently and effectively.

Table 17.2 also contains a simple checklist to help you make sure you hit all the important components of Monroe's motivated sequence.

TABLE 17.2 Monroe's Motivated Sequence Checklist

Step in the Sequence	Yes	No
Attention Step		
Gained audience's attention	☐	☐
Introduced the topic clearly	☐	☐
Showed the importance of the topic to the audience	☐	☐
Need Step		
Need is summarized in a clear statement	☐	☐
Need is adequately illustrated	☐	☐
Need has clear ramifications	☐	☐
Need clearly points the audience	☐	☐
Satisfaction Step		
Plan is clearly stated	☐	☐
Plan is plainly explained	☐	☐
Plan and solution are theoretically demonstrated	☐	☐
Plan has clear reference to practical experience	☐	☐
Plan can meet possible objections	☐	☐
Visualization Step		
Practicality of plan shown	☐	☐
Benefits of plan are tangible	☐	☐
Benefits of plan relate to the audience	☐	☐
Specific type of visualization chosen (positive method, negative method, method of contrast)	☐	☐
Action Step		
Call of specific action by the audience	☐	☐
Action is realistic for the audience	☐	☐
Concluding device is vivid	☐	☐

3.2 Problem-Cause-Solution

Another format for organizing a persuasive speech is the problem-cause-solution format. In this specific format, you discuss what a problem is, what you believe is causing the problem, and then what the solution should be to correct the problem.

Specific Purpose: To persuade my classroom peers that our campus should adopt a zero-tolerance policy for hate speech.

Main Points:

   I. Demonstrate that there is distrust among different groups on campus that has led to unnecessary confrontations and violence.

   II. Show that the confrontations and violence are a result of hate speech that occurred prior to the events.

   III. Explain how instituting a campus-wide zero-tolerance policy against hate speech could stop the unnecessary confrontations and violence.

In this speech, you want to persuade people to support a new campus-wide policy calling for zero-tolerance of hate speech. Once you have shown the problem, you then explain to your audience that the cause of the unnecessary confrontations and violence is prior incidents of hate speech. Lastly, you argue that a campus-wide zero-tolerance policy could help prevent future unnecessary confrontations and violence. Again, this method of organizing a speech is as simple as its name: problem-cause-solution.

3.3 Comparative Advantages

The final method for organizing a persuasive speech is called the comparative advantages speech format. The goal of this speech is to compare items side-by-side and show why one of them is more advantageous than the other. For example, let's say that you're giving a speech on which e-book reader is better: Amazon.com's Kindle or Barnes and Nobles' Nook. Here's how you could organize this speech:

Specific Purpose: To persuade my audience that the Nook is more advantageous than the Kindle.
Main Points:

I. The Nook allows owners to trade and loan books to other owners or people who have downloaded the Nook software, while the Kindle does not.

II. The Nook has a color-touch screen, while the Kindle's screen is black and grey and noninteractive.

III. The Nook's memory can be expanded through microSD, while the Kindle's memory cannot be upgraded.

As you can see from this speech's organization, the simple goal of this speech is to show why one thing has more positives than something else. Obviously, when you are demonstrating comparative advantages, the items you are comparing need to be functional equivalents—or, as the saying goes, you cannot compare apples to oranges.

KEY TAKEAWAYS

- There are three common patterns that persuaders can utilize to help organize their speeches effectively: Monroe's motivated sequence, problem-cause-solution, and comparative advantage. Each of these patterns can effectively help a speaker think through his or her thoughts and organize them in a manner that will be more likely to persuade an audience.
- Alan H. Monroe's (1935) motivated sequence is a commonly used speech format that is used by many people to effectively organize persuasive messages. The pattern consists of five basic stages: attention, need, satisfaction, visualization, and action. In the first stage, a speaker gets an audience's attention. In the second stage, the speaker shows an audience that a need exists. In the third stage, the speaker shows how his or her persuasive proposal could satisfy the need. The fourth stage shows how the future could be if the persuasive proposal is or is not adopted. Lastly, the speaker urges the audience to take some kind of action to help enact the speaker's persuasive proposal.
- The problem-cause-solution proposal is a three-pronged speech pattern. The speaker starts by explaining the problem the speaker sees. The speaker then explains what he or she sees as the underlying causes of the problem. Lastly, the speaker proposes a solution to the problem that corrects the underlying causes.
- The comparative advantages speech format is utilized when a speaker is comparing two or more things or ideas and shows why one of the things or ideas has more advantages than the other(s).

EXERCISES

1. Create a speech using Monroe's motivated sequence to persuade people to recycle.
2. Create a speech using the problem-cause-solution method for a problem you see on your college or university campus.
3. Create a comparative advantages speech comparing two brands of toothpaste.

4.   CHAPTER EXERCISES

SPEAKING ETHICALLY

Doreen is delivering a speech on the topic of donating money to help feed the children of AIDS victims in Africa. She set up her speech using Monroe's motivated sequence. She sails through attention, need, and satisfaction. She starts delivering her visualization step, and she goes a little crazy. She claims that if more people would donate to this cause, the world would be devoid of hunger, children in Africa could all get an education, and we could establish world peace. She then makes claims that not feeding the children of AIDS victims in Africa could lead to world chaos and nuclear war.

1. Is it ethical to create unrealistic expectations during the visualization step?
2. Should you try to exaggerate the visualization stage if you know, realistically, that the possible outcomes are not that impressive?
3. If Doreen was your friend, how would you respond to this section of her speech? Should you point out that her argument is unethical?

END-OF-CHAPTER ASSESSMENT

1. Which of the following is one of the reasons why Richard Perloff (2003) believes students should study public speaking today, more so than in the past?

    a. The number of persuasive communications has decreased with media consolidation.

    b. Persuasive messages take longer to travel today.

    c. Persuasion has become less institutionalized.

    d. Persuasive communication has become more subtle and devious.

    e. Persuasive communication is more obvious and blatant today.

2. Which theory of persuasion poses that if the discrepancy between the idea proposed by the speaker and the opinion of an audience member is too great, then the likelihood of persuasion decreases dramatically?

    a. social judgment theory

    b. social exchange theory

    c. cognitive dissonance theory

    d. psychodynamic theory

    e. elaboration likelihood model

3. While attempting to persuade an audience, Anne realizes that some of her audience members really like to engage in critical thinking and information processing. Knowing this, Anne makes sure her speech has very sound arguments that are completely supported by relevant research. Which of the five factors that lead to high elaboration discussed by Frymier and Nadler (2007) is shown here?

    a. personal relevance

    b. accountability

    c. personal responsibility

    d. incongruent information

    e. need for cognition

4. Jose gives a speech in which he argues that laws applying to traveling carnivals should not be the same as laws applying to amusement parks because the two are clearly different entities. What type of claim is Jose making?

    a. definitional claim

    b. factual claim

    c. policy claim

    d. value claim

    e. attitude claim

5. During a speech Paula states, "If my plan is enacted, our community will simply be safer. Families will be able to walk with their children without fear of gang violence. Parents and children will be able to go to the park without fear of drug dealers." What part of Monroe's motivated sequence is Paula using?

    a. attention

    b. need

    c. satisfaction

    d. visualization

    e. action

ANSWER KEY

1. d
2. a
3. e
4. a
5. d

ENDNOTES

1. Perloff, R. M. (2003). *The dynamics of persuasion: Communication and attitudes in the 21st Century* (2nd ed.). Mahwah, NJ: Lawrence Erlbaum, pp. 5–6.

2. Frankish, K. (1998). Virtual belief. In P. Carruthers & J. Boucher (Eds.), *Language and thought* (pp. 249–269). Cambridge, UK: Cambridge University Press.

3. Frymier, A. B., & Nadler, M. K. (2007). *Persuasion: Integrating theory, research, and practice*. Dubuque, IA: Kendall/Hunt.

4. Sherif, M., & Hovland, C. I. (1961). *Social judgment: Assimilation and contrast effects in communication and attitude change*. New Haven, CT: Yale University Press.

5. Festinger, L. (1957). *A theory of cognitive dissonance*. Evanston, IL: Row, Peterson, & Company.

6. Frymier, A. B., & Nadler, M. K. (2007). *Persuasion: Integrating theory, research, and practice*. Dubuque, IA: Kendall/Hunt.

7. Festinger, L., & Carlsmith, J. M. (1959). Cognitive consequences of forced compliance. *Journal of Abnormal and Social Psychology, 58*, 203–210.

8. Petty, R. E., & Cacioppo, J. T. (1986). The elaboration likelihood model of persuasion. *Advances in Experimental Social Psychology, 19*, 123–205.

9. Frymier, A. B., & Nadler, M. K. (2007). *Persuasion: Integrating theory, research, and practice*. Dubuque, IA: Kendall/Hunt.

10. German, K. M., Gronbeck, B. E., Ehninger, D., & Monroe, A. H. (2010). *Principles of public speaking* (17th ed.). Boston, MA: Allyn & Bacon, p. 236.

11. Micciche, T., Pryor, B., & Butler, J. (2000). A test of Monroe's motivated sequence for its effects on ratings of message organization and attitude change. *Psychological Reports, 86*, 1135–1138.

12. Monroe, A. H. (1935). *Principles and types of speech*. Chicago, IL: Scott Foresman.

CHAPTER 18
Speaking to Entertain

THE NATURE OF ENTERTAINMENT

Often the speaking opportunities life brings our way have nothing to do specifically with informing or persuading an audience; instead, we are asked to speak to entertain. Whether you are standing up to give an award speech or a toast, knowing how to deliver speeches in a variety of different contexts is the nature of entertaining speaking. In this chapter, we are going to explore what entertaining speeches are; we will also examine two specific types of entertaining speeches: special-occasion speeches and keynote speeches.

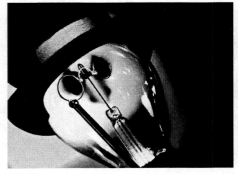

© Thinkstock

1. UNDERSTANDING ENTERTAINING SPEECHES

LEARNING OBJECTIVES

1. Understand the purpose of entertaining speeches.
2. Explain the four ingredients of a good entertaining speech.

In broad terms, an **entertaining speech** is a speech designed to captivate an audience's attention and regale or amuse them while delivering a message. Like more traditional informative or persuasive speeches, entertaining speeches should communicate a clear message, but the manner of speaking used in an entertaining speech is typically different. Entertaining speeches are often delivered on special occasions (e.g., a toast at a wedding, an acceptance speech at an awards banquet, a motivational speech at a conference), which is why they are sometimes referred to as special-occasion speeches. However, they can also be given on more mundane occasions, where their purpose is primarily to amuse audience members or arouse them emotionally in some way. Remember, when we use the word "entertain," we are referring not just to humor but also to drama. The goal of an entertaining speech is to stir an audience's emotions.

Of all the types of speeches we come in contact with during our lives, the bulk of them will probably fall into the category of entertainment. If you spend just one evening watching a major awards show (e.g., the Grammys, the Tonys, the Oscars), you'll see dozens of acceptance speeches. While some of these acceptance speeches are good and others may be terrible, they all belong in the category of speaking to entertain.

© Thinkstock

Other speeches that fall into the entertaining category are designed to inspire or motivate an audience to do something. These are, however, different from a traditional persuasive speech. While entertaining speeches are often persuasive, we differentiate the two often based on the rhetorical situation itself. Maybe your school has hired a speaker to talk about his or her life story in an attempt to inspire the audience to try harder in school and reach for the best that life has to offer. You can imagine how this speech would be different from a traditional persuasive speech focusing on, say, the statistics related to scholastic achievement and success later in life.

Entertaining speeches are definitely very common, but that doesn't mean they don't require effort and preparation. A frequent trap is that people often think of entertaining speeches as corny. As a result, they don't prepare seriously but rather stand up to speak with the idea that they can "wing it" by acting silly and telling a few jokes. Instead of being entertaining, the speech falls flat. To help us think through how to be effective in delivering entertaining speeches, let's look at four key ingredients: preparation, adaptation to the occasion, adaptation to the audience, and mindfulness about the time.

entertaining speech

Speech designed to captivate an audience's attention and regale or amuse them while delivering a clear message.

1.1 Be Prepared

First, and foremost, the biggest mistake you can make when standing to deliver an entertaining speech is to underprepare or simply not prepare at all. We've stressed the need for preparation throughout this text, so just because you're giving a wedding toast or a eulogy doesn't mean you shouldn't think through the speech before you stand up and speak out. If the situation is impromptu, even jotting some basic notes on a napkin is better than not having any plan for what you are going to say. Remember, when you get anxious, as it inevitably happens in front of an audience, your brain doesn't function as well as when you are having a relaxed conversation with friends. You often forget information. By writing down some simple notes, you'll be less likely to deliver a bad speech.

1.2 Be Adaptive to the Occasion

Not all content is appropriate for all occasions. If you are asked to deliver a speech commemorating the first anniversary of a school shooting, then obviously using humor and telling jokes wouldn't be appropriate. But some decisions about adapting to the occasion are less obvious. Consider the following examples:

- You are the maid of honor giving a toast at the wedding of your younger sister.
- You are receiving a Most Valuable Player award in your favorite sport.
- You are a sales representative speaking to a group of clients after a mistake has been discovered.
- You are a cancer survivor speaking at a high school student assembly.

How might you adapt your message and speaking style to successfully entertain these various audiences?

Remember that being a competent speaker is about being both personally effective and socially appropriate. Different occasions will call for different levels of social appropriateness. One of the biggest mistakes entertaining speakers can make is to deliver one generic speech to different groups without adapting the speech to the specific occasion. In fact, professional speakers always make sure that their speeches are tailored for different occasions by getting information about the occasion from their hosts. When we tailor speeches for special occasions, people are more likely to remember those speeches than if we give a generic speech.

1.3 Be Adaptive to Your Audience

Once again, we cannot stress the importance of audience adaptation enough in this text. Different audiences will respond differently to speech material, so the more you know about your audience the more likely you'll succeed in your speech. One of our coauthors was once at a conference for teachers of public speaking. The keynote speaker stood and delivered a speech on the importance of public speaking. While the speaker was good and funny, the speech really fell flat. The keynote speaker basically told the public speaking teachers that they should take public speaking courses because public speaking is important. Right speech, wrong audience!

1.4 Be Mindful of the Time

The last major consideration for delivering entertaining speeches successfully is to be mindful of your time. Different entertaining speech situations have their own conventions and rules with regard to time. Acceptance speeches and toasts, for example, should be relatively short (typically under five minutes). A speech of introduction should be extremely brief—just long enough to tell the audience what they need to know about the person being introduced in a style that prepares them to appreciate that person's remarks. In contrast, commencement speeches and speeches to commemorate events can run ten to twenty minutes in length.

It's also important to recognize that audiences on different occasions will expect speeches of various lengths. For example, although it's true that graduation commencement speakers generally speak for ten to twenty minutes, the closer that speaker heads toward twenty minutes the more fidgety the audience becomes. To hold the audience's attention and fulfill the goal of entertaining, a commencement speaker would do well to make the closing minutes of the speech the most engaging and inspiring portion of the speech. If you're not sure about the expected time frame for a speech, either ask the person who has invited you to speak or do some quick research to see what the average speech times in the given context tend to be.

2. SPECIAL-OCCASION SPEECHES

LEARNING OBJECTIVES

1. Identify the different types of ceremonial speaking.
2. Describe the different types of inspirational speaking.

Many entertaining speeches fall under the category of special-occasion speeches. All the speeches in this category are given to mark the significance of particular events. Common events include weddings, bar mitzvahs, awards ceremonies, funerals, and political events. In each of these different occasions, speakers are asked to deliver speeches relating to the event. For purposes of simplicity, we've broken special-occasion speeches into two groups: ceremonial speaking and inspirational speaking.

© *Thinkstock*

2.1 Ceremonial Speaking

Ceremonial speeches are speeches given during a ceremony or a ritual marked by observance of formality or etiquette. These ceremonies tend to be very special for people, so it shouldn't be surprising that they are opportunities for speech making. Let's examine each of the eight types of ceremonial speaking: introductions, presentations, acceptances, dedications, toasts, roasts, eulogies, and farewells.

ceremonial speech

Speeches given during a ceremony or a ritual marked by observance of formality or etiquette.

Speeches of Introduction

The first type of speech is called the **speech of introduction**, which is a minispeech given by the host of a ceremony that introduces another speaker and his or her speech. Few things are worse than when the introducer or a speaker stands up and says, "This is Joe Smith, he's going to talk about stress." While we did learn the speaker's name and the topic, the introduction falls flat. Audiences won't be the least bit excited about listening to Joe's speech.

Just like any other speech, a speech of introduction should be a complete speech and have a clear introduction, body, and conclusion—and you should do it all in under two minutes. This brings up another "few things are worse" scenario: an introductory speaker who rambles on for too long or who talks about himself or herself instead of focusing on the person being introduced.

For an introduction, think of a hook that will make your audience interested in the upcoming speaker. Did you read a news article related to the speaker's topic? Have you been impressed by a presentation you've heard the speaker give in the past? You need to find something that can grab the audience's attention and make them excited about hearing the main speaker.

The body of your introductory speech should be devoted to telling the audience about the speaker's topic, why the speaker is qualified, and why the audience should listen (notice we now have our

speech of introduction

Speech given by the host of a ceremony that introduces another speaker and his or her speech.

three body points). First, tell your audience in general terms about the overarching topic of the speech. Most of the time as an introducer, you'll only have a speech title and maybe a paragraph of information to help guide this part of your speech. That's all right. You don't need to know all the ins and outs of the main speaker's speech; you just need to know enough to whet the audience's appetite. Next, you need to tell the audience why the speaker is a credible speaker on the topic. Has the speaker written books or articles on the subject? Has the speaker had special life events that make him or her qualified? Lastly, you need to briefly explain to the audience why they should care about the upcoming speech.

The final part of a good introduction is the conclusion, which is generally designed to welcome the speaker to the lectern. Many introducers will conclude by saying something like, "I am looking forward to hearing how Joe Smith's advice and wisdom can help all of us today, so please join me in welcoming Mr. Joe Smith." We've known some presenters who will even add a notation to their notes to "start clapping" and "shake speakers hand" or "give speaker a hug" depending on the circumstances of the speech.

Now that we've walked through the basic parts of an introductory speech, let's see one outlined:

Specific Purpose: To entertain the audience while preparing them for Janice Wright's speech on rituals.

Introduction: Mention some common rituals people in the United States engage in (Christmas, sporting events, legal proceedings).

Main Points:

I. Explain that the topic was selected because understanding how cultures use ritual is an important part of understanding what it means to be human.

II. Janice Wright is a cultural anthropologist who studies the impact that everyday rituals have on communities.

III. All of us engage in rituals, and we often don't take the time to determine how these rituals were started and how they impact our daily routines.

Conclusion: I had the opportunity to listen to Dr. Wright at the regional conference in Springfield last month, and I am excited that I get to share her with all of you tonight. Please join me in welcoming Dr. Wright (start clapping, shake speaker's hand, exit stage).

Speeches of Presentation

The second type of common ceremonial speech is the **speech of presentation**. A speech of presentation is a brief speech given to accompany a prize or honor. Speeches of presentation can be as simple as saying, "This year's recipient of the Schuman Public Speaking prize is Wilhelmina Jeffers," or could last up to five minutes as the speaker explains why the honoree was chosen for the award.

When preparing a speech of presentation, it's always important to ask how long the speech should be. Once you know the time limit, then you can set out to create the speech itself. First, you should explain what the award or honor is and why the presentation is important. Second, you can explain what the recipient has accomplished in order for the award to be bestowed. Did the person win a race? Did the person write an important piece of literature? Did the person mediate conflict? Whatever the recipient has done, you need to clearly highlight his or her work. Lastly, if the race or competition was conducted in a public forum and numerous people didn't win, you may want to recognize those people for their efforts as well. While you don't want to steal the show away from winner (as Kanye West did to Taylor Swift during the 2009 MTV Music Video Awards, for example http://www.mtv.com/videos/misc/435995/taylor-swift-wins-best-female-video.jhtml#id=1620605), you may want to highlight the work of the other competitors or nominees.

Speeches of Acceptance

The complement to a speech of presentation is the **speech of acceptance**. The speech of acceptance is a speech given by the recipient of a prize or honor. For example, in the above video clip from the 2009 MTV Music Video Awards, Taylor Swift starts by expressing her appreciation, gets interrupted by Kanye West, and ends by saying, "I would like to thank the fans and MTV, thank you." While obviously not a traditional acceptance speech because of the interruption, she did manage to get in the important parts.

There are three typical components of a speech of acceptance: thank the givers of the award or honor, thank those who helped you achieve your goal, and put the award or honor into perspective. First, you want to thank the people who have given you the award or honor and possibly those who voted for you. We see this done every year during the Oscars, "First, I'd like to thank the academy and all the academy voters." Second, you want to give credit to those who helped you achieve the award or honor. No person accomplishes things in life on his or her own. We all have families and friends and colleagues who support us and help us achieve what we do in life, and a speech of acceptance is a great time to graciously recognize those individuals. Lastly, put the award in perspective. Tell the people listening to your speech why the award is meaningful to you.

Speeches of Dedication

The fourth ceremonial speech is the **speech of dedication**. A speech of dedication is delivered when a new store opens, a building is named after someone, a plaque is placed on a wall, a new library is completed, and so on. These speeches are designed to highlight the importance of the project and possibly those to whom the project has been dedicated. Maybe your great-uncle has died and left your college tons of money, so the college has decided to rename one of the dorms after your great-uncle. In this case, you may be asked to speak at the dedication.

When preparing the speech of dedication, start by explaining how you are involved in the dedication. If the person to whom the dedication is being made is a relative, tell the audience that the building is being named after your great-uncle who bestowed a gift to his alma mater. Second, you want to explain what is being dedicated. If the dedication is a new building or a preexisting building, you want to explain what is being dedicated and the importance of the structure. You should then explain who was involved in the project. If the project is a new structure, talk about the people who built the structure or designed it. If the project is a preexisting structure, talk about the people who put together and decided on the dedication. Lastly, explain why the structure is important for the community where it's located. If the dedication is for a new store, talk about how the store will bring in new jobs and new shopping opportunities. If the dedication is for a new wing of a hospital, talk about how patients will be served and the advances in medicine the new wing will provide the community.

> **speech of dedication**
>
> Speech delivered when a new store opens, a building is named after someone, a plaque is placed on a wall, when a new library is completed, and so on.

Toasts

At one time or another, almost everyone is going to be asked to deliver a **toast**. A toast is a speech designed to congratulate, appreciate, or remember. First, toasts can be delivered for the purpose of congratulating someone for an honor, a new job, or getting married. You can also toast someone to show your appreciation for something they've done. Lastly, we toast people to remember them and what they have accomplished.

When preparing a toast, the first goal is always to keep your remarks brief. Toasts are generally given during the middle of some kind of festivities (e.g., wedding, retirement party, farewell party), and you don't want your toast to take away from those festivities for too long. Second, the goal of a toast is to focus attention on the person or persons being toasted—not on the speaker. As such, while you are speaking you need to focus your attention to the people being toasted, both by physically looking at them and by keeping your message about them. You should also avoid any inside jokes between you and the people being toasted because toasts are public and should be accessible for everyone who hears them. To conclude a toast, simply say something like, "Please join me in recognizing Joan for her achievement" and lift your glass. When you lift your glass, this will signal to others to do the same and then you can all take a drink, which is the end of your speech.

> **toast**
>
> Speech designed to congratulate, appreciate, or remember.

Roasts

The **roast** speech is a very interesting and peculiar speech because it is designed to both praise and good-naturedly insult a person being honored. Generally, roasts are given at the conclusion of a banquet in honor of someone's life achievements. The television station Comedy Central has been conducting roasts of various celebrities for a few years.

In this clip, watch as Stephen Colbert, television host of *The Colbert Report*, roasts President George W. Bush.

http://www.youtube.com/watch?v=BSE_saVX_2A

Let's pick this short clip apart. You'll notice that the humor doesn't pull any punches. The goal of the roast is to both praise and insult in a good-natured manner. You'll also see that the roaster, in this case Stephen Colbert, is standing behind a lectern while the roastee, President George W. Bush, is clearly on display for the audience to see, and periodically you'll see the camera pan to President Bush to take in his reactions. Half the fun of a good roast is watching the roastee's reactions during the roast, so it's important to have the roastee clearly visible by the audience.

How does one prepare for a roast? First, you want to really think about the person who is being roasted. Do they have any strange habits or amusing stories in their past that you can discuss? When you think through these things you want to make sure that you cross anything off your list that is truly private information or will really hurt the person. The goal of a roast is to poke at them, not massacre them. Second, when selecting which aspects to poke fun at, you need to make sure that the items you choose are widely known by your audience. Roasts work when the majority of people in the audience can relate to the jokes being made. If you have an inside joke with the roastee, bringing it up during roast may be great fun for the two of you, but it will leave your audience unimpressed. Lastly, end on a

> **roast**
>
> Speech designed to both praise and good-naturedly insult a person being honored.

positive note. While the jokes are definitely the fun part of a roast, you should leave the roastee knowing that you truly do care about and appreciate the person.

Eulogies

eulogy

Speech given in honor of someone who has died.

A **eulogy** is a speech given in honor of someone who has died. (Don't confuse "eulogy" with "elegy," a poem or song of mourning.) Unless you are a minister, priest, rabbi, imam, or other form of religious leader, you'll probably not deliver too many eulogies in your lifetime. However, when the time comes to deliver a eulogy, it's good to know what you're doing and to adequately prepare your remarks. Watch the following clip of then-Senator Barack Obama delivering a eulogy at the funeral of civil rights activist Rosa Parks in November of 2005.

http://www.youtube.com/watch?v=pRsH92sJCr4

In this eulogy, Senator Obama delivers the eulogy by recalling Rosa Parks importance and her legacy in American history.

When preparing a eulogy, first you need to know as much information about the deceased as possible. The more information you have about the person, the more personal you can make the eulogy. While you can rely on your own information if you were close to the deceased, it is always a good idea to ask friends and relatives of the deceased for their memories, as these may add important facets that may not have occurred to you. Of course, if you were not very close to the deceased, you will need to ask friends and family for information. Second, although eulogies are delivered on the serious and sad occasion of a funeral or memorial service for the deceased, it is very helpful to look for at least one point to be lighter or humorous. In some cultures, in fact, the friends and family attending the funeral will expect the eulogy to be highly entertaining and amusing. While eulogies are not roasts, one goal of the humor or lighter aspects of a eulogy is to relieve the tension that is created by the serious nature of the occasion. Lastly, remember to tell the deceased's story. Tell the audience about who this person was and what the person stood for in life. The more personal you can make a eulogy, the more touching it will be for the deceased's friends and families. The eulogy should remind the audience to celebrate the person's life as well as mourn their death.

Speeches of Farewell

speech of farewell

Speech designed to allow someone to say good-bye to one part of his or her life as he or she is moving on to the next part of life.

A **speech of farewell** allows someone to say good-bye to one part of his or her life as he or she is moving on to the next part of life. Maybe you've accepted a new job and are leaving your current job, or you're graduating from college and entering the work force. Whatever the case may be, periods of transition are often marked by speeches of farewell. Watch the following clip of Derek Jeter's 2008 speech saying farewell to Yankee Stadium, built in 1923, before the New York Yankees moved to the new stadium that opened in 2009.

http://www.youtube.com/watch?v=HJrlTpQm0to

In this speech, Derek Jeter is not only saying good-bye to Yankee Stadium but also thanking the fans for their continued support.

When preparing a speech of farewell, the goal should be to thank the people in your current position and let them know how much you appreciate them as you make the move to your next position in life. In Derek Jeter's speech, he starts by talking about the history of the 1923 Yankee Stadium and then thanks the fans for their support. Second, you want to express to your audience how much the experience has meant to you. A farewell speech is a time to commemorate and think about the good times you've had. As such, you should avoid negativity during this speech. Lastly, you want to make sure that you end on a high note. Derek Jeter concludes his speech by saying, "On behalf of this entire organization, we just want to take this moment to salute you, the greatest fans in the world!" at which point Jeter and the other players take off their ball caps and hold them up toward the audience.

2.2 Inspirational Speaking

inspirational speech

Speech designed to elicit or arouse an emotional state within an audience.

The goal of an **inspirational speech** is to elicit or arouse an emotional state within an audience. In Section 2, we looked at ceremonial speeches. Although some inspirational speeches are sometimes tied to ceremonial occasions, there are also other speaking contexts that call for inspirational speeches. For our purposes, we are going to look at two types of inspirational speeches: goodwill and speeches of commencement.

Speeches to Ensure Goodwill

Goodwill is an intangible asset that is made up of the favor or reputation of an individual or organization. **Speeches of goodwill** are often given in an attempt to get audience members to view the person or organization more favorably. Although speeches of goodwill are clearly persuasive, they try not to be obvious about the persuasive intent and are often delivered as information-giving speeches that focus on an individual or organization's positives attributes. There are three basic types of speeches of goodwill: public relations, justification, and apology.

Speeches for Public Relations

In a public relations speech, the speaker is speaking to enhance one's own image or the image of his or her organization. You can almost think of these speeches as cheerleading speeches because the ultimate goal is to get people to like the speaker and what he or she represents. In the following brief speech, the CEO of British Petroleum is speaking to reporters about what his organization is doing during the 2010 oil spill in the Gulf of Mexico.

http://www.youtube.com/watch?v=cCfa6AxmUHw

Notice that he keeps emphasizing what his company is doing to fix the problem. Every part of this speech is orchestrated to make BP look caring and attempts to get some amount of goodwill from the viewing public.

Speeches of Justification

The second common speech of goodwill is the speech of justification, which is given when someone attempts to defend why certain actions were taken or will be taken. In these speeches, speakers have already enacted (or decided to enact) some kind of behavior, and are now attempting to justify why the behavior is or was appropriate. In the following clip, President Bill Clinton discusses his decision to bomb key Iraqi targets after uncovering a plot to assassinate former President George H. W. Bush.

http://www.youtube.com/watch?v=6mpWa7wNr5M

In this speech, President Clinton outlines his reasons for bombing Iraq to the American people and the globe. Again, the goal of this speech is to secure goodwill for President Clinton's decisions both in the United States and on the world stage.

Speeches of Apology

The final speech of goodwill is the speech of apology. Frankly, these speeches have become more and more commonplace. Every time we turn around, a politician, professional athlete, musician, or actor/actress is doing something reprehensible and getting caught. In fact, the speech of apology has quickly become a fodder for humor as well. Let's take a look at a real apology speech delivered by professional golfer Tiger Woods.

http://www.youtube.com/watch?v=Xs8nseNP4s0

When you need to make an apology speech, there are three elements that you need to include: be honest and take responsibility, say you're sorry, and offer restitution. First, a speaker needs to be honest and admit to doing something wrong. The worst apology speeches are those in which the individual tries to sidestep the wrongdoing. Even if you didn't do anything wrong, it is often best to take responsibility from a public perception perspective. Second, say that you are sorry. People need to know that you are remorseful for what you've done. One of the problems many experts saw with Tiger Woods's speech is that he doesn't look remorseful at all. While the words coming out of his mouth are appropriate, he looks like a robot forced to read from a manuscript written by his press agent. Lastly, you need to offer restitution. Restitution can come in the form of fixing something broken or a promise not to engage in such behavior in the future. People in society are very willing to forgive and forget when they are asked.

Speeches for Commencements

The second type of inspirational speech is the **speech of commencement**, which is designed to recognize and celebrate the achievements of a graduating class or other group of people. The most typical form of commencement speech happens when someone graduates from school. Nearly all of us have sat through commencement speeches at some point in our lives. And if you're like us, you've heard good ones and bad ones. Numerous celebrities and politicians have been asked to deliver commencement speeches at colleges and universities. One famous and well-thought-out commencement speech was given by famed *Harry Potter* author J. K. Rowling at Harvard University in 2008.

http://www.youtube.com/watch?v=nkREt4ZB-ck

J. K. Rowling's speech has the perfect balance of humor and inspiration, which are two of the main ingredients of a great commencement speech.

goodwill
An intangible asset that is made up of the favor or reputation of an individual or organization.

speech of goodwill
Speech given in an attempt to get audience members to view the person or organization more favorably.

speech of commencement
Speech designed to recognize and celebrate the achievements of a group of people.

If you're ever asked to deliver a commencement speech, there are some key points to think through when deciding on your speech's content.

- If there is a specific theme for the graduation, make sure that your commencement speech addresses that theme. If there is no specific theme, come up with one for your speech. Some common commencement speech themes are commitment, competitiveness, competence, confidence, decision making, discipline, ethics, failure (and overcoming failure), faith, generosity, integrity, involvement, leadership, learning, persistence, personal improvement, professionalism, reality, responsibility, and self-respect.

- Talk about your life and how graduates can learn from your experiences to avoid pitfalls or take advantages of life. How can your life inspire the graduates in their future endeavors?

- Make the speech humorous. Commencement speeches should be entertaining and make an audience laugh.

- Be brief! Nothing is more painful than a commencement speaker who drones on and on. Remember, the graduates are there to get their diplomas; their families are there to watch the graduates walk across the stage.

- Remember, while you may be the speaker, you've been asked to impart wisdom and advice for the people graduating and moving on with their lives, so keep it focused on them.

- Place the commencement speech into the broader context of the graduates' lives. Show the graduates how the advice and wisdom you are offering can be utilized to make their own lives better.

Overall, it's important to make sure that you have fun when delivering a commencement speech. Remember, it's a huge honor and responsibility to be asked to deliver a commencement speech, so take the time to really think through and prepare your speech.

KEY TAKEAWAYS

- There are eight common forms of ceremonial speaking: introduction, presentation, acceptance, dedication, toast, roast, eulogy, and farewell. Speeches of introduction are designed to introduce a speaker. Speeches of presentation are given when an individual is presenting an award of some kind. Speeches of acceptance are delivered by the person receiving an award or honor. Speeches of dedication are given when a new building or other place is being opened for the first time. Toasts are given to acknowledge and honor someone on a special occasion (e.g., wedding, birthday, retirement). Roasts are speeches designed to both praise and good-naturedly insult a person being honored. Eulogies are given during funerals and memorial services. Lastly, speeches of farewell are delivered by an individual who is leaving a job, community, or organization, and wants to acknowledge how much the group has meant.

- Inspirational speeches fall into two categories: goodwill (e.g., public relations, justification, and apology) and speeches of commencement. Speeches of goodwill attempt to get audience members to view the person or organization more favorably. On the other hand, speeches of commencement are delivered to recognize the achievements of a group of people.

EXERCISES

1. Imagine you've been asked to speak before a local civic organization such as the Kiwanis or Rotary Club. Develop a sample speech of introduction that you would like someone to give to introduce you.

2. You've been asked to roast your favorite celebrity. Develop a two-minute roast.

3. Develop a speech of commencement for your public speaking class.

3.   KEYNOTE SPEAKING

LEARNING OBJECTIVES

1. Understand the purpose of keynote speeches in society.
2. Explain the basic objective of an after-dinner speech.
3. Describe the purpose and types of motivational speeches.

The last type of entertaining speech we will examine is the keynote speech. A **keynote speech** is delivered to set the underlying tone and summarize the core message of an event. Keynotes are often given at the end of an event; there can also be a number of keynote speeches delivered throughout a longer event that lasts for several days. People who deliver keynote speeches are typically experts in a given area who are invited to speak at a conference, convention, banquet, meeting, or other kind of event for the purpose of setting a specific tone for the occasion. Some keynote speakers will actually work for a **speakers bureau**, an agency that represents celebrity and professional speakers. One very important organization for all aspiring keynote speakers is the National Speaker's Association (NSA, http://www.nsaspeaker.org). NSA also publishes a widely respected magazine for professional speakers called *Speaker* magazine, which can be accessed for free from their website (http://www.nsaspeaker-magazine.org).

© *Thinkstock*

In the world of professional public speaking, there are two common types of keynotes: after-dinner speeches and motivational speeches. Let's look at each of these unique speeches.

3.1   After-Dinner Speaking

After-dinner speaking gets its name from the idea that these speeches historically followed a meal of some kind. After-dinner speakers are generally asked to speak (or hired to speak) because they have the ability both to speak effectively and to make people laugh. First and foremost, after-dinner speeches are speeches and not stand-up comedy routines. All the basic conventions of public speaking previously discussed in this text apply to after-dinner speeches, but the overarching goal of these speeches is to be entertaining and to create an atmosphere of amusement.

After-dinner speaking is probably the hardest type of speaking to do well because it is an entertaining speech that depends on the successful delivery of humor. People train for years to develop **comic timing**, or the verbal and nonverbal delivery used to enhance the comedic value of a message. But after-dinner speaking is difficult, not impossible. Here is the method we recommend for developing a successful after-dinner speech.

First, use all that you have learned about informative or persuasive speeches to prepare a real informative or persuasive speech roughly two-thirds the length of what the final speech will become. That is, if you're going to be giving a ten-minute speech, then your "real" informative or persuasive speech should be six or seven minutes in length.

Next, go back through the speech and look for opportunities to insert humorous remarks. Table 18.1 lists various forms of verbal humor that are often used in the textual portion of a speech.

keynote speech

Speech delivered to set the underlying tone and summarize the core message of an event.

speakers bureau

Agency that represents celebrity and professional speakers.

after-dinner speaking

Speech that is informative or persuasive but also designed to elicit laughter from one's audience.

comic timing

The verbal and nonverbal delivery that someone uses to enhance the comedic value of a message.

TABLE 18.1 Forms of Verbal Humor

Type of Humor	Example
Acronym/Abbreviation	CIA—Certified Idiots Anonymous
	LAPD—Lunatics And Punishment Dispensers
Humorous Advertisement or News Headline	"Tiger Woods Plays with Own Balls, Nike Says"
	"A-Rod Goes Deep, Wang Hurt"
	"Federal Agents Raid Gun Shop, Find Weapons"
Aside	They are otherwise known as oxymorons, which are not people who don't know how to use acne medication.
	Colostomy, wasn't he one of the Greek Gods?
Definition	"A banker is a fellow who lends you his umbrella when the sun is shining and wants it back the minute it begins to rain." Mark Twain
	Spoiled rotten, or what happens to kids after spending just ten minutes with their grandparents.
Oxymoron	Scheduled emergency
	Gourmet spam
	Recreational hospital
Pleonasm	Frozen ice
	Sharp point
	Killed dead
Malapropism	He's a vast suppository of information (*suppository* should be *repository*).
	This is bound to create dysentery in the ranks (*dysentery* should be *dissent*).
One-Liner or Quotation	Better to remain silent and be thought a fool, than to speak and remove all doubt. —Abraham Lincoln
	A computer once beat me at chess, but it was no match for me at kick boxing. —Emo Philips
	Men occasionally stumble over the truth, but most of them pick themselves up and hurry off as if nothing had happened. —Winston Churchill
	In the first place God made idiots; this was for practice. Then he made school boards. —Mark Twain
Self-Effacing Humor	I looked over at my clock and it said 7:30, and I had to be at work by 8:00. I got up, got dressed, and sped to the office. Only then did I realize that it was 7:30 p.m. and not 7:30 a.m.
	"Thomas Jefferson once said, 'One should not worry about chronological age compared to the ability to perform the task.'…Ever since Thomas Jefferson told me that I stopped worrying about my age." —Ronald Reagan
Word Combination with Unusual Visual Effects	That kid was about as useful as a football bat.
	He was finer than frog hair.

Each of these is a possible humor device that could be implemented in a speech. Read the following speech delivered by Mark Twain on his seventieth birthday for a good example of an after-dinner speech (http://etext.lib.virginia.edu/railton/onstage/70bday.html).

Once you've looked through your speech, examining places for verbal humor, think about any physical humor or props that would enhance your speech. Physical humor is great if you can pull it off without being self-conscious. One of the biggest mistakes any humorist makes is to become too aware of what his or her body is doing because it's then harder to be free and funny. As for props, after-dinner speakers have been known to use everything from oversize inflatable baseball bats to rubber clown noses. The goal for a funny prop is that it adds to the humor of the speech without distracting from its message.

Last, and probably most important, try the humor out on real, live people. This is important for three reasons.

First, the success of humor depends heavily on delivery, and especially timing in delivery. You will need practice to polish your delivery so that your humor comes across. If you can't make it through one of your jokes without cracking up, you will need to either incorporate the self-crackup into your delivery or forgo using that joke.

Second, just because you find something unbelievably funny in your head doesn't mean that it will make anyone else laugh. Often, humor that we have written down on paper just doesn't translate when orally presented. You may have a humorous story that you love reading on paper, but find that it just seems to drone on once you start telling it out loud. Furthermore, remember there is a difference between written and verbal language, and this also translates to how humor is interpreted.

Third, you need to make sure the humor you choose will be appropriate for a specific audience. What one audience finds funny another may find offensive. Humor is the double-edged sword of public speaking. On one side, it is an amazing and powerful speaking tool, but on the other side, few things will alienate an audience more than offensive humor. If you're ever uncertain about whether a piece of humor will offend your audience, don't use it.

The following are some other tips for using humor from people who have professionally given after-dinner speeches and learned the hard way what to do and what to avoid:

- Personalize or localize humor when possible.
- Be clear about which words need emphasis with verbal humor.
- Be sure the punch line is at the end. Don't let on where the joke is going.
- Don't announce, "This is funny." or "I'm not very good at telling jokes, but…"
- Don't try to use humor that you don't know well.
- Don't use humor that you personally don't find funny.
- Don't apologize if others don't laugh.
- Don't try to explain the humor if it fails—just move on.
- Don't drag it out! Remember, brevity is the soul of wit.
- Know when to stop joking and be serious.
- Be natural and have fun!

3.2 Motivational Speaking

The second common form of keynote speaking is motivational speaking. A **motivational speech** is designed not only to make an audience experience emotional arousal (fear, sadness, joy, excitement) but also to motivate the audience to do something with that emotional arousal. Whereas a traditional persuasive speech may want listeners to purchase product X or agree with ideology Y, a motivational speech helps to inspire people in a broader fashion, often without a clearly articulated end result in mind. As such, motivational speaking is a highly specialized form of persuasive speaking commonly delivered in schools, businesses, religious, and club or group contexts. *The Toastmasters International Guide to Successful Speaking* lists four types of motivational speeches: hero, survivor, religious, and success.[1]

The **hero speech** is a motivational speech given by someone who is considered a hero in society (e.g., military speakers, political figures, and professional athletes). Just type "motivational speech" into YouTube and you'll find many motivational speeches given by individuals who can be considered heroes or role models. The following clip presents a speech by Steve Sax, a former major league baseball player.

    http://www.youtube.com/watch?v=R4ITFlbcu8g

In this speech, Sax talks about his life as a baseball player, along with issues related to leadership, overcoming obstacles, and motivation.

The **survivor speech** is a speech given by someone who has survived a personal tragedy or who has faced and overcome serious adversity. In the following clip, cancer survivor Becky M. Olsen discusses her life as a cancer survivor.

    http://www.youtube.com/watch?v=zuo1u_C9_3g

Becky Olsen goes all over the country talking with and motivating cancer survivors to beat the odds.

The **religious speech** is fairly self-explanatory; it is designed to incorporate religious ideals into a motivational package to inspire an audience into thinking about or changing aspects of their religious lives. One highly sought-after religious speaker in the United States is Joel Osteen, head minister at Lakewood Church in Houston, Texas. In this clip, Joel is talking about finding and retaining joy in life.

    http://www.youtube.com/watch?v=qp8KixxAk60

The crux of Osteen's speech is learning how to take responsibility of one's own life and let others take responsibility for their lives.

motivational speech

Speech designed not only to make an audience experience an emotional arousal (fear, sadness, joy, excitement) but also to motivate the audience to do something with that arousal.

hero speech

Type of motivational speech given by someone who is considered a hero in society (e.g., military leader, political figure, professional athlete).

survivor speech

Type of motivational speech given by someone who has survived a personal tragedy or has faced and overcome serious adversity.

religious speech

Type of motivational speech designed to incorporate religious ideals into a motivational package to inspire an audience into thinking about or changing aspects of their religious lives.

The final type of motivational speech is the **success speech**, which is given by someone who has succeeded in some aspect of life and is giving back by telling others how they too can be successful. In the following clip the then CEO of Xerox, Anne Mulcahy, speaks before a group of students at Dartmouth College discussing the spirit of entrepreneurship.

http://www.youtube.com/watch?v=IlnLfKWAPnw

In this speech, Mulcahy shares the leadership lessons she had learned as the CEO of Xerox.

KEY TAKEAWAYS

- Keynote speeches are delivered to set the underlying tone and summarize the core message of an event.
- After-dinner speeches are real informative or persuasive speeches with a secondary objective of making the audience laugh. Effective after-dinner speakers must first know how to effectively write a speech and then find appropriate humor to add to the presentation.
- Motivational speeches are designed not only to make an audience experience emotional arousal (fear, sadness, joy, excitement) but also to ask the audience to do something with that emotional arousal. There are four types of motivational speeches: the hero, the survivor, the religious, and the success.

EXERCISES

1. Take one of the speeches you've delivered in class and think of ways to add humor to it. Ultimately, you'll turn your original speech in to an after-dinner speech.
2. Think about your own life. If you were asked to give a motivational speech, which type of motivational speaker would you be: hero, survivor, religious, or success? What would the specific purpose of your speech be?

4. CHAPTER EXERCISES

SPEAKING ETHICALLY

Virginia is asked to roast one of her bosses at the annual company meeting. Virginia collects a range of stories from people about her boss and a few of them are definitely quite embarrassing. She finds out about her boss's ex-husband and some of the marital difficulties they had that are quite funny. She also finds out that when her boss broke her leg, it actually happened while sliding down a slide and not on a ski trip as she had told her office. As Virginia prepares her speech, she starts questioning what information she should use and what information is going too far.

1. How should a roaster ethically go about collecting funny stories for his or her roast?
2. What type of information would be ethical for a roaster to use? What type of information would be unethical for a roaster to use?
3. At what point does a roast go from being good-natured to being meanspirited?

END-OF-CHAPTER ASSESSMENT

1. Which type of speech is designed to captivate an audience's attention and regale or amuse them while delivering a clear message?

   a. informative

   b. actuation

   c. persuasive

   d. indoctrination

   e. entertaining

2. "Darla has been a great asset to our community. She has worked on numerous projects including the housing beautification project, the community advancement project, and the community action league. As such, it is with great honor that I present Darla with the Citizen of the Year award." This is an example of what type of speech?

   a. presentation

   b. introduction

   c. acceptance

   d. goodwill

   e. dedication

3. Sarah, a representative to a state legislature, has been forced to explain her reasoning behind voting for a new law. While she realizes the law isn't perfect, she really believes that the benefits of the law truly outweigh the problems. Sarah is going to deliver what type of goodwill speech?

   a. speech of public relations

   b. speech of justification

   c. speech of apology

   d. speech of trusting

   e. speech of competence

4. "That guy was an inept expert" is an example of which type of humorous language?

   a. pleonasm

   b. malapropism

   c. oxymoron

   d. eulogy

   e. simile

5. When presidents finish their presidency, they are often hired by a speakers bureau to speak for various groups. What type of motivational speeches would ex-presidents most likely give?

   a. hero

   b. survivor

   c. religious

   d. success

   e. inspirational

ANSWER KEY

1. e
2. a
3. b
4. c
5. a

ENDNOTES

1. Slutsky, J., & Aun, M. (1997). *The Toastmasters International® guide to successful speaking: Overcoming your fears, winning over your audience, building your business & career.* Chicago, IL: Dearborn Financial Publishing.

CHAPTER 19
Your First Speech

1. THE PUBLIC SPEAKING PYRAMID

© Thinkstock

Ancient Egyptians believed that the shape of a pyramid was very important and sacred because the triangular shape would help guide the deceased's body toward the stars into the afterlife. While this belief has long since disappeared, the idea of a structure guiding people in a specific direction toward greatness has remained.

FIGURE 19.1 Public Speaking Pyramid

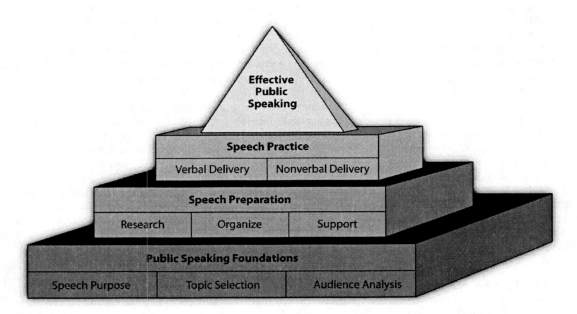

In this brief appendix, we hope to start you on the path toward effective public speaking. To help us understand the basic process of public speaking, we have chosen to use a pyramid-based model of public speaking (Figure 19.1). The rest of this chapter is going to briefly explain the basic public speaking process. We hope that this chapter will provide a simple overview of public speaking to help you develop your first speech. Each of the concepts explored in this chapter is fully developed elsewhere in *Stand Up, Speak Out*, so don't assume that this one chapter covers everything you need to know.

2. FOUNDATIONS OF PUBLIC SPEAKING

Every speech has to start somewhere, and one of the most common questions we hear from students in a public speaking course is, "Where do I start?" Well, your public speaking teacher will definitely give you some specific guidelines for all the speeches in your class, but all speeches start with the same basic foundation: speech purpose, topic selection, and audience analysis.

2.1 Speech Purpose

The very first question you'll want to ask yourself is this: what is the basic purpose of the speech you're about to give? As far back as the ancient Greeks, scholars of public speaking have realized that there are three basic or general purposes people can have for giving public speeches: to inform, to persuade, and to entertain.

To Inform

The first general purpose people can have for public speaking is to inform. When we use the word "inform" in this context, we are specifically talking about giving other people information that they do not currently possess. Maybe you've been asked to tell the class about yourself or an important event in your life. For example, one of our coauthors had a student who had been smuggled out of a totalitarian country as a small child with her family and fled to the United States, seeking asylum. When she told the class about how this event changed her life, she wasn't trying to make the class do or believe anything, she was just informing the class about how this event changed her life.

Another common type of informative speech is the "how-to" or demonstration speech. Maybe you'll be asked to demonstrate something to the class. In this case, you'll want to think about an interesting skill that you have that others don't generally possess. Some demonstration speeches we've seen in the past have included how to decorate a cake, how to swing a golf club, how to manipulate a puppet, and many other interesting and creative speeches.

To Persuade

The second general purpose that public speakers can have is to persuade. When you persuade another person, you are attempting to get that person to change her or his thought process or behavior. In the first case, you're trying to get someone to change her or his opinion or belief to what you, as the speaker, want that person to think or believe after the speech. For example, maybe you belong to a specific religious group that doesn't always get the greatest press. In your speech, you could try to tell your classmates where that negative press is coming from and all the good that your religious sect does in the world. The goal of this speech isn't to convert people, it's just to get people to think about your group in a more positive fashion or change their thought process.

The second type of persuasive speech, the more common of the two, is to get someone to change her or his behavior. In this case, your goal at the end of the speech is to see your audience members actually do something. When we want an audience to do something at the end of the speech, we call this a "call to action" because we are actually asking our audience members to act on what we've said during the speech. For example, maybe you're an advocate for open-source (or free) software packages. So you give a speech persuading your classmates to switch from Microsoft Office to OpenOffice (http://www.openoffice.org). In your speech, you could show how the cost of Microsoft Office is constantly rising and that OpenOffice offers the exact same functionality for free. In this case, the goal of your speech is to have your classmates stop using Microsoft Office and start using OpenOffice—you want them to act.

To Entertain

The third general purpose people can have for public speaking is to entertain. Some speeches are specifically designed to be more lighthearted and entertaining for audience members. Quite often these speeches fall into the category of "after-dinner speeches," or speeches that contain a serious message but are delivered in a lively, amusing manner that will keep people alert after they've finished eating a big meal. For this reason, most speeches that fall into the "to entertain" category are either informative or persuasive, but we categorize them separately because of reliance on humor. Effective speeches in this category are often seen as the intersection of public speaking and stand-up comedy. The speeches themselves must follow all the guidelines of effective public speaking, but the speeches must be able to captivate an audience through interesting and funny anecdotes and stories. Some common entertaining speech topics include everything from crazy e-mails people have written to trying to understand our funny family members.

Not all entertaining speeches include large doses of humor. Some of the most memorable speakers in the professional speaking world fall into the entertaining category because of their amazing and heart-wrenching stories. The more serious speakers in this category are individuals who have experienced great loss or overcome enormous hurdles to succeed in life and who share their stories in a compelling style of speaking. Audience members find these speakers "entertaining" because the speakers' stories captivate and inspire. In the professional world of speaking, the most commonly sought after form of speaker is the one who entertains an audience while having a serious message but delivering that message in a humorous or entertaining manner.

2.2   Topic Selection

Once you have a general purpose for speaking (to inform, to persuade, or to entertain), you can start to develop the overarching topic for your speech. Clearly, some possible speech topics will not be appropriate for a given general purpose. For example, if you've been asked to give an informative speech, decrying the ills of social policy in the United States would not be an appropriate topic because it's innately persuasive.

In a public speaking class, your teacher will generally give you some parameters for your speech. Some common parameters or constraints seen in public speaking classes are general purpose and time limit. You may be asked to give a two- to three-minute informative speech. In this case, you know that whatever you choose to talk about should give your listeners information they do not already possess, but it also needs to be a topic that can be covered in just two to three minutes. While two to three minutes may seem like a long time to fill with information, those minutes will quickly disappear when you are in front of your audience. There are many informative topics that would not be appropriate because you couldn't possibly cover them adequately in a short speech. For example, you couldn't tell us how to properly maintain a car engine in two to three minutes (even if you spoke really, really fast). You could, on the other hand, explain the purpose of a carburetor.

In addition to thinking about the constraints of the speaking situation, you should also make sure that your topic is appropriate—both for you as the speaker and for your audience. One of the biggest mistakes novice public speakers make is picking their favorite hobby as a speech topic. You may love your collection of beat-up golf balls scavenged from the nearby public golf course, but your audience is probably not going to find your golf ball collection interesting. For this reason, when selecting possible topics, we always recommend finding a topic that has crossover appeal for both yourself and your audience. To do this, when you are considering a given topic, think about who is in your audience and ask yourself if your audience would find this topic useful and interesting.

2.3   Audience Analysis

To find out whether an audience will find a speech useful and interesting, we go through a process called audience analysis. Just as the title implies, the goal of audience analysis is to literally analyze who is in your audience. The following are some common questions to ask yourself:

- Who are my audience members?
- What characteristics do my audience members have?
- What opinions and beliefs do they have?
- What do they already know?
- What would they be interested in knowing more about?
- What do they need?

These are some basic questions to ask yourself. Let's look at each of them quickly.

Who Are My Audience Members?

The first question asks you to think generally about the people who will be in your audience. For example, are the people sitting in your audience forced to be there or do they have a choice? Are the people in your audience there to specifically learn about your topic, or could your topic be one of a few that are being spoken about on that day?

What Characteristics Do My Audience Members Have?

The second question you want to ask yourself relates to the demographic makeup of your audience members. What is the general age of your audience? Do they possess any specific cultural attributes (e.g., ethnicity, race, or sexual orientation)? Is the group made up of older or younger people? Is the group made up of females, males, or a fairly equal balance of both? The basic goal of this question is to make sure that we are sensitive to all the different people within our audience. As ethical speakers, we want to make sure that we do not offend people by insensitive topic selection. For example, don't assume that a group of college students are all politically liberal, that a group of women are all interested in cooking, or that a group of elderly people all have grandchildren. At the same time, don't assume that all topic choices will be equally effective for all audiences.

What Opinions and Beliefs Do They Have?

In addition to knowing the basic makeup of your audience, you'll also want to have a general idea of what opinions they hold and beliefs they have. While speakers are often placed in the situation where their audience disagrees with the speaker's message, it is in your best interest to avoid this if possible. For example, if you're going to be speaking in front of a predominantly Jewish audience, speaking about the virtues of family Christmas celebrations is not the best topic.

What Do They Already Know?

The fourth question to ask yourself involves the current state of knowledge for your audience members. A common mistake that even some professional speakers make is to either underestimate or overestimate their audience's knowledge. When we underestimate an audience's knowledge, we bore them by providing basic information that they already know. When we overestimate an audience's knowledge, the audience members don't know what we're talking about because they don't possess the fundamental information needed to understand the advanced information.

What Would They Be Interested in Knowing More About?

As previously mentioned, speakers need to think about their audiences and what their audiences may find interesting. An easy way of determining this is to ask potential audience members, "Hey, what do you think about collecting golf balls?" If you receive blank stares and skeptical looks, then you'll realize that this topic may not be appropriate for your intended audience. If by chance people respond to your question by asking you to tell them more about your golf ball collection, then you'll know that your topic is potentially interesting for them.

What Do They Need?

The final question to ask yourself about your audience involves asking yourself about your audience's needs. When you determine specific needs your audience may have, you conduct a needs assessment. A needs assessment helps you to determine what information will benefit your audience in a real way. Maybe your audience needs to hear an informative speech on effective e-mail writing in the workplace, or they need to be persuaded to use hand sanitizing gel to prevent the spread of the flu virus during the winter. In both cases, you are seeing that there is a real need that your speech can help fill.

3. SPEECH PREPARATION

Once you've finished putting in place the foundational building blocks of the effective public speaking pyramid, it's time to start building the second tier. The second tier of the pyramid is focused on the part of the preparation of your speech. At this point, speakers really get to delve into the creation of the speech itself. This level of the pyramid contains three major building blocks: research, organization, and support.

3.1 Research

If you want to give a successful and effective speech, you're going to need to research your topic. Even if you are considered an expert on the topic, you're going to need do some research to organize your thoughts for the speech. Research is the process of investigating a range of sources to determine relevant facts, theories, examples, quotations, and arguments. The goal of research is to help you, as the speaker, to become very familiar with a specific topic area.

We recommend that you start your research by conducting a general review of your topic. You may find an article in a popular-press magazine like *Vogue*, *Sports Illustrated*, *Ebony*, or *The Advocate*. You could also consult newspapers or news websites for information. The goal at this step is to find general information that can help point you in the right direction. When we read a range of general sources, we'll start to see names of commonly cited people across articles. Often, the people who are cited across a range of articles are the "thought leaders" on a specific topic, or the people who are advocating and advancing how people think about a topic.

© Thinkstock

Once you've identified who these thought leaders are, we can start searching for what they've written and said directly. At this level, we're going from looking at sources that provide a general overview to sources that are more specific and specialized. You'll often find that these sources are academic journals and books.

One of the biggest mistakes novice public speakers can make, though, is to spend so much time reading and finding sources that they don't spend enough time on the next stage of speech preparation. We recommend that you set a time limit for how long you will spend researching so that you can be sure to leave enough time to finish preparing your speech. You can have the greatest research on earth, but if you don't organize it well, that research won't result in a successful speech.

3.2 Organization

The next step in speech preparation is determining the basic structure of your speech. Effective speeches all contain a basic structure: introduction, body, and conclusion.

Introduction

The introduction is where you set up the main idea of your speech and get your audience members interested. An effective introduction section of a speech should first capture your audience's attention. The attention getter might be an interesting quotation from one of your sources or a story that leads into the topic of your speech. The goal is to pique your audience's interest and make them anticipate hearing what else you have to say.

In addition to capturing your audience's attention, the introduction should also contain the basic idea or thesis of your speech. If this component is missing, your audience is likely to become confused, and chances are that some of them will "tune out" and stop paying attention. The clearer and more direct you can be with the statement of your thesis, the easier it will be for your audience members to understand your speech.

Body

The bulk of your speech occurs in what we call "the body" of the speech. The body of the speech is generally segmented into a series of main points that a speaker wants to make. For a speech that is less than ten minutes long, we generally recommend no more than two or three main points. We recommend this because when a speaker only has two or three main points, the likelihood that an audience member will recall those points at the conclusion of the speech increases. If you are like most people, you have sat through speeches in which the speaker rambled on without having any clear organization. When speakers lack clear organization with two or three main points, the audience gets lost just trying to figure out what the speaker is talking about in the first place.

To help you think about your body section of your speech, ask yourself this question, "If I could only say three sentences, what would those sentences be?" When you are able to clearly determine what the three most important sentences are, you've figured out what the three main points of your speech should also be. Once you have your two or three main topic areas, you then need to spend time developing those areas into segments that work individually but are even more meaningful when combined together. The result will form the body of your speech.

Conclusion

After you've finished talking about the two or three main points in your speech, it's time to conclude the speech. At the beginning of the speech's conclusion, you should start by clearly restating the basic idea of your speech (thesis). We restate the thesis at this point to put everything back into perspective and show how the three main points were used to help us understand the original thesis.

For persuasive speeches, we also use the conclusion of the speech to make a direct call for people change their thought processes or behaviors (call to action). We save this until the very end to make sure the audience knows exactly what we, the speaker, want them to do now that we're concluding the speech.

For informative speeches, you may want to refer back to the device you used to gain your audience's attention at the beginning of the speech. When we conclude back where we started, we show the audience how everything is connected within our speech.

Now that we've walked through the basic organization of a speech, here's a simple way to outline the speech:

    I. Introduction

        A. Attention getter

        B. Thesis statement

    II. Body of speech

        A. Main point 1

        B. Main point 2

        C. Main point 3

    III. Conclusion

        A. Restate thesis statement

        B. Conclusionary device

           ■ 1. Call to action

           ■ 2. Refer back to attention getter

3.3 Support

You may think that once you've developed your basic outline of the speech, the hard part is over, but you're not done yet. An outline of your speech is like the steel frame of a building under construction. If the frame isn't structurally sound, the building will collapse, but no one really wants to live in an open steel structure. For this reason, once you've finished creating the basic structure of your speech, it's time to start putting the rest of the speech together, or build walls, floors, and ceilings to create a completed building.

For each of the two or three main points you've picked in your speech, you need to now determine how you are going to elaborate on those areas and make them fully understandable. To help us make completed main points, we rely on a range of supporting materials that we discovered during the research phase. Supporting materials help us define, describe, explain, and illustrate the main points we selected when deciding on the speech's organization. For example, often there are new terms that need to be defined in order for the audience to understand the bulk of our speech. You could use one of the sources you found during the research stage to define the term in question. Maybe another source will then help to illustrate that concept. In essence, at this level we're using the research to support the different sections of our speech and make them more understandable for our audiences.

Every main point that you have in your speech should have support. For informative speeches, you need to provide expert testimony for why something is true or false. For example, if you're giving a speech on harmfulness of volcanic gas, you need to have evidence from noted researchers explaining how volcanic gas is harmful. For persuasive speeches, the quality of our support becomes even more important as we try to create arguments for why audience members should change their thought processes or behaviors. At this level, we use our supporting materials as evidence in favor of the arguments we are making. If you're giving a speech on why people should chew gum after meals, you need to have expert testimony (from dentists or the American Dental Association) explaining the benefits of chewing gum. In persuasive speeches, the quality of your sources becomes very important. Clearly the American Dental Association is more respected than Joe Bob who lives down the street from me. When people listen to evidence presented during a speech, Joe Bob won't be very persuasive, but the American Dental Association will lend more credibility to your argument.

4. SPEECH PRACTICE

Once you've finished creating the physical structure of the speech, including all the sources you will use to support your main points, it's time to work on delivering your speech. The old maxim that "practice makes perfect" is as valid as ever in this case. We are not downplaying the importance of speech preparation at all. However, you could have the best speech outline in the world with the most amazing support, but if your delivery is bad, all your hard work will be lost on your audience members. In this section, we're going to briefly talk about the two fundamental aspects related to practicing your speech: verbal and nonverbal delivery.

© Thinkstock

4.1 Verbal Delivery

Verbal delivery is the way we actually deliver the words within the speech. You may, or may not, have noticed that up to this point in this chapter we have not used the phrases "writing your speech" or "speech writing." One of the biggest mistakes new public speakers make is writing out their entire speech and then trying to read the speech back to an audience. You may wonder to yourself, "Well, doesn't the president of the United States read his speeches?" And you're right; the president generally does read his speeches. But he also had years of speaking experience under his belt before he learned to use a TelePrompTer.

While reading a speech can be appropriate in some circumstances, in public speaking courses, the goal is usually to engage in what is called extemporaneous speaking. Extemporaneous speaking involves speaking in a natural, conversational tone and relying on notes rather than a prepared script. People who need to read speeches typically do so for one of two reasons: (1) the content of their speech is so specific and filled with technical terminology that misspeaking could cause problems, or (2) the slightest misspoken word could be held against the speaker politically or legally. Most of us will not be in either one of those two speaking contexts, so having the stuffiness and formalness of a written speech isn't necessary and can actually be detrimental.

So how does one develop an extemporaneous speaking style? Practice! You've already created your outline, now you have to become comfortable speaking from a set of notes. If you put too much information on your notes, you'll spend more time reading your notes and less time connecting with your audience. Notes should help you remember specific quotations, sources, and details, but they shouldn't contain the entire manuscript of your speech. Learning how to work with your notes and phrase your speech in a comfortable manner takes practice. It's important to realize that practice does not consist of running through your speech silently in your mind. Instead, you need to stand up and rehearse delivering your speech out loud. To get used to speaking in front of people and to get constructive feedback, and we recommend that you ask a few friends to serve as your practice audience.

4.2 Nonverbal Delivery

In addition to thinking about how we are going to deliver the content of the speech, we also need to think about how we're going to nonverbally deliver our speech. While there are many aspects of nonverbal delivery we could discuss here, we're going to focus on only three of them: eye contact, gestures, and movement.

Eye Contact

One of the most important nonverbal behaviors we can exhibit while speaking in public is gaining and maintaining eye contact. When we look at audience members directly, it helps them to focus their attention and listen more intently to what you are saying. On the flip side, when a speaker fails to look at audience members, it's easy for the audience to become distracted and stop listening. When practicing your speech, think about the moments in the speech when it will be most comfortable for you to look at people in your audience. If you have a long quotation, you'll probably need to read that quotation. However, when you then explain how that quotation relates to your speech, that's a great point to look up from your notes and look someone straight in the eye and talk to them directly. When you're engaging in eye contact, just tell yourself that you're talking to that person specifically.

Gestures

A second major area of nonverbal communication for new public speakers involves gesturing. Gesturing is the physical manipulation of arms and hands to add emphasis to a speech. Gestures should be meaningful while speaking. You want to avoid being at either of the extremes: too much or too little. If you gesture too much, you may look like you're flailing your arms around for no purpose, which can become very distracting for an audience. At the same time, if you don't gesture at all, you'll look stiff and disengaged. One of our friends once watched a professor (who was obviously used to speaking from behind a lectern) give a short speech while standing on a stage nervously gripping the hems of his suit coat with both hands. Knowing how to use your hands effectively will enhance your delivery and increase the impact of your message.

If you're a new speaker, we cannot recommend highly enough the necessity of seeing how you look while practicing your speech, either by videotaping yourself or by practicing in front of a full-length mirror. People are often apprehensive about watching video tapes of themselves speaking, but the best way to really see how you look while speaking is—well, literally to see how you look while speaking. Think of it this way: If you have a distracting mannerism that you weren't conscious of, wouldn't you rather become aware of it *before* your speech so that you can practice making an effort to change that behavior?

Movement

The last major aspect of nonverbal communication we want to discuss here relates to how we move while speaking. As with gesturing, new speakers tend to go to one of two extremes while speaking: no movement or too much movement. On the one end of the spectrum, you have speakers who stand perfectly still and do not move at all. These speakers may also find comfort standing behind a lectern, which limits their ability to move in a comfortable manner. At the other end of the spectrum are speakers who never stop moving. Some even start to pace back and forth while speaking. One of our coauthors had a student who walked in a circle around the lectern while speaking, making the audience slightly dizzy—and concerned that the student would trip and hurt herself in the process.

When it comes to movement, standing still and incessant pacing are both inappropriate for public speaking. So how then should one move during a speech? Well, there are a range of different thoughts on this subject. We recommend that you plan out when you're going to move while speaking. One common way is to purposefully move when you are making the transition from one major point of your speech to the next. You might also take a step toward the audience at the moment when you are intensifying a point, or take a step back when saying something like, "Let's back up and think about this for a moment." However, we don't recommend moving when discussing important, complex ideas during your speech because the movement could be distracting and prevent audience members from fully understanding your message. Overall, you should practice movement so that it becomes comfortable for you and second nature.

5. CONCLUSION

In this appendix, we have introduced you to the basics of effective public speaking. We discussed building an appropriate foundation for your public speech, preparing your speech, and practicing your speech. All the concepts discussed in this appendix will be more fully discussed in the other chapters in this book. We hope this introduction will give you a boost as you start your journey toward effective public speaking.

Index